The Earliest English

LEARNING ABOUT LANGUAGE

General Editors:
Geoffrey Leech & Mick Short, Lancaster University

Already published:

Analysing Sentences (2nd edition) Noel Burton-Roberts

Words and Their Meaning Howard Jackson

An Introduction to Phonology Francis Katamba

Grammar and Meaning Howard Jackson

An Introduction to Sociolinguistics (2nd edition) Janet Holmes

Realms of Meaning: An Introduction to Semantics Th. R. Hofmann

An Introduction to Psycholinguistics Danny D. Steinberg

An Introduction to Spoken Interaction Anna-Brita Stenström

Watching English Change Laurie Bauer

Meaning in Interaction: An Introduction to Pragmatics Jenny Thomas

An Introduction to Cognitive Linguistics Friedrich Ungerer and Hans-Jörg Schmid

Exploring the Language of Poems, Plays and Prose Mick Short

Contemporary Linguistics: An Introduction William O'Grady, Michael Dobrovolsky and Francis Katamba

An Introduction to Natural Language Processing Through Prolog Clive Matthews

An Introduction to Child Language Development Susan Foster-Cohen

The Sounds of Language: An Introduction to Phonetics Henry Rogers

An Introduction to Foreign Language Learning and Teaching Keith Johnson

Varieties of Modern English Diane Davies

Patterns of Spoken English Gerald Knowles

The Earliest English Chris McCully and Sharon Hilles

The Earliest English

An Introduction to Old English Language

Chris McCully and Sharon Hilles

Harlow, England • London • New York • Boston • San Francisco • Toronto • Sydney • Singapore • Hong Kong
Tokyo • Seoul • Taipei • New Delhi • Cape Town • Madrid • Mexico City • Amsterdam • Munich • Paris • Milan

Pearson Education Limited

Edinburgh Gate
Harlow CM20 2JE
United Kingdom
Tel: +44 (0)1279 623623
Fax: +44 (0)1279 431059
Website: www.pearsoned.co.uk

First edition published in Great Britain in 2005

ISBN 0 582 40474 6

British Library Cataloguing-in-Publication Data
A CIP catalogue record for this book can be obtained from the British Library

Library of Congress Cataloging-in-Publication Data
McCully, C. B.
The earliest English : an introduction to the English language from the beginnings to the twelfth century / Chris McCully and Sharon Hilles.
p. cm. — (Learning about language)
Includes bibliographical references and index.
ISBN 0–582–40474–6 (pbk.)
1. English language—Old English, ca. 450–1100. 2. English language—Old English, ca. 450–1100—Grammar. 3. English language—Middle English, 1100–1500. I. Hilles, Sharon. II. Title. III. Series.

PE135.M23 2004
429′.82—dc22

2004050356

10 9 8 7 6 5 4 3 2 1
08 07 06 05 04

Set by 35 in 10/12.5pt Palatino
Printed in Malaysia, PJB

The Publishers' policy is to use paper manufactured from sustainable forests.

Contents

Acknowledgements

'Of making many books there is no end. . . .' wrote the poet of *Ecclesiastes*, 'and' (he added, with all the professional weariness of a scholar) 'much study is a weariness of the flesh'. On the other hand, the making of this book was attended by both luck and good fortune, and they made the weariness of the flesh almost a delight. First, we'd like to thank Richard Hogg, of the University of Manchester, who, more years ago than seems decent to mention, unwittingly began this project with three pamphlets he'd originally intended for the use of his first-year 'Old English' students. Richard's work eventually was developed into his *Introduction to Old English* (2002). Some of the early units here contain one or two expansions, or re-presentations, of Richard's original texts and ideas, and while we hope he forgives our reinterpretations of his work, we hope he will find the current text worthy of his plans, and consistent with them. In the same departmental context, some of the material we introduce in Unit 8 owes its existence to a teaching pamphlet originally prepared by Carole Weinberg and David Denison, though they can't have foreseen the redeployment of their work on the *Peterborough Chronicle* in quite the present format. We are grateful to them, and again to Richard Hogg, for allowing us to make use of some of the original questions they posed on the language of the 1137 and 1140 entries in the *Chronicle*. Second, Olga Fischer saw a very early draft version of the text and made many suggestions for improvement in both conception and detail. We thank her, and her students at the Universiteit van Amsterdam, for having worked with the pre-original version, and for having been so generous with their time and comments. We are also grateful to have discussed, with both Olga and with Nikolaus Ritt, of the University of Vienna, some of the ideas that eventually brought some of this text into its current shape. Third, we thank Mary Ellen Ryder, of Boise State University, who reviewed the proposal that underlay this text, for having commented at such length, and so constructively, about it. Fourth, we thank Professor Wilhelm Busse, of the University of Düsseldorf, who allowed us to make use of some tables of Old English inflections that were originally developed for a *Workbook* he and his colleagues used until recently with their 'Old English' students, and we thank, too, Noel Burton-Roberts for his permission to allow us to adapt the lay-out of some tables that were designed for use many years ago in the School of English at the University of Newcastle-upon-Tyne. We also thank those other colleagues with whom we've been privileged to discuss some of the issues contained in the text. Among these faces and voices are Donka Minkova, Roger Lass, Bob Stockwell, Ricardo Bermúdez-Otero, Heinz Giegerich and Paula Fikkert. Monika Schmid, of the Vrije Universiteit, Amsterdam, functioned simultaneously as critic, proofreader, library contact and source of many constructive ideas for setting the text, particularly the fiddly parts. Osamu Koma, Honorary Research Fellow in the University of Manchester (2002–03), painstakingly spotted some typos and other errors in Unit 5. Two readers for Pearson Education made very detailed and critical comments on the penultimate draft of the text, and we are greatly obliged to them for requiring us to cut or to simplify some of our analyses and reorder several sections of our draft. In the publishing context, Melanie Carter and Helen MacFadyen handled one very complicated manuscript and one almost equally complicated – that is, an exasperating – author with enviable, and very much appreciated, professional skill. And finally we'd like to thank the students who have made successive proposals for this book, and successive redraftings of it, such a thoughtful pleasure. They have patiently endured our desperate last-minute photocopying, our computer glitches and our mysterious changes of heart, analysis and font size. None of these students and scholars can be blamed, of course, for whatever errors of judgement, interpretation or presentation we may have made here. Much though we'd like to blame others for our faults, those errors are ours alone.

Publisher's acknowledgements

We are grateful to the following for permission to reproduce copyright material:

Maps 2, 3, 4 and 5 after maps from http://www.trin.cam.ac.uk/sdk13/RPMaps/MapPolDev.jpg, reproduced by permission of Professor Simon Keynes; Figure 5.3 adapted from *Course in Phonetics, 4th Edition*, reproduced by permission of Thomson Learning Global Rights Group (Ladefoged, P. 2001); Table 8.1 adapted from *Hugo: Dutch in Three Months*, reproduced by permission of Dorling Kindersely Ltd. (Fenoulhet, J. 1997).

In some instances we have been unable to trace the owners of copyright material, and we would appreciate any information that would enable us to do so.

Terminology

List of symbols and a note on conventions

While we have tried to keep symbols and abbreviations to a minimum, no one writing on or working with language, particularly on the earliest, and thus reconstructed, forms of English, can do so without making systematic use of some scholarly apparatus. Following long-established convention, for instance, we cite written forms in italics, as in Old English *rōd*, cross. We also make use of the following conventions of transcription:

/ / phonemic transcription, e.g. /pɪn/, pin
[ ] phonetic transcription, e.g. [pʰɪn]
< > graphemes, e.g. <pin>

(For a fuller account of phonemes, that is, underlying sound segments, see Units 1 and, particularly, 2 (consonants and vowels) and 5 (vowel length). On syllable structure and stress in (Old) English, see Unit 5.)

A macron (length-mark) appears over long vowels in their orthographic (written) forms, as in Old English *dōm*, judgement (phonemic /do:m/). On the analysis of long vowels as they appear in syllables, see especially Unit 5.

A single asterisk * marks either a historically reconstructed or an ungrammatical form; the context will make it clear which is intended.

Morphemes – for the present, morphemes can be taken to be 'meaningful parts of words' – are, where necessary, separated by hyphens, as in *cyning-as*, kings, where *cyning* is the lexical root and *-as* the nominative plural inflection.

Abbreviations

(a) Languages (and some varieties of languages)

AmE American English

We use this label as a convenient, though over-simple, cover-term for varieties of English spoken today in large parts of the North American continent. The cover-term is used in a sense equivalent to how linguists might deploy the term 'GA' – 'General American'

A-N Anglo-Norman
BrE British English

Again, we use this label as a convenient, though over-simple, cover-term for varieties of English spoken today in the British Isles. Usually, and with our intended readerships and their learning histories in mind, we will use the terms 'BrE' and 'AmE' for the purposes of explicational contrast. Thus, for example, we shall be able to contrast 'AmE speakers', many of whom have the phonological feature of rhoticity, or post-vocalic /r/, with BrE speakers, many of whom do not have such a phonological feature as parts of their grammars. We're well aware of the over-simple nature of such contrasts, but it's difficult to avoid making them during the course of a textbook intended to get you thinking – perhaps for the first time – about the nature of 'Englishes'

Du Dutch
E English
eME early Middle English
eModE early Modern English
F French
G German
Gmc Germanic
Ice Icelandic
IE Indo-European
L Latin
ME Middle English
N Northern
Nbr Northumbrian
NGmc North Germanic
OE Old English
OHG Old High German
OIce Old Icelandic
OLG Old Low German
ON Old Norse
OS Old Saxon
PDE Present-day English
PrGmc Proto-Germanic
WGmc West Germanic
WS West Saxon

(1) Generally, where you encounter 'PD' as part of an abbreviation of a language, you can gloss it as 'present-day', thus PDG, Present-day German
(2) Generally, where you encounter 'L' as the first part of an abbreviation of a language, you can gloss it as 'late', thus LL, Late Latin, LME, Late Middle English

(3) Generally, where you encounter 'e' as part of an abbreviation of a language, you can gloss it as 'early', thus eME, early Middle English

(b) Other terms

In our experience, beginning students can often be baffled by the use of even commonly used scholarly abbreviations, and very often misuse these pieces of equipment in written assignments. Here are some of the most common:

c Latin *circa*, about (thus 'c1000', around the year 1000)
cf Latin *compare*, confer
eg Latin *exempli gratia*, for example
ff following pages
fn. footnote, plural *fnn.*, footnotes
ie Latin *id est*, that is
IPA International Phonetic Alphabet
MS manuscript, plural *MSS.* manuscripts
n note, plural *nn.* notes
nb Latin *nota bene*, note well
pp pages
pret preterite – another word for past tense form of a verb
RP Received Pronunciation [RP is, or was, a prestige spoken variety of British English. For decades of the 20th century it was considered to be a spoken 'standard'.]

[NB. If you're going to use grammatical terms to describe the structures and functions of the English language, there is one spelling mistake which students commonly make. The word <**auxiliary**> is spelt with ONE <l>. It isn't spelled *<auxilliary>, nor yet *<auxillary>, however much you might want it to be.]

(c) Abbreviations used for grammatical concepts

The meaning of the abbreviations will become clear as we work:

acc accusative
adj adjective
dat dative
fem feminine
gen genitive
ind indicative
masc masculine
neut neuter
nom nominative

NOM nominal (group)
NP noun phrase
obj object
pl plural
ppl past participle
prep preposition
pres present
sb subjunctive
sg singular
VP verb phrase

Using this book

This book is organised into eight units, with an Interlude after Unit 4. Each unit is intended to generate sufficient work to occupy one week's study, although of course the time taken to complete each unit will depend on whether you're studying alone, or with others, in a university seminar, or in a school or college classroom. It will also depend on whether you're working through this book as part of the American quarter system, the UK semester or term system, or the system in use in some parts of Europe, namely a number of 90-minute study periods. We have tried, with some difficulty, to accommodate each of these possibilities, and a unit, in our view, is equivalent to roughly 4–5 hours' full-time work, in class and/or out of it. Naturally, however, students and their tutors will want to tailor the work done within each unit to both the time available, the nature of the group and the focus of the course. Our preferred structure is a compromise, and like many compromises, it's intended to be taken with a certain amount of patience . . . and good humour.

Each unit includes exercises and further reading, together with some suggested web links. Some of the early units contain passages for translation. It's important to stress that the exercises are there in order to introduce you not only to 'the earliest English', but also to invite you to work in detail with some of the most important tools of the craft that is historical linguistics – such as OED2 (the 2nd edition of the great *Oxford English Dictionary*). (You'll find that 'Working with dictionaries' is the topic introduced in the Interlude between Units 4 and 5.) In order to fulfil this book's aims for yourself, it's necessary to work through each exercise before moving on to the next.

You're also encouraged, at the end of each chapter, to browse in some suggested websites. It must be admitted that websites can range from the egregious to the inspiring. What we've done here is simply pick out the ones that include the most useful material (such as maps of early England), or the most concise histories (such as the history of the Norman Conquest), or are best keyed in to the points we raise in the text. We don't, alas, receive any endorsements or fees from the websites we mention, and likewise their inclusion here doesn't necessarily imply any endorsement on our part. We have simply tried to be multiply functional, and maximally helpful.

Unit One

Thinking about the earliest English

1.0 Preliminaries

This book is primarily about the earliest English language, the language used for 400 or so years before, and for some time after, AD 1066 in many parts of what is now England, southern Scotland and the Welsh borders. But the book has another purpose: if it's 'about' the earliest English language, it's also about the people who spoke it, and about the gradual, the rapid or even the catastrophic changes in that society – changes that came radically to affect the historical development of English.

To get an idea of what the earliest English sounded like, before you go any further, try browsing the websites listed at the end of this chapter. You'll hear Old English (OE) being spoken – that is, reconstructed. No one is completely sure how OE sounded, but scholars have a pretty good idea. (On how and why scholars have a good idea of how OE sounded, read further in Unit 1, and see also Units 2 and 5.) What you'll hear is a best guess about how OE was pronounced. You may be surprised that it doesn't sound like Chaucer (who was writing at the end of the 14th century), Shakespeare (who was writing around the end of the 16th) or the King James Version of the Bible (1611). Students frequently remark that OE sounds more like German than present-day English (PDE). A language spoken 1000 or more years ago may seem very distant. What could people living in the 21st century possibly have in common with what might seem, on a mere and ignorant acquaintance, to be what one of our more unenlightened students called 'the remote grunts of an unwashed peasantry'? Contrary to what we might expect, surviving manuscripts from the OE period do not reveal a linguistically primitive version of 'modern mankind'. Instead, a rather vivid picture emerges of a people in love with language; a people who prize not only a good story, but a story cleverly, beautifully and well told; a people who employ a vigorous language, often rich with stylistic density and metaphor. We'll see a complex, often aristocratic and highly organised society, with values, ideals and ideas about the world and life that can seem hauntingly contemporary. By the time you finish this book, we think that you'll agree with us: neither the human spirit, nor the conditions with which it engages, have changed much, if at all, in the last 1500 years. Some of the best as well as the worst parts of our culture have a long history, and one that is often singularly expressed in the English language.

1.1 Uniformity and change

These remarks have an immediate linguistic point. What we do in these pages, as generations of scholars working in the fields of OE and, more recently, historical linguistics have done, is to reconstruct part of the history of a language. But we immediately wonder whether we are *re*constructing, or simply constructing? To talk about history at all, whether it's a linguistic history or the history of royal dynasties, is essentially to relate a narrative, to tell a story. Even though it might not be immediately apparent, if we think about it for a moment it becomes clear that all narratives have a theoretical framework – that is, a set of surrounding assumptions, that helps to make the story plausible. A story isn't a story, by our standards, unless it can be told within such a framework. One linguistic assumption of our theoretical framework, an assumption that is at least intuitively attractive, is that speakers of OE, and of early Middle English (eME), had the same vocal equipment as ours, and used it in very much the same ways. For example, just as there is a constraint in present day English to the effect that (crudely) 'no syllable may end in the sound segments */-pdf/' (there are no English words such as **mupdf* or **ipdf*), then we might expect, on quite general articulatory grounds, that no syllables ended that way in OE or eME either. The combination of speech sounds */pdf/ is of course 'difficult to say', but it also, more importantly, violates the enduring principles that determine what speech sounds may precede or follow one another to make up a well-formed English syllable. One issue we will track in these pages is this: *what is, linguistically, impossible today was probably impossible in earlier periods of the language*. There are, as always, exceptions to this. OE *cniht*, boy, was pronounced with syllable-initial /kn-/, that is, both the /k/ (corresponding to written <c>) and the /n/ were pronounced; OE *hring*, ring, was pronounced with initial /h/ followed by an /r/. These syllable-initial combinations of speech sounds are impossible in present day English, but were certainly possible in OE, just as they are today – and this is a key point – in *other* European languages. Nevertheless, despite these and other apparent exceptions, we'll continue to believe, at least generally, that *what's linguistically impossible today* ***was probably*** *impossible yesterday*. Put differently, what currently obtains in a language in terms of possible word orders, sounds, sound systems and so forth was possible, even probable, in the language long ago. Though it may be a depressing truth for those who believe in the evolutionary betterment of the human condition, language users don't change much.

This principle is in fact so important that the historical linguist Roger Lass devotes a great deal of Chapter 1 of his book *Historical linguistics and language change* to it (Lass 1992:4–43, see especially Section 1.5). There, Lass calls it the *General Uniformity Principle*: 'No linguistic state of affairs (structure, inventory, process, etc.) can have been the case only in the past' (1992:28). This is linked with a weaker principle, which Lass dubs the *Uniform Probabilities Principle*: 'The . . . likelihood of any linguistic state of affairs (structure, inventory, process, etc.) has always been roughly the same as it is now.'

To illustrate the first principle, the General Uniformity Principle, consider the OE word *heofon*. You might make a reasonable, and correct, assumption that this word can be translated as 'heaven'. But notice that the OE form is spelled with <f>. Why isn't it spelled with <v>? The answer is two-fold. First, we have evidence that Anglo-Saxon scribes (on the distinction between 'Old English' and 'Anglo-Saxon', see below) didn't have access to the letter shape <v>. They used the written symbol <f> to do duty both for the speech-sound /f/ (as in *fisc*, fish or *faran*, to travel, cf. PDE to *fare*) and the speech-sound /v/ (as in *heofon* or *lufian*, to love). For reasons that needn't concern us at the moment, it appears that the letter written as <f> in OE was pronounced in two different ways. It was pronounced /f/ when it was initial or final in the word and as /v/ when it occurred between voiced sounds. ('Voicing' is explained in the following paragraphs.) These two voiced sounds were frequently vowel shapes. Vowels are always – under normal circumstances, excluding whispering – voiced in English, so if the sound was written as an <f>, it was pronounced as a /v/ when it occurred between two vowels and as an /f/ elsewhere.

This notion isn't quite as arbitrary as it might seem. As it turns out, the two sounds /f/ and /v/ are almost identical. They're pronounced in exactly the same way, using exactly the same articulatory organs (most clearly, the lips and teeth), in exactly the same place. There's only one clear difference. In production of ('realisation of') the sound /f/, the vocal cords don't vibrate; in the realisation of /v/, they do. To feel this for yourself, *whisper* the first sound in the word *fat*, and then the first sound in the word *vat*. Do this very slowly. You'll see – feel – that they sound exactly the same. Do it again and pay close attention to where your teeth are with respect to your lips during both sounds. They should be in exactly the same place. Now notice how much air comes out when you pronounce both sounds. Again it should be the same. That's because the speech sounds /f/ and /v/ are very similar except for the feature of production that linguists call *voicing*.

To illustrate that point more precisely, put your fingers gently on the side of your throat next to your Adam's apple. This time *say* (i.e. don't whisper) the first sounds in both of those words (*fat* and *vat*). You should feel a vibration (and hear a buzzing sound) on the first sound of the second word, *vat*. In other words, one sound is voiced, or produced with vibration of the vocal cords, and the other sound is voiceless, that is, produced without vibration of the vocal cords. Put differently, and slightly more technically, we might say that '/v/ is the voiced counterpart of /f/'.

Thinking about matters this way leads us to a basic theoretical concept in linguistics. Languages might have one *underlying* speech-sound that is realised differently (in this case, as either voiced or voiceless) depending on where the sound appears in the word. In the case of OE, we might want to think about the claim that there was one *underlying* speech-sound, /f/, which speakers and writers thought of, and wrote, as <f>, and which could be realised in speaking *either* as [f] (a voiceless sound) *or* as [v] (a voiced sound), depending on the context in which it appeared. In fact, in OE it seems to have been pronounced [f] everywhere *except* when it occurred between two vowels, or any two other voiced sounds. In other words, /f/ – we might argue – *became* voiced most characteristically when it occurred between voiced sounds.

Exercise 1.1.0

At this point we'd like to invite you to discover some evidence for Lass's General Uniformity Principle. Remember, this is the hypothesis that we should be able to find evidence in the present for what we are claiming existed long ago. If we apply this to our study of the history of the earliest English, we might say that if a sound, written as <f>, was voiced or voiceless depending on its location in a word in OE, there should be some evidence of this phenomenon in present-day English (PDE – we'll use this abbreviation from here on). Luckily we won't have to look at any languages other than PDE for evidence, because there are some word pairs in PDE in which this still happens.

There was an ending in OE that changed certain nouns into the infinitive form of a verb. That ending was <*-ian*>, and it had the effect of putting the final sound of a noun's root (for now, 'root' = most basic form of the word, the 'citation form') between two vowels. In OE, for instance, the word for the noun 'cloth' was *clāð* (where the symbol <ð> is pronounced like voiceless 'th', as in PDE *cloth*), and the verb 'to clothe' was formed by adding '-ian' to give us *clāðian*, to clothe.

> How do you think the 'th' sound in the second word was pronounced in OE?
> And why might it have been pronounced in this way?

We hope you answered 'like the th-sound in *clothe*' – because the sound written as 'th' came between two vowels in OE (the vowel shapes written <ā> and <i>) and therefore became voiced. So one survivor of the OE system is the word pair *cloth* (noun) and *to clothe* (the verb form) in which the noun form ends in a voiceless 'th' but the verb form ends in a voiced 'th'. There are other word pairs that came either directly or indirectly from this OE principle, where a sound is very often voiced between two voiced sounds, and voiceless everywhere else.

Exercise 1.1.1

Look at the pairs of PDE words shown in table 1.1 and put a tick (AmE check) by those that seem to have this voiceless/voiced alternation; that is, pairs in which the voiceless sound suggested by <th> (as in ***thigh***) becomes the voiced (still suggested by the <th> spelling, as in ***thy*** or ***then***), or where the sound /f/ becomes /v/. Don't look at the comments until you have finished the exercise.

Table 1.1 Alternating noun/verb pairs in PDE

Nouns	Verbs	Singular	Plural
teeth	teethe	life	lives
breath	breathe	sheaf	sheaves
house	house	loaf	loaves
advice	advise	oath	oaths
bath	bathe	wife	wives
		half	halves
		laugh	laughs

Comment on Exercise 1.1.1

The words we were looking for among the noun/verb sets were *teeth, breath, bath*. In each of these cases, when the word becomes a verb, the voiceless, final sound of the noun becomes voiced. In PDE we can turn nouns into verbs via the process of incorporation, where nouns are simply used as verbs. For example:

(1) Mary put butter on her biscuit.
(2) Mary buttered her biscuit.
(3) The twins took a photograph of their mother.
(4) The twins photographed their mother.

In PDE we also use derivational affixes such as *-ise* (spelled <-ize> in AmE) to turn a noun into a verb.

(5) We cooked the onions in butter until the sugar began to turn to caramel.
(6) We caramelised the onions.

In the second group of words found in the above exercise (right-hand columns), the singular and plural nouns, the words we were looking for were *life, sheaf, loaf, wife* and *half*. Nowadays it may seem peculiar that the plural of 'wife' isn't 'wifes' – after all, most words form the plural with an 's' or 'es', but don't change root-final consonants from a voiceless to a voiced version as they do so. The reason that the plural form of 'wife' has a 'v' sound, of course, is because of the history of the word, namely that OE principle regarding /f/ and /v/. That these alternations still exist in PDE is evidence of Lass's uniformity principles. These words are like linguistic fossils – forms that are relics of an earlier existence.

Later, we'll say more about the principles we've just sketched. For the moment, both principles can be roughly summarised under one heading as the *Uniformitarian Hypothesis*, which will function as part of the theoretical framework we're going to need in order to tell the story of – that is, (re)construct – the earliest English, and act as a check on the wilder excesses of historical speculation.

1.2 Initial terminology

We've already said that this text is primarily intended to help you read, study and enjoy the earliest English language and aspects of its culture, especially its literary culture. We're assuming that you don't have much, if any, prior knowledge of the subject, although, as we'll soon see, whether English is your first or second language, you already possess a great deal of tacit knowledge of the earliest English (and even certain aspects of its historical culture). Just as human beings are inseparable from their personal histories – our individual pasts are part of our identities at this moment, today – it's impossible for languages and cultures to leave their pasts behind.

For the moment, let's think about the earliest English by adopting a straightforward distinction between the terms *Anglo-Saxon* and *Old English*. Some scholars use the terms interchangeably, but we won't. In this book we'll use the term *Old English* to mean one or other of the varieties of the language widely spoken in England in the six centuries between the approximate dates of 449 and 1150. We'll use the term *Anglo-Saxon* to refer to everything else, such as the people(s), culture and archaeology. We might speak, for example, of 'an Anglo-Saxon brooch' or 'an Anglo-Saxon king'. We won't speak of an 'Old English king' – the phrase is in any case ambiguous – but we will talk about entities such as the 'Old English vocabulary' and 'Anglo-Saxon kings'.

We'll also use some abbreviations (initial lists, of both abbreviations for languages and for some grammatical terms, are given at the beginning of the book). OE, as you'll have already noticed, will stand for Old English, the language spoken across most areas of what's now, geographically, England from the 5th to the 12th centuries. *Beowulf*, one of the most famous epic poems in what can be called English, is an example of OE, as is Cædmon's *Hymn,* which was composed in the late 7th century (a West Saxon version of this text can be found later in this unit). ME will stand for Middle English, the version of English spoken in roughly the same area from around 1100 to about 1500. Chaucer's *Canterbury Tales* is written in a London dialect of what we're calling Middle English. Early Modern English (eModE) will cover roughly 1500 to c.1800, and includes the language of Shakespeare, Spenser, Milton and the King James Bible.

Now, you'll find abbreviations such as OE, eME, eModE and PDE in many standard handbooks. It's convenient to divide the history of the English language up in such a way but, of course, such divisions are a gross simplification and involve much fudging. This fudging is often concealed in terms such as 'roughly 1500 to c.1800'. In fact, there is both a range and a variety of 'Englishes'. Think about the differences between British, American, Canadian and Australian English, or the English spoken in Texas as compared to the English spoken in Liverpool. The Englishes spoken in the Philippines, Nigeria and India are also instances of 'English', but may be somewhat different from the variety of English with which you are familiar. Sometimes you can understand another variety of English easily, sometimes not. In other words, 'English' is a convenient but inaccurate and vague notion. Which English are we talking about? In this book, we're largely going to ignore this complex issue and will usually write as if there were one English language. But of course that isn't true, except for the purposes of analytical convenience. We'll hint at the complex nature of the true state of affairs when we begin to study the linguistic foundations of what were to become the dialects that made up the earliest English.

We're going to ignore something else. Linguists tell us that all languages change over time. This is a completely natural, unstoppable process. Most linguists will argue that languages don't decay, become degraded or, conversely, become less primitive and somehow 'improve'. They just change. Common sense will tell you that these changes won't be abrupt, but will be gradual and almost imperceptible to the users of the language.

These worries and simplifications notwithstanding, we'll speak of OE as 'lasting' up to c.1150, and ME 'starting' in c.1150. In fact, of course, English didn't change on one particular date. It would be a great falsification to say that English changed on 1 January 1150, or on the day that the first Viking long-ships were sighted off Lindisfarne (late 8th century), or on the day after the Battle of Hastings (see Unit 8). Vikings and Normans had a very significant impact on the language, true, but their full linguistic importance is revealed later, often very much later, than the signal events of their first arrivals. The language changed slowly, over time, in different ways and at varying rates in different varieties, though, nevertheless, the general direction of these linguistic changes seems fairly clear. The dates we have decided to use in this book are for convenience, imposed by linguists to facilitate, organise and manage a discussion and study of the changes in English. The dates aren't, and can't be, linguistic turning-points. They are wholly arbitrary and exist for the purposes of story-telling. We're going to use them anyway.

Exercise 1.2.0

For most in-text exercises in this book we're going to provide 'comments' after we've set the exercises themselves. For the following exercise, however, we're not going to do so. The exercise below simply asks you to become more aware of your own, and others', dialect(s) of English. It asks you to begin to think about your own, possibly tacit, knowledge of the history of the English language.

1. One reason we are making a distinction between OE and Anglo-Saxon is because of the ambiguity in a sentence like 'He was an old English king'. If that sentence were spoken, what might the ambiguity be?
2. You may not have lived sufficiently long to notice changes in English (and change in one's own lifetime, however long, can be hard to identify precisely), but if you know The Lord's Prayer, or any other passages from the King James version of the Bible, or passages from Shakespeare, recite them to yourself, or to the other members of your group, to give a sense of how English has changed. Can you think of any other *evidence* that English has changed over time?
3. Our students have told us that they think one way to keep everything straight is to start a time-line early and add to it as you go along. Take out a piece of notebook paper, turn it sideways and sketch in the times and events (or general periods) that we've mentioned already. For example, When was the Old English period? Middle English? When did the Vikings come to England? If necessary, look up what you think are key dates in an encyclopedia or history textbook. As you progress through this book, you'll probably have to tape additions to your piece of notebook paper.

1.3 Old English poetry

We're now going to turn our attention to OE poetry, and to Cædmon's famous *Hymn* as a case in point. This last was composed in the second half of the 7th century in Whitby, in what is now North Yorkshire (part of the OE kingdom of Northumbria). The *Hymn*, famous since it's the first extant (written, surviving) poem on a religious subject in the English language, was clearly held to be important by Cædmon's contemporaries. During the decades after its composition, at least four copies of the poem were made. Since most OE poems survive in just one copy (although of course other copies may have been lost), the copying of the *Hymn* indicates its literary and cultural value.

Although the *Hymn* is one of the first extant and datable poems in English, that's not of course to suggest in any way that it's the first poem ever to have been composed and recited. There was a very long and rich tradition of poetry before Cædmon recited a line. This can be inferred from the existence of scraps of language, such as charms, riddles and inscriptions, found in similar forms all over northern Europe, and also from references within surviving OE poetry.

The earliest, pre-Cædmon poetry was composed and recited by peoples whose culture was sometimes if not largely, pagan. One important point to notice was that poetry, at this early date, seems to have had one very characteristic form: it was composed in a line which had a two-part structure. The two parts of the line were linked by alliteration (we'll look at this in more detail in Unit 5). In Anglo-Saxon England, at least, poetry had this one form: it had no other. The uniqueness of this situation is expressed by Strang (1970:323):

> There are several reasons in the nature of OE verse why it should, to a greater extent than later poetry, develop a language distinct from that of prose. The most radical is not often mentioned, and is difficult for readers accustomed to later literature to grasp. It is that OE had a straightforward distinction between metre, which had a single, unique form, and non-metrical writing, i.e. writing not in this form. This is indeed a situation rare in any literature; normally, if one decides to write in verse, one can also decide which verse-form to write in. In ME, though forms derived from OE metre survived, the essential of the situation was changed, for the poet always had a choice of metres open to him. His verse might be alliterative or rhyming; the lines might contain any number of feet, of various types, uniform or in mixed patterns; they might be arranged in stanzas of various types, or not in stanzas at all. Before 1100 these alternatives did not exist as choices. There was one metre; you used it or you did not. You might compromise and conform to some but not all of its rules, writing a kind of semi-verse, and you could add patterning of your own selection to the basic form; but you could not write a verse of a different form.

Since OE poetry appears to have been associated with one, and only one, particular form, that form functioned as a *cultural sign* ('this form of discourse = poetry'). In addition, this form seemed to be somehow ideally suited to the language in which it was composed. (We explore this issue more fully in Unit 5.)

These factors bear on the fame of Cædmon's *Hymn*, and help to explain its contemporary importance. There are other factors we might want to begin to consider: even though pre-Cædmonian poetry embodied non-Christian subject-matter, and though the earliest praise-poems were reserved for secular rulers, Cædmon apparently composed a short poem in praise of a specifically Christian God. This in itself was unusual. But even more unusual was the fact that this praise-poem was composed in the very form, and using the same verbal strategies and forms of diction, as had been earlier employed in Germanic, that is, pagan verse. More unusual still, Cædmon was by no means the scop (*scop*, shaper, poet) of a tribe or court, one versed in the techniques of Germanic poetry (and paid to reproduce them), but an illiterate animal husbandman.

The story of Cædmon is found in Bede's *History of the English Church and People*, or *Ecclesiastical History* (completed around 731). Bede wrote his *History* in Latin, but Cædmon's *Hymn* is given in an English version in his original manuscript. As well as the versions that exist in different manuscripts of the 8th century, the text was several times reproduced, in different varieties of OE, during the 10th, 11th and 12th centuries.

1.4 Reading passage

The only details of Cædmon's life are known from Bede, who related that Cædmon was a member of the secular community of the monastery whose abbess was called Hild (abbess 657–680), at Whitby. He was a man, recounted Bede, well advanced in years, and he had never learnt any of the arts of poetry-making and song-craft. On one occasion (Bede's narrative continues) Cædmon was attending a *gebēorscipe* (beer-party). A harp was passed around and each of those present was expected to recite something to the accompaniment of the harp. Cædmon, in the full knowledge of his own poetic incompetence (or perhaps because of the lewd subject-matter of the songs being recited) left the party and went out to sleep with the animals whose care was entrusted to him that night. During his sleep, a figure, perhaps an angel, appeared to him and commanded him to sing something. 'I don't know how to sing anything,' replies Cædmon ('Ne con ic nōht singan'), 'and that was why I left the party and came here.' The figure isn't about to be appeased by Cædmon's embarrassment. 'Yet you shall be able to sing to me.' Cædmon is half-persuaded. 'What must I sing?' The figure replies, 'Sing to me of the beginning of creation.' At that point, and divinely inspired, Cædmon recites his *Hymn*.

Since we'll be looking later at several specimens of OE written in West Saxon dialect, the text is given here not in the original Northumbrian, but in a West Saxon version. (Should you want to compare the West Saxon version with the original Northumbrian, turn to page 205.) Editorial punctuation, capital letters and length-marks (over relevant vowels) have been supplied. Notice that each line of the poem has been split into two halves. That division reflects a structural principle of the verse: as we'll see in Unit 5, each half-line is a self-contained metrical entity.

Cædmon's *Hymn* (WS version)

First half-line	**Second half-line**	
Nū sculon herigean	heofonrīces Weard,	**Line 1**
Meotodes meahte	ond his mōdgeþanc,	**Line 2**
weorc Wuldorfæder,	swā hē wundra gehwæs,	**Line 3**
ēce Drihten,	ōr onstealde	**Line 4, etc.**
Hē ærest scēop	eorðan bearnum	
heofon tō hrōfe,	hālig Scyppend.	
Þā middangeard	monncynnes Weard,	
ēce Drihten,	æfter tēode	
fīrum foldan,	Frea ælmihtig.	

Word for word translation

Now (we) must praise	Heaven-kingdom's Guardian
(the) Maker's powers	and his mind-thought,
works of the glory-father	as he (the) wonders of each
eternal Lord	installed (the) beginning.
He first shaped	of earth for the children
heaven as a roof,	holy Maker.
Then middle-yard	mankind's Guardian,
eternal Lord,	afterwards created
for men of earth,	Lord Almighty.

Prose translation

Now we must praise the Guardian of the heavenly kingdom, the powers of the Creator and his conception, the works of the Father of glory, since he, the eternal Lord, established the beginning of every wonder. The Holy Creator first shaped heaven as a roof for the children of men. Then afterwards the Guardian of mankind, eternal Lord, and God Almighty, made this world for the people of earth.

Before we comment on the poem, complete the following exercise.

Exercise 1.4.0

Study the OE version of the text above and highlight the elements in each verse-line that alliterate. Though we comment on this in more detail shortly (and look at it in far more detail in Unit 5), for the moment we define alliteration as involving the initial consonant(s) of words that begin with the same sound, such as PDE *sin*, *suffering* and *scent*. (Notice that in *scent*, the two letters shapes <sc> are realised as one speech-sound, /s/.) Don't look at the comments until you've tried to pick out the alliterating sounds.

Comment on Exercise 1.4.0

Your answer probably looks something like this, where we've supplied some of the alliteration in boldface type:

Nū sculon **h**erigean	**h**eofonrīces Weard,	(alliteration on /h/)
Meotodes **m**eahte	ond his **m**ōdgeþanc,	(alliteration on /m/)
weorc **W**uldorfæder,	swā hē **w**undra gehwæs,	(alliteration on /w/)
ēce Drihten,	ōr onstealde.	(alliteration?)
Hē ǣrest scēop	eorðan bearnum	(alliteration?)
heofon tō **h**rōfe,	**h**ālig Scyppend.	(alliteration on /h/)
Þā **m**iddangeard	**m**onncynnes Weard,	(alliteration on /m/)
ēce Drihten,	æfter tēode	(alliteration?)
fīrum **f**oldan,	**F**rea ælmihtig.	(alliteration on /f/)

There doesn't, on the face of it, seem to be much system here. Some half-lines have one alliterating element, others have two. And in some lines alliteration seems to be absent altogether.

Yet with a slightly deeper understanding of the conventions that governed this metre, a system does emerge. There are three key points to notice, though we'll have cause to modify these points, particularly the point about apparent vowel alliteration, as we proceed:

- alliteration is a property of stressed syllables
- where they occur at the beginning of a stressed syllable, any vowel seems to alliterate with any other vowel (thus the vowel shapes written <ē> and <ō> in line four)
- the second half-line may only contain one alliterating syllable

'Alliteration is a property of stressed syllables.' It's difficult at this stage in our work to formulate this with any more precision, but perhaps we could say that, where a syllable is stressed, alliteration is a property of one or more sound segments initial in that syllable. And, apparently, any vowel, whatever its phonetic quality, can be allowed to alliterate with any other vowel. Take line 4, *ēce Drihten ōr onstealde*. Here it looks as if the line is alliterating on the *ē* of *ēce* and the stressed monosyllable *ōr*. (You might guess that the *on-* of *onstealde* might figure here, but it doesn't. Can you work out why not?) Something similar applies to line 5, *ǣrest scēop eorðan bearnum*, where the sound represented by the written shape <*ǣ*> seems to be alliterating with the sound represented by written <*eo*>. And again, in line 8, *ēce Drihten æfter tēode*, where *ē* seems to be alliterating with *æ*.

There's much more to say about OE metre, but we've said enough here to hint at the richness, density and compression of this form of composition. Part of Cædmon's 'miracle' is that an unlettered stockman could be divinely inspired not simply to sing of the Creation, but to do so using all the conventions, constraints and apparatus embodied in the verse of the Germanic heroic – and pagan – past. As with all poetry, in any language, it's not just 'the thing said' that matters; it's *how* the thing is said. The form of a poem is part of its meaning.

Turning to the theme of the *Hymn*, the poem is in the tradition of the eulogy, or praise-poem. This form was familiar from the Germanic past, where secular kings were lauded for their power, their purpose, their generosity and the breadth of their conception. Here, the conception involves not just the military success of a tribe, but the creation of all things. Notice too the local details: God first shaped heaven 'as a roof'; then he turned his attention to *middangeard*, literally to the 'middle-yard', where earth is conceived as being poised between heaven and whatever lies below; and then to the inhabitants of *middangeard, moncynn*, mankind. The movement is from heavenly conception to the everyday textures of the human. It's a sophisticated achievement in so small a space.

Of Cædmon's later career, Bede's translator tells us that Cædmon woke from his dream, 'and all that he had sung while sleeping he remembered, immediately adding many words in praise of God in the same manner'. On waking, Cædmon visited his overseer, who immediately took him to the abbess, Hild, who told him, in the presence of learned men and scholars, to repeat the *Hymn* and reveal the source of his inspiration. They gave Cædmon further religious material and asked him if he could turn it into 'the best poetry'. He did so the following morning. 'All those things he was able to learn by ear he remembered,' wrote Bede, remarking that Cædmon was in the habit of musing on them 'like a clean beast chewing the cud' while turning them 'into the sweetest poetry. . . . His songs and poems were so lovely to hear that teachers themselves learnt from his dictation, and wrote down his words.'

1.5 Words, words, words

Although languages change over time, and sometimes they change radically, it's also true to say that the history of any language involves continuity as well. One area of the English language where continuity is particularly evident is in its vocabulary. The term *vocabulary* is used more or less synonymously with the term *lexicon*. The lexicon of a language includes all the words used in that language, from nouns (*book, window, eye*) and verbs (*to go, to read, to learn, to teach*) to prepositions (*by, with, from, in*) to pronouns (*he, she, it, they, them*) and determiners (words which typically introduce, and often specify, a following noun – examples are *a, an, the, this*). (Note: the italicised examples are merely a selection taken from PDE. Technically, a lexicon contains other elements, but they won't concern us for the moment. We'll explain the terms *noun, verb* and so on later, and with more precision. Unit 3 focuses on the structure of OE nouns, Unit 4 on OE verbs.)

The lexicon (or total 'mental dictionary') of PDE includes many words that were used in OE. One rough-and-ready way of finding English words whose ancestry can be traced back into OE is to find PDE monosyllables, words containing one and only one syllable, particularly monosyllabic words which have 'dictionary meanings', that is, words that are easily defined or imagined, such as *knife, ear, arm* or *sword*, as opposed to words that are difficult to define or imagine, such as *the, a* or *of*. Words that belong to the first set are sometimes called *content words* (or 'lexical words', though here we prefer the former term since it's less ambiguous). Words that belong to the second set are sometimes called *function words* (or 'non-lexical words', or 'grammatical words'). Unlike content words, which have dictionary meanings (e.g. cat = adult feline quadruped), grammatical words are words to which it's difficult or even impossible to ascribe meanings, but they do have a clear grammatical function within the sentence.

Consider, for example, a word like *hound*. It can be glossed (that is, defined) as something like 'adult canine quadruped' (noun). Example: 'Jasper had an old hound that always howled at the moon.' The word could also be glossed as a verb, meaning 'to follow or chase; to pursue relentlessly'. Example: 'Chris was hounded by debt collectors.' If you know German, you'll also know that German has a similar word, *Hund*, denoting the same entity. You might make a plausible guess that the English word *hound* and the German word *Hund* have a common history, and you'd be right. (*Hound* and *Hund* are called cognate words, where *cognate* is descended from Latin *co-natus*, born together.) In fact, OE and Old German (usually called Old High German, OHG, in reference works) have a common ancestor and, in some ways, Old English is more like present-day German than PDE. That's one of the reasons why studying OE seems, paradoxically perhaps, sometimes easier for native speakers of German than for native speakers of English.

Exercise 1.5.0

Given the explanation of *content words* and *function words* above, which of the following items do you think might be content words? On what grounds might you decide this? Once you have decided which items are content words and which are function words, look at the content words. What are the parts of speech that comprise this category?

Hints: You might have to use your intuitions to decide which words are nouns, which verbs and which adjectives. We urge you to think about the *linguistic behaviour* of the words to which you're applying those intuitions. For example, you might claim that *apple* is a noun. Why? It *behaves* like a noun: it can be preceded by an article (*an* or *the*); its sense can be modified by a preceding adjective ('the *bad* apple'); it takes a plural form in *-s* ('apples'), and so on. Verbs, too, show characteristic forms of linguistic behaviour: they have infinitive form in *'to X'* – *to* *eat, to find, to swim* (but not, notice, **to apple* or **to quickly*); they take endings if they occur with a preceding third person singular pronoun (*he, she* or *it*) – *he swims, she finds*, and so on. And adjectives? Adjectives don't usually take endings (*the dry towel* is fine, but **the drys towels* is not); often, but not always, they stand in front of the head noun whose sense they are modifying; and so on. . . . Using your hunches is, then, a matter of careful observation of linguistic *behaviour*. That said, here's the list of words:

an	apple	for	cat	find
swim	eat	chair	sweet	top
quickly	go	coat	dry	fast
of	should	terrible	must	unusual
buy	this	why	slowly	seldom
since	early	beautiful	frequently	suddenly

Exercise 1.5.1

For this you'll need a good dictionary. A *Shorter Oxford* or *Concise Oxford* dictionary would be suitable, as would the *Encarta World English Dictionary* or *The American Heritage Dictionary*, College Edition. What you need is a dictionary that indicates word etymologies (or origins). The *Pocket Oxford Dictionary*, for example – a text that just happens to be on the desk in Amsterdam at the moment these words are written – uses the abbreviation E to indicate words which are native English (that is, were used in, and survive from, the OE period, or even earlier), but that's not really adequate for the purpose of this exercise. Other dictionaries, and usually more detailed and extensive ones – such as the *New Oxford* that has just been pulled from the bookshelf – will use the abbreviation OE to refer to native words. The *Encarta World Dictionary* and *The American Heritage Dictionary* also use the abbreviation OE, and will usually give the OE word from which the PDE word came.

Once you have access to a good dictionary, turn up the entries for the letter <W>. In the exercise, you should find at least ten *monosyllabic* words beginning with the letter <W> which can be traced back to OE (reminder: the brackets < > indicate the written letter, not its sound). Copy down the words that come from OE and, if your dictionary has the OE word, write that down as well. Don't look at the comments in the following section until you've finished this exercise.

Comment on Exercise 1.5.1

We've no way of knowing which dictionary you've used, so our comments must be general, rather than tied to a particular page of your dictionary. But, as a specimen comment, consider the following, where the dictionary text used was *The Oxford Library of Words and Phrases, Vol. III: Word Origins*. The first word found there, *wabble*, isn't, of course, a monosyllable, so can be ignored. The next word, *Wacke*, is a rare word and used specifically in the field of geology. There isn't anything in the entry that unambiguously indicates that the word comes from OE (there's no E or OE in the indication of origins). Looking down the list, the first monosyllable that has OE in the gloss is *wade* ('go OE'). The word *wade*, then, is our first entry. Moving on down the list, we find that the word *wag* (stir, move) was originally derived from OE *wagian*, totter, sway; the word *wake* (watching, watch, vigil) was originally OE (*wācan*, arise, come to life, be born); the word *walk* (move about, journey) came from the OE word *wealcan* meaning 'to roll, turn about, rove'; and *wall* (rampart, defensive structure) from OE *weall* . . . and so on. (As some of you may have noticed, OE *weall* has a deeper history and may ultimately be a borrowing from Latin *vallum*, rampart. The word is so thoroughly nativised, however, that we include it here, rather arbitrarily, as an OE word.)

In this exercise, you've probably come across dictionary abbreviations like AF, OHG, ON and so on. Like the abbreviation OE, these indicate the original language from which a word came. You'll find many of these abbreviations treated in the list of abbreviations at the front of this book, and you'll find a short account of the relationships between many European languages in Unit 2. For the moment, we want to emphasise that many PDE monosyllabic content words can trace their history back into the OE period. Of course, there are many monosyllables which can't and don't, but they're not altogether as numerous as those which can. On the other hand, many polysyllabic words, i.e. words containing more than one syllable, can be traced to borrowings from French, or from Latin, or any other number of languages, such as aboriginal Australian (*wallaby*) or even Hindi (*wallah*). English is, and always has been, a great borrower. In fact, this lexical fecundity is a distinctive feature of English, and the kinds of words borrowed, the dates at which they were borrowed and the languages from which they were borrowed are of considerable help in piecing together the story of English. Nevertheless, in spite of the numerous borrowings, it's quite possible to find a core OE vocabulary that has lasted to the present day. Once we're aware of this, then the fact that we can quickly find native words in the dictionary, and can see that they form a core vocabulary (consider how words such as *walk* or *wall* not only occur frequently but are of everyday currency), should help us to realise that even as speakers of PDE we're often using words of OE provenance. Even though it may sound and look very different today, OE is all around us. The English language has, over the centuries of its evolution, retained much of its original lexicon. It would be almost true to say that 'we speak Old English without knowing that we do': our linguistic present includes many aspects of the linguistic past.

Exercise 1.5.2

Study the following paragraph and, using your dictionary, find all the *monosyllabic* content words that can trace their origin back to OE. What general conclusion might you draw about the longevity of the OE lexicon? Again, don't look at the comments until you have finished the exercise.

> Nick slipped off his pack and lay down in the shade. He lay on his back and looked up into the pine trees. His neck and back and the small of his back rested as he stretched. The earth felt good against his back. He looked up at the sky, through the branches, and then shut his eyes. He opened them and looked up again. There was a wind high up in the branches. He shut his eyes again and went to sleep.
>
> (from Ernest Hemingway, *Big Two-hearted River*:1)

Comment on Exercise 1.5.2

Ignoring the proper name, *Nick*, obvious monosyllables to investigate are: *pack, lay, down, shade, back, pine, trees, neck, small, earth, felt, good, sky, shut, eyes, wind, high, went, sleep*. In total, then, there are at least 20 words we can investigate. *Pack* is originally a loan-word from Dutch and therefore non-native in the sense we've defined; *lay* is clearly a form of the verb *lie*, which is OE; *down* derives from OE; *shade* is derived from OE; *back* is likewise native; *pine* is recorded as existing in OE, but was probably a loan-word from Latin into OE; *tree* derives directly from OE, as do the words *neck, small, earth, felt* (from *feel*), *good, shut, eye, wind, high, went* and *sleep*. If you've looked up the word *sky* you've probably found the abbreviation ON, indicating that the word was borrowed into English from Old Norse, the language used by the Vikings.

So of the original list of 20 words only two, a loan-word from Dutch and a loan from ON, appear to be 'non-OE'. The vocabulary employed in this excerpt is, then, overwhelmingly native in origin, and emphasises the point that the English language has an enduring lexicon, much of it derived directly from the OE period (or even earlier, in the common Germanic word-stock; see Unit 2).

These observations help, perhaps, to explain something of Hemingway's prose style. It is considered as a much less ornate style than that of many of his contemporaries. In addition to Hemingway's preference for short, and simple, sentences, he also prefers the familiar, everyday word – the native word, whose origin is OE – over lexical choices that involve borrowing from Latin and Greek.

1.6 Pronouncing Old English

The first step isn't merely learning how to pronounce OE words, but in having the confidence even to begin such an exercise. Be assured that the exercise is worthwhile: OE is often clearer to understand when it's spoken – it often feels closer to PDE and less like a stern, remote, philologically minded relative. For those of you lucky enough to have taken a course of instruction in English phonology (that is, on the patterning of English speech-sounds), we've put the IPA (International Phonetic Alphabet) symbols between brackets. If the symbols in brackets are unfamiliar to you, feel free to ignore them at this point. In any case, we've tried to give examples in both American and British English. Here are a few pronunciation tips for OE.

1. Pronounce everything: <hl> for example has two sounds, both the <h> followed by the <l>. OE *hlāf*, loaf, is pronounced with syllable-initial /hl-/. The same rule-of-thumb applies to double consonants: OE *settan*, to set, should be pronounced with a 'long' /t/; you can hear how a 'long /t/' might sound if you pronounce PDE *set to*, as opposed to PDE *rating* (where the /t/ is a single speech-sound). A 'long /t/' such as that found in OE *settan* is referred to as a double consonant (technically, what is known as a geminate consonant).
2. <c> is usually pronounced as /k/ when it's syllable-initial or -final, as in *care* (OE *caru*) or *king* (OE *cyning*). However, before or after <ie>, after <e> or diphthongs that begin with <ie> or <ea> and in some cases that are dictated by the prehistory of OE, <c> is pronounced as 'ch' as in ***ch**urch*. IPA /ʧ/ (American /č/). (Scholars working in the US tend to use the symbol /č/, while those working in Europe and elsewhere often use /ʧ/. From now on, and simply because the present book is being finished in the heart of Old Europe, we'll use /ʧ/.) Example: OE *cyrice*, church, or *ēce*, eternal.
3. <ð> is a new(ish) symbol to you. It's called *eth* and pronounced 'th', as in ***th**igh* or ***th**y*, that is either /θ/ or /ð/, depending on its location in a word. OE *forð*, forth. It's worth noting that Anglo-Saxon scribes sometimes use <þ> for voiceless /θ/, and <ð> for voiced /ð/, but scribal practice is by no means consistent.
4. <Ð> is also a new symbol, but it's just a capital eth and pronounced exactly like eth. Example: OE *Ðēodric*, Theodoric (a proper name)
5. <þ> is used interchangeably with <ð> by most, though not all, OE scribes. It's called *thorn* and, like eth, it is also pronounced as either the 'th' in ***th**igh* or the 'th' in ***th**y*. Example: OE *þæt*, the, that.
6. <h> is usually pronounced /h/ when it occurs as a single consonant at the beginning of a word (*hālig*, holy), but when it appears after a vowel it's often pronounced like the 'ch' sound found in Scots English *loch* and (some varieties of) PDGerman *ni**ch**t*, /x/ (or /χ/, depending on the spoken variety employed).
7. We'll talk more about vowels later, but let's begin with a couple that might be a little difficult. The OE letter shape <y> represents a high front lax vowel, and OE <ȳ> a high front tense vowel. Don't worry too much at this stage if terms like 'tense' and 'lax' seem unfamiliar. To pronounce a kind of generic high front vowel shape, one of the shapes symbolised by OE <y>, pronounce /ɪ/, the vowel sound in the word

sit, but round your lips like you're saying 'oh' at the same time. Good practice for this sound is the OE word *cyssan*, which means 'to kiss'. Another example would be the vowel shape found in French *tu*, or German *küssen*, to kiss. To pronounce the sound corresponding to the letter shape <ȳ>, produce the sound /iː/ (which is the long vowel shape heard in the words *seat, tea, meet*) and round your lips at the same time, just like you did for <y>. Good practice for this vowel shape is the OE word for 'little', *lȳtel*.

We also have to consider *ligatures* and *digraphs*. An example of a *ligature* is the written shape <æ>; this corresponds to a single vowel shape. *Digraphs* are formed by two letter-shapes that together correspond to one sound. You've already encountered some digraphs – the <sc> of OE *scip*, for example (/ʃɪp/).

8. <æ> is called *ash* and has the sound in BrE of the vowel symbolised by the <a> in slightly old-fashioned pronunciations of *cat*. In many varieties of American English, ash has the sound of *a* in words like *hat*, *map* and *bad*. IPA /æ/.
9. <cg> sounds like the <dg> combination in *edge*. IPA /ʤ/. OE *ecg*, edge.
10. <sc> is pronounced like the <sh> in *ship*. IPA /ʃ/ or American /š/ (we'll use /ʃ/). Think also, for example, of OE *fisc*, fish.
11. Where you encounter it at the beginning of the root of a word, as in a word such as *geþyld*, patience, <ge> is pronounced like *yuh*, with an initial shape corresponding to how the <y> in PDE *yes* is pronounced. If you speak German, watch this one because it is pronounced in OE differently from the way it is pronounced in German.

You're now ready to try some reading and translation. (For more detail on the form and pronunciation of OE speech-sounds, see Units 2, 3 and 5.) In the following exercises, help yourself by pronouncing each word slowly and carefully, or, if you're working as part of a seminar group, help each other out by reading the words aloud to each other. If there is a *macron* (a horizontal line over a vowel, for example <ā>), that means that the written shape corresponds to a long vowel. (Since they're rather more complex entities than they seem, long and short vowels are further discussed, in considerably more detail, in Unit 5.)

Exercise 1.6.0

Study and pronounce the following OE words. The key is practice, so repeat the exercise until you are able to pronounce each word automatically, without having to stop and think about each individual sound. Look back to the pronunciation guide if necessary.

ecg	scip	biscop	lȳtel	yfel	þū
stān	fæder	ic	heofonlīce	hīerde	eorðe
cwēn	niht	hrōf	hors	miht	þīn
nama	rīce	willa	dæg	forgif	hrycg
wisse	wæs	drīfan	wīse	gelǣd	mōnað

Comment on Exercise 1.6.0

The words you've just pronounced should (for the most part) be immediately recognisable as words familiar in PDE: *edge, ship, bishop* are transparent as long as you remember that the letter shape <cg> is pronounced like PDE <dg> and <sc> like PDE <sh>. *lȳtel* may have to be said several times to get that high front tense rounded vowel. (Try for German u-umlaut, pronounced long, if you know that vowel shape.) This word will eventually become PDE 'little'. *yfel*, evil, is a double challenge. It begins with the sound of the vowel in 's**i**t', but with your lips rounded, and the <f> is pronounced as [v] because it comes between two voiced sounds. *þū* can be glossed as 'you' or 'thou'; remember that the initial 'th' sound is voiceless, like the 'th' in ***th**in* or ***th**ink*.

stān, with its long vowel, survives into PDE as 'stone' (and has a noteworthy dialectal variant in Scots English, *stane*). *fæder* is just about recognisable as PDE *father*, though there has been change both in the quality of the vowel and in the word-medial consonant, which has changed from <d> to <th> (speakers of BrE should also note that in OE the word-final <r> is pronounced as /r/). *ic* sounds like PDE 'itch', but is in fact the OE version of the first person pronoun, I. (This pronoun has an interesting history, in which the final 'ch' became pronounced as /k/ in some dialects of (early Middle) English. The final /k/ was often dropped in front of words beginning with a consonant (thus ME *I cam*, I came), from which point the usage was generalised. The short vowel left by this process was subsequently lengthened and diphthongised during the later ME period.)

heofonlīce is challenging. The <f> is pronounced as a [v] because it is between two vowels, the <c> is pronounced like 'ch' because it comes after <i>, and the final <e> is also pronounced. This last shape sounds, unpromisingly, like 'uh'. The suffix 'līc(e)' will eventually become 'ly' in PDE. The whole word means 'heavenly'. *hīerde* is a verb form, the past tense of 'to hear'. Don't forget to pronounce the final syllable which, as mentioned previously, has the (still deeply unpromising, but nevertheless significant) sound of 'uh'. The difficulty in the next word, *eorðe*, is the 'new' symbol <ð>, which is pronounced here as a voiceless 'th' as in the words ***th**ick* and ***th**ink*. Don't forget to pronounce the final <e> ('uh' again). The word can be glossed as 'earth' – notice the voicelessness of the (root-) final <th> shape in PDE.

cwēn is recognisable as PDE 'queen', but note that the letter combination <qu> wasn't used by Anglo-Saxon scribes, hence the initial <cw>. *niht*, with its characteristic post-vocalic pronunciation of <h> (recall German *nicht*) is recognisable as PDE 'night' (the vowel lengthened as a consequence of the [x] being dropped and subsequently diphthongised in the later ME period). And *hrōf* gives PDE 'roof'. Don't forget to pronounce both the <h> and the <r>. *hors* obviously yields 'horse' in PDE. *miht* is the OE word that will eventually evolve into 'might' or 'power'. (Think of the German word for 'power', *Macht*.) Again, the <h> is pronounced [x] or [χ], and the word rhymes with *niht*, which we looked at earlier. *þīn* will become 'thine', which, if you were brought up, for example, on the King James version of the Bible, you will recognise as a possessive pronoun, corresponding to 'your' in PDE.

The next word, *nama*, becomes 'name' in PDE. *rīce* (pronounced with a 'ch' and an 'uh' as the last two sounds) means 'kingdom'. We see a survival of OE *rīce* in PDE *bishop**ric***, which is an area (diocese) ruled over by a bishop. Take the 'a' off the next word, *willa*, and it is clear that it means 'will'. The vowel sound in the next word, *dæg*, sounds like the 'a' in AmE *h**a**t*, *c**a**t* or *d**a**nce*. The final sound is roughly the same sound that starts the word *you*. Eventually this word will become PDE 'day'. The next word, *forgif*, has two syllables. The first is *for* and sounds very much like the word 'for' in PDE. The '*g*' here sounds like the first sound in ***y**ou* or ***y**et*, and the final 'f' is just an [f]. It's not a [v] because it isn't between two voiced sounds. This word will become 'forgive'. In the next word, *hrycg*, we see <hr>, a possible initial consonant cluster in OE (/hr/, cf <hring>, mentioned earlier). We lose the 'h' later in the development of English, but for now it's pronounced [hr-], as both letter shapes <h> and <r> suggest; don't forget how the digraph 'cg' is pronounced. This word will become 'ridge', and here it sounds remarkably like '"ridge" with an "h" at the beginning'.

The first word in the last line of the exercise, *wisse*, has two syllables and, because each respective 's' is not *itself* between two vowels, the sound remains /s/ and is pronounced long, as a double consonant (a geminate) – as the <ss> spelling suggests. The last sound is the 'uh' of a word-final, unstressed 'e' in OE. This is a form of the verb 'to know'.

The next word, *wæs*, is probably recognisable to you as PDE 'was', and the only two things you have to look out for is the vowel (which is the sound of /æ/ we mentioned for *dæg* above) and the final 's'. Nowadays, 'was' ends in a 'z' sound. In OE, <s> was /s/ unless it came between two voiced sounds, where it occurred in speech as voiced, namely as [z]. But in OE, what you see in the spelling is very much what you get in the pronunciation: *wæs* ends in a voiceless sound.

The next word, *drīfan*, may be recognisable to you as 'drive'. The 'f' represents a [v] sound and the vowel is the spoken realisation of a high front tense 'ee' sound, /iː/.

The following word, *wīse*, means 'wisely'. It is pronounced with the same vowel as the previous word, but this time the <s> represents a [z] – it comes between two vowels.

gelǣd, the penultimate word, begins with the very common OE prefix 'ge'. As we've seen before, this prefix is *always* pronounced 'yuh' and is never stressed. The root of the word – *-lǣd* – has the same low front lax vowel, /æ/, that we've talked about already. This root isn't glossed as 'lad' – though that would be a good guess. Well, a fair guess. Actually, it wasn't even a reasonable guess. It is a verb, 'lead'.

The pronunciation of the last word in the series, *mōnað*, should be obvious. The vowel is a little different from the present-day version found in *month*. In OE, this vowel is a pure, and tense, 'o' sound (it's crudely similar to that heard in PDE *mow* or *hoe*). The final sound of *mōnað* corresponds in pronunciation to a voiceless 'th' sound (at least partly because <ð> doesn't come between two voiced sounds).

Exercise 1.6.1

Attempt to pronounce, then to translate, the following OE phrases. Don't look at the comments until you've given the exercise a fair trial by yourself.

(1) se cyning wæs swift
(2) se biscop wæs dēad
(3) se fisc swam under þæm stāne
(4) se cyning lufaþ þā cwēn
(5) sēo cwēn lufaþ þone cyning
(6) se biscop hīerde þā cwēn
(7) þone cyning cyseþ sēo cwēn
(8) þæt hors gelǣdde se biscop

Comment on Exercise 1.6.1

(1) The king was swift. (2) The bishop was dead. And? (3) The fish swam under the stone. Correct – but you may have noticed a couple of difficulties with this last sentence. We'll comment on the difficulties shortly. First, a more general comment. The function word *se* is an article, a definite article, equivalent (roughly, and here) to PDE 'the'. Now in PDE there's one and only one definite article, 'the'. Simple enough. But in OE, as still in many other European languages, the definite article changed its form depending on its grammatical function in the sentence and the *gender* of the noun to which it was attached. This apparent changing-ness, of form, function, gender, can be one of the things that makes the earliest English initially seem difficult to study. But in fact there's a system that underlies the apparent changing-ness, and that makes our job as scholars much easier. As it happens, we've loaded the analytical dice with these practice sentences, because in the first three practice sentences above, the nouns we've chosen belong to the masculine gender.

The term *gender* here needs explanation. We're not speaking of biological gender – men are masculine, women feminine. As linguists, we use the word *masculine* as a (perhaps unfortunate) grammatical term that refers to historically inherited patterns of *linguistic behaviour*. The gender of a noun, though sometimes coinciding with natural gender, has linguistically speaking little to do with the biological gender of the object or with speakers of a language *imputing* biological gender to particular nouns. In fact, biological gender and grammatical gender do not necessarily match, and, in the case of non-biological objects, grammatical gender is virtually inexplicable in biological terms. In OE, the noun *man* is masculine, for example, but the word *scip*, ship, is neuter (though notice that ships can be 'feminine' in PDE nautical terminology – 'She's a fine boat'). Even more tellingly, OE *duguð*, troop of retainers, belongs linguistically to the feminine gender. As we'll see, each linguistic gender belongs to a *system*, and the articles in front of a noun change according to the gender of the noun. Another way to look at it is that 'articles can signal the gender of the noun'. For example, we might want to speak of (masculine, subject position) *se cyning*, the king, but in a corresponding place – the subject position – in a different sentence we would speak of 'the ship' as (neuter, subject) *þæt scip* (not **se scip*) or (feminine, subject) *sēo duguð*, the troop (not **se duguð* or *þæt duguð*).

Se, *þæt* and *sēo* are all glossed as 'the', but *se* is used with grammatically masculine nouns, *þæt* with grammatically neuter nouns and *sēo* with grammatically feminine nouns.

Bearing this in mind, let's go back to sentence (3) above. *Se fisc* – this part's fine, so long as we remember that the letter cluster (digraph) <sc> is pronounced in OE as /ʃ/. Then there's *swam* – also fine; it's a verb and just as it looks (past tense of *swim*). Then there's the harmless-looking word *under*, which you no doubt translated, correctly, as 'under'. But this apparently guileless word introduces a change in case-relations into the sentence. While we can speak, correctly, of the little phrase *se fisc* as being the subject of the sentence – the fish is the thing doing the swimming, and occurs in a position which we associate with subject-hood in PDE (cf. '*the rat* ate the cheese'; '*the cheese* was bad'; '*the rat* died') – *under*, here in our sentence (3), announces not the subject, but a different linguistic structure. We'll define the structure in question more closely in Unit 4 and thereafter, where we'll start calling it a dative construction; but for the present, it's important just to notice the difference. This difference is indicated grammatically in OE in the phrase *þæm stāne*. The word *stone* is linguistically masculine in OE; its root, its basic form, is *stān*, so we might expect the article *se* to stand in front of the word. But notice in (3) that the word, which has here the form *stan-e*, occurs with a final -e (that unpromising, but nevertheless significant, 'uh' sound), and is preceded by the article *þæm*. Inoffensive it seems, yet this combination of change in article and change in ending, which, following venerable tradition, we'll call *inflection*, carries a great deal of grammatical information. Despite the form of the article *þæm*, which seems closer to 'them' than anything else, it still means 'the'; it's still the definite article. Yet its form isn't the one we expected to indicate 'masculine noun, and subjecthood'; that would be *se*. So we can see that the change of form – in the form of the word and in the article – does carry a great deal of grammatical information.

If you've translated the practice sentences (4–6) as 'the king loves the queen', 'the queen loves the king' and 'the bishop heard the queen' you'd be right. Why do you suppose that in sentences (4) and (6) the noun phrase 'the queen' is 'þā cwēn' but in (5) it's 'sēo cwēn'?

In (7), who is doing the kissing and who is getting kissed? How do you know? And who was doing the leading in (8)? How do you know? Remember that *se* marks grammatically masculine subjects and *sēo* marks grammatically feminine subjects. *Cyning* is masculine, and if it were the subject it would be marked with *se*. However, here it is marked with *þone* so the king can't be doing the kissing. He is getting kissed. (8) is slightly more difficult because *hors* is a neuter noun and *þæt*, the article ('the' again), can be used for both neuter subjects and certain kinds of neuter non-subjects; however, *biscop* is masculine, and you can tell that *biscop* has to be the subject, regardless of where it comes in the sentence, because it has the subject designation for masculine nouns, *se*, in front of it. If the horse were doing the leading, what would be the marker before the noun *biscop*?

Exercise 1.6.2

Read the following aloud, and then see if you can translate it. We talked about some of the words in Exercise 1.6.0. Try to work out at least what the text is (many of you will be able to do this if you can understand the first two words) before you look at the comments.

The text is given here in a West Saxon form of OE.[1] (West Saxon was – or came to be – a prestige written dialect of the language, and one that was the source for a *standard literary form* of the language for about 200 years. On the notions *dialect* and *standard*, with particular reference to the prestige of West Saxon, see Unit 7.)

In the following, notice particularly the ways in which this OE version differs from any later version familiar to you, and try to analyse what the inflectional endings might be here, particularly those that occur on nouns.

[1] The text we use is in fact taken from G.L. Brook (1955), who noted that this version is based on MS. Corpus Christi College Cambridge 140, 'a manuscript written at the beginning of the eleventh century' (1955:113, n.3).

Fæder ūre
þū þe eart on heofenum
sī þīn nama gehālgod.
Tōbecume þīn rīce.
Gewurþe ðīn willa on eorðan
swā swā on heofenum.
Urne gedæghwāmlican hlāf
syle ūs tō-dæg.
And forgyf ūs ūre gyltas,
swā swā wē forgyfað ūrum gyltendum.
And ne gelǣd þū ūs on costnunge,
ac ālȳs ūs of yfele.
Sōþlīce.

Comment on Exercise 1.6.2

If you were brought up in the Christian tradition, this text may be familiar to you as the Lord's Prayer (*Matthew* vi, 9–13). If you aren't familiar with the Lord's Prayer, you might want to look it up in the *Bible*, or on-line, or see if anyone in your group can recite it from memory. There are some immediate points of recognition between this version and almost any later version. The word *fæder*, for example, is readily translatable as 'father' (we met this word earlier), though notice that original <d> is today pronounced as [ð] – a clear indication of a change in the pronunciation of the relevant consonant that must have taken place at some time after the 11th century. Then there's the word *ūre*, our, and the word *þū*, thou, both pronouns. Both survive into PDE, although *þū*, the 'thou' form, is now used only in a very few spoken dialects of English, or in the most archaic or religious, or quasi-religious language; its range of functions has largely been taken over by the pronoun *you*. We will be tracing some of the reasons for this change later in this book (in Unit 7, in particular).

Next comes the form *þe*. On the face of it, this looks suspiciously like 'the', but in fact we've already noticed that the definite article has a range of forms in OE (recall the brief discussion of *se* and *þæm*, above). In fact this is an undeclinable (non-form-changing) relative pronoun, and can be translated as 'that' or 'who'. Relative pronouns in PDE change their forms, of course. Think of *who*, *whom* and *whose: The man who helped me, the man whom I helped, the man whose help was invaluable*. (Question: if *þe* can be glossed as 'that' or 'which', how would you translate *þē*? The macron over the vowel is no mere graphical detail. It makes an entirely new word. Hint: The two words aren't related in meaning and *þē* belongs to the same word class as *ūs* or *ūre*. The answer is . . . ? The pronoun, 'thee'.)

Next, the word *eart*, recognisable with only a little imagination as archaic 'art', a verb. (Notice: *þū* and *eart* yield 'thou art') Next, the innocuous *on*, which you might be tempted to translate as 'on'. Like many prepositions in OE, this one does in fact have a range of meanings (see Unit 4):

it could indeed mean 'on', but was rather more likely to mean 'in' or even 'into'. And then there's the word *heofenum*. If you remembered that <f> was pronounced as [v] when it occurred between vowels, this would give you 'heaven' followed by the inflection, *-um*. The word as a whole then has the morphological ('word-part') structure *heofen-um*, where *heofen* is the lexical root and *-um* the inflexion. You may notice a structural similarity here between *on heofenum*, and *under . . . þæm stāne*, which we discussed earlier. In the last example, we said that the preposition *under* introduced a phrase that couldn't be the subject, and that this 'non-subject-hood' was indicated by the inflection *-e* on the root, *stān-*, and by the use of the article *þæm* instead of *se*. Something similar is happening with *on heofenum*: the preposition is accompanied by an inflection on the following noun. (Later, we'll speak more explicitly of these words inflecting in the dative case, see Unit 4.)

Exercise 1.6.3

At this point, we'll ask you to look again at the nouns in the passage and try to make an educated guess as to which ones occur with an inflection (that is, an ending that indicates the noun's role in the sentence). We repeat the passage for convenience:

> Fæder ūre þū þe eart on heofenum sī þīn nama gehālgod. Tōbecume þīn rīce. Gewurþe ðīn willa on eorðan swā swā on heofenum. Urne gedæghwāmlican hlāf syle ūs tō-dæg. And forgyf ūs ūre gyltas, swā swā wē forgyfað ūrum gyltendum. And ne gelǣd þū ūs on costnunge, ac ālȳs ūs of yfele. Sōþlīce.

Comment on Exercise 1.6.3

Nama looks as if it might have the structure *nam* + *a*, but in fact *nama* is itself, in its bisyllabic entirety, the lexical root. *Rīce* once again looks as if it might have the structure *rīc-e* but, once again, *rīce* is itself the root. *Willa* patterns with *nama*, i.e. there's no inflection here. Then there's *eorðan*, whose structure seems plausibly to be *eorð*, earth, followed by the inflection *-an*. Then *heofenum* again, already discussed. The next noun in the sequence is *hlāf*, a word that underlies PDE 'loaf' (though here, *hlāf* means 'bread'). There's no apparent inflection in this word, though. The next noun is *gyltas*. Here, it looks as though we're dealing with a lexical root *gylt*, guilt or offence, followed by an inflection *-as*. The plural inflection *-as* is one that gives rise to the fact that later forms of English pluralise nouns largely by 'adding an s': plural 's' is a survival of OE *-as*. Next in sequence is the unfamiliar word *gyltendum*, though it's clearly somehow related to *gylt*. We might in fact translate *gyltendum* as 'offenders' – forgive our offences, just as we forgive our offenders. (The King James version of the Bible captures this parallelism too – 'forgive us our *trespasses*, as we forgive those who *trespass* against us'.) Next, another unfamiliar word, *costnunge*. There's no clear relationship between this word and anything in PDE, and we have to have access to a glossary or specialist dictionary for this one: 'temptation'. Nevertheless, we might make a reasonable guess that the root of the word is *costnung* and the inflection once again that apparently harmless *-e*. The last word is *yfele*. Intervocalic <f>, remember, is pronounced [v], and this allows us to suggest that the root of the word *yfele* is *yfel*, evil (see Exercise 1.6.0).

We've by no means exhausted the linguistic possibilities or the literary merits of the Lord's Prayer, but we think we've said enough to convince you that this short text is composed in a highly structured language, parts of which are recognisable from our experience of PDE. There are fairly direct survivals, such as *fæder*, or *yfel*, and there are words whose meaning can be readily inferred, like *gylt*, or *gyltendum*, while others are unfamiliar (*costnung*) or have subtly altered their meaning(s), e.g. *hlāf* (consider the PDE distinction between 'loaf' and 'bread').

Whatever the survivals or the changes, the text itself has literary merits just as great as any later version. There's the direct invocation of the loving Father (notice the employment of the *þū* pronoun), the fact that he has a *rīce*, just as many Anglo-Saxon kings had a *rīce*. Moreover, this heavenly *rīce* should not just 'come', it should *tōbecume*, literally 'to-become', or 'come about'. There's the homely invocation of *hlāf*. And there's the parallelism between 'offence' and 'offender' we've already discussed. There's the relative shortness of the phraseology, the avoidance of long-winded diction, and there are the repetitions. It's a piece that invites the divine into the commonplace, and does so with considerable, and memorable, power.

Summary

In Unit 1 we've looked at a key principle of historical reconstruction, the Uniformitarian Hypothesis; we've begun to pronounce OE; we've made an important distinction between content words and function words; and we've looked briefly at some of the conventions of OE poetry, beginning our understanding with Cædmon's *Hymn*.

What follows is a list of study questions, which you may like to complete for yourself, or discuss in class; some websites in which you might like to browse; and some suggestions for further reading. We firmly invite you to complete some of this work before turning to Unit 2.

Study questions

1. What does the abbreviation *OE* stand for? How is that different from *Anglo-Saxon*? Give an example of how both might be used.
2. One important hypothesis that linguists use in reconstructing a language – how it might have sounded, and how it might have changed over the years – is Lass's *Principle of Uniform Possibilities*. Describe this in your own words, and explain how it might help linguistic historians.

3. During what period (more or less) was OE spoken? What was the geographical range of spoken OE? Give an example of a piece of literature recorded in OE.
4. Consider the letters, or letter-combinations, <sc>, <f>, <s>, <cg> and <c>. How might they have been pronounced in OE? Are they pronounced similarly in PDE, or have new sound-spelling conventions been introduced into the language at some time after the OE period?
5. We claimed in this chapter that you as a speaker of English already know a great deal of OE, perhaps without realising that you do. What factors might have allowed us to make such a claim?
6. Why did we imply that there are, in truth, many 'Englishes' rather than one English? Do you agree or disagree? Explain your position.
7. If someone claimed that the English language had become 'degraded' since Shakespeare's time, what might a linguist say in response?
8. What does the term *lexicon* mean to a linguistic historian? In what ways might the term denote something different from the word *dictionary*?
9. What are *content words*? What examples can you find from PDE, and how many of these might have been survivals from OE? Have any such survivals changed their meanings and, if so, how?
10. List five lexical words in PDE that come from OE. Use new examples, i.e. examples you haven't already studied as part of this unit.
11. What does it mean to say that OE nouns had 'grammatical gender'? Name three nouns mentioned in this unit and identify their gender. Does grammatical gender match biological gender? Can you think of any other languages that have grammatical gender?
12. How could you tell 'who was doing what to whom' in OE? In other words, how could you tell grammatical relationships? How do you tell grammatical relationships in PDE? How was word order (that is, crudely, the order in which the subject, verb and object appear in a sentence) different in OE from PDE?

Websites that you may find useful

For some good examples of spoken OE, we suggest:

- http://www.wwnorton.com/ – go towards the end of the page; there are excerpts from several OE texts, including poems, riddles, etc. An excellent site
- http://www.engl.virginia.edu/OE/Guide.Readings/Colloquy.html – go to the pronunciation practice section
- http://www.georgetown.edu/cball/oe/paternoster_oe.html – there is a continuous reading of the Lord's Prayer and a line by line play back of it. General information on OE and links to other helpful sites
- www.anglo-saxon.demon.co.uk – by following the link *Welcome to Anglo-Saxon England* you can browse in various projects currently running on

Old English language, literature and culture. There's a valuable link, for example, to 'Anglo-Saxon resources on the net', and by following it you're able to download some images from 'Anglo-Saxon language and documents', including a reproduction page from the *Anglo-Saxon Chronicle,* which will give you some idea of how a page of Old English looked as it issued from the scribes' hands

- http://www.towson.edu/~duncan/hellinks.html – impressive collection of links to a number of sites dealing with every aspect of the history of English. The information ranges from the general to the specific, including a link to an on-line course in OE from the University of Calgary
- www.kami.demon.co.uk/gesithas/readings/readings.html – this is the homepage for the *Ængliscan Gesīðas,* a 'society . . . for people interested in all aspects of Anglo-Saxon language and culture'. It includes interesting information on runes, the Anglo-Saxon calendar, a bibliography and links to other helpful sites
- http://www.georgetown.edu/cball/oe – you'll find everything put on-line by Professor Ball and her students and colleagues useful and interesting
- www.ling.upenn.edu/~kurisuto/germanic/bright.html – Bright's OE glossary. This is really a wonderful site. It is an OE dictionary based on Bright's text of 1891

We suggest that you try various search engines and keywords such as Old English, Anglo-Saxon, etc.

References and suggestions for further reading

There are several widely used introductions to the Old English language. The most extensive, and currently, we think, the most popular, is that by Bruce Mitchell and Fred C. Robinson, *A guide to Old English* (5th edition, 1992). This has a useful discussion of some issues concerned with history, language and culture; see especially Section 6, pp.118ff. At this stage in our work, the linguistic detail Mitchell and Robinson provide is rather too advanced, but we'll return to sections of their text again in later units, since its scope is fairly comprehensive and its selected passages of Old English well-chosen and clearly edited (Part Two, Section 3, pp.182ff., for example, contains Ælfric's *Colloquy on the occupations,* which we'll be looking at in the next unit, and Section 9, pp.220ff., contains Bede's account of Cædmon. Both sections have short introductory passages that help to put the work into their contexts).

Introductions to the earliest periods of the English language may be found in C.L. Barber, *The English language: a historical introduction*, 1993, especially Chapter 4, while Chapters 3–5 of Albert Baugh and Thomas Cable's *A history of the English language,* 4th edition, 1993, or the subsequent edition

(2001), have earned their status as straightforward readings of the development of Old English. David Crystal's handsome *The Cambridge encyclopedia of the English language* (1995) contains much interesting and useful information on Old English, how it arrived in England and about the people who spoke it. The text is also accompanied by excellent images. Thomas Pyles and John Algeo's *The origin and development of the English language* (1993) is widely used, particularly in the US, and is invaluable, while the relevant sections of Jeremy Smith's *An historical study of English* (1996) should also be consulted. A further useful and readable guide is Chapter 3 of Graddol, Leith and Swann (*English: history, diversity, change,* 1996) where Dick Leith traces the origins of English, and his work contains a word for word translation of Cædmon's *Hymn* (pp.111–112), a further section on OE vocabulary and OE grammar, and some reasons why the grammar of OE began to change (pp.112–120).

On language change, Roger Lass's work, cited earlier in Unit 1, should be accompanied by a reading of April McMahon, *Understanding language change* (1994).

For those wanting to begin to read Old English poetry, and to form some idea of the range, tone and variety of this form of verse, an interesting selection of texts, with the original OE faced by a page of translation, may be found in Andrew Hamer, *A choice of Anglo-Saxon verse* (1970), but this is out of print and may only be obtained through a library. In addition to the material provided in Graddol, Leith and Swann (see above), Cædmon's *Hymn* is valuably commented on in Strang (1970:369), from which parts of our translation(s) have been taken. Barbara Strang's *A history of English* (1970) remains one of the best introductions to the history of the English language, though it's by no means a populist work, and is very concisely written. A scholarly edition of Cædmon's *Hymn,* together with two slightly later Northumbrian poems, is that of A.H. Smith, *Three Northumbrian poems* (2nd edition, 1978).

Unit Two

History, culture, language origins

2.0 Reading passage

We begin with an excerpt from what has come to be known as Ælfric's *Colloquy*. A forerunner of this passage was originally written in Latin by Ælfric, one of the most important churchmen, scholars and educators of the late 10th and early 11th centuries. The piece we're about to use, and the other dialogues that accompany it, were intended for the instruction of school-boys learning Latin. Some time after Ælfric's death, an anonymous monk translated the text into Old English. During the 19th century, the great English philologist Henry Sweet revised the exercise, casting it into idiomatic Old English prose.[1] It's on Sweet's version that Mitchell and Robinson base their 1992 text and on which we base ours (see below). First, read the piece aloud, then attempt to translate it using the glossary given below. Not every word is glossed, so in some cases you'll have to make a contextually based guess.

An effective method for translating is to begin with a word by word translation, called a transliteration. Follow this by putting each sentence or phrase into everyday, idiomatic modern English. Don't use archaisms or stilted language, but try to render the passage into the most natural PDE. Many of our students in both the US and the UK have found starting a notebook dedicated to translations particularly helpful. We've done the first line for you to give you an idea of what we're suggesting. And to help you further, we've given a full translation in the apparatus that concludes this unit. (You're strongly advised not to look at that until you've had a go at the present exercise. 'No cheating' is after all a good rule for life. Usually.) The text given here, part of a dialogue between a narrator and a fisherman, is a shortened adaptation of that found in Mitchell and Robinson's *Guide to Old English* (1992).

[1] Henry Sweet. 1897. *First steps in Anglo-Saxon*. Oxford: The Clarendon Press.

Exercise 2.0.0

The Fisherman	
Hwelcne cræft canst þū?	1
Which occupation know-how-to you?	
What's your occupation?	
Ic eom fiscere.	2
Hwæt begietst þū of þīnum cræft?	3
Bīleofan ic mē begiete, and scrūd, and fēoh.	4
Hū gefēhst þū þā fiscas?	5
Ic gā on mīnne bāt, and rōwe ūt on þā ēa, and weorpe mīn nett on þā ēa.	6
Hwīlum ic weorpe angel ūt mid ǣse, oþþe spyrtan;	7
and swā hwæt swā hīe gehæftaþ ic nime.	8

Hwæt dēst þū gif hit unclǣne fiscas bēoþ?	**9**
Ic weorpe þā unclǣnan ūt, and nime þā clǣnan mē to mete.	**10**
Hwǣr cīepst þū þīne fiscas?	**11**
On þǣre ceastre.	**12**
Hwā bygþ hīe?	**13**
Þā ceasterware. Ne mæg ic hira swā fela gefōn swā ic sellan mæg.	**14**
Hwelce fiscas gefēhst þū?	**15**
Ǣlas, and hacodas, and scēotan, and ealle ōþre fiscas þe on	**16**
þǣm ēam swimmaþ . . .	**17**

Selective glossary

angel	hook
ǣlas	eels
ǣse	bait, food
bāt	boat
begietst	from the verb *begietan*, to acquire, to receive
bīleofan	from *bīleofa*, sustenance, food
ceastre	town
cīepst	from the verb *cīepan*, to sell
cræft	occupation
ēa	water
(ge)fēhst	from the verb *(ge)fōn*, to catch
fiscas	fish(es)
fiscere	fisher(man)
gefēhst	since *ge-* is a prefix, look this word up under <f>
hacodas	pike (a kind of fish, identical to the American Northern Pike)
hwīlum	sometimes
mete	food
nime	from the verb *niman*, to take
oþþe	or
scēotan	trout
spyrtan	from *spyrte*, eel-basket
weorpe	from the verb *weorpan*, to throw

You probably found that, although there are several words in the passage that look and sound similar to their PDE counterparts – *angel, nett, cræft* – there are several, perhaps many, others whose pronunciation and meaning only become clear with some knowledge of OE sound-structure, so we'll return to your translation once we've discussed some more aspects of that.

The systematic study of sound-structure in language is known as *phonology*. To study phonology isn't simply to study pronunciation (the study of the actual physical stream of speech is known as *phonetics*). Phonology implies pronunciation, surely, but it also includes the study of deeper principles: the ways in which sound-systems are characteristically, perhaps even universally, organised; the ways in which we can speak of *classes* of sounds (on a broad view, entities such as consonants and vowels); and the ways in which certain speech-sounds, or classes of sounds, may be deleted in some linguistic environments, inserted into others, and so on.

Here we're going to focus just on the consonant system of OE, partly as it is manifested in the above passage, partly as it is manifested at large. One question you might like to ask yourself at this stage is 'What is a consonant?' And, a supplementary but useful rider, 'How does a consonant differ from a vowel?' In the present context, our task is going to be to reconstruct the consonant system of OE. This is a more difficult question than perhaps it appears.

To what period of OE would our exercise refer? OE of the 7th century? Or the 11th? And what accent of OE would we want or need to refer to? After all, in PDE, both AmE and BrE, there are certain accents that contain consonants others do not contain and, contrariwise, there may be certain accents that lack a part or parts of the consonant inventory (roughly, a full list of consonant sounds) of others. (Certain BrE accents, for example, appear to lack the phoneme /h/, so you hear *'eart* for *heart*, *'ear* for *hear*, *'ome* for *home*.)

These problems notwithstanding, we can establish a working consonant inventory for 'Old English' with some rigour. One reasonable procedure would be to work out what consonants occur in the variety of the language given above, that is, in 11th century West Saxon – roughly the time and place in which our anonymous monk translated Ælfric's Latin *Colloquy*. The task is made easier by the fact that in most forms of OE, what you see in the written system is very much what you get in the spoken one. (Remember one of the pronunciation hints given in Unit 1: pronounce everything.)

Exercise 2.0.1

Look back at or, better, print out, the *Colloquy* excerpt. Work out what consonants occur, note where they occur (e.g. 'typically at the beginning/end of words', or 'between vowel sounds', or both) and try to model what the consonant inventory of 11th century West Saxon might have looked and sounded like. This exercise will prove to be a little more straightforward in theory than in practice because there are a few exceptions to our first rule of pronunciation ('pronounce everything'). We'll step around these problems by making some extra stipulations. These will seem arbitrary at first, but their analytical usefulness will become justified as we proceed.

The first stipulation is that <hw> (found in the first word of the text, written <Hwelcne>, line 1) is a digraph, that is, two letters written to represent one sound. The OE sound here was probably pronounced like the <wh> combination found in Scottish or Irish English *which* – it's a kind of breathy 'w' sound, produced with rounding of the lips. (Many Scottish and Irish English speakers are able to contrast the words *which* and *witch*, but for many speakers of other varieties of both BrE and AmE, there's no such contrast.) For the sake of convenience, let's represent the relevant sound with the symbol /ʍ/.

Staying with the word <Hwelcne>, we also have the sound /l/, which we find in PDE words like *like* and *help*, and the letter <c>, which you will recall from Unit 1 sometimes has the sound 'ch' like the last sound in the word *which*. (In fact, this letter shape is very often pronounced as 'ch' when it occurs in the last position of the syllable, as here – if you say the word 'Hwelcne' slowly, you'll probably hear a syllable division like 'Hwelc + ne', where '+' marks the syllable boundary.) Again, to avoid confusion, we'll designate the symbol /ʧ/ to stand for this sound.

Ignoring all the vowel sounds, the last consonantal sound occurring in <Hwelcne> is /n/. So, in the first word, we have these consonantal sounds: /ʍ/, /l/, /ʧ/, /n/.

In the next word, the initial written <c> isn't /ʧ/. Remember that written <c> is often pronounced /ʧ/ when this occurs *finally* in the syllable. Here, the <c> symbol occurs *initially* in the syllable and word. This is the sound that you hear in words like *cat, kind* and *call*. We'll use /k/ to designate this sound.

Go ahead and finish the line, remembering that the letter shape <þ> is pronounced as voiced or voiceless 'th': we'll use /θ/ to designate the voiceless sound sometimes indicated by written <þ>. (Remember voicing, from Unit 1?)

In line 2, remember that the combination of letters <sc> – another digraph – is pronounced like the first sound in *ship* or *should*. Once again we need a special symbol to avoid confusion, so we'll use a symbol we introduced in Unit 1, IPA /ʃ/. Everything else will follow our rules until we get to line three.

The <g> in the second word of line 3 – the word written <begietst> – will sound pretty much like the first sound in *gate* – our students sometimes call this a 'hard *g*' – but when the <g> is part of the very common prefix 'ge' as we see in line 5, it is pronounced more like the sound written as <y> in *yes* or *yuck*.

This seems like another stipulation, but we can explain it. The letter shape <g>, when it stands initially in an OE syllable and where it's not followed by another consonant, is sometimes pronounced with 'hard *g*' (other OE examples are words such as <gān>, to go, <gāst>, spirit, cf. PDE ghost). However, if this same letter shape stands before what we'll eventually come to call a high or mid front vowel – vowel sounds often written in OE as graphic varieties of <i> or <e> or <ie> – then that letter shape <g> is there pronounced like the first consonant sound you get in PDE *yes* or *yard*. The phonemic symbol for such a sound is /j/. So by this stipulation, the OE word spelled <gē> is pronounced with the initial consonant /j/ – a fuller transcription of the whole word would be /je:/, and it's this pronunciation that underlies that of the (now antique) pronoun <ye> in PDE. 'O come! all *ye* faithful. . . .'

If we continue with the exercise, everything goes according to our rules-of-thumb – (i) 'what you see is pretty much what you get'; (ii) 'pronounce everything' – until the letter shape <f> in line 4 (you encounter this in the word <bīleofan>). <f> standing between two vowel shapes, in this case the vowels written as <eo> and <a>, is pronounced [v]. We talked about this in the last unit: remember the pronunciation of the OE spelling <heofon> (PDE heaven).

One more exception: in line 7, the <s> in the seventh word, the word spelled <ǣse>, occurs between two vowel shapes. Where it crops up between two vowels, the written consonant shape <s> is pronounced [z], as in the first consonants found in PDE words such as *zebra* and *zoo*.

Finally, we have no example of it in our reading, but in OE, when the written shapes <þ> or <ð> occur between two vowels, their spoken instantiations are voiced, and sound like the 'th' in PDE *then* or *this* or *bother*. We'll use the phonemic symbol /ð/ to designate this voiced counterpart of /θ/. (We introduced this matter briefly in Unit 1, where we began to suggest that although /f/ and /v/ contrasted in PDE, they didn't do so in OE, where [f] and [v] were contextually determined pronunciations of *one* underlying speech-sound.)

At this point, we have an emerging inventory of OE consonants. To help you complete the exercise, we give a fuller – but still not quite complete – inventory in table 2.1. Some of these sounds we discussed in Unit 1. The written symbols you'll find in the 'grapheme' column (if it isn't already clear, *graphemes* are letter-shapes of the conventional alphabet). The phonemes (the speech-sounds and their symbols) you can find in the left-hand column, headed 'sounds'. And in the right-hand column, we've given examples that help to illustrate each sound as you might expect to encounter it in PDE, along with some OE examples. We've underlined the relevant PDE graphemes in the 'example' column:

Table 2.1 Some Old English consonants

Sounds Phonemes in / /	**OE grapheme(s)** Graphemes in < >	**Example**
/ʍ/	<hw>	what, where, which
/l/	l	like, lean
/ʧ/	c	which, itch
/n/	n	now, neat
/k/	c	craft, kind
/r/	r	reach, craft
/f/	f	craft, find, fish
/t/	t	craft, sit, take
/s/	s	sit, list
/θ/	þ	thin, thigh
/m/	m	mine, mean
/ʃ/	sc	ship, should (OE *fisc*)
/g/	g	guard, good
/d/	d	dog, deed
/x/	h	ach (German), loch
/p/	p	pie, pond
/j/	g(e)	yup (OE *giet*, yet)
/ð/	þ or ð	then, this
/w/	w	work (OE *weorc*; see below)
[/v/	f	knives (OE *heofon*, etc.)]
[/z/	s	zeal, zip]

Exercise 2.0.2

Have any of these *sounds* disappeared from (your variety of) English? If you find that certain speech-sounds have disappeared, can you guess why they might have done so? Are there any graphemes that have disappeared from English? Which digraphs (two letters representing one sound) are pronounced differently in PDE and OE? Go back to Unit 1 and add to your general inventory of OE sounds any sounds that were listed before, but not mentioned in the last exercise. Now reread the passage (Exercise 2.0.0.) aloud. Are there any words you couldn't make out before, but can now?

Some difficulties might be these:

- The symbol <c> in the word spelled <cīepst>, line 11. We stated that the symbol <c> is sometimes pronounced /k/, and sometimes /ʧ/ (PDE ***itch***). (If you look into the table above, you'll see that the written symbol <c> is related to two possible, and different, pronunciations.) In the word <cīepst>, though, notice that the initial consonant is followed by a vowel shape spelled with an <i>. What we're in fact looking at is the same sort of thing we noted when we thought through how the letter shape <g> was pronounced: in some environments, written <g> was pronounced as /j/, while in others, it was pronounced as 'hard *g*', /g/. With the letter shape <c>, things aren't radically different: when it's followed by the vowel shape written <i> (<ī>, or just <i>), <c> gets pronounced as /ʧ/. If you pronounce the word spelled <cīepst> with this initial sound, you'll probably pronounce a word something like 'cheapst' (with that lump of consonants at the word-end). That's along the right lines because the word actually means 'sell' ('Where do you sell your fish?'), and you may notice a resemblance between the concept of selling and the PDE word *cheap*. Think also of the London street name *Cheapside*. This wasn't (and certainly isn't) a place where you could go bargain-hunting. It was a place where goods were bought and sold.
- Another thing that merits attention is the symbol <w>, which you'll have found in the word <weorpe> in line 10. We already have the symbol <hw>, whose pronunciation we established as /ʍ/ – a 'breathy sort of *w*'. But the symbol <w>, though it's related to a sound which is produced in the same kind of way as /ʍ/ (the production of both 'w' and /ʍ/ sounds is modulated by rounded lips), isn't 'breathy'. It's pronounced in much the same way as it looks, and the relevant symbol for the spoken sound is /w/. It appears, then, that OE had two varieties of 'w-like' sounds, /w/ and /ʍ/. As we've noted, some varieties of English still contain such a contrast, and that contrast helps to distinguish *witch* from *which*, or *why* from (a river name) *Wye*.

- A final sound we ought to consider is the sound suggested by the <h> of the word spelled <hacodas> in line 16. If you look at the table above, you'll see that we give the pronunciation /x/ for <h>. But in the example spelled <hacodas>, that doesn't seem right. For one thing, there are no PDE words that *begin* with the speech sound /x/, and vanishingly few (again, in PDE) that actually *end* with such a speech sound. What we might suggest is that where the letter shape <h> occurs initially in a syllable, as it does in our example <hacodas>, as in other words not given in our passage (e.g. OE *hring*, ring, or OE *hǣlan*, to heal), then it's pronounced as its written form suggests, as /h/. Therefore we now have two pronunciations for the letter shape written as <h>: we have /h/ when the relevant sound occurs syllable-initially and /x/ when it occurs before a (final) consonant (OE *niht*, night) or syllable-finally (OE *sōhte*, sought). Notice that quite often, PDE spellings containing <gh> – just as in PDE <night> or <sought> – suggest an earlier pronunciation in /x/.

Having looked at the consonant system of OE, let's now have an initial look at the production of vowel shapes. In all known languages, vowel sounds (i.e. entities including school-room 'a, e, i, o, u') are produced, like the vast majority of speech-sounds, on an egressive (out-breathing) air-stream which originates, of course, in the lungs. (It's very difficult to produce any meaningful speech sounds at all when you're breathing *in*.) There are several places along the vocal tract at which the shape of this egressive air-stream can be modified. One place is the mouth or *oral cavity*. Here the shape of the air-stream can be changed by movements of the tongue and lips. In the case involving the production of certain consonants, the tongue may actually touch the roof of the mouth (the *hard palate*), or the bony ridge behind the upper teeth (the *alveolar ridge*), or the teeth themselves, in order to produce certain types of speech-sound. Modification of the air-stream through movements of the tongue, teeth, lips (the active *articulators*), as well as modifications to the size and shape of the oral cavity, produce recognisably distinctive speech-sounds. 'Distinctive' is here a key word. The sounds /s/ and /z/, for example, differ only in terms of their voicing (/s/ is voiceless, /z/ voiced). Yet this apparently trivial difference leads to meaningful contrast – 'seal' and 'zeal' are 'different words' in English, largely because /s/ and /z/ are distinctive speech-sounds within the system of English phonology.

If you think for a moment of the production of *vowels* in English, you'll find that when vowels are produced, the blade of the tongue (the part of the tongue between the centre and the tip of the tongue) and tip of the tongue aren't actually touching any of the other articulatory organs. The sides of the tongue may be touching the upper and/or lower teeth (try thinking about the position of your tongue while simultaneously pronouncing a lengthened version of the vowel-shape 'eeee' to make this last point clear), but this doesn't seem to be a decisive factor in vowel-production or vowel recognition. What seems to count, in the production of vowel shapes, is simply the relative height of the body and blade of the tongue, and whether the tongue is moved toward the front of the mouth or whether it's medial or retracted. These movements affect the shape of the oral cavity, and therefore the resonance of the vowel shape produced.

We can begin to diagrammatise this. The shape in figure 2.1 is known as a *vowel trapezium*. The vowel trapezium is a stylised diagram of a human mouth, as this might be seen from the left-hand side. The labels are self-explanatory: they refer to the front, centre and back of the oral cavity. If you look at this shape, you'll find certain vowel shapes symbolised in different parts of the trapezium. For example, you'll find the symbol /i/ in the front/close position, in the top left corner of the trapezium. 'Close' is a technical term that refers to the closeness of the front part of the blade of the tongue to the upper/front part of the oral cavity. Therefore, the diagram suggests, when a vowel shape such as '/i/' is produced (we'll refine the discussion of this sound and its symbol later), the tongue is *fronted* and *raised* into the 'close' position.

If you now look into the bottom right corner of the trapezium, you'll find a shape symbolised '/ɑ/'. You can easily infer from the vowel trapezium that when such a vowel shape is produced, the (body/blade of the) tongue is *lowered* and *retracted*: it is in the fully 'open' position.

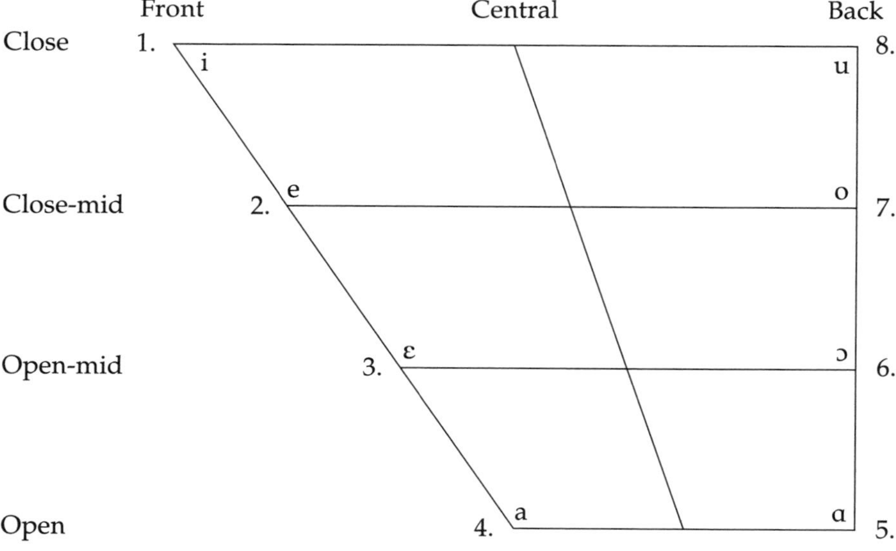

Figure 2.1 A first vowel trapezium

Notice that the symbols you find in this trapezium suggest nothing about vowel *length*. We'll have to do some more work on that problem in Unit 5 since, clearly, speakers and hearers are readily able to identify 'long' and 'short' vowel shapes and to deploy them contrastively. For the moment, all we're doing is beginning to illustrate how linguists think about defining vowel shapes. Further, you might notice that, since OE spelling involves 'what you see is what you get', a vowel spelled, for example, <i> or <ī> by an Anglo-Saxon scribe will usually imply that some high, front, close vowel shape is indicated by the relevant grapheme. Similarly, a vowel spelled as <u> or <ū> by an Anglo-Saxon scribe will usually imply some high, back, close vowel shape.

Turning back to *consonants*, we can observe that these are in some ways more spectacular entities than vowels. Virtually all consonants involve some kind of more or less radical constriction of the air-stream, or even its total, albeit momentary, stoppage. Part of what distinguishes one sound from another is exactly *how* the egressive air-stream is modified. This 'how' can be put in more technical (and more accurate) terms as the 'manner of articulation'.

Consider for a moment the speech-sound 'p', or better, to give it its proper phonological symbolism, /p/. In the production of this sound the air-stream is *stopped* by closed lips; the nasal cavity is also shut, so no air can escape through the nose. Both lips are the active articulators, the critical 'place of articulation', and the way in which the air stream is modified is by stopping it. Thus we could classify /p/ as a *bilabial stop*, specifying first the *place* in which the air-stream is modified and, second, the *manner* in which it is interfered with. *Place* of articulation and *manner* of articulation are two factors linguists specify when providing a technical description of a sound.

Now consider the speech-sound /s/. In producing this sound, we think you'll find that the body of the tongue is raised towards the roof of the mouth, with the sides of the tongue touching the upper teeth. The tip of the tongue lies just behind the bony ridge behind the upper teeth (the *alveolar ridge*), but doesn't actually touch it. The air-stream, in production of /s/, is forced into the millimetric gap between tongue-tip and alveolar ridge, and friction results. We hear this friction as an audible hiss. Further, unlike the production of the speech-sound /p/, in producing /s/ the air-stream is not stopped. /s/ involves continuation of the air-stream, not its stoppage. Sounds that are produced by modifying the air-stream in this way are called *fricatives*. Fricatives are a particular class of sound, namely that class of sound which involve friction in their production. Along with /s/, consonants such as /f/, /v/, /z/ and several others involve friction, and thus would be classed as fricatives.

If we develop this just a little further, we can begin to understand what linguists do when they describe consonants and state how consonants contrast with each other. We have a three-way classificatory system now in play: we can specify the *place* of articulation, the *manner* of articulation and the *class of sound* to which the speech sound belongs. Taking /p/, /s/, /f/ and /v/ as three contrasting speech sounds, this is what their linguistic classification might begin to look like:

Table 2.2 The three-way classification of English consonants

	Place	Manner	Class of sound
/p/	Lips	Stoppage of air-stream	Stop
/s/	Tongue/alveolar ridge	Friction	Fricative
/f/	Lips/teeth	Friction	Fricative
/v/	Lips/teeth	Friction	Fricative

Exercise 2.0.3

In the above classificatory table, notice that /f/ and /v/ have exactly the same specifications. Both are produced in the same place, using the same active articulators (lips and (bottom) teeth); the production of both involves friction, and both sounds are classed as fricatives. What, then, is the factor that crucially allows us to distinguish between the two sounds /f/ and /v/?

Comment on Exercise 2.0.3

It's *voicing*, which you'll recall from Unit 1. Voicing involves vibration of the vocal cords as a sound is uttered. If you conduct the same experiment we asked you to conduct in Unit 1, putting your fingers lightly either side of your Adam's apple as you produce the relevant sound(s), you'll be able to feel voicing, that vibration in the vocal folds. Try the experiment with the speech sound /v/ (a voiced sound), and now with /f/ (a voiceless sound). Switch from 'ffffff' to 'vvvvv' without a pause.

What you've just done is help to establish another way in which consonants contrast. As well as contrasting in their place and manner of articulation, they can contrast in their voicing. Thus /f/ and /v/.

The distinction between voiced and voiceless sounds is of great significance for English – in fact, for all languages. Consonants, for example, all involve some kind of occlusion or stricture in the air-stream, as we've just established, but typically (note: 'typically' . . . but not always) they fall into *pairs* of sounds, the one voiced, the other voiceless. /s/ and /z/, for example, don't differ in their *place of articulation*, nor in their *manner of articulation*, but they do differ in terms of *voicing*.

Exercise 2.0.4

Go back to your inventory of consonants in OE. Which of these consonants seem to be voiced/voiceless pairs? (In other words, which consonants *don't* differ in place or manner of articulation, but *do differ only* in whether or not they're voiced?) You might object 'How will I know? I don't speak Old English . . . !' But you can complete this exercise quite satisfactorily by using your knowledge of your own variety of PDE . . . and your common sense.

Comment on Exercise 2.0.4

There are several pairs you could have chosen: /t/ and /d/ would be one case, while /k/ and /g/ ('hard *g*') would be another. Both members of each pair are produced in the same way, in the same part of the oral cavity, using the same articulators. They differ just in terms of voicing. Obviously, even self-evidently, we have voiceless/voiced pairs in PDE as well: /f/ and /v/, /p/ and /b/, /t/ and /d/, /k/ and /g/, where the first member of each pair given here is voiceless. The same could be said of /θ / and /ð/ in PDE. (Recall that these symbols stand respectively for the voiceless 'th' sound (PDE ***thigh***) and its voiced counterpart (PDE ***then***).)

Exercise 2.0.5

One further issue concerning consonants. In PDE, the sounds /p/ and /b/, /s/ and /z/, /f/ and /v/, /θ/ and /ð/ are *contrastive*. This means that the contrast between two sounds is *meaningful*. To illustrate more precisely what we mean by this, consider the following frame. Which single consonants can be inserted into the gap (the underscored space) in order to produce meaningful monosyllables, that is, different words, in PDE?

<____in> (insert a consonant, so that a meaningful English word is produced)

Two obvious candidates are /p/ and /b/ (PDE ***pin*** and ***bin***). Two further candidates are /t/ and /d/ (PDE ***tin*** and ***din***). We could also insert /s/ (PDE *sin*), though there's no PDE syllable *zin*. Similarly, we could insert /θ/ (PDE ***thin***), though again there's no PDE /ðɪn/. We could add other speech-sounds: the voiceless /f/ of *fin*; the sound that forms the initial 'g' in ***gin*** (/ʤɪn/); and so on. These consonantal differences are, as we've seen, *contrastive*, in the narrow sense in which we're beginning to use that term. That is, these sounds are *phonemes*.

You might want to try the same kind of exercise using the following frame:

<pi____> (insert a consonant, so that a meaningful English word is produced

In this frame, certainly, you could have inserted /t/ (*pit*), or /s/ (*piss* – note that <ss> is a digraph and stands for a single consonant phoneme), or /n/ (*pin*). But you could also have inserted a speech sound such as /ʧ/ (*pitch*).

By means of this exercise, we're beginning to establish the consonant phonemes, the systematically functional speech-sounds, of PDE, and along the analytical way we're saying some useful things about the sound system of OE, too. And here let's risk a more precise definition of what a phoneme is. It's *a minimal sound-unit which is meaningful in the linguistic system of a given language.*

Given some of the background we've introduced at the front end of this unit, let's reconsider the opening line of the *Colloquy*: *Hwelcne cræft canst þū*? Focus for the moment on *cræft* and *canst*. How is the <c> pronounced in each case? And is the speech-sound suggested by this written <c> actually a phoneme in, say, 11th century West Saxon?

<c> occurs initially in both syllables, but in the first word it's followed by <r>. So this consonant can (i) stand alone while initial in the syllable (*canst*) or (ii) combine with a following consonant in the same syllable-initial position (*cræft*). These two observations hint that the speech-sound symbolised by written <c> may here turn out to be a distinctive phoneme. What's more, we have PDE pronunciation to help us: OE *cræft* eventually yields PDE craft, and *canst* (from the OE verb *cunnan*, to know how to) is related to PDE *can*. (Speakers of German might also like to note PDG *ich kann Deutsch*, 'I know (how to speak) German'.) In both these PDE words, orthographic <c> is pronounced with the (back of the) blade of the tongue raised to the soft palate and the air-stream is momentarily stopped, leading to a rapid plosive release. Graphic <c>, then, here translates into the speech sound /k/.

If we have a /k/, is its voiced counterpart, /g/, found in the passage? We already know from Exercise 2.0.5 that it is. Consider line 6, and the phrase *ic gā*, I go. The <g> is here clearly initial in its syllable, and PDE pronunciation again helps us. Graphic <g> is here related to phonemic /g/. It would appear, then, that /k/ and /g/ are paired: they are distinctive phonemes in 11th century West Saxon. In this case, voicing (as expected) produces a phonemic distinction.

Would that historical reconstruction were always so simple. Complications arise with graphic <f> and with graphic <þ>. (If you remember our work from Unit 1, then you might be able to guess what they are.) We'll comment later on what these complications involve. Despite your howls of protest, and your insistent request for further work on (Old) English phonology, we're going to turn now to another topic.

2.1 Some history

We've referred to the earliest English language and to 'the peoples who used it'. The plural, *peoples*, was used deliberately. The term *Anglo-Saxon* contains two words, and this might give us a hint that when we think into the pre-Conquest past we're not looking at a particularly settled or homogeneous society. The concept of 'England' and 'the English people' is in fact a relatively late one. Before the early 10th century, very few Anglo-Saxons would have thought of themselves as particularly 'English'. This is so because the history of the English peoples in the OE period (again, roughly 500–1150 – though we don't believe in periods except as arbitrary constructs, do we?) is largely a history of tribal loyalties and treacheries, of warring kingdoms, of conquest and settlement. At that time, and certainly in the period before the later 9th century, a person's loyalties were to a local tribe and king rather than to a nation. Geographically as well as culturally (and linguistically) it makes more sense to think of these times in terms of kingdoms and their local difficulties, rather than large native conglomerates with common laws, rights, duties and language, although, as we'll see, the term *English* was used from an early period in order to denote the language of all the Anglo-Saxons.

This pattern, of factions, conquests and settlement, can clearly be seen when we look at the coming of the Angles, Saxons and others to what Rome called 'Britannia', many parts of which are now called England. The Anglo-Saxons didn't arrive en masse, or even with well-defined ideas of conquest and government. They arrived by invitation and, thereafter, almost by a determined, if continuing, kind of accident. Some notes on history may help us to understand the accident.

From the Roman historian Tacitus, in his *Germania* (see also Section 3.1 below), we know that by the first century AD, Germanic tribes had long been settled in northern Europe. These tribes seem to have been organised on a local basis, forming larger units only when militarily or politically expedient.

Until the early 5th century most of 'Britain' formed part of an extended Roman Empire. The native inhabitants were Celtic peoples, whose languages are the direct parents of the surviving present-day Celtic languages. Very few Celtic words survive into PDE, but this isn't altogether surprising. If there were bilingual Latin/Celtic speakers in that long-ago Britain, the Celtic language was virtually eclipsed as Celtic society vanished or was incorporated into a Romanised infrastructure. That isn't to say that we can't find *any* influence from Celtic or from Latin words borrowed into the English language via Celtic. Place-names, for example, are one lexical field where words of Celtic provenance are still in use. County names such as Kent, Devonshire, Cumbria and Cornwall all contain Celtic elements. Many river names (Ae, Avon, Aire, Esk, Usk, Wye, among others) were originally Celtic;

and names for natural features such as hills and mountains may often be Celtic in origin (*tor*, mound; *combe*, valley; *crag*, rock or hill; *luh* (loch, lough), lake are representative). This geographical pattern isn't accidental.

Exercise 2.1.0

On a map of England, shade in the areas – the counties – mentioned in the last paragraph. You'll notice a geographical pattern. Why do you think this pattern exists?

Comment on Exercise 2.1.0

You can download maps of England from the Internet. Many websites are devoted to maps and, with a bit of ingenuity, you can download and print historical maps of England, including maps of Celtic Britain, or maps of the early Anglo-Saxon settlements, or maps of the Anglo-Saxon kingdoms as they might have existed in 700, or 900 . . . Below, in map 1, you'll find we provide a bare template outline of the UK mainland. We provide this outline so that you can make copies of it. On the first of your copies you should have marked in the counties we mentioned in the previous paragraphs.

The answer to the question we asked lies, of course, in the settlement of Anglo-Saxon England. The Anglo-Saxon incomers largely settled in, and spread from, the south-east and east. As they did so, it seems that Romano-Celtic languages and culture were largely subsumed in the invasions, or driven ever westerly.

In map 2 you'll see the Anglo-Saxon kingdoms as they were during the period of the Heptarchy. Notice the important boundary that runs between Carlisle and Jarrow, and also what is going to be another important boundary, running south of Chester towards Hereford. In map 3 ('The Mercian Supremacy'), you'll see that this boundary is marked as Offa's Dyke. In both maps, you'll find the names of some important religious sities (such as Lindisfarne, Jarrow and Canterbury). Try to remember these and to picture their position in relation to English cultural geography.

In maps 3 and 4, which show the Anglo-Saxon kingdoms as they existed in 1800 and in the 10th century, you'll see the emergence of what, by the early 11th century, is almost a unified country.

In these maps we've gone well beyond the Anglo-Saxon settlements and anticipated much later developments in political and cultural history – some of which we discuss in later Units. Nevertheless, the maps should give you some idea of how 'England' emerged from what were the early incursions of the Angles and Saxons.

Once you've looked at these maps, complete the next exercise (2.1.1), then begin to think with us about the nature and extent of the Anglo-Saxon settlements themselves.

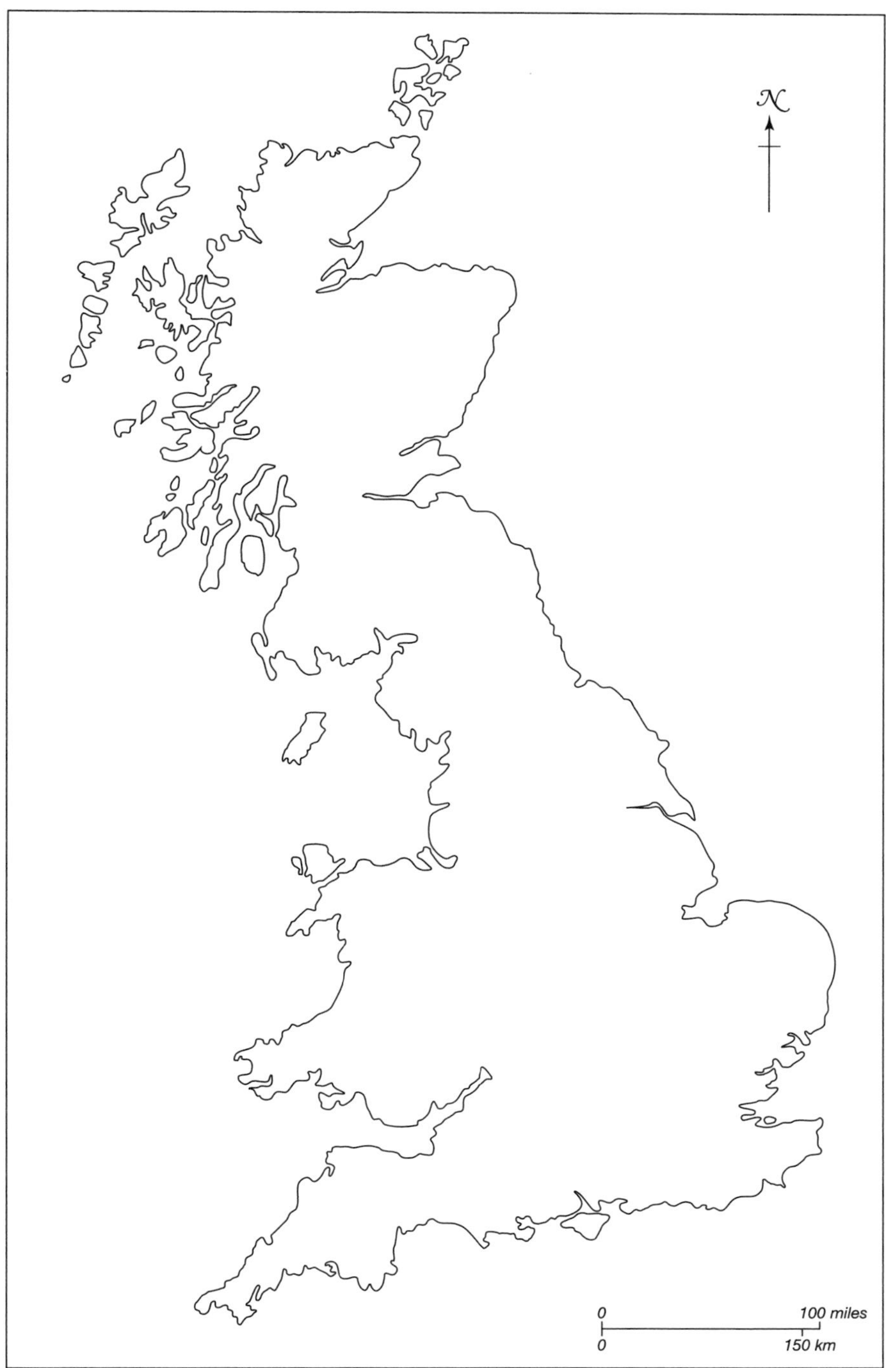

Map 1 Outline of Great Britain

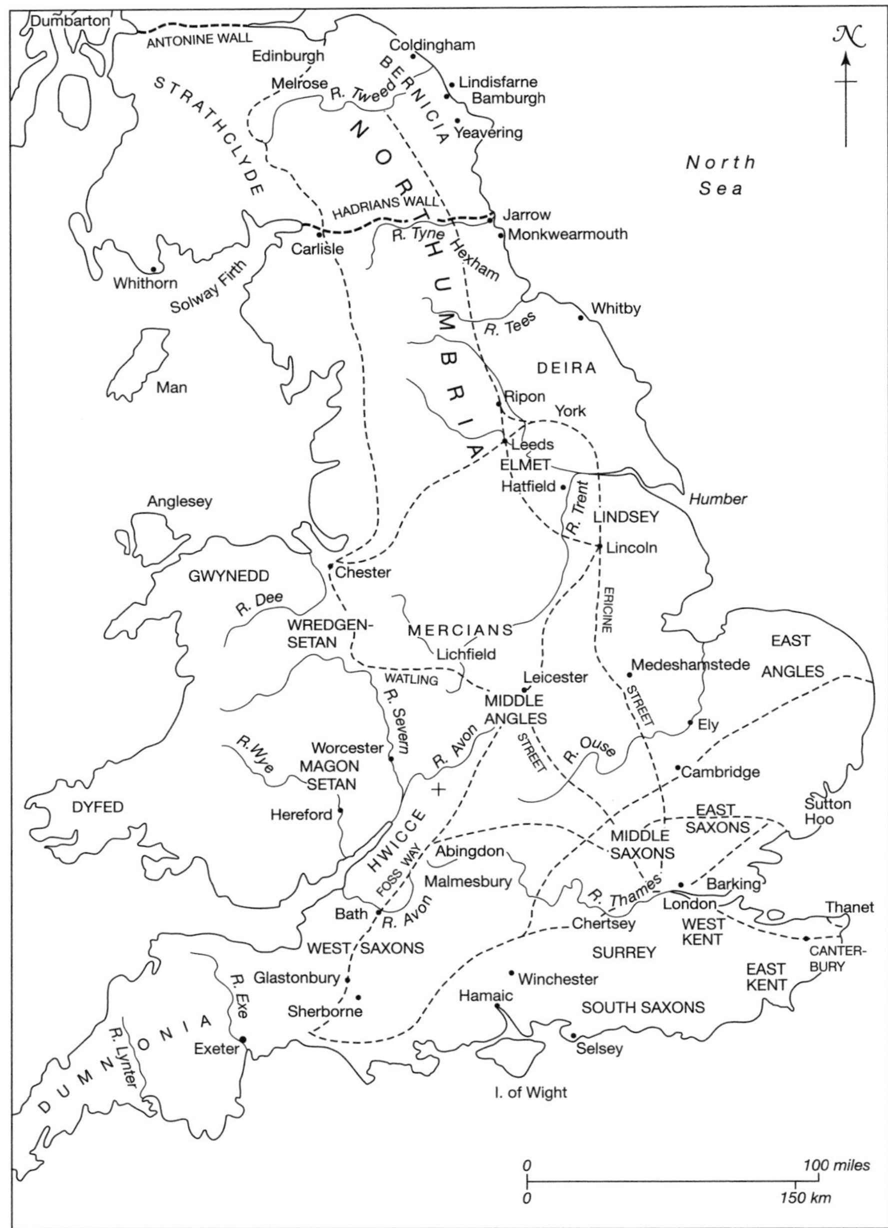

Map 2 The period of the Heptarchy

Source: After map 'The Heptarchy' (c.700) from http://www.trin.cam.ac.uk/sdk13/RPMaps/MapPolDev.jpg. Reproduced by permission of Professor Simon Keynes.

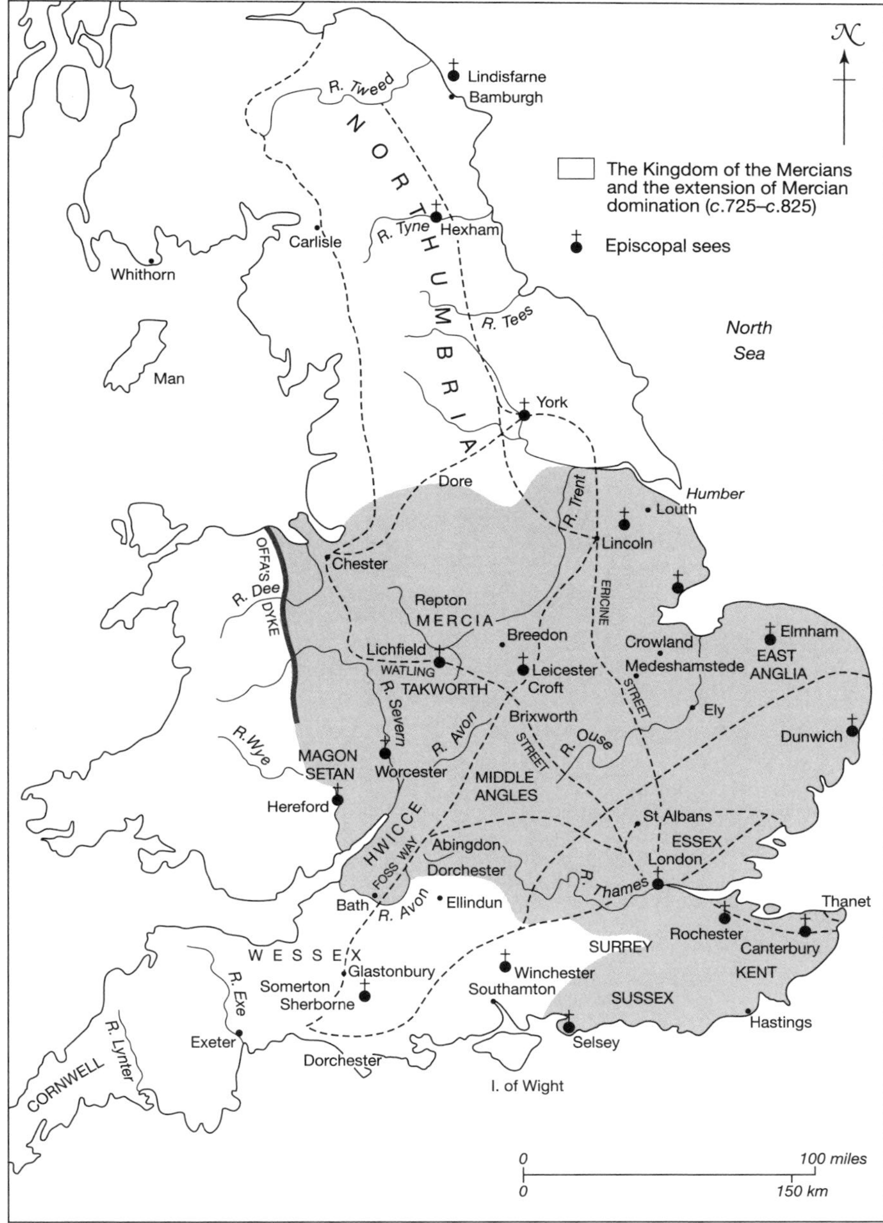

Map 3 The Mercian Supremacy

Source: After map 'The Mercian Supremacy' (c. 800) from http://www.trin.cam.ac.uk/sdk13/RPMaps/MapPolDev.jpg. Reproduced by permission of Professor Simon Keynes.

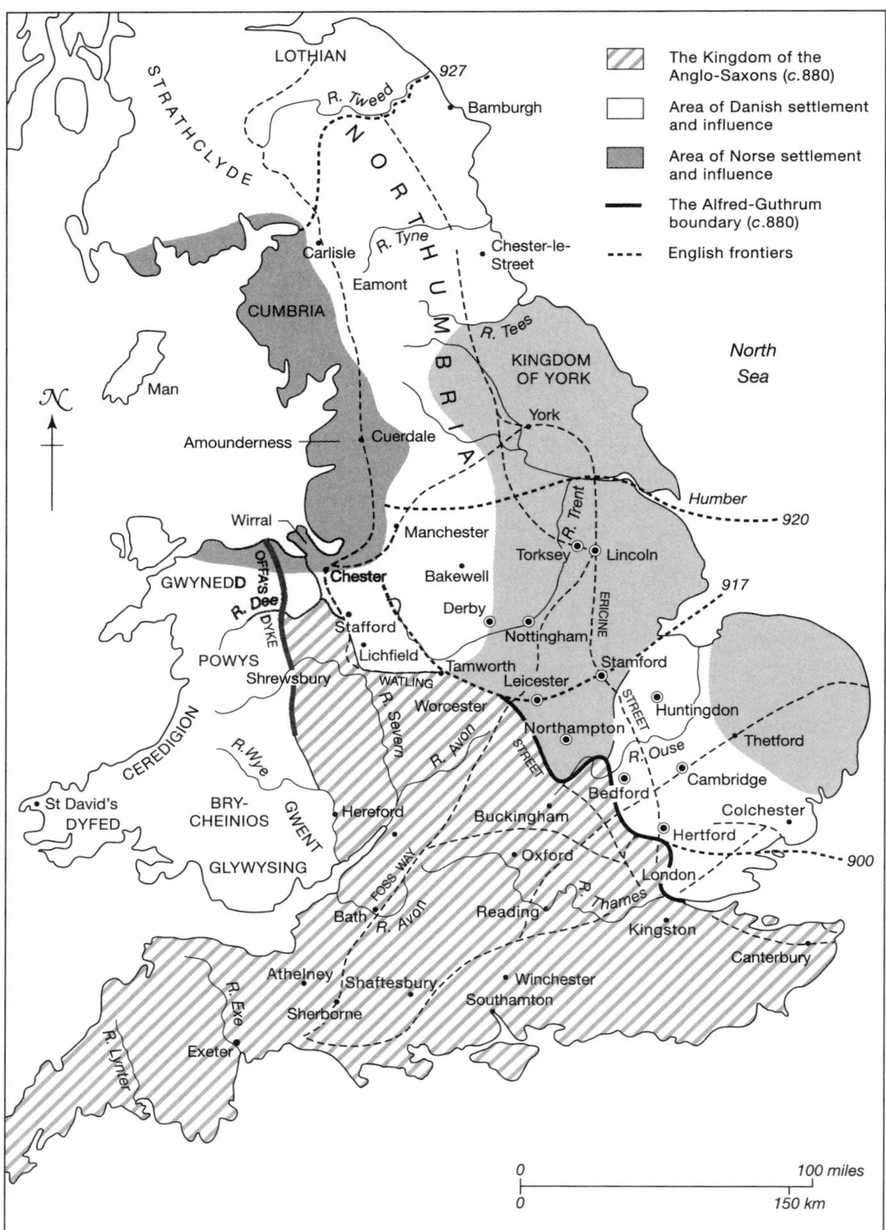

Map 4 The tenth century

Source: After map 'The Kingdom of the Anglo-Saxons' (c.900) from http://www.trin.cam.ac.uk/sdk13/RPMaps/MapPolDev.jpg. Reproduced by permission of Professor Simon Keynes.

Exercise 2.1.1

The following passage is adapted into English from the account given, in Latin, by Bede (often known as the 'Venerable Bede', c.671–735) in his great work, *Historia Ecclesiastica Gentis Anglorum*, the *History of the English Church and Peoples*, completed in 731. We encountered Bede in Unit 1: it's in his *History* that the story of Cædmon is first found.

In the following extract, Bede is writing about something that occurred roughly 300 years before his lifetime. Study the passage carefully.

> In the year of our Lord 449, Martian became Emperor with Valentinian and forty-sixth successor to Augustus. In his time the Angles or Saxons came to Britain at the invitation of King Vortigern in three longships, and were granted lands in the eastern part of the island on condition that they protected the country. Nevertheless, their real intention was to attack it. At first they engaged the enemy advancing from the north, and having defeated them, sent back news of their success to their homeland, adding that the country was fertile and the Britons cowardly. Whereupon a larger fleet quickly came over with a great body of warriors, which, when joined to the original forces, constituted an invincible army. They also received grants of land and money from the Britons, on condition that they maintained the peace and security of the island against all enemies.
>
> These newcomers were from the three most formidable races of Germany, the Saxons, Angles, and Jutes. From the Jutes are descended the people of Kent and the Isle of Wight, and those in the province of Wessex opposite the Isle of Wight are called Jutes to this day . . . Their first chieftains are said to have been Hengist and Horsa . . .
>
> (trans. Leo Sherley-Price, Penguin Classics, 1955 or later edition)

Bede was a careful historian, and his account seems to be a relatively accurate rendering of what happened three centuries earlier. Bede's achievement as a chronicler seems all the more astonishing when you consider that he was writing about a time for which there were no contemporary records and whose history was recorded orally and passed down from one generation to another, often in song or verse. As Bill Bryson puts it in his interesting little book, *Mother tongue* (1991:41), when we think about what Bede was trying to achieve, it 'is rather like us writing a history of Elizabethan England based on hearsay'.

One of the significant things we might consider is that Bede used the term 'Angles' in the title of his great work. By the time he was writing, 'Angles' was a term used indiscriminately for Angles, Saxons and Jutes. This word is closely related to the word 'English', which was used from the beginning to describe the language of the settlers, whatever their origins. From 'Angle', too, comes the compound *Angel-cynn*, race of the Angles, and *Engla-land*, land of the Angles, which around 1000 becomes the commonest term to describe the country itself.

Given all the evidence – evidence from Bede, evidence from existing place-names, archaeological evidence – it's likely that the invaders/settlers came from the area of north-west Germany and Denmark, perhaps even north-east Holland, the area known today as Friesland. Indeed Frisian, still spoken by about 300,000 people in this part of the Netherlands, is the language to which English is most closely related historically. The incomers seem first to have made incursions along the south coast, and also settled along the east coast, south of the Humber, especially in East Anglia. Soon they spread westwards and northwards, and by the end of the 7th century the Anglo-Saxons (as we now call them) had settled almost all of England and southern Scotland, with the exception of Cornwall and, perhaps, the extreme north-west of England.

You can find something of the pattern of settlement in today's county names: Essex (= East Saxons), Sussex (= South Saxons), East Anglia (= land of the Angles) and 'Wessex', which survives as a county name only in Thomas Hardy and later Hardiana (= West Saxons).

2.2 A language-family tree

What of the language, English, spoken by the invaders? We've already begun to explore what some of the consonants of that language must have been. This language must have been similar to the Germanic languages spoken at the same time on the European mainland. It's convenient, as well as accurate, to think of this group of languages – which includes the ancestors of present-day Dutch, Frisian and German – as a *language-family*. The early invaders probably spoke mutually intelligible Germanic *dialects*, much as a speaker of AmE from Texas might today be able to hold some kind of conversation with a BrE speaker from Tyneside, despite the marked linguistic differences between those two dialects.

During the past 1500 years, English has become less overtly 'Germanic'. Indeed we could argue that, in terms of its borrowing of words from French and Latin, its modern syntactic patterning and its loss of many originally Germanic inflections, it has become almost *un*-Germanic and more like a Romance language. Nevertheless, it's important to emphasise that careful thought, reading and scholarship can find some very clear continuities between OE and PDE. English has never shaken off – nor, perhaps, will it ever shake off – its Germanic past. We'll demonstrate some of the survivals and continuities as we proceed.

Let's return to the idea of a language-family. Robinson (1992:5–6) puts this very well:

> [T]wo languages are said to be genetically related if they are divergent continuations of the same earlier language. The known or hypothesized language that serves as a common ancestor is called a *proto-language*, or sometimes, to use kinship terminology, a *parent language*, in which case the divergent

continuations are frequently referred to as *daughter languages*. A parent language and its daughters constitute a language family.

Languages participating in a language-family are sometimes called *cognate* languages ('cognate' = descended from a common ancestor . . . kindred, akin . . .), and it's worthwhile looking at the grouping, since it not only has a bearing on where OE came from, but also on how OE, and even ME, developed.

Exercise 2.2.0

We're going to construct a family tree of English, starting with Proto-Germanic, the daughter of an Indo-European (IE) language. Proto-Germanic (PrGmc) was probably spoken some time around 500 BC. It's important to know what the abbreviations are for different languages; we have repeated them so that you can begin to learn them now. When you look at the tree in figure 2.2, you'll see blanks in some of the spaces where you'd expect to find the name of a parent language. We leave these blanks deliberately. Study the clues which will be given over the next few pages and write the name of the language and/or the abbreviation in the appropriate blank on the tree. Remember, this is just a general sketch, and there are many issues surrounding this type of construction that we're blithely going to ignore.

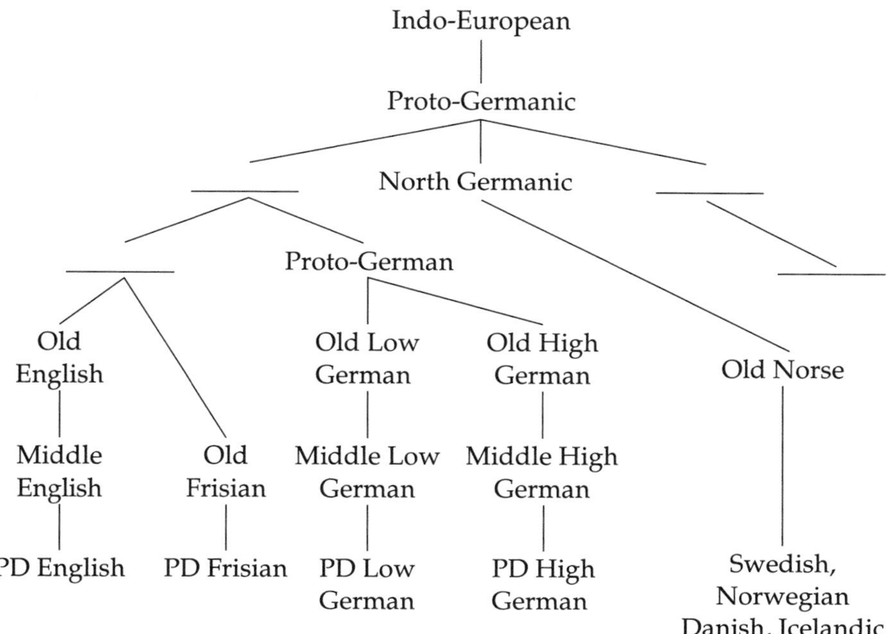

Figure 2.2 A language-family tree

If you'd like to go into the genealogy of English and the problems involved in constructing such a family tree in more detail, we refer you to the readings listed at the end of the chapter.

We can think of PrGmc, a daughter language of IE, as the mother of all Germanic languages. Most scholars suggest that PrGmc evolved into three daughter languages: West Germanic, North Germanic and East Germanic. When the Angles, Saxons and Jutes arrived in what is now called England in AD 449, they probably spoke a variety of a West Germanic (and daughter) dialect which scholars call Anglo-Frisian. We don't have any manuscript records of WGmc, which is discouraging, but we do have some fragments of its daughter language. These fragments are found in letter shapes carved into stone or wood. The letter shapes themselves are drawn from an alphabet of *runes* and are known as runic inscriptions. An alphabet called the *futhorc* comprised the runic set and is called the *futhorc* since those symbols spell out the first letters in the (English) runic alphabet, thus the first six letter shapes spell out F-U-TH-O-R-C. This early alphabet was typically used sparingly, for a sentence or two, but probably not for entire manuscripts or extended written discourse. Runes were in use long before any significant portion of the population was literate and were probably known to only a relatively select few. Runes were usually employed as a maker's or owner's mark used for incantations and other spells or charms, or for inscriptions on gravestones. The word *rune* itself is glossed as 'secret'. According to Bolton (1982:105), '[e]ven in the late Anglo-Saxon period, when runes appeared in manuscripts, they were used in riddling or secret applications: an Old English riddle in the Latin alphabet may have the solution appended in runes, or a poem will have its otherwise anonymous author's name interwoven in the text with runic letters.'

Scholars have pointed out that the angular shape of the runes suggests that they were probably carved in wood or stone, so that cross-strokes stood out predominantly against the grain of the materials being used. The dating, interpretation and even transcription of runic inscriptions are to some degree uncertain. Yet much can be inferred, even from small runic fragments, which allows some insight into the prehistory of the Germanic languages.

Bryson (1991:39–40) gives a nice example of a translated English rune. Having called the earliest Anglo-Saxons 'functionally illiterate' – a neat phrase, which we would completely endorse – he writes the following:

> In 1982, a gold medallion about the size of a 10p piece [or a US quarter:McC] was found in a field in Suffolk. It had been dropped or buried by one of the very earliest of the intruders, sometime between AD 450 and 480. The medallion bears a runic inscription which says (or at least is thought to say): 'This she-wolf is a reward to my kinsman.' Not perhaps the most profound of statements, but it is the earliest surviving example of Anglo-Saxon writing in Britain. It is, in other words, the first recorded sentence in English.

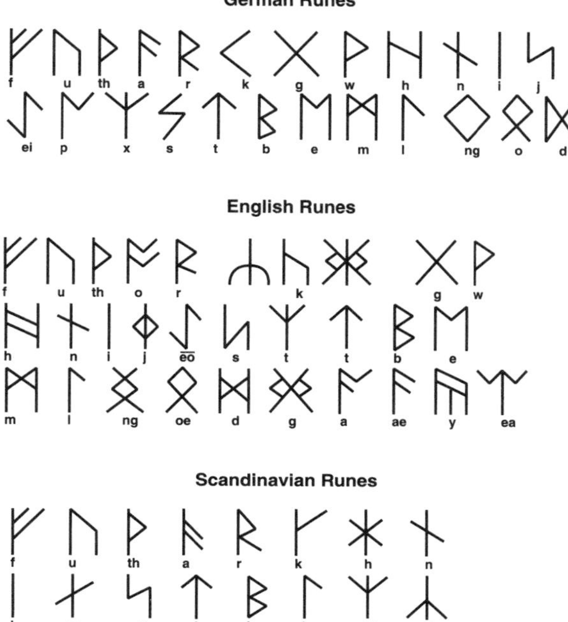

If you look back at the language-family tree, you'll see that we've suggested that Old Norse (ON) – the language of the Vikings – was a daughter of an earlier, North Germanic language, which was itself a sister of West Germanic. In fact, if there *was* an earlier North Germanic language of this kind, then it's impossible to find evidence for it. Our tree is therefore a fudge: we're implying that a parent language exists, but without being able to prove it. It's merely 'likely'. To all intents and purposes, ON *is* the earliest form of North Germanic that we can reconstruct.

ON is principally represented in writing by Old Icelandic (OIce), an ON language which was first recorded in the 12th century, although clearly the language had been spoken for much longer, and there are runic inscriptions from much earlier periods. Icelandic is, chronologically speaking, a conservative language. By that we mean Modern Icelandic has changed relatively little from its medieval forbear: unlike speakers of PDE who attempt to read OE, Icelanders can read OIce with little difficulty. OIce is closer in structure to OE than to ME, a language with which it was partially contemporary. Runic inscriptions dating from the period when the Vikings invaded England (beginning in the late 8th century) suggest that the language of the Vikings was similar to OE, although probably by that date the two languages were not altogether mutually intelligible. *Dialects* of the two languages, however, might well have been. Eventually, North

Germanic languages will include Icelandic, Swedish, Danish, Norwegian and Faroese.

Gothic came from (i.e. seems to have been a daughter language of) East Germanic. The only example we have today of Gothic is from a translation of the Bible from Greek into Gothic which was done in the 5th century by a Bishop in the Roman Catholic church named Ulfilas or Wulfila. The language was still relatively close to Proto-Germanic, as the early date of its records suggests. Gothic was still spoken in the Crimea as late as the 16th century, but is extinct today.

An example of an Old Low German (OLG) language was Old Saxon (OS), which was first recorded in the 8th century. It was influenced by OHG, and like OHG it retained older forms of WGmc which would become lost in OE. One famous poem, *Hildesbrandslied* (The song of Hildebrand), was written in OS, though there are also some OHG forms in the text. The OS poem *Genesis* was translated into OE. Even after c.400 years the two languages, OE and OS, must have been similar, at least in terms of their lexicon and their morphology (their principles of word-building), because some OS forms are retained in the OE translation.

Old High German has written records from the 8th century AD. It evolved from the same language as OLG, namely Proto-German. That makes OHG and OLG sister languages. OHG was a collection of dialects (presumed to be mutually intelligible). Unlike OE, no one variety appears to have been culturally dominant. The term *Low German* covers those languages which were spoken in the northern part of Germany, and *High German* the languages of the south. As Robinson (1992:242) points out, 'It should be noted that the terms "High" and "Low" are not evaluative terms, but geographical ones, the High German dialects being spoken on the higher ground of southern Germany and Switzerland,' and the Low German dialects being spoken in the northern low lands. Even today, speakers of German in the lowlands of the Rhine refer to their dialect as 'Platt-Deutsch'.

Old Frisian was first recorded in c.1200, making it contemporary with ME (rather than OE). Based on the written records, this is the language closest to OE. Robinson (1992:182) states that most of the Old Frisian documents deal with laws and goes on to say that '. . . with their volume and explicitness, these texts far surpass the legal texts of any other Old Germanic language. Second, despite their relatively late date, they reveal a singularly Germanic point of view about the righting of wrongs, specifically an emphasis on monetary compensation rather than corporal punishment of the offender'. This is a cultural value obtaining in Anglo-Saxon England as well. Old Frisian evolved into Frisian (which is, as we've noted, still spoken today in some parts of the Netherlands and north-west Germany), just as OHG evolved into High German and Yiddish, and OLG evolved into Low German, and into Dutch.

As we've seen, Proto-Germanic is the ancestor of all the Germanic languages. Its 'date' – the period at which one might expect some form of this language to have been spoken – can be placed very roughly around 500 BC. There aren't any written records for this proto-language. It must be reconstructed by comparing early forms of other Germanic languages. Such reconstruction is a delicate and often difficult task, but if, for example, two or more early languages share some common feature, then it's likely that such a feature was also part of the structure of the earlier proto-language. Where early languages don't appear to share the same feature, then the philologist looks for reasons why that might be.

Using careful reconstructive methods, it's possible to incorporate the tree we constructed above into a chronological structure encoding even earlier history. Proto-Germanic, for example, was an IE language. Most of the languages of Europe, and some of the languages of the Middle East and India, are also IE languages. Proto-Germanic differs, though, from many of these languages, which is another way of saying that these languages are only very distant relations. The Germanic languages, considered as a group, seem to have been subject to one particular historical change (more properly, a set of changes) which made them distinct from other IE languages.

This isn't the place to investigate such a change or changes in detail, even though the changes are spectacularly systematic. (If you'd like to know more, see the reading suggested at the end of this section.) However, just to give you some idea of what might have been involved, consider the following.

OE is, as we've seen, an example of a Germanic language, and Latin is an example of a non-Germanic language. Both languages come, via various routes, from a common, but very distant, ancestor: Indo-European. However, words beginning in Latin with the letter <p>, such as *piscis*, fish, or *pater*, father, often turn up in OE beginning in <f> (OE *fisc*, *fæder*). Similarly, words in Latin and other IE but non-Germanic languages beginning with the letter <d> – *decem*, ten – often turn up in OE and other Germanic languages beginning with the letter <t> (OE *tien*, OS *tehan* – compare these with PDE *ten*, Modern Danish *ti*). We can make inferences from such data (which are of course far more extensive than our mere two examples suggest) and claim that the Germanic languages underwent, as a group, changes that other IE languages did not undergo.

Another change, the effect of which still lasts into PDE, is the tendency for word-stress in the Germanic language-family to attach itself to the *first syllable* of a word (more accurately, to the first syllable of a word's most basic – what linguists call its *root* – form). It seems that the Germanic language-family – but not other languages or families within the IE grouping – was subject in the remote past to a regularising stress-shift. This shift has significant consequences for the history of the Germanic languages in general, and for English in particular. There were several other changes – in terms of loss of original inflections, or in terms of preferred syllable shapes, or even in terms of possible syntactic organisation – that seem to have set Proto-Germanic apart from IE. Perhaps this was due to tribes splitting off and migrating to another area and to their version of IE undergoing changes that other varieties (daughters) of IE did not.

Since OE and Old Frisian share certain linguistic developments they're grouped together as having come from WGmc, just as Proto-German did. (You'll recall that this makes Anglo-Frisian and Proto-German sister languages.) One of the developments Old Frisian and OE share is the change of the original Gmc vowel sound <a>, which was regularly written <æ> in Anglo-Frisian and early OE. Other changes include a vowel-change (a change in the quality of the vowel) before nasal consonants such as those written <n> or <m>.

As we've mentioned, Old Frisian was first recorded in c.1200, making it contemporary with early ME (rather than OE). For this reason we have again to be circumspect about terminology – it might be better, for example, to term this language Middle Frisian. Yet, on the written records, this is the closest language to OE. You can see something of the closeness the two languages, English and Frisian, have maintained by looking at a fragment of modern Frisian vocabulary (taken from Biddulph 1995):

PDE	**PD Frisian**
thanks	bitanke
bread	bread
thus	dos
ears	earen
tell	fortel
green	grien

We stated that when Angles, Saxons and Jutes arrived in England they spoke dialects of WGmc. In the 250 years between their arrival and the development of early written records, the language had changed and become a distinct form of (daughter of) WGmc. Within OE – and related to the geographical and cultural pattern of the settlements – there were four principal dialects: Kentish, West Saxon, Mercian and Northumbrian. All have a claim on our attention, but you might like to note that it's the last two, Mercian (a Midlands form) and Northumbrian – Mercian and Northumbrian are collectively called Anglian – which have the strongest claim to be the 'ultimate ancestors' of PDE. On the other hand, we know that West Saxon (WS) was a highly prestigious variety of the OE language. Many poems, and prose works, are composed in WS, and WS became the standard written language after Viking raids had destroyed (or at least, curtailed) English literary culture in other parts of the kingdom. King

Alfred (known as 'the Great', who ruled the kingdom of Wessex 870–899) is, likewise, an important cultural figure as well as a historically important military leader. His prose works (written personally or commissioned by him) are all composed in WS, although Alfred also painstakingly learned Latin when he was already middle-aged. Such prose forms an important record of life and times in the mid-Anglo-Saxon period. We'll be studying one of these prose texts later, where we'll also be tracking some of the linguistic features that allow us to distinguish Northumbrian forms of OE, or Mercian forms, from WS.

Given the existence of dialects of OE, how can we speak of a unified 'OE language'? Again we must turn to careful philological reconstruction. It seems to be the case, for instance, that the speech sound(s) represented by Gmc <sk> became 'sh' in OE, so that OE (and later English) has the word <ship> as opposed to the NGmc equivalent spelled with <s> plus a 'hard k', <skip>. One intriguing example where this difference eventually gives rise to two different word-forms is the word for 'shirt'. NGmc languages kept the original /sk/ sound, whereas the OE consonant(s) underwent the change to 'sh', to give ModE *shirt*. After the Norse incursions into England, however, the original word, beginning /sk/, was loaned back to OE. Now we have two PDE words, ***sk**irt* and ***sh**irt*, both of which arise from the same Gmc root, but which respectively show one of the reasons why OE is distinguished as a WGmc language, whereas ON is characterised as NGmc.

2.3 The Anglo-Saxon Heptarchy

The consolidation of the Anglo-Saxon settlement is symbolised by what scholars call the period of the Heptarchy, or the seven kingdoms: Wessex, Essex, Sussex, Kent, East Anglia, Mercia and Northumbria. (The word 'heptarchy' derives partly from the Greek loan-word *hepta*, seven.)

Exercise 2.3.0

To get some idea of how the Heptarchy looked, we're going to work with another map, map 5. On this map of Anglo-Saxon England notice the following important towns, constructions and religious foundations: Canterbury, Rochester, Winchester, Exeter, Malmesbury, Worcester, Lichfield, York, Whitby, Durham, Jarrow, Lindisfarne, London, Offa's Dyke and Hadrian's Wall. Also spot, and if necessary mark out more clearly (on a duplicate map), the courses of the rivers Humber, Severn, Tees, Tyne and Thames.

Comment on Exercise 2.30

The reasons we've asked you to work with another map are several. First, you might like to ask yourself about the linguistic reality of geographical

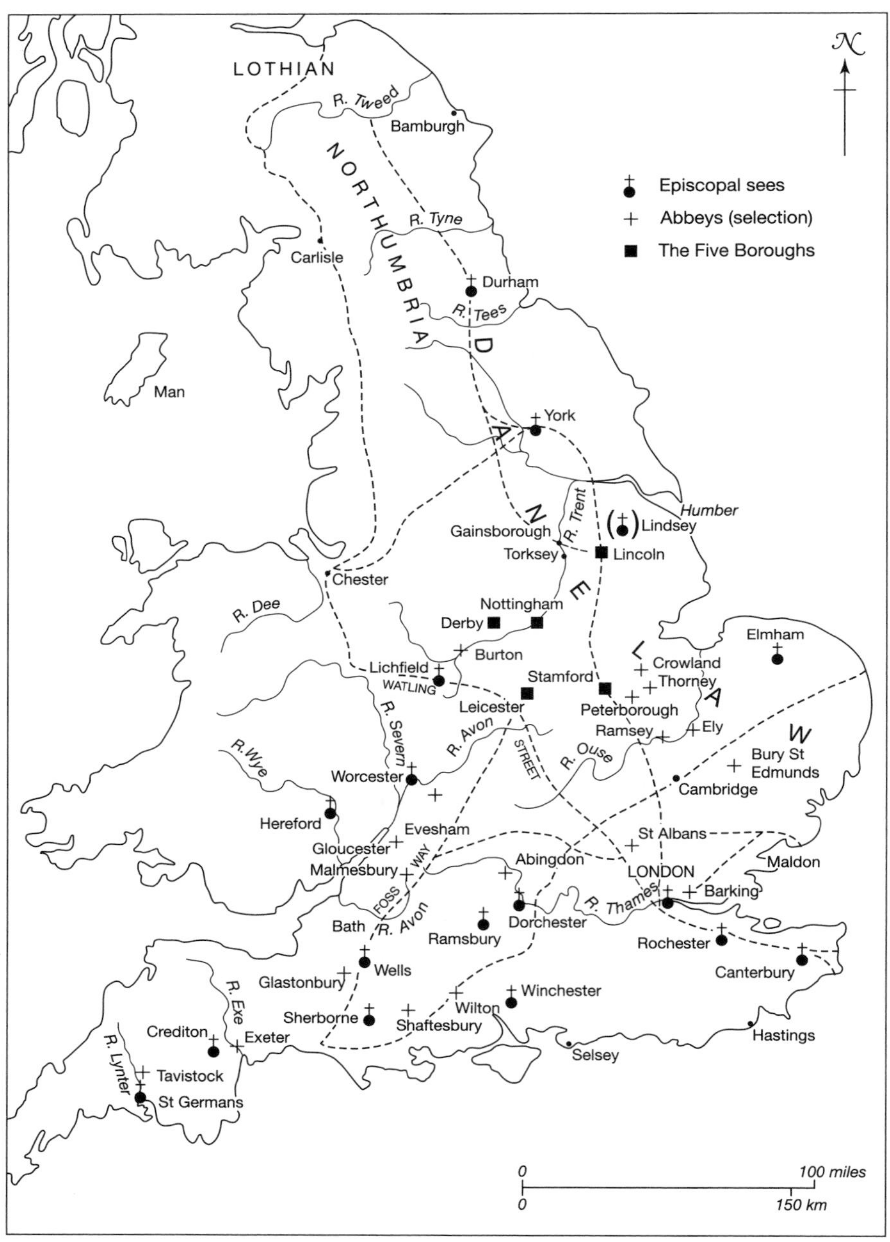

Map 5

Source: After map 'The Kingdom of the English' (c.1000) from http://www.trin.cam.ac.uk/sdk13/RPMaps/MapPolDev.jpg. Reproduced by permission of Professor Simon Keynes.

boundaries. If Wessex is bounded by Mercia (to the north), and Mercia is bounded by Northumbria (again, to the north), then are the *linguistic* boundaries between these geographical areas (these OE kingdoms) the same as the *geographical* boundaries? If not, why not? That's one question. Another question relates to extra-linguistic circumstances, and how those circumstances – such as invasion and settlement – relate to the development of prestige varieties of OE. Why, for example, did WS eventually become a – one might say 'the' – prestige variety, and not, say, Northumbrian? The answer, which we'll explore in Units 6 and 7, relates to the existence of the kingdom of Wessex in the 9th and 10th centuries. A third issue relates to the spread of Christianity and literacy. When we ask the question 'Where does English literacy come from?' then we need to have some idea of the geography that might be involved, and be able to have some mental picture of those key places and sites where literacy was developed, and from where it spread.

Summary

We've covered a great deal of ground in this unit, and done some strikingly different kinds of work with the earliest English.

We began the unit with a discussion of a strategy you might use to translate OE. To put that strategy into practice, we read, and began to translate, a passage of dialogue (Ælfric's *Colloquy*, in an OE version) between a narrator and a fisherman. We remind you that you can find a full translation at the end of this unit, after the sections of Study Questions and References.

Next, we talked about consonants and vowels, and, while focussing on consonant sounds, we began to reconstruct what the consonant inventory of OE might have been. We introduced some new symbols, and noticed that some graphemes apparently have disappeared from English over the years and that some digraphs are pronounced differently in PDE from how they were pronounced in OE. We discussed how sounds are produced and some of the technical terms used in describing sound production.

Next, we talked briefly about the conquest of the Celts by the Romans, the Roman 'occupation'. We then turned our attention to the Germanic tribes, the Angles, the Saxons and the Jutes, and their arrival in what is now England. We talked about the history of the language that the Germanic invaders (or settlers, depending on your perspective) spoke, and constructed a language family tree.

Study questions

1. What are some of the problems you encountered as you worked with us on reconstructing the consonant system of OE?

2. Pronounce the following as they might have occurred in OE. Which letter shapes here have more than one pronunciation, and under what circumstances can a single letter shape be pronounced as two different speech sounds?

   <hw> <sc> <c> <þ> <ge> <hl> <tt>

3. In providing a technical description of a consonant speech-sound, what three factors do linguists consider?
4. What is the definition of *phoneme*?
5. In table 2.3, we give a full list of the consonants of OE. We've taken the list that appears on table 2.1 (p. 37), and added the items to it that we discussed in the Comment to Exercise 2.02. Look through the list again, and then answer the question that follows:

Table 2.3 OE consonants (Table 2.1 extended)

Sounds Phonemes in / /	**OE grapheme(s)** Graphemes in < >	**Example**
/ʍ/	<hw>	what, where, which
/l/	l	like, lean
/ʧ/	c	which, chin (OE *cynn*)
/n/	n	now, neat, chin
/k/	c	craft, kind, back
/r/	r	reach, craft, barrel
/f/	f	craft, find, fish, staff
/t/	t	craft, sit, take
/s/	s	sit, list
/θ/	þ	thin, thigh
/m/	m	mine, mean
/ʃ/	sc	ship, should (OE *fisc*)
/g/	g	guard, good
/v/	f	knives (OE *heofon*, etc.)
/d/	d	dog, deed
/x/	h	ach (German), loch
/p/	p	pie, pond
/j/	g(e)	yup (OE *giet*, yet)
/z/	s	zee, zip
/ð/	þ or ð	then, this
/w/	w	work (OE *weorc*)
/h/	h	hot (OE *hāt*)
/b/	b	bath (OE *bæþ*), nub

Note: we have included /z/ and /v/ here as 'honorary' speech sounds. In OE, as we've mentioned, it seems likely that the pair [f] and [v] were contextually determined realisations of one underlying phoneme, and ditto with [s] and [z]. This much is at least implied by OE spelling practice, where there is one letter shape, <s>, for both [s] and [z] and one letter shape, <f>, for [f] and [v].

This looks undiscriminating. Can you restructure the list so that most of it falls into *pairs of consonant phonemes*? Think of speech-sounds, rather then of letter shapes. We'll start you off. As we discussed in the unit, there's good reason to suppose that /b/ and /p/ form a contrastive pair of consonant speech sounds. What are the others? (Once you've established that, you might want to think about the consonant phonemes that *don't* seem to fall neatly into pairs and, in particular, *why* they don't.)

6. Add to your timeline (if you haven't already) to include the items mentioned in this chapter.

Websites you may find useful

There's a great deal on the web about many of the topics we have discussed in this unit. In fact, there are so many relevant sites that it's hard to know where to begin. We suggest that you begin your own search under topics such as *Anglo-Frisian, runes, Germanic,* etc. You might also like to look at:

- http://www.english.uga.edu/~methelie
- http://www.redbad.tripod.com
- http://www.towson.edu/~duncan/germanic
- http://www.wodanaz.com/runes
- http://www.anthro.mankato.msus.edu/prehistory
- http://www.lonestar.texas.net/~jebbo/learn-as
- http://www.avesta.org

References and suggestions for further reading

Barber, C.L. 1993. *The English language: a historical introduction*. Cambridge: Cambridge University Press. [See especially Chapter 3.]

Baugh, A.C. and Thomas Cable. 1993. *A history of the English language.* 4th edition. London: Routledge and Kegan Paul. [Read Chapters 2 and 4, or selected parts of Chapters 2 and 4, before progressing to Chapter 3 which is on OE proper.]

Biddulph, Joseph. 1995. *Notes on Frisian*. Pamphlet, available from 32 Strŷd Ebeneser, Pontypridd, CF37 5PB, Cymru (Wales). ISBN 1 897999 03 8

Bryson, Bill. 1991. *Mother tongue*. London: Penguin. [Chapter 4, 'The first thousand years', is useful.]

Fennell, Barbara. 2001. *A history of English: a sociolinguistic approach*. Oxford: Blackwell.

Graddol, David., D. Leith and J. Swann, eds. 1996. *English: history, diversity and change*. London: Routledge.

Hunter Blair, Peter. 1970. *An introduction to Anglo-Saxon England*. Cambridge: Cambridge University Press (CUP). [Look up 'Bede' in the Index. Good historical introduction.]

Leith, D. 1983. *A social history of English*. London: Routledge and Kegan Paul.

Sherley-Price, Leo. 1955. *Bede: A History of the English church and people*. London: Penguin Classics. [A useful translation. See especially Book I, chapter 15.]

Strang, B.M.H. 1970. *A history of English*, London: Methuen.

If you're interested in following up a Latin reference (translated into readable English) which gives an account of the Germanic tribes, see *Tacitus: the Agricola and the Germania*, trans. with an introduction by H. Mattingly, trans. revised by S.A. Handford. 1970. London: Penguin Classics.

And finally . . .

Translation (Exercise 2.0.0)

The Fisherman	
Hwelcne cræft canst þū?	1
Which occupation know-how-to you?	
What's your occupation?	
Ic eom fiscere.	2
I am fisher	
I'm a fisherman	
Hwæt begietst þū of þīnum cræft?	3
What gainest thou from thine craft?	
What do you gain from your occupation?	
Bīleofan ic mē begiete, and scrūd, and fēoh.	4
Sustenance I for myself gain, and clothing, and money	
I gain food, clothing and money	
Hū gefēhst þū þā fiscas?	5
How catchest thou the fishes?	
How do you catch the fish?	

Ic gā on mīnne bāt, and rōwe ūt on þā ēa, and weorpe mīn nett on þā ēa.	**6**
I go into mine boat, and row out on the water, and cast mine net into the water	
I go into my boat, row out on the water and cast my net into the water	
Hwīlum ic weorpe angel ūt mid ǣse, oþþe spyrtan; and swā hwæt swā	**7**
Sometimes I throw hook out with bait, or basket, and so-what-so	
Sometimes I throw out a baited hook, or an eel basket, and whatever	
hīe gehæftaþ ic nime.	**8**
them seizes I take	
those catch, I take	
Hwæt dēst þū gif hit unclǣne fiscas bēoþ?	**9**
What do-est thou if it unclean fishes is?	
What do you do if you catch unclean [spawning? inedible?] fish?	
Ic weorpe þā unclǣnan ūt, and nime þā clǣnan mē to mete.	**10**
I throw those unclean out, and take those clean for myself to food	
I throw away the bad ones and take the clean ones for food	
Hwǣr cīepst þū þīne fiscas?	**11**
Where sell-est thou thine fishes?	
Where do you sell your fish?	
On þǣre ceastre.	**12**
In the town	
In the town	
Hwā bygþ hīe?	**13**
Who buy-eth them?	
Who buys them?	
Þā ceasterware. Ne mæg ic hira swā fela gefōn swā ic sellan mæge.	**14**
The town-people. Nor may I of them so many catch as I to-sell may	
The citizens. I can't catch as many as I can sell	

Hwelce fiscas gefēhst þū?	**15**
Which fishes catch-est thou?	
What sort of fish do you catch?	
Ǣlas, and hacodas, and scēotan, and ealle ōþre fiscas þe on	**16**
Eels, and pikes, and trouts, and all other fish which in	
Eels, pike and trout, and all kinds of other fish that	
þǣm ēam swimmaþ. . . .	**17**
the water swimmeth	
swim in the water	

Unit Three

Nouns

3.0 Mercenaries and settlers

In 402 the Roman garrison began to withdraw. By 410, the province the Romans had administered lay virtually unprotected and Romano-British society was in decline. What happened next is unclear. Scholars disagree on exactly how to interpret the evidence, or on what constitutes 'evidence'. Following Davies (1999) we're going to suggest that Britannia now had no defence, no clear leadership and virtually no way to maintain order. Davies (1999:174) suggests that there was probably 'radical deterioration' in Britannia – economically, politically and socially. In the local Roman Christian church there was also chaos, evidenced by the spread of the Pelagian heresy (a position, developed by the 5th century British monk Pelagius and his followers, that denied the doctrine of original sin).

Various groups and individuals vied with one another to fill the power vacuums left by the departure of the Romans. The vulnerability of 'Britannia' to attacks from the north (the Picts), the north-west (the Irish) and from continental Europe (the Angles and Saxons) was a pattern that was to repeat itself for centuries.

Civil war broke out in the mid-5th century. One of the key figures appears to have been a powerful warlord referred to by various names, including the one by which Bede calls him, Vortigern. Vortigern was clearly strategically over-stretched. His solution to military and tactical problems was to invite his continental neighbours as allies into what was not yet 'England'.

In spite of our admiration for Bede's version of events, modern scholarship suggests that the Germanic tribes who composed the 'Anglo-Saxon invasion' were not merely the Angles, the Saxons and the Jutes, but rather more like six or seven different tribes. Further, the 'Jutes' may not in fact have hailed from Jutland ('Jute-land'; see also Stenton, 1947:14)). The date Bede gives, AD 449, for the Germanic incursion is most likely incorrect, though, interestingly, this date was also given by the 9th century *Anglo-Saxon Chronicle* and has been adopted as the date of the Anglo-Saxons' first arrival by much subsequent scholarship. Still, however they came, and for whatever set of purposes, the Germanic tribes who migrated in the

5th century to the promising territory formed by Britain's local conflicts had, undeniably, arrived, and arrived to stay.

3.1 The *Germania*

Brundage (1990:125) describes the beginning of the sixth century as follows: 'The Germanic settlers brought with them their own laws, customs, and traditional practices, but they did not seek to impose their law on their new neighbours; on the other hand, the Germans had no desire to adopt Roman ways, including Roman laws, as their own. As a result, the West became culturally and legally pluralistic'.

In other words, when they arrived in Britannia the Anglo-Saxons kept their own Germanic traditions and culture. A great deal of what we can infer about that culture comes from the *Germania*, a work Tacitus completed in the middle of the first century AD (Mattingly, revised by Handford, 1970). The work is far from unbiased. It is, to some extent, a vehicle for criticising the moral decline of Rome by ostensibly describing tribes of barbarians, who were 'uncorrupted by the temptations of public shows or the excitements of banquets' and who didn't (unlike, Tacitus hints, his decadent Roman colleagues) find vice amusing or call seduction 'up-to-date' (1970:117). But Tacitus wasn't reluctant to criticise these same barbarians for indolence (1970:114), and for indulging in 'drinking-bouts lasting all day and all night' (1970:120).

Germanic tribal leaders were surrounded by what Tacitus calls a *comitatus*, an inner circle of warriors who would serve and protect a warlord or chieftain, or would die trying to save him. '[T]o leave a battle alive after their chief has fallen means lifelong infamy and shame. To defend and protect him, and to let him get the credit for their own acts of heroism, are the most solemn obligations of their allegiance. The chiefs fight for victory, the followers for their chief . . . For the Germans have no taste for peace; renown is more easily won among perils, and a large body of retainers cannot be kept together except by means of violence and war' (1970:113). This theme, of loyalty unto, and then beyond, death, is one of the prime topics of much subsequent Anglo-Saxon poetry and prose. The celebration of physical endurance, moral steadfastness and courage also has its converse side, cowardice, degeneracy and betrayal, and these also feature in Anglo-Saxon literature.

3.2 The *Germania* and the Anglo-Saxons

Woolf (1976:64) characterises the *Germania* as 'part ethnographical treatise, part primitive Utopia'. It's a matter of record that Tacitus was a man of letters, a historian, a senator, a consul and a governor, a successful orator and the son-in-law of Agricola, one-time governor of Roman Britain. There's independent evidence supporting many of Tacitus' comments, and it's agreed that Tacitus is generally accurate. If this is the case, one must then ask to what extent his description of the Germanic tribes in the first century was applicable to the Germanic tribes who went to Britain in the fifth. Scholars seem to agree that the description was more applicable, rather than less.

This can be seen in the existence of texts inscribed in the runic alphabet, which was a peculiarly Germanic artefact. As we mentioned in the last unit, the runic alphabet (the *futhorc*) eventually runs into disuse in England but is the source for the letter-shape thorn, <þ>, which was incorporated into the later OE written system to symbolise a 'th' sound. There's other evidence. Germanic society appears to have been based on a tribal structure, with tribes held together by allegiance to a leader or lord (OE *hlaford*, a word ultimately deriving from *hlāf* + *weard*, guardian of the bread), usually reinforced by ties of kinship. The nature of lordship and loyalty, of blood-ties and treachery, are enduring and much-visited themes of OE poetry and prose (see, for example, the prose passage beginning on p. 74; this is an entry from the *Anglo-Saxon Chronicle*, relating to the 8th-century feud – a blood-feud that lasted for three decades – between Cynewulf and Cyneheard, members of the royal house of Wessex).

Apparently this tribal structure was transported to Britain with the Anglo-Saxon settlements, and we see over the next few centuries the evolution of powerful lords into provincial kings, who command the loyalty of the local leaders in their area of dominion. The term 'king' (OE *cyning*), however, is perhaps a little misleading in this context, since it has connotations of a more fully developed feudal structure of the type we associate with the later medieval period. Only with Alfred 'the Great', king of Wessex from 871–899, do we begin to see a gradual emergence of national kingship, and Cnut, a Danish ruler, has a good claim (notwithstanding the prior claims of Edgar) to be the first king to reign over a politically unified England (beginning of the 11th century; see also Units 6 and 7). Similarly, it is only later in the 10th century that a recognisable governmental infrastructure begins to emerge.

We can infer uncertainly from Tacitus, and know more certainly from later records, that Anglo-Saxon chieftains were surrounded by a group of counsellors known in OE as the *witan* (OE *wita*, wise man, *witan*, plural, wise men). The deliberations of the *witenagemōt* – the meeting of the wise – were important forums for the discussion and ratification of laws. Kings also held meetings of their councils at the national, rather than purely at the local, level. Hunter Blair (1970:221) notes that 'the king's council met on at least seventy occasions during the tenth and eleventh centuries and no doubt there were many other meetings of which no record remains'. Such meetings were usually attended, it seems, by about sixty or seventy of the most influential members of the nobility and clergy.

3.3 Local shires and their politics

If we skip forward to political organisation as we find it in the 10th and 11th centuries, we find that Anglo-Saxon administration involved local *shires*, OE *scir* [OED2 (*Oxford English Dictionary*, Second Edition – see also Interlude) gives the first attestation of the term in its sense of 'province or district' as occurring in 893]. 'Shire' is an important word, since one consequence of the division of the country into large provinces such as Wessex, Northumbria and Mercia was the subsequent development of what were to be, for many centuries, the county shires of England. Shire affairs were administered by the shire court, which was the body through which the provincial or national king's commands could be effected, but which also transacted local business. The president of the shire court was the *ealdorman* of the shire, an important (and, in some cases, extremely powerful) local magnate whose responsibilities were wide and included the raising and leading of shire troops (note that the PDE word *alderman* comes from *ealdormann* and the word *sherriff*, from shire + 'reeve', steward). By the later OE period, *ealdormen* were often earls in their own right and may have had jurisdiction over a group of several shires. One such *eorl* is Byrhtnoth, who appears in *The Battle of Maldon* (written in, or very soon after, 991). Byrhtnoth functions in this poetic text as a Germanic war-lord rather than as county official: he's surrounded by all the trappings of high rank, including what is effectively a *comitatus*, an inner circle of councillors and warriors who fight to the death in his defence. According to the anonymous poet, some of Byrhtnoth's *comitatus* engage in hawking on their way to battle. Hawking was at this period a particularly aristocratic pastime.

If, by the late 10th century, the role of *ealdorman* had sometimes been translated into that of *eorl*, then there was a need for a functionary to fulfil the original role of court-president. This functionary was the shire-reeve, the sheriff, who operated rather as a chief county magistrate, settling disputes, adjudicating important wills and supervising the (often conflicting) claims of church and local politics.

Behind the provinces, the shires. And behind the shires? Here, smaller local governmental units, called *hundreds* or, later, and in areas of Scandinavian influence, *wapentakes* (OE *wæpentæc*, ON *vápnatak*), transacted smaller matters of local business and law. Theft, and its redress and restitution, seems to have been a perennial concern. In the system of justice administered in wapentakes, prosecution and defence were in the hands of 12 'dooms-men' (PDE *doom* is etymologically related to *dēman*, to judge, cf. PDE *deem*), a body which to some extent underlies the modern twelve-person jury.

We can gain a good picture of life in early England from written records relating to the organisation of shires and hundreds, from wills and charters, and especially from law codes (which exist from early in the Anglo-Saxon period). Land-rights, rights of pasture, theft, the procedure for raising and maintaining war-bands, the duties owed to secular officials (from lowest to highest), the adjudication of wills and the settlement of blood-feuds – these show that the Anglo-Saxon system of local government was by no means some haphazard brutality, but a well-articulated structure with known procedures and precedents. It was also a stable system. Many of the local features of such a governmental system were incorporated into the Norman administration of England (whose census was the *Domesday Book*, the 'Book of Assessment') and the Norman, feudal, organisation of society.

3.4 Women

The records give us a picture of a society which, concerned with land, territorial possession and war, was bound to have been male-dominated. And whatever we may infer from Tacitus about the place of women in early Germanic society, it's difficult to say much about the place of women in Anglo-Saxon England. Yet as early as the 7th century we find a prominent woman such as Hild, Abbess of Whitby, whom you will recall from the story of Cædmon in Unit 1, who owed her position not to her husband but to herself (and to her family connections). Women had an important role in education and ecclesiastical matters, and there are many charters and, in particular, wills which show that it was clearly possible, indeed common, for widows to lead independent and influential lives. One such will, dating from the late 10th century, is that of Æthelgifu, a widow with estates in the English midlands.

Æthelgifu clearly had large estates of which to dispose. She disposed of them liberally, even royally, since she bequeathed to the king, Æthelred ('Un-ræd'), 30 mancuses of gold (a *mancus* was a unit of currency equivalent in value to an ox) and two stallions, together with her deerhounds; a further 30 mancuses were gifted to the queen. Her herd of swine, along with its swineherd and a number of slaves, went to a religious foundation at St Albans, together with lavish payment for her funeral (a further 30 mancuses), oxen, cows and 150 sheep. Personal bequests to relatives included gifts of land, cattle and slaves, and bequests to kinswomen included her own effects – saddle gear, cups, horns, dresses and head-dresses. Æthelgifu, then, clearly had considerable powers of patronage. Her deposition also makes it clear that she had control over the lives of her slaves. Perhaps it's worthwhile pointing out that slavery was not altogether a matter of mud and chains in Anglo-Saxon England. Rather, slavery was an accepted and important part of the social system. Since landowners were obliged to supply their slaves with food and clothing, people sometimes chose to be sold into slavery during difficult times – times of famine or disease. Their freedom could subsequently be bought when their, or their society's, circumstances improved.

3.5 Reading passage

The following excerpt is taken from the *Anglo-Saxon Chronicle*. The *Chronicle*, or, perhaps better, chronicles, were probably started under King Alfred's direct patronage around 891 and continued up until 1154. (We'll look at another, 12th century, excerpt in Unit 8.) Since entries are written retrospectively, they cover history before 891 as well as contemporary events. They constitute important philological and literary evidence. The *Chronicle* used many sources, including Bede, other records and annals, oral histories and popular tales. Alfred was, as far as we know, the first quasi-national leader to encourage and legitimise the use of the vernacular, and the *Anglo-Saxon Chronicle* was written in (often eloquent) Old English, rather than in Latin.

We're going to look at a fragment of an entry for the year 755. Greenfield (1965:45) notes that this particular entry '. . . is detailed in an archaic prose that suggests an oral narrative tradition or an earlier written source'. Mitchell and Robinson say that '[t]he narration is so swift and breathless, the selection of detail so adroit, that some scholars have felt that the chronicler was recording a saga refined by many retellings in oral tradition' (1992:208).

Before we actually begin this chapter's reading selection, perhaps we should briefly review some Germanic law. Brundage (1990:125) suggests that Germanic law

> . . . was based on two foundations: the collective responsibility of the kindred for the actions of its members and the principle of reciprocal revenge. The extended kinship group was prominent in archaic German society and remained fundamental to Germanic institutions for generations following the invasions. The kindred bore responsibility for fulfilling the obligations incurred by any of its members and for seeing to it that each member both paid what he owed and received what he had a right to . . . Reciprocal revenge meant in effect that wrongs were avenged by inflicting injury upon the person responsible for the damage, or, failing that, upon some other member of his or her household, or their kin.

With this in mind, let's get on to the passage. The entry tells of Cynewulf, who became king of the West Saxons after Sigebryht, the former king, was ousted by Cynewulf and members of his *wiotan* (a variant spelling of *witan*) for what the chronicler calls *unryhtum dǣdum* (wrongful deeds). Although Sigebryht was deprived of his kingdom, he was allowed to retain some land and remain in the province. This proved to be a mistake. Sigebryht subsequently committed one wrongful deed too many by killing Cumbra, his own most loyal retainer. Sigebryht was then exiled by King Cynewulf to the forest of Andred (in what's today part of the Hampshire Weald). It is fitting that Cumbra's death be avenged, and avenged it was by *ān swān* (a swineherd, loyal to his overseer, Cumbra) who stabs Sigebryht to death *æt Pryvetes flōdan* (by the stream at Privett, a place in Hampshire).

In terms of the 'rules' of blood-feud, if Sigebryht, as a deposed and slain king, had surviving kin, then it would be their prime duty to avenge his death. Sigebryht indeed had a brother, Cyneheard, who was not only obligated to avenge his brother's death, but was also a pretender to the throne of Wessex.

According to the chronicler, after Sigebryht's death 31 winters passed. Cynewulf spent his time fighting 'great battles against the Britons' (probably the Cornish, on the western borders of Wessex), while Cyneheard waited for the appropriate moment for revenge. After 31 years, however, Cynewulf decided – for reasons left unclear by the chronicler – to expel the dangerous pretender, Cyneheard, from the kingdom, just as he had expelled Sigebryht so long before.

Cyneheard apparently discovered the plan and decided on a pre-emptive strike: while Cynewulf was *on wīfcȳþþe* (literally, 'in woman-knowing', visiting his mistress) in Merton, Cyneheard and his men crept into the village and surrounded the woman's house. The king – surprised in the half-light of dawn – realised he was under attack, went to the door and 'valiantly defended himself' until he saw his rival, Sigebryht's brother. At that point he rushed out, severely wounding the pretender to his throne. The skirmish continued and finally Cyneheard's men killed the king. Our reading will open at this point, with the screams of the dead king's mistress.

Exercise 3.5.0

In the following, we've given a relatively literal translation under each line of text. Using this, and the glossary, try to construct a more fluent translation in the line below our literal version. We have completed lines 1–3 for you.

Ond þā on þæs wīfes gebǣrum onfundon þæs cyninges þegnas	1
And then in the woman's cries discovered the king's thanes	
And then the king's companions discovered from the woman's cries	

þā unstillnessse ond þā þider urnon swā hwelc swā þonne gearo wearþ	**2**
the disturbance and then thither ran so-which-so then ready had-become	
the disturbance, and whoever had become ready most quickly ran there.	
ond radost. Ond hiera se æþeling gehwelcum feoh ond feorh gebēad,	**3**
and quickest. And of-them the prince to-each money and life offered,	
. . . And the prince offered money and life to each of them,	
ond hiera nænig hit geþicgean nolde; ac hīe simle feohtende wǣran	**4**
and of-them none it to-accept not-wished, but they continually fighting were	
oþ hīe alle lǣgon būtan ānum Bryttiscum gīsle, ond sē	**5**
until they all lay-dead except one British hostage, and that one	
swīþe gewundad wæs.	**6**
very-much wounded was.	
þā on morgenne gehīerdun þæt þæs cyninges þegnas þe him	**7**
Then in morning heard it the king's companions who them	
beæftan wǣrun, þæt se cyning ofslægen wæs. þā ridon hīe þider	**8**
behind were, that the king slain was. Then rode they thither	
ond his aldorman Ōsrīc, ond Wīferþ his þegn, ond þā men	**9**
and his alderman Osric, and Wiferth his thane, and those men	
þe hē beæftan him læfde ǣr, ond þone æþeling on	**10**
which he behind them had-left before, and the prince in	
þǣre byrig mētton þǣr se cyning ofslægen læg	**11**
the village encountered where the king killed lay	

Selective (and simplified) glossary

ǣr	before, previously
ac	but
ānum	one, a, only
æþeling	prince
beæftan	behind
Bryttiscum	British
būtan	except
byrig	stronghold
feoh	money
feohtende	fight(ing)
feorh	life
gearo	ready
gebǣrum	outcries; screams
gebēad	offered
gehīerdun	heard
geþicgean	accept
gehwelcum	each one
gewundad	wounded
gīsle	hostage
hīe	pronoun; they, them
hiera	pronoun; their
hit	pronoun; it
lǣfde	left
lǣgon	they lay (dead)
mētton	meet; encounter
morgenne	morning
nǣnig	none, no one
nolde	contraction of *ne wolde* – would not
ofslægen	killed
on	on; in
Ond þā	and then
onfundon	realise
oþ	until
þā	the
þǣr	where
þæs wīfes	the woman's
þegnas	thanes, companions
þider	thither; in that direction; there
þone	the
þonne	then
radost	quickest
ridon	ride

se	the
sē	pronoun; here 'he', 'that one'
simle	continuously; always
swā hwelc swā	whoever
urnon	ran
unstillnesse	disturbance
wǣrun	were
wæs	was
wearþ	became

NB: from this point we'll refer to Cynewulf by name, or by 'the king', while we'll refer to Cyneheard, the pretender to the throne, as 'the prince', cf. the translation of *æþeling* in the glossary above.

Idiomatic translation

And then the king's thanes discovered the disturbance from the woman's cries, and whoever could get ready quickest ran there. And the prince offered money and life to each of them, but none of them wanted to accept the offer. So they [Cynewulf's men] continued to fight, until all of them lay dead, except for one British hostage, although he was severely wounded.

When the following morning Cynewulf's thanes – the ones who had been left behind the previous night – heard that the king had been killed, they rode to Merton. These men included Osric, the king's alderman, and Wiferth, his thane, and those (other) men he'd left behind, and they encountered the prince in the village where the king lay slain.

It has to be admitted that this isn't the easiest passage of OE we could have chosen, but it – and the rest of the *Chronicle* entry for the year 755 – does give some idea of the savagery of the duties of parts of Anglo-Saxon society, a society in which life always has a price, bribery and revenge are leitmotifs of 'correct' action, and internecine feuding sometimes rumbles on for decades. If you think that these features are somehow 'primitive', or belong solely to Anglo-Saxon society, think again. Their human landscape is reminiscent of *The Godfather*.

One thing you may have found tricky is the fact that OE seems to have so many words meaning 'the'. Look back at the glossary and there you'll find the kinds of words we mean – words like *se*, or *þone*, *þæs* or *þā*. To understand how these words function, we need to think about the behaviour of OE nouns. We need, in fact, to understand more about the nature of the OE grammatical system itself. That understanding is best served by first turning to the topic of OE *inflections*.

3.6 Inflections, nouns and grammatical roles

When we compare OE with PDE, one of the first things we notice is that some kinds of OE words change their shape or form much more frequently and radically than they do today. When we say 'change their . . . form' you might like to think of PDE nouns. One of the things we do to indicate grammatical *possession*, for example, is to affix the basic noun (the root) with an apostrophe + <s>:

(1) The **king's** men were spoiling for a fight (the men 'belonging to' the king)
(2) They searched the **car's** interior (the interior of the car)

And again, one of the things we do to indicate *number* (one, as against more than one – singular, as against plural) is to affix the root of nouns with <s>:

(3) There were three **kings** present (king + s)
(4) Several **factors** were discussed by the committee (factor + s)

'Add an **s**' is in fact an inadequate rule for plurality. Consider the three plural forms *book + s, hand + s, church + es,* where each inflectional suffix is *pronounced* differently, despite having the same, graphic <(e)s> shape.) These changes of shape or form, changes carrying grammatical information, are called *inflection,* from ME *inflecten,* to bend, curve, alter. We can say, therefore, that in PDE, nouns normally inflect for number (singular and plural) and possession (= apostrophe + <s>).

It's important to realise at the outset that inflections are one of the ways in which languages can indicate the relationships between parts of a sentence (crudely, who is doing what to whom); that is, inflection is a part of the grammatical system of the language. Consider, for example, the following Latin sentence:

(5) Domini monent pueros (the masters advise the boys)

There are three main lexical elements in the sentence, that is, three 'content words', each having its own root. Respectively, these roots are *domin-*, *mon-* and *puer-*. Roots are the most basic, i.e. the uninflected, part of the lexical word. Endings – inflections – are added to the roots so that we can find which word is the subject, which word is the verb and which the object. For example, in (5) the *-i* affixed to *domin-* tells us that 'the masters' are likely to be the subject of the sentence, and the *-os* affixed to *puer-* tells us 'the boys' are likely to be the object of the sentence; the termination *-ent* on *mon-* not only tells us that this is the verb of the sentence, but also that it's consistent with – technically, it 'agrees with' – and, therefore, points to its subject, the preceding plural, *domin + i.*

Inflections carry vital grammatical information. Notice, too, that once inflections are added to roots, the word-order of the phrase, clause or sentence can be relatively free. For example, consider the following:

(6) Pueros monent domini
(7) Domini pueros monent
(8) Pueros domini monent

Though they may differ in terms of their emphasis, (6), (7) and (8) have the same cognitive content as (5), in spite of the change in the order of the words. In each sentence, the masters are advising the boys. We can recover the identity of 'those being advised' and 'those doing the advising' from the endings with no hesitation or ambiguity.

In PDE, if the word order is changed, the roles of the two elements in the sentence, the boys and the masters, change too. Compare (9) and (10):

(9) The masters advise the boys
(10) The boys advise the masters

In PDE, we rely largely on *word-order* to tell us who is doing the advising and who is being advised – to tell us who is the subject and who the object. In (9–10), the advisers come before the main verb; they are the *subject* of the sentence; the advisees come after the main verb, and are the *object* of the advising. Word-order is the key: there are no additional inflectional endings in these particular PDE sentences to indicate subject-hood or object-hood.

We rarely think of the internal construction of PDE (unless, as here, we wish to begin to work professionally with its form and history). The inflectional system of PDE nouns is very simple and contains little of the detail, relatively speaking, that it did in the OE period. This is because PDE uses word-order as one of its important constitutive grammatical principles, while OE primarily uses inflections to carry a great deal of grammatical information. But we know that some inflectional endings do still survive into PDE – <s> plural ending(s), <'s> possessives. The story of English thus far is, partly, the story of a language moving from one that relies on a complex and developed inflectional system (technically, a *synthetic language*, as in OE) to one that expresses sentence roles largely via word-order (technically, an *analytic language*, as in PDE).

3.7 Inflections in other languages

Inflection plays a part in the grammatical systems of cognate languages such as German, Dutch and Danish. In modern Danish, for example, nouns may belong to the common gender, which can be signalled by the presence of the indefinite article *en* before a noun (thus *en mand*, a man), or the neuter gender, signalled by the presence of *et* before the noun (thus *et loft*, a ceiling). Present-day Dutch also distinguishes between common and neuter genders (*het huis*, a house, neuter; *en tuin*, a garden, common gender). It's worth noting again that gender in these grammatical systems usually has nothing to do with biological gender in 'real life'. There are complex historical reasons for words belonging to one gender or another, but one thing is certain: the inflected languages we're now looking at don't have a system of natural or biological gender, gender corresponding to maleness, femaleness or other attributes of the 'real world'. This is one of the reasons why inflected languages can seem hard to learn for speakers of PDE. In Danish, Dutch and German, for example, the gender of each noun must be remembered as well as the root itself.

The reason we're speaking of other Germanic languages at this point is that we wish to be consistent with some of the principles we sketched in Unit 1. There, we noted that when we reconstruct languages, we rarely find anything that is unprecedented. Generally speaking, languages have recognisable strategies for constructing grammatical systems, and so it's interesting that OE has just such a recognisable strategy, sharing its strategic propensities with its Germanic relatives. In terms of language history, it's also interesting to begin to think now about how OE was to change, and lose many of its inflections, becoming a more analytic language. After all, some of its sister languages didn't change in quite the same way, and evolved different grammatical strategies to the ones adopted by later English, and it's useful to start thinking about why these differences might have arisen. (We look at this issue again in Units 7 and 8.)

One language that has retained a rich inflectional system is modern German. OE is, as we've noted, rather like modern German, since both languages regularly have two *numbers* (singular and plural), three *genders* (masculine, feminine and neuter) and four *cases* (nominative, accusative, genitive and dative – we'll discuss these shortly).

In contemporary French, the best signs of number and gender are found not in the roots but in the definite article preceding them, that is to say, the French equivalent of PDE *the*. Thus, in French, masculine singular *le*, feminine singular *la* and plural (all genders) *les*. In Danish, the same would hold good for *et* (neuter, singular) and *en* (common, singular). Danish forms plurals, incidentally, by affixing words with *-e* or *-er* (indefinite plural, thus *blomster*, flowers) or, for plurals including 'definiteness', with a further *-ne* or *-ene* (definite plural, thus *blomsterne*, the flowers). In German, too, one can infer number and gender from the articles preceding the noun roots: *der Bruder*, masculine singular, the brother; *die Sonne*, feminine singular, the sun; *das Glas*, neuter singular, the glass, and so on.

3.8 Articles in OE

Articles are a sub-class, and furthermore a closed class, of *determiners* (grammatical words that typically pre-modify nouns) and, in PDE, the definite or indefinite articles (*the*, definite; *a*, *an*, indefinite) invariably precede the noun.

(11) **The** flowers were from **an** expensive florist on **the** west side
(12) She always enjoyed **a** good book

This ordering, where an article is followed by the noun or nominal group it introduces, isn't always or necessarily the case in all modern Germanic languages. Present-day Danish, again, like other Scandinavian languages, tacks an article onto the *end* of the root when definiteness is required, thus *universitet*, university, and *universitet* + *et*, the university. That is a linguistic strategy favoured by the North Germanic group of languages. But the article + noun precedence is invariably true for PDE, and the same holds good for OE: articles almost always precede their nouns.

Articles often index, or point to, the 'definiteness' (or contrariwise, encode the indefiniteness) of the noun they introduce. By definiteness we mean whether the noun is a specific one, known to both speaker and hearer, to the speaker only, to the hearer only, or to neither. For example, if someone utters the sentence in (13) below, it is assumed that both the speaker and the hearer have a particular book in mind, and (13) refers to that one book.

(13) Hand me **the** book, please

On the other hand, (14) assumes that neither speaker nor hearer is referring to one definite, specific car (hence 'indefinite article'):

(14) I need **a** new car

So we have a class of determiners, which includes two kinds of article in PDE, definite and indefinite. It's easiest at this stage to think of *the* and *a* as illustrative of definite and indefinite articles respectively, but there are several other words that also function as determiners (the words *some* and *any*, for example, can also behave in this way).

3.9 More on OE articles, noun inflections and grammatical case

Although we speak of articles in OE, what we're calling 'articles' probably seem more like – and they certainly behave similarly to – PDE demonstratives (*this*, *that*, *these*, *those*). This notwithstanding, we'll translate the relevant bits of structure in front of nouns as definite articles and refer to them as such from this point forward: *se* + *cyning*, article + noun, the king. (It's also worth noting that OE generally didn't have what we would recognise as the indefinite article *a*. The evolution of the indefinite article system is a feature of later English. It's true that you sometimes encounter phrases such as *ān swān* (a swineherd, a swain) in OE, but here *ān* means 'a certain', 'one particular').

With these notes and comments in mind, let's turn again to the inflectional system of OE itself. Since both the definite article, and OE nouns inflect, it's extremely important that you should know the inflectional *paradigm* (or pattern) of the OE definite article, which is laid out in table 3.1. As you study this paradigm, you may be puzzled by the exact meaning of the terms 'Accusative', 'Genitive' and so forth. If so, don't panic. They will be explained directly. OE examples (all nominative singular): *se cyning* (masculine, the king), *sēo cwēn* (feminine, the queen), *þæt scip* (neuter, the ship).

Table 3.1 The OE article system

	Singular			**Plural**
	Masculine	**Feminine**	**Neuter**	(all genders)
Nominative	se	sēo	þæt	þā
Accusative	þone	þā	þæt	þā
Genitive	þæs	þǣre	þæs	þāra
Dative	þǣm	þǣre	þǣm	þǣm

A word now, as promised, on the labels *Nominative*, etc., which appear in the left-hand column of the table above. These labels indicate grammatical **cases**, which may be thought of as roles in a sentence that nouns and noun phrases can play, such as 'the noun phrase (NP) that represents the one performing the action' or 'the noun phrase that represents the one "receiving" the action' or 'the noun phrase that indicates possession'. To make things easier, let's just refer to *Noun Phrases* in general. We'll call them NPs rather than nouns, because nouns in OE sentences often have at least one thing (= piece of structure) in front of them, such as an article, and may even have more, such as an adjective or adjectives (these can occur both in front of and after the head noun), and what applies to noun phrases will apply to nouns as well. Here are some examples of NPs in PDE:

(15) **The paintings** intrigued her (NP contains definite article + plural noun)
(16) All she wanted to produce was **a painting** (NP contains indefinite article + singular noun)
(17) **Ugly paintings** delighted him (NP contains no apparent article + adjective + plural noun)

And now some examples in OE:

(18) **se cyning** ācwealde him (the king killed him; NP contains article inflecting for case [nominative], number [singular] and gender [masculine])

(19) Hē ācwealde **þone cyning** (he killed the king; NP contains article inflecting for case [accusative], number [singular], and gender [masculine])

(20) **Se gōd cyning** wæs Ōswold gehāten (the good king was called Oswald; NP contains a definite article [nominative, singular, masculine], an adjective [no ending] and an apparently uninflected head noun)

(21) Hē ācwealde **þone gōdne cyning** (he killed the good king; NP contains a definite article [accusative, singular, masculine], an adjective [root + accusative singular masculine inflection -ne], and an apparently uninflected head noun)

(22) Hē rǣdde **bēc** (he read books; notice that the word *bēc* is an NP consisting of a single word head noun. The root of the plural form *bēc* is *bōc*, book. This is one of those nouns that changes its vowel to indicate plurality, cf. PDE *mouse* (singular), *mice* (plural)

There are other reasons for thinking of single nouns with no modification as instances of noun phrases, but they need not concern us here. Take it on faith, if you will, that when we say NP, we mean 'a noun with whatever, if anything, comes with it'. (As we've claimed, nouns will often be preceded by articles, and/or by adjectives, but you'll already have noticed that nouns may also be followed by units of structure, cf. PDE *The book **of Fate***.) A graphic illustration of the structure we're invoking here may be found in figure 3.1, where the NP does, as claimed, include the root of the noun 'and whatever comes with it', i.e. in this instance whatever article precedes it.

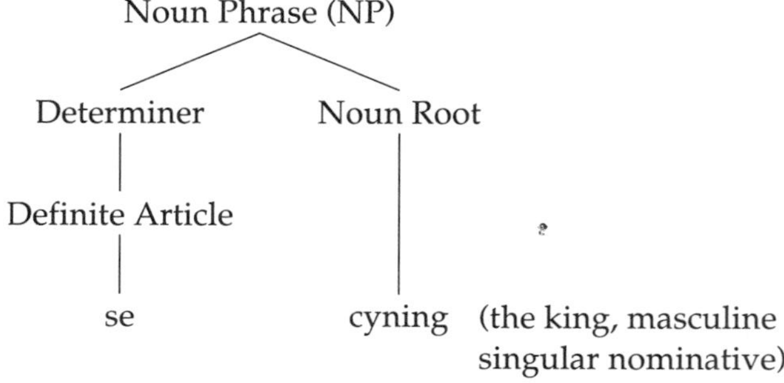

Figure 3.1

This said, the term *nominative case* is used to refer to the NP that is the subject of the sentence. *Accusative case* refers to the NP that functions as the direct object of the sentence. *Genitive case* indicates an NP that shows possession. And *dative* can be analysed (not altogether satisfactorily) as the case of the NP that is the indirect object (*They gave* ***Sharon*** *a present*, where 'Sharon' is the indirect object of the giving, and the present is the thing given, i.e. the direct object.)

Take some more PDE examples.[1] Study the following:

(23) The brilliant tutor bought a red Ferrari
(24) His mother's red Ferrari
(25) The student bought his mother a red Ferrari.

In (23), it's the brilliant tutor who initiates the action of the sentence; the tutor also provides the introductory 'topic' and focus of the whole sentence. On these grounds we can say that the brilliant tutor is the subject of the sentence.[2] *Bought*, on the other hand, is a verb. We know this because like many other verbs in PDE it changes its root vowel to form the past tense (present tense *buy*, past tense *bought*). As a verb – and, moreover, a verb that needs some unit of structure to follow it (consider the ill-formedness of the (im)possible sentence **the tutor bought*) – it introduces, and is itself the first member of, a verb phrase. And as a verb, it doesn't itself have case, because only elements within NPs have case. Nestling within the verb phrase, however, is another phrase, 'a red Ferrari'. It is this, the red Ferrari, which is the direct object of the buying, and it's this NP which is grammatically-speaking the direct object – and which in other circumstances might be said to have 'accusative case' (though cf. fn.1).

(24) is not a sentence (there's no tensed verb in it) but it *is* a self-contained phrase. The red Ferrari belongs to 'his mother', as indicated by the possessive inflection <'s>. NPs that show possession are said to have or 'be in' the genitive case.

(25) is slightly more complex. *the student*, on positional and other grounds, can be identified as the subject of the sentence and therefore might be said to be in the nominative case. Again the verb (which of course has no case) introduces a verb phrase. Nestling within the verb phrase are two further phrases, 'a red Ferrari' (the direct object of the buying and therefore in

[1] In what follows, we use PDE sentences as examples to help us begin thinking about terms such as 'nominative', 'accusative' and so on, though we're only too well aware that this distorts some of the simplicity of PDE, which has relatively fixed word-order and only limited case-marking. We adopt this tactic merely for expositional clarity.

[2] If you think about this for even a moment, you'll undoubtedly notice that our definition of subject won't stand up when we start thinking about 'empty' subjects such as 'It's always noisy on the 3rd floor' or 'There are some things we need to talk about.' Clearly these sentence aren't 'about' *it* or *there*. For this reason many linguists argue that the only inclusive definition of 'subject' is a formal one that specifies its position in a tree diagram.

accusative case) and *his mother*, which is the indirect object of the student's magnanimity and therefore in the dative case.

If we paraphrase the last sentence (25) as (26) below, notice how the preposition *for* appears as we unpack the sentence. When we translate OE dative cases, for example, we will often find the dative introduced by, or implicit from, the presence of a preposition such as *to*, *for*, *in*, etc.

(26) The student bought a red Ferrari **for** his mother

We're now in a position to make slightly more rigorous sense of table 3.1 and figure 3.1. If, for example, we have a masculine singular noun in OE which appears in subject position (= nominative case), we expect the noun to be accompanied and introduced by the article *se*. This is quite correct. Consider the following from our reading in this chapter:

(27) Ond hiera **se æþeling** gehwelcum feoh ond feorh gebēad

And of-them **the prince** to each money and life offered

And the prince offered money and life to each of them

We know from the presence of the article *se* that *se æþeling* can be nothing but nominative singular (and masculine, to boot). Further, because of its case, nominative, we know that *se æþeling* must be the subject of the sentence, even though it isn't the first item of structure in the sentence. Now consider (28). If we find a masculine noun introduced by the article *þone*, we know that it will be accusative case and most likely the direct object of the sentence (and another masculine noun):

(28) Hē ofslōg **þone aldormon**
He slew the alderman

That's exactly what we find. The alderman is the direct object of the killing, and, grammatically, can be nothing other than accusative singular.

Exercise 3.9.0

Using the above information, and relying only on reconstruction from the form of the definite article, state as precisely as you can the number, case and gender of the following nouns. Note: for some of these examples, there are two possibilities, i.e. some examples could accurately, and therefore satisfactorily, be analysed as either, say, 'nominative singular neuter' *or* 'accusative singular neuter'. For this exercise, you'll need to make careful use of table 3.1, so revisit that before you start or, better still, make a copy and have it in front of you as you work.

se stān
þæt bedd

þæs naman
þæt word
þone hyll
þā word
þǣre lufe
þǣm lufum
þǣm fingrum
þāra sweorda

Comment on Exercise 3.9.0

Many of these examples are straightforward. Thus *se stān* is singular, nominative, masculine. *þone hyll* is singular, accusative, masculine. Others are only slightly ambiguous: *þæt bedd* is either nominative or accusative (it's not possible to tell here), singular, neuter, and the same is true of *þæt word*, while *þæt naman* is either masculine or neuter, genitive singular. Others are more complex. *þā word* could be feminine, accusative singular or nominative or accusative plural, with any gender. But we've already seen that *þæt word* is neuter, and therefore *þā word* can only be nominative or accusative plural (it could only be accusative singular if it were feminine). At first glance, that seems rather puzzling. After all, we expect plural nouns to have some kind of plural inflection, but here, *word* isn't apparently inflected. That's because some OE nouns have *zero inflections*. You'll find that some PDE nouns behave in the same way – items like *deer* (**deers*), or *sheep* (**sheeps*), or *salmon* (**salmons*), or the word *fish* (which has zero-inflection *fish* alongside *fishes* as its possible plural realisations). So we might say that the internal structure of *þā word* in our example is a 'plural article that pre-modifies a noun which has a zero [plural] inflection'. We can in fact make greater structural use of 'zero inflections', and will be incorporating them into our analysis of other kinds of nouns, see table 3.2 in the next section, 3.10.

Continuing with the exercise, since *þǣre lufe* must be feminine singular, and either genitive or dative, the several possibilities for *þǣm lufum* come down in the end to feminine, dative plural. *þāra sweorda* has to be genitive plural, but could be any gender. Can you work out why *þǣm fingrum* has to be dative plural? (This last requires more information than we've given you so far, but one clue is that the noun is masculine.)

3.10 Inflections on OE nouns

The answer to the last puzzle comes not from the paradigm of the definite article (*þæm* could be masculine or neuter, dative singular or dative plural in all genders), but from the fact that nouns also inflect for number and case, although usually not in such clear-cut ways as the definite article.

Table 3.2 Inflections for OE strong masculine nouns

	Singular	Plural
Nominative	hund **ø**	hund**as**
Accusative	hund **ø**	hund**as**
Genitive	hund**es**	hund**a**
Dative	hund**e**	hund**um**

Note: ø indicates no inflection, or what some linguists call zero inflection.

The most common ways in which nouns decline is as shown in table 3.2 where we use the word *hund*, dog, for the purpose of explication (cf. our earlier remarks on the relationship with German *Hund*).

If you look closely at this table, and compare the OE word *hund* with PDE *hound*, you should be able to see that these two words are much more alike than seems at first to be the case. Ignoring the respective vowel qualities of the root syllable, the nominative plural form *hundas* is different from *hounds* only in that in PDE the vowel of the second syllable – the <a> of the inflection <-as> – has been lost. Otherwise, the two words are morphologically identical, each comprising root + plural affix.

Exercise 3.10.0

We mentioned earlier that we have two inflections for nouns in PDE: plural, which is often, though not always, realised through the suffix <s>, and possessive, which is often realised as <'s>. What do you think the source of these two inflections might be? Hint: look at the table for *hund* above.

Comment on Exercise 3.10.0

If you suspect that the OE inflection *-as* is the source of '*s*-plurals' in PDE you would of course be quite right. (We actually said the same thing in Unit 1, so don't run riot with self-congratulation.) The same is true of genitive singular *hundes* compared with PDE possessive *hound's*. (The terms genitive and possessive are, you'll recall, virtually interchangeable, at least at this point in our study.) Furthermore, there's no difference in the OE (masculine) forms between the nominative and accusative, in both singular and plural.

What all this means is that there are only three OE inflections here, in the masculine paradigm, which are drastically different from anything in PDE – the dative singular and plural, and the genitive plural. Even with these there is a further simplifying factor, since the dative plural of *every* noun in (almost all varieties of) OE ends in *-um*, and nowhere else can any noun ever end in *-um*. This is why we were able to say *þǣm fingrum* was dative plural.

We could, if we wished, refer quite succinctly and transparently to the declension to which *hund* belongs (and other nouns behaving like it, such as *stān, biscop, cyning*) as the '-as plural declension.' This makes the point that the nominative plural is formed by adding *-as* to the singular form. Most masculine nouns in OE which have one- or two-syllable roots follow this pattern, more or less. Similarly, if we wanted to we could say that PDE *hound* belongs to the present-day -*s*-declension, since it forms its plural by adding the letter -*s*.

'If we wished . . .'? 'If we wanted . . .'?

Exercise 3.10.1

The last kind of statement about declension isn't in fact very useful for PDE, since, in many varieties of our English, almost all nouns decline in the same way. Unfortunately it's very important for OE, where nouns can decline in a variety of ways. Consider, for example, the nouns *word* and *god*, presented in table 3.3 (notice the short vowel and single, word-final consonant in this last example):

Table 3.3 OE strong neuter nouns

	Singular	Plural	Singular	Plural
Nominative	word	word	god	god**u**
Accusative	word	word	god	god**u**
Genitive	word**es**	word**a**	god**es**	god**a**
Dative	word**e**	word**um**	god**e**	god**um**

In what ways do these nouns behave differently to *hund*? And how do they differ from each other?

The main difference between, for example, *word* and *hund* relates to grammatical gender (as the caption to table 3.3 will have told you). Interestingly, nouns belonging to the masculine and neuter genders show respectively different, and highly typical, patterns of inflection. Can you spot where the differences lie?

Comment on Exercise 3.10.1

The only differences occur in the nominative and accusative plural. There, recall that *hund* has *-as*. In table 3.3, *word* has no ending in the nominative and accusative plural, and, in the same cases, *god* has the ending *-u*. The reason for this is the difference between *masculine* nouns like *hund* and *neuter* nouns like *word* and *god*, which have either -u or zero. The earlier example *þæt word* (nominative singular) may have helped you to spot that

that word was neuter. There is in fact a principled reason why *-u* appears as a plural inflection in some neuter nouns and not others. If we give you neuter nominative plural *scipu*, ships, as additional information, can you work out what the reason might be? (Clue: think syllables, and their internal structure.)

Further comment on Exercise 3.10.1

The answer lies in the shape of the root. Where that root is composed of a short vowel followed by one, and only one, word-final consonant, as in *scip* or *god*, then, in neuter nouns, an inflectional *-u* appears in nominative and accusative plural. On the other hand, where the root has a short vowel and *two* following consonants (or where the root vowel is itself long), then the nominative and accusative plural form is simply zero, as in the nominative and accusative plural forms of OE *word*. It appears, then, that *syllable shape* also interacts with OE morphology (word-building).

3.11 Additional noun declensions in OE

The last section should have helped you to work out some of the structures you find in noun declensions in OE. From this point you should be able to go on to look at other noun declensions with confidence. Of these, the most important declensions are as follows:

- the so-called *strong feminine* or -e plural declension, shown by a noun such as *glofu* glove
- the *weak* or -n declension, to which a noun such as *nama*, name, belongs (this declension survives in a few PDE words such as *oxen*; it is still a productive manner of forming plurals in other Germanic languages, notably Dutch)
- a group of *irregular* nouns such as OE *mann*, plural *menn*. This group is distinguished as irregular since it forms its plurals not by adding an inflectional affix, but by changing the vowel of the root. We met an example from this group earlier, with the word *bōc*, plural *bēc*. This group of OE irregular plurals can be compared with a very similar, but much smaller, group in PDE. Think, for example, of the plurals of nouns such as *louse* and the joke-plural *spouse/spice*

You'll be happy to know – well, you won't exactly be happy, but you may well be at least *relieved* to know – that there's a one-page summary of the chief OE article, adjective and noun inflections at the end of this unit. If you turn to this, concentrate at this point on the shape of the noun inflections. Concentrating on those, and beginning to learn the structure of the OE inflected article system, are key skills in working with the earliest English.

We wish there was some easy short-cut to learning these patterns, but there isn't anything fail-safe we can suggest beyond *memorising the paradigms* for each class of noun, e.g. 'strong masculine nouns like *stān*', 'weak nouns like *nama*', and so on. Nevertheless, as you work with each paradigm, we hope you find the summary (increasingly) helpful. It's also replicated in Appendix 1, pp. 294–95.

3.12 Pronouns

Finally in this unit, an initial look at OE personal pronouns. These are shown in table 3.4. The terminology used to talk about pronouns makes reference to 1st person, 2nd person and so on. Thus, all forms of the *I* pronoun (*ic, me, min, me*) are '1st person singular', while the forms *we, us* and so on are 1st person plural. The *you* pronouns are the 2nd person forms, singular and plural (and see below), and the *he, she, it* ones are third person singular, while the *they* forms are 3rd person plural. (Notice from the table that *him* in OE can in principle mean 'him' or 'them'.)

For OE, rather than thinking of the syntactic *position* of the pronoun, it's rather more satisfactory to correlate pronouns with the *grammatical categories* into which they can 'fit'. The subject position of a sentence may be filled by any kind of nominative pronoun (***I** told you, **She** enjoys sailing, **It**'s a barracuda*), while the direct object position may be filled by any kind of accusative pronoun, and the indirect object by any dative pronoun. In table 3.5 below you'll find some constructed examples from OE.

Notice the form of the word 'pronoun' itself: 'pro + noun'. A pronoun is a word that may 'stand for' a noun – more specifically a NP, of the kind we introduced above. Compare the two OE sentences shown in figure 3.2.

Table 3.4 OE pronouns

	1sg.	2sg.	1pl.	2pl.
Nom	ic, I	þū, you	wē, we	gē, you
Acc	mē	þē	ūs	ēow
Gen	mīn	þīn	ūre	ēower
Dat	mē	þē	ūs	ēow
	3sg. masc.	**3sg. fem.**	**3sg. neut.**	**3pl.**
Nom	hē, he	hēo, she	hit, it	hī, they
Acc	hine	hī	hit	hī
Gen	his	hire	his	hira
Dat	him	hire	him	him

Table 3.5 Subject and object pronouns in OE

Hē	*ascode* (*asked*)	*them*	(He asked them)
Subject Nom. 3rd person Singular Pronoun		Object Acc. 3rd person Plural Pronoun	
Hēo	*ācwelde* (*killed*)	*þone þegn*	(She killed the retainer)
Subject Nom. 3rd person Singular Pronoun		Object Acc. (masc.) – Singular Noun	
Hī	*timbrodon* (*built*)	*hit*	(They built it)
Subject 3rd person Plural Pronoun		Object 3rd person Singular Pronoun	

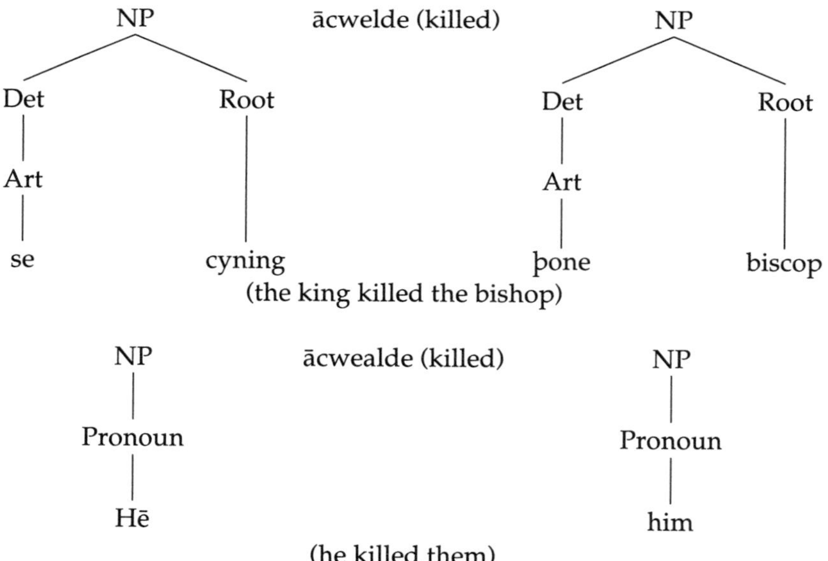

Figure 3.2 Pronouns and NP in OE

Exercise 3.12.0

What major differences can you see between the OE personal pronoun system and the present-day one, particularly in terms of pronouns that have been lost over time, and also in terms of the case-system? Also, can you make any generalisation about the actual forms of the 3rd person pronouns, both in the singular and the plural, as they occur in OE?

Comment on Exercise 3.12.0

One important difference between OE and PDE is the existence of a second person singular form in OE, namely *þū*. This second person singular form, as you'll have realised, is the antecedent of the archaic or dialectal form in PDE, *thou*. It's important to notice that *þū* is strictly singular. *gē* on the other hand (archaic 'ye', as in 'O **ye** of little faith!') is strictly plural. In OE there's no difference of meaning such as there is between French *tu* and *vous* (one being the polite form), German *du* and *Sie*, or Spanish *tu* and *usted*. (Note: it's very useful for a language to have a pronominal distinction in the 2nd person singular and plural. Some current British and American English dialects have, or are even reintroducing, a distinction between singular *you* and plural *youse*. Consider also here American English dialectal *you*, plural *y'all*.) In terms of cases, the OE system for the 1st and 2nd person is strongly analogous to that obtaining in PDE (as well it might be, since the prior forms underlie the present-day system!). Only in the 3rd person is there distinctive dative case-marking in OE.

Exercise 3.12.1

The 3rd person pronouns can cause some difficulties when translating. This arises in part because they all have the characteristic of starting with <h>. This leads to possible ambiguity. For example, what different things can OE *hī* mean? Or *him*? Also, unfortunately, there's a good deal of spelling variation in OE scribal practice – as you may already have found in your work on the story of Cynewulf and Cyneheard – so that, for example, alternative spellings for *hī* include both *hīe* and *hī*.

There are two OE pronoun forms we didn't put in table 3.4. These are the special (and rather rare) *dual* forms used for the 1st and 2nd person when referring to two persons only. *wit* means 'we two' and *unc* 'us two'.

Now you know something of the structure of the OE pronoun system, consider the ways in which the OE system changed into the system familiar in your dialect of PDE. What do you think caused the changes? When did the changes take place? And what does your account suggest about the relationship between OE and other Germanic languages?

3.13 NPs, nominals, strong and weak adjectives

We've said something about inflected articles and nouns. We've also mentioned adjectives. One way to begin to think about the network of relationships that exists within the NP is to think of the *function* of its internal constituents. The function of determiners, for instance, is to introduce the head noun, 'head' meaning 'the grammatical, and often the semantic, focus of the phrasal constituent as a whole'. In the NP *se gōd cyning*, *se* is the article and *cyning* the noun. In terms of the function of these two words, though, the article functions as a determiner, i.e. it pre-modifies the noun, and the noun functions as the head of the whole phrase. Consider also the adjective *gōd*. Its function is again that of a pre-modifer; it 'belongs with' the following noun. Thus, the article *se* doesn't actually pre-modify just the next word along in the string (**se gōd* wouldn't make much sense on its own and we'd want to ask 'the good what?'), but actually pre-modifies the group of two words, *gōd cyning*, of which *cyning* is the head. We can schematise this by looking at figures 3.3 and 3.4, one adapted from Section 3.9 above and

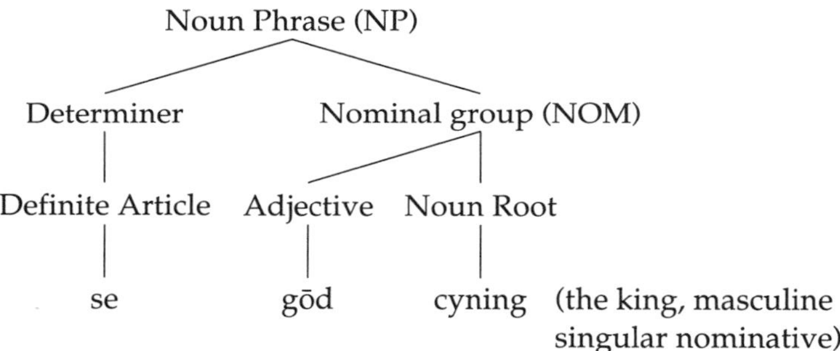

Figure 3.3 Constituents within a NP

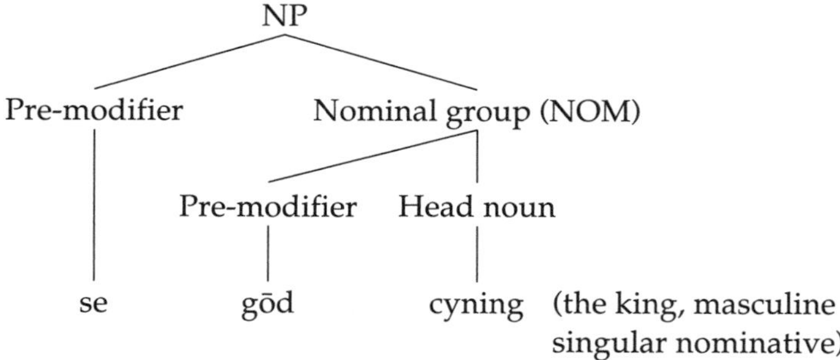

Figure 3.4 The *function of the constituents* within the same NP

the other encoding the same structure, not in terms of the labels 'article, adjective, noun', but in terms of the *function* of these items within the NP. In figure 3.3, we've given a label to the piece of language formed by the adjective and the noun. Since the adjective and noun seem to belong together, we've called them a *nominal group* (sometimes abbreviated to NOM).

So within this NP, the function of *se* is to pre-modify the stretch of language that has *cyning* as its head, while the function of *gōd* is to directly pre-modify the following head noun. The words participate in *a network of relationships*. Thinking about these relationships helps us to understand what a noun actually is. We've often heard it said that a noun is 'the name of a person, place or thing', but for the purposes of working with language such a definition is inadequate. Is 'beauty' a person, a place or a thing? Is 'happiness'? These may indeed be human attributes, but you might observe that such nouns don't *behave* quite like other nouns such as 'garden' or 'fence'. For one thing, gardens and fences can be counted, while it's difficult to pluralise 'happiness' (*happinesses). Nevertheless, beauty and happiness are nouns and they may be analysed that way *because they behave in that way*, i.e. they participate in many of the key relationships we expect nouns to participate in. They can be pre-modified by articles ('the happiness he felt was astounding'); and they can stand as the heads to adjectives ('great happiness is a delusion'). So what we call 'noun' is really a way not only of identifying a word's cognitive *content*, but a way of thinking about its *behaviour*.

The reason we're thinking about structure and function, and about the differences between the two, is because this helps us understand the behaviour of NPs in general, and adjectives in particular. For example, Mitchell and Robinson claim quite properly that adjectives in OE have two forms, one 'strongly declining' form and one 'weakly declining' form: 'Most adjectives can be declined strong or weak . . . The strong form is used when the adj. stands alone, e.g. "The man is old" *se mann is eald*, or just with a noun, e.g. *ealde menn*. The weak form follows when the adj. follows a dem[onstrative], e.g. 'that old man' *se ealda mann*, or a poss[essive] adj., e.g. 'my old friend' *mīn ealda frēond*. You can remember that the strong forms stand alone, while the weak forms need the support of a dem. or poss. pron[oun]' (Mitchell and Robinson 1992:30–31).

All this is quite true, but we need to understand why. Let's think of the idea of 'strong adjective' by thinking of a 'fully inflected adjective', and conversely, think of 'weak adjective' as a 'less inflected adjective'. Why should there be a difference in the two patterns?

Inflected definite articles carry a great deal of grammatical information – about case, number and, often, about gender. This information relates to the head noun that it's the function of the article to introduce. Thus *se* in *se cyning* carries the unambiguous information that *cyning* must be a masculine noun, that we're dealing with a singular entity and that the case we're studying is the nominative.

If an article carries all this information, then an adjective that appears in the same NP doesn't really need to carry the same information. This would lead merely to redundancy, and languages don't appear to tolerate too much grammatical redundancy.

However, in the absence of an inflected definite article before a noun, it's somewhat more difficult to ascertain information about gender, or number, or case. Sometimes it's possible to infer some information about these things just from the inflectional ending on the noun, but often it's not. Therefore, if an adjective stands (usefully) in a modifying relationship with a head noun, i.e. in a nominal group, and if that nominal group isn't preceded by an article, then it's extremely useful to a synthetic language if grammatical information can be coded, via inflection, onto the adjective. So the phrase 'good kings' (nominative or accusative plural) in OE would be *gōd-e cyning-as*, with an inflectional *-e* on the adjective and the expected nominative plural inflection *-as* on the head noun.

If we're trying your patience at this point, we'll gently remind you that you will find a table of inflections on nouns and adjectives at the end of this unit. The at-a-glance summary should help you further in your understanding of how the earliest English was put together.

Summary

We've covered a great deal of ground in this unit. We noted that Romano-British society went into decline after the withdrawal of the Roman garrison. We also had our first glimpse of those Germanic tribes who were, two or three centuries later, to begin settling what was to become Anglo-Saxon England. Our principal source for that glimpse – though he was writing at least three centuries before the Anglo-Saxon conquest and settlement of England – was Tacitus, whose *Germania* is a wry, but apparently accurate, account of the ways of life of 'the Germans'. We also said something about the development of the kingdoms of Anglo-Saxon England, and noted that those kingdoms underlie, to some extent, the shape of what were to be, for many centuries, the English counties ('shires'). We also devoted one section of text to the role of women in early Germanic society. This seems to have been, at least in the case of the well-born and the aristocracy, far more powerful than might have been expected.

In terms of the language of the Germanic peoples, we developed the work done in Unit 2 by devoting a relatively great deal of space to a preliminary analysis of the OE inflectional system. We did this for two main reasons. First, inflections often form a set of small but irritating obstacles to the student who wants to begin to read the earliest English. And second, in terms of the development of English, we will need to look later at patterns of inflectional loss. Some understanding of the inflectional system of OE is, then, important if we're subsequently going to take on interesting work concerning linguistic evolution. An analysis of the erosion of the inflectional system of OE will occupy parts of Units 6 and 8.

We also introduced our readers to the system of articles that existed in OE and, with that introduction, we also began to think about grammatical case (nominative, accusative, genitive and dative), since case-relations are at the heart of the OE grammatical system just as they're at the heart of the grammatical systems of some other Germanic languages. And, finally, we asked you to start thinking about the pronoun system of OE. Again, we did this for two good reasons. First, the pronoun system contains some ambiguities (remember *hī* and *him*?) and these need spotting, if only in order to help you with your translation of relatively difficult passages like the *Chronicle* entry we asked you to examine in this unit. And, second, the pronoun system of OE will undergo modification during our period – think, for example, of what the 3rd person singular feminine pronoun was in OE and what its equivalent would be today – and we need to understand the structure of the prior system in order to apprehend the nature of the changes it was subsequently to undergo.

Study questions

1. Study table 3.2 again (you'll find it in Section 3.10). How many inflections have been lost from that particular paradigm? Why do you think that loss might have taken place? Do you think all inflections were lost at the same rate?
2. Study the lists of pronouns given above (table 3.4, Section 3.12). Which of those pronouns have survived into PDE, and which have been lost? What pronouns have been added to the system? Can you begin to guess why any language might need to add to its pronoun system?
3. The definite article in OE is highly inflected. If we claim, as many scholars would claim, that OE articles 'inflected for gender, number and case' what, precisely, would that phrase mean? And can you give examples of articles inflecting for gender, number and case?
4. We claimed in the Summary that case-relations are at the heart of the grammatical system of OE. If you are a non-native speaker of English, your native language may also have case-relations and a grammatical system more or less dependent on inflections. Could you begin to describe your own language in terms of inflections and case-relations?
5. We introduced OE nouns, and suggested that nouns have internal structure as well as participating in grammatical relationships with other words of the clause or sentence. As we've seen, for example, nouns may be preceded by an inflected article; they may also be preceded by (one or more) adjectives. Do you think, from what you've read here so far, that these adjectives would also show inflection? (Native and non-native

speakers of German and Dutch might like to consider this question particularly closely.)

6. In PDE, nouns may also be followed by constituents (ranging from single words to entire sentences) that post-modify their sense, e.g. ***The car I bought*** *was too expensive, They visited* ***the restaurant at the end of the street***. How would you begin to describe such patterns? And do you think that such patterns of post-modification were available to a speaker of OE?

Websites you may find useful

You might like to look again at some of the websites we listed at the end of Unit 2 (p. 63, if you missed them first time round). Most of these sites don't go into the kind of linguistic detail we need, although all will provide some further introduction to early Germanic and, specifically, to Anglo-Saxon, society and culture:

- http://www.english.uga.edu/~methelie
- http://www.redbad.tripod.com
- http://www.towson.edu/~duncan/germanic
- http://www.wodanaz.com/runes
- http://www.anthro.mankato.msus.edu/prehistory
- http://www.lonestar.texas.net/~jebbo/learn-as
- http://www.avesta.org

References and suggestions for further reading

Barber, C.L. 1993. *The English language: a historical introduction*. Cambridge: Cambridge University Press. [See especially Chapter 3.]

Baugh, A.C. and Thomas Cable. 1993. *A history of the English language*. 4th edition. London: Routledge and Kegan Paul. [Read Chapters 2 and 4, or selected parts of chapters 2 and 4, before progressing to Chapter 3, which is on OE proper.]

Fennell, Barbara. 2001. *A history of English: a sociolinguistic approach*. Oxford: Blackwell.

Hogg, Richard. 1992. *A grammar of Old English. Vol.1: Phonology*. Oxford: Blackwell Publishers. [This is an advanced grammar, but full of indispensable detail. p.63ff., for example, on unstressed vowels, is full of interesting reconstruction of the development of the vowel shapes of many OE inflections, tracing their forms back into PrGmc. However, you may want to wait until you've read this text thoroughly before embarking on such a specialist read.]

Hunter Blair, Peter. 1970. *An introduction to Anglo-Saxon England*. Cambridge: Cambridge University Press.

Mattingly, H., (trans.), revised by S.A. Handford. 1970. *Tacitus: the Agricola and the Germania*. London: Penguin Classics. [Repeated from the suggested reading given in Unit 2.]

Quirk, Randolph and C.L. Wrenn. 1957. *An Old English grammar*. London: Methuen. [Concise and handy student grammar, with the pronouns set out on p.38, and an introduction to the origins and function of the case system of OE in Part III, p.59ff.]

Sherley-Price, Leo. 1955. *Bede: A History of the English church and people*. London: Penguin Classics. [A useful translation. See especially Book I, Chapter 15.]

Strang, B.M.H. 1970. *A history of English*. London: Methuen.

And finally . . .

Appendix 1: At-a-glance guide to OE inflections – nouns and adjectives

Tables 3.6 and 3.7 present a somewhat simplified guide to OE article, adjective and noun inflections, as these might be expressed in classical WS.

Table 3.6 Nouns and strongly declining adjectives

If you wish to find the strongly declining adjective, together with the inflections on the head noun, then just cover the left-hand part of table 3.6 (i.e. the articles). If an article is present in a given NP, then of course the following adjective will decline weakly, if present, and you should look up the relevant inflection in table 3.7.

We use the abbreviations M(asculine), F(eminine) and N(euter) and, in the left-hand rows, N(ominative), A(ccusative), G(enitive) and D(ative). N+A here means 'both nominative and accusative'.

Inflections appearing in parentheses are often phonologically conditioned, e.g. they appear after light syllables in roots. Thus *scip* (neuter, n+a sg., with zero inflection) and *scipu* (n+a pl.)

	Articles (the/that)			**Adjectives**			**Nouns**		
	M	**N**	**F**	**M**	**N**	**F**	**M**	**N**	**F**
Sg.N	se	þæt	sēo	–	–	(-u)	–	–	(-u)
A	þone	þæt	þā	-ne	–	-e	–	–	-e
G	þæs		þære	-es		-re	-es		-e
D	þæm		þære	-um		-re	-e		-e
Pl.N+A		þā		-e	(-u)	-a	-as	(-u)	-a
G		þara			-ra			-a	
D		þæm			-um			-um	

Table 3.7 Weakly declining adjectives (and nouns)

Recall that weak adjectives are preceded by a definite article or possessive pronoun. Here's how adjectives behave in that circumstance. Nouns – 'weak nouns' – inflect this way as well. Notice the prevalence of the inflectional ending *-an*.

	M	N	F
Sg.N	-a	-e	-e
A	-an	-e	-an
G		-an	
D		-an	
Pl.N+A		-an	
G		-ena	
D		-um	

Unit Four

Verbs

4.0 The conversion of England

The story of the Christian conversion of England is so well known that it warrants no more here than the bare facts – although it's worth repeating, since the conversion has a profound effect not only on the development of the English people, but also on their language.

At the end of the 6th century Pope Gregory dispatched his emissary, Augustine, to Britain together with a company of monks (said by Bede to number 40 souls) in 597. (This Augustine isn't to be confused with the earlier great cleric and writer Augustine of Hippo who lived in the 4th century and who authored the famous *Confessions*, a seminal Christian work.) Even under Augustine's determined leadership this group almost turned back: 'Having undertaken this task at the Pope's command and progressed a short distance on their journey, they became afraid, and began to consider turning home. For they were appalled at the idea of going to a barbarous, fierce, and pagan nation, of whose very language they were ignorant . . .' (Bede, *History*, trans. Sherley Price 1955:66). It was only after papal encouragement and reassurance that Augustine and his monks landed on Thanet (Kent), together with interpreters they'd acquired from the Franks. Their mission lay with the king of Kent, Æthelbert. Æthelbert 'had already heard of the Christian religion, having a Christian wife of the Frankish royal house named Bertha . . .' (69), and he received Augustine hospitably, not only allowing him freedom to preach but also granting him a house in Canterbury from where their mission could be sustained. It's no accident, therefore, that Canterbury became a significant religious site and the most important of all English arch-episcopal sees (the word *see* is derived from Latin *sedere*, to sit). According to Bede, '. . . great numbers gathered each day to hear the word of God, forsaking their heathen rites, and entering the unity of Christ's holy Church as believers' (71).

4.1 Influence of the Celtic church

The success of the Roman mission to England is so apparent, and legitimised by such a powerful source, the Pope in Rome, that it's difficult not to think of it as the prime event in the conversion of England. On the other hand, we know from Bede that Augustine and his followers had to rely (at least initially) on interpreters, and it's also significant that Augustine's mission was to a royal court, rather than to a people. Perhaps the mission was as much about successful diplomacy as it was about evangelical zeal. Therefore we should also be conscious of another religious source for the conversion of England. This source lay in Ireland.

Although Britain had been partly Christianised during the Roman occupation (the empire of Rome had after all been itself Christianised, and forms of Christian worship had touched even the far north of Britain) pagan worship obviously still lingered. In Ireland, however, in the four centuries following the death of Christ, a form of Christian worship was developing that was to have a momentous impact on the peoples (note: peoples, not courts) that it eventually touched.

After the departure of the Romans, Christianity had remained, if not thriven, in those parts of Britain not over-run by pagan Anglo-Saxon settlement. In particular, it lasted in Ireland under the auspices of Patrick (mid-5th century) and Columba (born c.520). During this period, the north of Ireland and the south of what's now Scotland (Galloway and parts of Argyll) formed a distinct kingdom, and there was frequent travel and contact between peoples on either side of what is now the Irish Sea. Of special note was the fact that Columba formed a monastic house and church at Iona, a small island off the south-west tip of Mull. From this base, Columba and his followers, whose Christianity was marked by evangelism, teaching and, in many religious foundations, extreme asceticism, preached to and converted the peoples of the north.

If Iona's influence had stopped there, that would have been remarkable enough and a testimony to how Christianity survived on the remote western fringes of European dark-age civilisation. But, because of a series of political and military accidents in Northumbria, the impact of Celtic Christianity was to be felt across the whole of the north of England, as far south as the English midlands, and eventually penetrated, through evangelism and scholarship, to most areas of England. It was even to make its mark on Rome.

4.2 The convergence of the Celtic and Roman traditions

In the 7th century the strongest, and culturally the most important, of the Anglo-Saxon kingdoms in the emerging Heptarchy was Northumbria. In the years 616–632 the Northumbrian kingdom was ruled by one of the most powerful kings of that era, Edwin, who was well acquainted with Christianity. He had married a Christian daughter of the Kentish royal house,

Æthelberg, in 626, and later the following year was converted to the 'worship of the true God' (Bede). He was publicly baptised by the Christian bishop Paulinus, who – by a convenient twist – had been one of a band of clerics sent to England by Pope Gregory to bolster Augustine's original Kentish mission. Bede also recounted how Paulinus, as bishop of York, in the years to follow preached to and baptised many hundreds of converts on the banks of the rivers Glen and Swale.

Edwin had gained power in 616 when he and his powerful East Anglian ally, Rædwald (who may well have been the leader whose remains archaeologists discovered at the famous burial site at Sutton Hoo), slaughtered the Northumbrian ruler, Æthelfrith, in battle. On the death of their father, Æthelfrith's two sons, Oswald and Oswy, escaped to the Irish (Scottish) kingdom of Dalriada. 'By the time of Oswald's arrival in Dalriada in 616, the monastery on Iona, or I-Columcille, had been established for some fifty years and was approaching the period of its greatest importance. The island Bede called Hii had long been a sacred site before the coming of Columcille . . .' (Marden 1992:109). While on Iona, Oswald and his brother were instructed in the Christian faith and, possibly, in methods of Christian teaching.

After Edwin and his sons died in battle in 632, there followed a turbulent year of claim, counter-claim, siege and violent feud in Northumbria when many of the recently converted peoples relapsed into pagan forms of worship (Bede called 632 'the ill-omened year'). Oswald, however, had a strong claim to the Northumbrian crown and, together with his brother, Oswy, a small company of loyal retainers, a Dalriadic warband and whatever loyal Northumbrians were prepared to join him, he confronted his opponents in 633 near what is now Chollerford, at a place Bede and other chroniclers called 'Heaven's field'. On the eve of the approaching battle Oswald is said to have received a vision of Saint Columba which promised his forces victory. Thus encouraged, and after erecting a cross on the battlefield, Oswald duly slew Cadwallon, the leader of the opposing forces, and a large part of Cadwallon's army. (As recorded by Bede, and by a much later biographer, Ælfric, in his *Life of Saint Oswald*, the cross on the battlefield was subsequently held to have miraculous properties.) Oswald, therefore, assumed the Northumbrian kingship not merely as a successful general but as a Christian warrior-saint whose success had been promised and endorsed by heavenly showing. Oswald reigned from 633–642.

One of Oswald's first actions as king was to send back to Iona for missionaries who would convert, or re-convert, the northern peoples. Eventually he was sent a cleric named Aidan, who had been Irish-trained, and granted him a religious site on the tidal island of Lindisfarne: a Northumbrian Iona.

One of the consequences of the Celtic mission was the development of an educational system that trained native English in the elements of the faith, the transmission and maintenance of that faith, and monastic rule. In short, it was this mission that was to ensure the lasting survival of Christianity in the north; that led directly to the foundation of important monasteries such as Jarrow and Monkwearmouth; that guaranteed that such houses would be repositories of scholarship, filled with treasures and reliquaries; that informed all subsequent literacy in the north of England; and that made the Northumbria of the later 7th and early 8th centuries one of the greatest cultural centres of Western Europe. It was the Golden Age of Northumbria. The age of Bede.

Oswald was succeeded by his brother, Oswy, who reigned from 642–670. Oswy is credited with bringing together the Celtic and the Roman Christian traditions, motivated by issues close to home. Though they were both Christians, Oswy, an observer of the Celtic tradition, and his wife, an observer of the Roman tradition, celebrated Easter at different times. This may seem rather a minor point today, but at the time it was of supreme importance because this was one of the issues that symbolised the separation of the two Christian churches and deeply affected daily life, which was closely tied to the church calendar. King Oswy formally adopted the Roman position at the Synod of Whitby (664), an adoption that led the way to a joining of the two factions, confirming the stature of the Christian Church in the Anglo-Saxon kingdoms.

Exercise 4.2.0

You might like to get some idea of the geography of some key sites mentioned in Section 4.2. Look at map 6. The map shows some important religious sites. Pay particular attention to the sites of (a) Canterbury, (b) Lindisfarne, (c) Jarrow/Monkwearmouth and (d) – for future reference in Unit 6 – Ruthwell.

We've already noted that parts of what is now England had been Christianised during the Roman occupation, and in fact this form of worship was sometimes deeply imbued in the peoples who used it. Areas of Wales and Scotland had also accepted the Christian religion, as had large parts of Ireland, and it's possible that these peoples and forms of worship had a greater effect on the retention of Christianity than had Augustine's papally endorsed mission. Hunter Blair writes, for example, that the triumph of the Roman Church (= Roman Catholicism) 'belonged less to the age of the conversion than to the succeeding age of Bede' (1970:126).

From our point of view, the fact that the Anglo-Saxons were Christianised in the 7th and following centuries is something of momentous importance. The coming of Christianity brought with it a system of writing (which almost completely replaced the earlier runic alphabet), a sense of history, a literature, a European cultural dimension and a set of ethics that eventually

Map 6 Some key religious sites in Anglo-Saxon England

twined with the Germanic social code, which had originally been based rather more on heroism and worldly renown than on moral responsibility. As the 7th century turned into the 8th, England – and one area in particular, Northumbria – could justifiably claim to lead European culture and scholarship, a pre-eminence not to be matched for many centuries.

4.3 Reading passage (1)

In the previous unit we suggested that the Germanic peoples arriving in Britannia as mercenaries, and (all too) quickly becoming colonists, appeared to have neither assimilated, nor to have been assimilated into, the surrounding Romano-British society. They brought with them their own religion, their own customs and their own societal values. Apparently they had no interest in changing those Romanised Celts who might have remained around them, nor in being changed by them. They appear to have learned neither Latin nor Celtic in any great numbers nor to any great degree. The result, at least for a time, was a culturally (linguistically, religiously and legally) divided society. Nowhere was this more apparent than in the conversion of Britannia. Davies (1999:197) points out that the

> Celtic Christians and the Germanic pagans had seven or eight generations in which to reinforce and to ritualize their cultural differences. From all accounts, the Celts were as loath to share their religion with pagans as the pagans were to accept it. What is more, when the [Germanic tribes] eventually accepted Christianity, they did so from Irish or Roman missionaries, not from their British neighbours. And they did so with the full weight of political and social power behind them.

Later in his text, Davies mentions that the ethos of the mission from the Roman church and its followers differed greatly from that of the Celtic Church. Augustine's mission was to the Germanic courts – although he converted just one court – in Britannia, and his '. . . Germanic converts were apt to adopt the new religion thinking that it would bring them political and material benefits' (Davies 1999:199). In Northumbria, by contrast, Bede tells us that Edwin was convinced personally by what Paulinus taught and that he both intended and earnestly desired to accept the new faith. First, however, he wanted to have *gesprec* and *geþeaht*, discussion and deliberation, regarding the matter with his *witan*, and wanted to know what they thought of this *nīwe lār*, new lore. That context forms the background of our next reading passage.

The format is the same as in previous units. We give a (very) literal translation in roman type, and a more fluent, idiomatic translation in bold type. As before, we give a full translation at the end of the unit, but again we urge you not to cheat . . .

Exercise 4.3.0

þā hæfde hē gesprec and geþeaht mid his witum and syndriglīce	1
Then had he discussion and deliberation with his witan and individually	
Then he deliberated with his counsellors, and kept asking them all individually	
wæs fram him eallum frignende hwylc him þūhte and gesawen	2
was from them all asking what to-them seemed and seen	
how this new learning seemed to them, and was seen by them,	
wæs þēos nīwe lār and þǣre godcundnesse bīgong þe þǣr lǣred wæs	4
was this new lore, and the divinity that there taught was.	
. . . along with the form of divinity that it taught.	
Him þā andswarode his ealdorbisceop, Cēfi wæs hāten:	5
Him then answered his high priest, Cefi was called:	
Then his (pagan) high priest, who was called Cefi, answered him:	
'Geseoh þū, cyning, hwelc þēos lār sīe þe ūs nū bodad is. Ic þē	6
sōðlīce andette þæt ic cūðlīce geleornad hæbbe þæt eallinga	7
nāwiht mægenes ne nyttnesse hafað sīo ǣfæstnes þe wē oð ðis	8
hæfdon and beēodon, for ðon nǣnig þīnra þegna nēodlicor ne	9
gelustfullīcor hine sylfne underþēodde tō ūre goda bīgange þonne	10

ic, and nōht þon lǣs monige syndon þā þe māran gefe and fremsumnesse	11
æt þē onfēngon þonne ic, and in eallum þingum māran gesynto hæfdon.	12
Hwæt, ic wāt, gif ūre godo ǣnige mihte hæfdon, þonne woldan hīe mē mā fultumian	13
forþon ic him geornlīcor þēodde ond hӯrde. For þon mē þynceð wīslic, gif þū	14
gesēo þā þing beteran and strangran þe ūs nīwan bodad syndon, þæt wē þām	15
onfon.' þæs wordum ōþer cyninges wita and ealdormann geþafunge	16
sealde, and tō þǣre sprǣce fēng and þus cwæð . . .	17

Selective glossary

Since we introduced you to concepts like case, gender and number in the last unit, in this glossary we've indicated these grammatical properties for nouns. We also indicate what items are verbs, and what tense and grammatical person these items show. We do this now because subsequent work in the unit is concerned with how OE verbs are structured.

In this glossary, you'll find words prefixed with *ge-* listed alphabetically, i.e. under the entries for <g>. This may help you to find the words in question, but such a listing isn't standard practice in OE glossaries and dictionaries, which list words prefixed with *ge-* generally under the initial letter of their root form. Thus in a standard OE glossary you'd look up *gesprec*, discussion, not under <g> but under <s>, since <s> is the letter that begins the root. In later units, we'll adopt the standard practice.

andette — verb; 1sg. past from verb infinitive *andettan*, to confess
ǣfæstnes — religion (fem. nom. sg.)
ǣnige — any
æt — prep.; from; assigns dat. case to its object
beēodon — verb; 1pl., past from infinitive *begān*, to perform, surround
bīgange — see *bīgong*
bīgong — worship (masc. nom. sg.)
bodad — verb; ppl. from *bodian*, to preach
cūðlīce — clearly
cyninges — king (masc. gen. sg.)
eallinga — utterly
eallum — all (dat. pl.)
fēng — verb; 1sg. past from *fōn*, to catch, seize; idiomatic phrase: *tō þǣre sprǣce fēng*, succeeded to the speech, i.e. took the floor
for ðon — because, therefore, and so
fram — prep.; from, by, away; assigns dat. case to its object
fremsumnesse — benefits (fem. pl. acc.)
frignende — verb; pres. participle from *frignan*, to ask, inquire
fultumian — verb; infinitive, to help, support
gefe — gifts (fem. acc. pl.)
geleornad — verb; ppl. from *geleornian*, to learn
gelustfullīcor — willingly (comparative form)
geornlīcor — eagerly, zealously, readily (comparative form)
gesawen — verb; ppl. from *gesēon*, to see
gesēo — verb; 1sg. pres. from *gesēon*, to see
geseoh — verb; imperative sg. from *gesēon*, to see
gesprec — conference, discussion (neut. acc. sg.)
gesynto — prosperity (fem. acc. sg.)
geþafunge — assent (fem. acc. sg.)
geþeaht — counsel, deliberation (neut. acc. sg.)
gif — if
goda — gods (neut. nom. pl.) [The word for non-Christian gods is neut. The word for the Christian God is masc.]
godcundnesse — divinity; godhead (fem. gen. sg.)
godo — gods (neut. nom. pl.)
hafað — verb; 3sg. pres. from *habban*, to have, hold

hāten	verb; ppl. from *hatan*, to call, command, name; idiomatic phrase: was called, was named
hæfde	verb; 3sg. past, see *habban*
hæfdon	verb; 1pl. past see *habban*
hīe	pronoun; 3pl. nom.; variant spelling of *hī*
him	pronoun; 3pl. dat., them
hine	pronoun; masc. acc. 3sg., him
hwelc	pronoun; fem. sg., what sort of, what, how
hȳrde	verb; 1sg. past from *hieran*, to obey, hearken to, hear
lār	teaching, doctrine, lore (fem. nom. sg.)
lǣred	verb; ppl. from *lǣran*, to teach, advise
lǣs	less; idiomatic phrase: *nōht þon læs*, nonetheless
mā	noun; more
māran	fem. acc. sg., comparative form of *micel*, great, large, much
mægenes	strength, power (neut. gen. sg.)
mihte	power, might (fem. acc. sg.)
monige	many, many a (nom. pl.)
nāwith	naught, nothing
nǣnig	none, no one
nēodlicor	comparative form of 'diligently'
nīwe	new (fem. nom. sg.)
nōht þon lǣs	see *lǣs*
nū	adverb of time; now, now that
nyttnesse	usefulness, benefit (fem. gen. sg.)
onfēngon	verb; 3pl. past from *onfōn*, to receive, accept, take up
onfōn	verb, infinitive; to receive, accept, take up
oð	prep.; up to, as far as (assigns acc. case)
ōþer	another, other
sealde	verb; 3sg. past from *sellan*, to give, sell
sīe	verb; 3sg. sb. from *bēon*, to be [On the distinction between ind. and sb. moods, see Section 4.13.]
sīo	determiner; fem. nom. sg. (variant spelling of *sēo*)
sylfne	self (masc. sg. acc.)
syndon	verb; 3pl. pres. from *bēon*, to be
syndriglīce	individually, separately, especially
þā	adverb of time; then
þǣre	determiner; fem. gen. sg.
þæs	demonstrative pronoun; neut. gen. sg., to that one's
þē	pronoun; 2sg., (to) thee
þegna	thane, retainer, warrior, nobleman (masc. gen. pl.)
þēodde	verb; 1sg. past from *þēowan*, to serve
þēos	demonstrative; fem. nom. sg., this
þing	things (neut. acc. pl.) [Note the presence of the zero-inflected plural in this neuter noun.]

þīnra	possessive pronoun; masc. pl. gen., thy
ðis	demonstrative pronoun; neut. acc. sg.
þonne	than
þūhte	verb; 3sg. past from *þyncan,* to seem
þynceð	verb; 3sg. pres. from *þyncan,* to seem
underþēodde	verb; 3sg. past from *underþēodan,* to subject, devote
wāt	verb; 1sg. pres. from *witan,* to know
wīslic	wise (neut. nom. sg.)
wita	counsellor (masc. nom. sg.)
wordum	words (neut. dat. pl.)

4.4 Word order and pronouns in OE

Probably one of the first things you noticed in the above reading and translation exercise is that even though OE prose sentences predominately had the word-order Subject-Verb-Object or, abbreviated, SVO (just as they do in PDE), that wasn't invariably the case. In situations like these, it's probably an effective translation strategy to follow the method we outlined in Units 2 and 3. Go sentence by sentence, or even clause by clause, and note the case of the nouns and the number (is it singular or plural?) and person (1st, 2nd, or 3rd) of the verb. That will help you get subjects and objects sorted out.

In terms of word-order itself, you'll notice, for instance, that the verb is in second place in the first sentence. Some linguists call languages that prefer the verb in the second position in a sentence 'V-2 languages'. OE probably isn't really a V-2 language, but Finegan (1987:97) points out that '. . . negative sentences introduced by the particle *ne* favour verb-second position, producing a VS order as in the first clause of *ne geseah ic næfre þā burg, ne ic þone sēap nāt,* I have never seen that city, nor do I know the well.' Sometimes we encounter a similar situation in PDE. Consider the two sentences below:

(1) I have never heard of such a thing
(2) Never have I heard of such a thing

The first shows typical ('unmarked'; normal) PDE word order. However, even in a language with fixed word order like PDE, if we move the negative adverb *never* to the front of the sentence as in (2), the action forces the subject *I* and the auxiliary verb *have* to invert or switch positions, thus putting the (auxiliary) verb *have* in second position. Only certain negative adverbs seem to trigger this in PDE, though any fronted adverbial will cause subject/auxiliary inversion in present-day German. The same thing happens in Dutch. And one of the almost invariable word-order patterns of OE was that after an adverb, or adverbial phrase, the tensed verb comes next:

(3) **Nū sculon** herigean (Now we have to praise)

Adverb, *nū*, followed by tensed verb

(4) **ðā onfēng** Ēadwine cyning gelēafan (Then king Edwin received the faith)
Adverb, *ðā*, followed by tensed verb

A second thing you might have noticed is that *him* doesn't always mean the same thing in OE that it does in PDE. We mentioned this problem in the last unit. *Him* can be a masculine, dative *singular* pronoun (him) but it can also be a 3rd person, dative *plural* pronoun (them). In the above text, it is, in our reading, the latter – the *them* form – in line 2 ('he asked . . . them . . . how it seemed to them . . .'), and the former – the *him* form – in line 4 ('Then the high priest answered him . . .'). The OE word for the masculine, accusative singular pronoun (the direct object, for which PDE has *him*) is *hine*.

4.5 OE verbs: present participles

If we put line 1 in the correct order for PDE, we get 'then he had discussion and deliberation with his counsellors and . . .' In line 2 we'll have to pick up 'individually', an adverb. Being an adverb, it will modify the sense of the verb phrase,[1] *wæs frignende*, which in this case contains a present participle. In PDE, a present participle is any verb + ing. Thus in the following sentences, all the *-ing* forms of the verb are present participles. Notice how versatile these present participles are: though they remain present participles, they can be used rather like nouns, as in (5), as adjectives, as in (6), or simply as main lexical verbs, as in (7):

(5) She enjoyed **swimming**
(6) The **running** gag fell flat
(7) They were **eating** too much chocolate

Although the -ing suffix is found in OE, it hadn't yet come to signal the progressive function. For this progressive function OE had the suffix *-ende*, which could be affixed to the root of the verb to form a present participle. Thus *frignan*, to ask, has the root form *frign-*, to which different suffixes can be attached. One such suffix is the *-an* that indicates the infinitive, the 'to-' form, of the verb (*frign + an*, to ask). Another is the suffix *-ende* (*frign + ende*, asking). A further example might be the verb *ascian* (*aski + an*, to ask), with the present progressive form *asci + ende*, asking.

[1] Though many would disagree with the nomenclature (and if at all pressed, we probably would too) in this book, for ease of explanation, we're going to call the main verb and any auxiliaries that might accompany it a verb phrase (VP).

Exercise 4.5.0

In the phrase *wæs frignende*, just as in PDE the *wæs* acts (more or less) like an auxiliary verb.[2] Auxiliary verbs are non-lexical verbs, one of whose functions is to indicate tense within the extended Verb Phrase (VP). You might like to think about the following three sentences from PDE. For each sentence, identify the auxiliary verb. Note what tense that verb carries. And then identify the main lexical verb in the same sentence. Once you've done that, repeat the same procedure for the next three OE phrases.

(8) They had gone
(9) She was eating too much chocolate
(10) She's injured her chances
(11) Hīe woldan mē mā fultumian (They would support me more)
(12) Ic hæbbe cūðlīce geleornod (I have truly learned)
(13) Hē is bebēodende (He is commanding)

Comment on Exercise 4.5.0

In (8) the auxiliary verb is *had*, a past tense form of the verb *have*; the main lexical verb is *gone*. This last is the past participle of the verb *go*. It can't be the past tense, for two reasons: (i) tense is shown once, and once only, in a VP (this holds good for both OE and PDE), and (ii) in standard varieties of English the past tense of the verb *go* is *went*.

In (9), the auxiliary verb is *was*, a past tense form of *to be*. The main lexical verb is *eating*, here in its present participle form. Now, that looks confusing, because *was* is in the past tense, while we gloss *eating* as 'present participle'. However, if you think about this for a moment, you'll realise that what's meant by the whole sentence is 'continuous action taking place in the past'. At the exact time she was eating chocolate, that time was for her the present. It's from the narrator's perspective that this binge can be put into the past. Therefore *was* is past tense, and we're quite justified in maintaining that *eating* is a present participle. Some scholars would call this kind of construction a 'past progressive', and we like the simplicity of that terminology. (In the same way, *is eating* would be called a present progressive construction, cf. also fn.2.)

[2] In PDE, the construction *am, is* or *are* together with a following verb + ing is called the present progressive construction. *Was* or *were* and a verb + ing is called the past progressive. Although line 2 looks very much like an OE example of past progressive, Jespersen (1965[1924]) notes that the PDE progressive/continuous construction '. . . owes very little to the OE construction' and arose from '. . . the construction of the verbal substantive with the preposition *on*: is on huntinge, is a-hunting, is hunting' (278). This is not entirely an uncontroversial explanation, but Mitchell and Robinson (1992) point out that the verb *to be* is '. . . found with the present participle as the ancestor of the ModE continuous tenses' (p. 110) and that it did not always mean the same thing as in PDE. In OE it could be similar to simple present, or could suggest an action continuing over time.

In (10), *'s* is an abbreviation of *has* (not *is*, cf. **She is injured her chances*), and *has* forms the auxiliary verb. It's in the present tense. *Injured* is the main lexical verb, and it occurs here in its past participle form. On the face of it, the form *injured* looks like it could be past tense, but recall the principle we just mentioned: tense can be marked once, and once only, in the VP, and in this sentence we've already marked tense on *has*.

The OE examples follow the same kind of pattern. The auxiliary verb comes first in the VP in these examples, and in each case it shows tense. (13) shows a present progressive construction, where the main lexical verb shows the *-ende* participle; (14) shows tense marked on *hæbbe*, with *geleornod* as the past participle. That past participle form, with *ge-* as a prefix and an *-od-* suffix on the verb root, is entirely characteristic of OE past participles. And that leaves sentence (11). We need to be cautious here, because although *woldan* looks suspiciously like PDE *would*, which itself is a particular kind of auxiliary verb, and although we've translated *woldan* as 'would', the verb *woldan* in OE, which is derived from the infinitive *willan*, behaved often rather like a main lexical verb, one meaning 'wish, intend, desire'. True, the PDE verb forms *will/would* do derive ultimately from OE *willan*, but we need to be aware that some verbs, though they're auxiliaries in PDE, may well have been more 'main-verb-like' in OE. Notice also that in sentence (11) the verb *fultumian* is in its infinitive form, not either of its participial forms.

If we continue with our translation for a few moments, we can expose some other features of the earliest English. Line 2 ends with another past participle, *gesawen*.[3] In line two, *him* is 3rd person dative plural. Dative case usually signals an indirect object. In PDE, an indirect object for 3rd person dative plural is *them*. We see that 'all' (*eall + um*) is also dative plural, thus agreeing with *him* (he went about individually asking them all). Thus far, then, in line 2, we have word by word 'was from them all asking how to them seemed and seen was'. Rendered into more idiomatic English we get 'was asking individually from them all, how seemed and was seen'.

At this point we should notice that we need a subject – *what* seemed? *what* was seen? We need a NP in nominative case. In line 3 we find two that fit the bill: *þēos nīwe lār*, this new teaching, and *bīgong*, worship. *Þǣre* is a definite article – the – and *godcundnesse* means 'godhead' or 'divinity'. *godcundnesse*

[3] If you speak a relatively standard English dialect, you'll always be able to find a past participle with the following frame: 'have ______'. Whatever verb form goes in the blank will be a past participle. If you try a few verbs like *eat, see, buy, like, go* you'll get 'have *eaten*, have *seen*, have *bought*, have *liked* and have *gone*.' The italicised words are past participles. *Have* + a past participle creates the present perfect. *Had* + a past participle is called the past perfect or pluperfect. Jespersen (1955[1905]) again: '[t]he use of have and had as an auxiliary for the perfect and pluperfect began in the Old English period, but it was then chiefly found with transitive verbs and the real perfect-signification had scarcely yet been completely evolved from the original meaning of the connexion.' (216)

is genitive, which means we can translate it with a possessive construction: either an inflection *'s* or a prepositional phrase with *of*. That yields 'the worship of the Godhead' or 'the Godhead's worship'. So, the first sentence could be rendered in PDE as follows: 'Then he had discussion and deliberation with his counsellors and was asking (or "kept asking") individually from them all, how this new doctrine and worship of the Godhead which was taught there seemed (to) and was seen (by) them.' We have to add two prepositions, *to* and *by*. Which brings us to how prepositions worked in OE.

What we do with prepositions and word order nowadays in PDE was often done in OE with case. As we've seen, languages that indicate grammatical roles in a sentence through inflections are called synthetic languages, while languages that indicate the roles through word order and prepositions, almost to the total exclusion of inflections, are called analytic languages. Part of the story of English is the story of a language in transition from a synthetic to an analytic language. One feature of this change is that, as grammatical case is eroded, prepositions seem to play a more significant role in indicating the grammatical relations involved in the sentence – and certainly, though they remain semantically versatile function words, prepositions come to take on a more fixed range of meanings.

Exercise 4.5.1

Go through the OE translation again and pick out from the original text all the prepositions that occur in the passage. Consider how you've translated them. Are there other ways in which you could have translated these prepositions?

Comment on Exercise 4.5.1

Prepositions are non-lexical words, a closed class in PDE. By 'closed class' we mean that prepositions are a fixed set. You can't invent a new preposition whenever you feel like it, though it's easy to invent new *lexical* items. They were a closed class in OE, too, and included words such as *tō, æt, mid* and *fram*. You probably spotted these as you completed the exercise:

mid *his witum*	**with** his witan
wæs ***fram*** *him eallum frignende*	kept asking (**from**) all of them
þæt wē ***oð*** *ðis hæfdon*	that we **until** now had
tō *ūra goda bīgange*	**to** the worship of our gods
æt þē	**from** thee
in *eallum þingum*	**in** all things

If you look at the case of each of the nominal elements that occurs after each preposition, you'll see that – with the possible exception of *oð ðis*, which forms a fixed expression in which *ðis* is accusative – each nominal group is in the dative case. Notice too, for example, that *æt* is the source for PDE *at*, but is here plausibly translated as *from*. This hints that, as we've claimed, prepositions in OE have a wider range of possible translations than you might think, and don't have the relatively fixed meanings we ascribe to them in PDE. In OE, *tō* can mean 'to' or 'towards' or 'into'; *æt* can mean 'at' or 'from' or even 'to' or 'into'.

4.6 Relative clauses

At the end of line 3 we have a relative clause. It begins with the OE indeclinable relative pronoun *þe* ('indeclinable' simply means that *þe* doesn't, and can never, inflect). The relative pronouns in PDE are *who, whom, whose, which, that,* together with zero. (For an instance of the zero relative, think of sentence types like *Andrews said* **that** *he was going* – where's there's an overt relative – and *Andrews said* **[zero]** *he was going*.) We'll use the empty set symbol (ø) to indicate the last possibility. All of these possibilities are further illustrated below. The relative clause is underlined, and the relative pronoun, that is the pronoun that introduces the relative clause, has been italicised.

(14) The student *who* produced a brilliant translation of Beowulf
(15) The student *whom* I met at a college party
(16) The student *that* I met at a college party
(17) The student *whose* translation was brilliant
(18) The translation *which* I found particularly useful will be published soon
(19) The translation *that* I found particularly useful will be published soon
(20) The translation *ø* I found particularly useful will be published soon

In PDE, different relative pronouns are used depending on the role they play in the relative clause. In (14), the relative pronoun, *who*, is the subject of the relative clause. In (15), the relative pronoun, *whom*, is the object of the relative clause. If we wanted to make a declarative sentence out of this sentence containing the relative clause, we'd say:

(21) I met the student at a party.

In (15), the verb is *met*. We ask 'who met the student?' and we get *I*, which is the subject. If we ask 'Who(m) did I meet?', the answer is 'the student.' Therefore, *whom* takes the place of the direct object, 'the student', in (15). In (16), *that* is the object in the relative clause, which is again 'the student'. *Whose* in (17) is a possessive determiner which has replaced *his* or *her*. In (18) the subject is replaced. In (19) and (20) an object is replaced, albeit with ø in (20).

In (14)–(17), we are talking about human subjects and objects. In (18)–(20) we are talking about non-human subjects and objects. Because we make a distinction between subjects and objects, and between humans and non-human, we wind up with a large range of relative pronouns in PDE, but each one has a somewhat limited distribution, with the exception of *that*, which can go just about anywhere, and ø, which can replace human or non-human objects.

Now for some good news. In OE, this is all made easier with just one unchanging and unchangeable relative pronoun, *þe*. In this function, *þe* is said to be indeclinable. And a good thing too.

4.7 *Thou* and *you* in OE

In line 5 Cefi addresses the king as 'thou' (*Geseoh þū, cyning*). If you speak German, or French or Spanish (and indeed a number of other languages), you'll know there is a distinction between a formal *you* and an intimate *you*. Cefi is not showing that he is on intimate terms with the king, nor is he addressing the king as one might address a child or a servant. As we said in the last unit, OE had more than one *you*, but the distinction was not simply 'formal' vs. 'intimate'. It was between one, two only, or more than two. In OE it was also possible to speak about 'we two' or 'you two.' Later in the history of English a distinction developed between *you*, used as a term of respect, and *thou*. As this happened, *thou* came increasingly to be used with those of lower status (or as a term of intimacy). This change seems to have taken place particularly in circles most influenced by medieval French. However, in our period, Cefi's use of *þū* simply means he is addressing Edwin, not Edwin and one other person, or the king and more than one other person.

You'll find more about the OE pronoun system and its interestingly varied development in eME, in Units 6 and 7.

4.8 OE and PDE verbs

You'll remember from Unit 3 that when we started work on nouns, we claimed that careless definitions of what nouns were ('names of persons, places or things') just weren't adequate for our purposes. The same goes for verbs. Sometimes defined as '*doing*-words', verbs are better defined as words that participate in a network of *temporal* and *aspectual* relationships. *Temporal* involves time-relations: *he arrived* is past tense, *he arrives* is present tense and these time-relations are signalled by inflections suffixed to the verb root. *Aspect* involves whether the network of relationships in which the verb(s) participate indicates action which is completed, or in process: *he has arrived* is present tense, perfect aspect (i.e. the action of the arriving is complete, finished; he has actually arrived); *he is arriving* is present tense, progressive aspect (i.e. he is actually in the process of arriving, the 'action' is ongoing).

Although OE verbs have a quite complex set of inflections that help us to work out grammatical features like tense and aspect, in practice verbal inflections often cause less difficulty than noun inflections. In part, this is because some verb inflections are recognisable from PDE equivalents or near-equivalents – thus you should be able to work out that OE *þū lūfast* is equivalent to archaic 'thou lovest'. But it is also because the OE verb system contains less intricacy than the PDE one. That doesn't mean that the OE verb system was 'simpler' (it still contained all the temporal and aspectual distinctions it needed); it's just that from our vantage point as scholars it seems less intricate: the range of modal verbs that we're familiar with in PDE isn't found in OE, for instance.

In OE there are only two tenses: present and past. In fact, this two-tense system is one of the aspects of the syntax that sets Germanic languages off from other Proto-Indo-European languages. The future is expressed simply by the present tense, e.g. 'I arise' can mean either 'I arise (now)' or 'I shall arise (tomorrow)'. We see the same thing in PDE. There is no morphologically encoded way to express future, that is, no future tense inflection. (22) expresses the future using a present tense verb. (23) uses a modal auxiliary, itself in the present tense, but which has nevertheless a sense of futurity. (24) uses present tense with progressive aspect, and (25) uses the phrasal modal *be going to*:

(22) The plane **leaves** at 8:30 tomorrow morning
(23) The plane **will leave**
(24) The plane **is leaving**
(25) The plane **is going to leave**

The continuous or progressive forms such as (24) are common in PDE, but don't exist as such in OE, although occasionally you'll come across the odd example that looks like such a form. They are found, for example, in the reading in the last chapter from the *Anglo-Saxon Chronicle* (the verb phrase *wæs feohtende*, continued to fight, that you found in the story of Cynewulf and Cyneheard), and there is one in the reading in this unit, in line 2, *wæs frignende*, which we would translate as past tense, progressive aspect, 'was asking', or, more idiomatically, 'kept asking'. Forms showing perfect aspect, that is, what shows up in PDE as *have* + past participle, are found rather less frequently in OE, since OE often prefers the simple past tense. Once again, however, there is an example in this unit's reading in line 6, *geleornad hæbbe*, have learned. The following PDE sentences show perfect aspect:

(26) I **have lost** my way (present tense, perfect aspect)
(27) They **had driven** for hours before they realised that they were lost (past tense, perfect aspect)

Before considering OE verb inflections in more detail, we have to consider another factor. We can do this best by looking firstly at PDE. Today we usually make a distinction between *regular* and *irregular* verbs. Typical regular verbs include *walk, love* and *hate*. The common characteristic of such verbs is that they form their past tenses by the simple addition of an ending or suffix which contains an alveolar stop consonant (that is to say, a *d* or a *t* sound, thus *love-**d**,* or *walk-**ed**,* where *-ed* is pronounced /t/):

(28) They **walked** to the university
(29) They **loved** the new library
(30) They **hated** the new administrative building

Exercise 4.8.0

Make an extended list of 20 or more verbs. Any verb will do. Now write the past tense of each verb. If this presents any kind of challenge, put the verb in the blank 'Yesterday he _______'. If you speak a dialect close to BrE or AmE standard, this frame will yield the past tense. (You might have to add some kind of complement to the frame such as 'well', 'good', 'in the hall', or 'the mayor'. The need for a particular kind of complement, or none at all, is a property governed by the verb.) Now *say* the past tense form of each verb. Listen for the sound of the ending. Group all of the regular verbs together.

Comment on Exercise 4.8.0

In your group of regular verbs, you have undoubtedly discovered that even though all of the endings may be spelled '-ed', they won't all be pronounced that way. You should have discovered some ending in a /t/ sound, as in the example we spotted in (28) (other examples would be *harped, fished, hacked, laughed . . .*). Some probably were like (29), ending in a /d/ sound (other examples would be *clubbed, plagued, named . . .*), and some were like (30) ending in an /ɪd/ sound (other examples would be *fainted, hunted, raided . . .*). They needn't all be pronounced in exactly the same way to technically qualify as regular verbs; the only requirement is that they form the past tense with a dental suffix.

4.9 'Less regular' verbs

Among the verbs that you listed there were, no doubt, verbs that weren't like (28), (29) or (30) in the past tense. Instead, they changed in some other way (*see, saw* or *go, went*) or they might not have changed at all (*hit, hit*). Verbs that aren't regular are considered 'less regular' by definition, though we'll shortly see that there are very different forms of 'irregularity'. What we can say, at least for the moment, is that verbs behaving 'less regularly' don't form their preterite (their past tense) with a dental or alveolar suffix.

Many PDE English verbs – on a rough count, around 200 of them – are in this sense 'less regular', for example (and notoriously) the verbs *to be* and *to go*. Note that their past tenses – *was/were* and *went*, respectively – appear to have no straightforward relationship with the present tense forms. These are called *suppletive* forms. But among the 'less regular' verbs there are some that appear to have a pattern, for example *sing*, with past tense *sang* and past participle *sung*.

Exercise 4.9.0

Verbs such as *sing* are critical for our purposes. In order to demonstrate that *sing* (or rather, *sing – sang – sung*) follows a pattern, think of three or four other PDE verbs that follow exactly the same pattern. You may have already listed those verbs in the previous exercise. Now try to construct a list of verbs in which the past tense is formed in any way other than with *-ed*. As you think of examples, the 'sing-sang-sung pattern' isn't, of course, the only one you'll find; there are others.

Comment on Exercise 4.9.0

You should in fact be able to identify (at least) six different patterns. Don't worry if the verbs you think of don't have three different forms like *sing* does; it's quite common for the past tense and past participle forms to be identical. But do make sure that none of your examples include the addition of a dental or alveolar consonant, e.g. *keep, kept*, or *buy, bought*, or *catch, caught*, where *t* is added.

Some verbs are exactly like *sing*. These include *ring – rang – rung; swim – swam – swum; drink – drank – drunk; sink – sank – sunk*. You may have thought of others. It's less important which particular examples you've picked, than that you've found sufficient to help you believe that these verbs all follow the same pattern, even if the total number of verbs is relatively small.

Other verbs which follow a *different pattern* from *sing* but which nevertheless follow *similar principles* include: *drive – drove – driven; choose – chose – chosen; steal – stole – stolen; meet – met – met* (note that the /t/ is already there in the present tense – it's not been added to the verb to form the past); *draw – drew – drawn; fall – fell – fallen*. Don't be concerned if you haven't picked these actual verbs as your examples, or if the verbs you have chosen show different patterns. The verbs we've used here have been selected for a particular reason, but the situation in PDE is that there is a large number of such patterns, and quite often only one or two verbs may follow any one specified pattern. That's why we consider them to be in some sense 'less regular' verbs.

We're going to call verbs forming their past tenses with a dental or alveolar suffix *weak verbs*, and ones behaving like *swim* or *drive*, strong verbs. It will be apparent that strong verbs form their past tenses by *changing the vowel in their root*. Once we've set up the strong/weak distinction, we should also notice that there are verbs which aren't just 'less regular', but appear to be *irregular*: these include *have*, *be* and *go*.

4.10 Still more on OE verbs

When we're reconstructing how verbs behave in PDE, it's useful to give *three* forms (or 'principal parts') of each verb: (i) infinitive (the 'to' form of the verb such as *to walk*, *to hate*, etc.), (ii) past tense, and (iii) past participle. From these all other verbal forms can be deduced, for example the present participle, the 'verb + ing' form mentioned above, is taken from the infinitive with the addition of the *-ing* suffix.

It's useful to give *four* principal parts of OE strong verbs: (i) infinitive, (ii) past tense singular, (iii) past tense plural, and (iv) past participle. Thus we have *sing**an*** – *sang* – *sung**on*** – *sung**en*** (inflectional suffixes boldened): 'to sing – he/she sang – they sang – sung'.

What we find in OE is that our 'less regular' verbs – usually, as we've just noted, called 'strong verbs' in order to distinguish them from weak verbs which form their past tense by the addition of a dental or alveolar consonant – fall into seven classes as shown in table 4.1.

One of our students once rather nicely described engaging with such patterns as 'like listening to a set of tunes'. These 'tunes' form the characteristic behaviour of the OE strong verbs. Further, these verbs are usually sub-classified according to the pattern of vowel changes (often called *gradation*) which occurs in each class. Thus *drīfan* is said to be a strong verb of class I, *cēosan* strong class II, *singan* strong class III, and so on. Each class has a particular vowel-gradation series found in the verb's root, a particular 'tune'. Thus Class I shows the gradation series 'ī – ā – i – i'. At this stage it's

Table 4.1 The characteristic behaviour of strong verbs in OE

	Infinitive	Past sg.	Past pl.	Past participle	
I	*drīfan*	*drāf*	*drifon*	*drifen*	(drive)
II	*cēosan*	*cēas*	*curon*	*coren*	(choose)
III	*singan*	*sang*	*sungon*	*sungen*	(sing)
IV	*stelan*	*stæl*	*stǣlon*	*stolen*	(steal)
V	*metan*	*mæt*	*mǣton*	*meten*	(meet)
VI	*dragan*	*drōg*	*drōgon*	*dragen*	(draw)
VII	*feallan*	*fēoll*	*fēollan*	*feallen*	(fall)

not so important that you learn the exact patterning of each class as that you realise that such patterning did and does occur, and that it's not very different from the 'strong' verbal patterns found in PDE.

An understanding of this will help you greatly in translating OE. It will be much easier to find, for example, *rād* in an OE glossary if you can tell that it belongs to strong class I and that therefore you need to look for the infinitive, *rīdan*.

Exercise 4.10.0

Let's now look at verb inflections. Recall that verbs inflect for grammatical information concerning number and tense. The present tense of a verb such as *drīfan* is as follows (the inflections have been put into boldface type):

1sg.	ic *drīf**e***	(I drive)
2sg.	þū *drīf**st**/drīf**est***	(thou drivest)
3sg.	hē/hēo/hit *drif(e)**þ***	(he driveth)
pl.	wē/gē/hī *drīf**að***	(they drive)

Look closely at the inflections. How many of them are still recognisable today?

Comment on Exercise 4.10.0

The 1st person verb form ('1sg.' is of course an abbreviation for 'first person, singular') is, at least in terms of spelling, almost identical to the PDE form. The 2nd person inflection is again recognisable as a modern English form, even if 'thou drivest' is archaic and/or only to be found in religious styles of English. And if you recall that in Shakespeare's time, or even later (though archaically), forms such as 'Love seeketh not itself to please' (Blake, *Songs of Experience*) occur, then you should be able to recognise the 3rd person singular form. After that, only the OE plural form seems strange (today, as you'll have noted from our gloss 'they drive', plural forms of verbs in the present tense take no ending).

Exercise 4.10.1

The past tense forms are:

1sg.	ic *drāf*	(I drove)
2sg.	þū *drifest*	(clumsily glossed, thou drovest)
3sg.	hē/hēo/hit *drāf*	(he drove)
pl.	hī *drifon*	(they drove)

There's a rather odd feature here, namely the change of vowel (compare carefully the present tense and past tense forms) in the 2nd person singular. Can you think why this happens? And can you think of any verb in PDE –

or a relatively archaic form of PDE – which behaves in the same way (there is only one, but it occurs very frequently)?

Comment on Exercise 4.10.1

There can only be one reason for the change of vowel in the 2nd person singular, given the principles on which strong verbs operate. This is that in this particular form the verb (rather oddly) takes its vowel from the past tense plural, not from the singular. The verb in PDE which works this way (when the archaic form *thou* is used) is the past tense of the verb *to be*. This is: *I was, thou wert, he/she was, they were*. There's no need to explain this odd behaviour here, but it is important to remember that in OE the past tense of all strong verbs observes this kind of pattern.

4.11 Weak verbs

So far we've not considered the OE equivalent of PDE regular, that is, weak, verbs. But there was an equivalent, and many OE verbs (but not the very commonest ones, like *to be* or *to go*) were of this type. In terms of inflection for number in the present tense, weak verbs behave much like strong verbs, so that we find, for example, that a weak verb such as *fēdan*, feed, has the following present tense:

1sg. ic *fēde*
2sg. þū *fēdest*
3sg. hēo *fēdeþ*
pl. hī *fēdaþ*

The past tense forms, as you would expect from PDE, are formed by the addition of an ending that includes an alveolar stop consonant. In verbs like *fēdan* this ending is *-de*. The inflections themselves are marginally different from strong verbs, so we find:

1sg. ic *fēdde*
2sg. þu *fēddest*
3sg. he *fēdde*
pl. hi *fēddon*

If this all seems a bit much to take in at present, you might like to notice the following points in particular, since these will help you to translate passages from OE:

- 2nd person singular forms have some kind of *-st* suffix in both present and past tenses
- 3rd person singular forms have an *-eth* (<-eð>) suffix in the present tense
- 3rd person plural forms have an *-ath* (<-að>) suffix in the present tense
- 3rd person plural forms have an *-on* suffix in the past tense

4.12 Reading passage (2)

Let's return to Edwin's 7th century Northumbrian court. If Cefi's counsel, as evidenced in the reading passage in Section 4.3, seems opportunistic, and less than lyrical, the words of the next counsellor to speak, as told to us by Bede's translator, more than make up for it. His evocative words, spoken 1500 years ago, have become famous for the inspired comparison they draw.

Exercise 4.12.0

'þyslīc mē is gesewen, þū cyning, þis andwearde līf manna	1
This-like by me is seen, O king, this present life of-man	
Such seems to me, O king, this present life of man	
on eorðan tō wiðmetenesse þǣre tīde þe ūs uncūð is:	2
on earth to with-measure-ness the time which to us unknown is:	
on earth in comparison to the time which is unknown to us:	
swylc swā þū æt swǣsendum sitte	3
if-so thou at banquets were to sit	
It's as if you were to sit at great feasts	
mid þīnum ealdormannum and þegnum on wintertīde,	4
with thine aldermen and nobles in wintertime	
in the winter with your high priests and nobles,	
and sīe fȳr onǣlæd and þīn heall gewyrmed,	5
and might-be fire kindled and thine hall warmed	
and a fire would be kindled and your hall warmed	
and hit rīne and snīwe and styrme ūte;	6
and it would rain and snow and storm outside	
while outside it would rain, and snow, and storm;	
cume ān spearwa and hrædlīce þæt hūs þurhflēo,	7

cume þurh ōþre duru in, þurh ōþre ūt gewīte. 8

Hwæt, hē on þā tīd þe hē inne bið 9

ne bið hrinen mid ðȳ storme þæs wintres; 10

ac þæt bið ān ēagan bryhtm and þæt lǣsste fæc, 11

ac hē sōna of wintra on þone winter eft cymeð. 12

Swā þonne þis monna līf tō medmiclum fæce ætȳweð. 13

Hwæt þǣr forgange, oððe hwæt þǣr æfterfylige, 14

wē ne cunnun. For ðon gif þēos nīwe lār 15

ōwiht cūðlicre ond gerisenlicre brenge, 16

þæs weorþe is þæt wē þǣre fylgen.’ 17

Selective glossary

In this glossary, we have been careful to give you the tense and number of the verb forms that appear in the passage. We also introduce a new term, *subjunctive*. For work on the indicative and the subjunctive, look at Section 4.13, 'Comments on the reading'. This directly follows the glossary.

Note also that in this glossary, and those that follow, we've adopted the usual practice of listing roots prefixed by *ge-* under the initial letter of their root. Here, then, you would look up *gewīte* not under <g>, but under <w>.

ān — a, an, one, only
æfterfylige — verb; follows after (3sg. pres. sb.)
ætȳweð — verb; appear (3sg.)
andwearde — adjective; present
bið — verb; 3sg. pres. from *beon*, to be
brenge — verb; bring (3sg. pres. sb.)
bryhtm — blink
cume — verb; (should) come (3sg. pres. sb.)
cūðlicre — comparative form, certain
cymeð — verb; come (3sg. pres. indicative)
duru — door
ēagan — eye
eft — again, afterwards
fæc — noun; interval (nom. sg. neut.)
forgange — verb; (might) precede (3sg. pres. sb.)
fylgan — 1pl. sb. of *fylgan*, to follow (assigns dat.)
hē — pronoun; masc. nom. sg.
hrædlīce — swiftly
hrinnen — touched (ppl.)
hūs — house (neut. acc. sg.)
hwæt — what – or a word for getting the attention of an audience
is gesewen — seems, is seen
lār — teaching, doctrine (fem. nom. sg.)
læsste — smallest (neut nom. sg.; superlative)
līf — life (neut. nom. sg.)
manna — of man (gen. pl.)
medmiclum — brief (dat. sg. neut.)
mid — prep.; by
monna — man (gen. pl.)
nīwe — new
of — prep. from (assigns dat.)
on — prep.; into, during, on, in
onǣlæd — kindle (ppl.)

ōþre . . . ōþre	one . . . the other
oððe	or
ōwiht	anything
rīne	verb; rain (3sg. sb.)
gerisenlicre	comparative form, suitable, proper
sīe	3sg. sb. of *beon*, to be
snīwe	verb; snow (3sg. sb.)
sōna	immediately
spearwa	sparrow (masc. nom. sg.)
swā	thus, so
swæsendum	banquets (dat. pl.)
swylc swā + subj.	as if
styrme	verb; storm (3sg. pres. sb.)
tīd	time (fem. acc. sg.)
tide	time (fem. gen. sg.)
tō	prep.; to, into, for, as a
þā	determiner; fem. acc. sg.
þære	pronoun; fem. dat. sg.
þæs weorþe is þæt	it is worthy that . . .
þæt	determiner; neut. acc. sg.
þonne	then
þurh	through, by means of
þurhflēo	verb; fly through (3sg. pres. sb.)
þyslīc	such
uncuð	unknown (neut. gen. sg.)
ūte	outside
weorþe	worthy
gewīte	verb; depart (3sg.)
gewyrmed	warmed (ppl.)
(*to*) *wiðmetenesse*	in comparison with (assigns gen.)

4.13 Comments on reading passage (2) – the subjunctive

There is a great deal that could be (and has been) said about this counsellor's moving words. Certainly one of the most memorable aspects of this passage, from the point of view of its linguistic construction, is that it is cast almost entirely in the *subjunctive mood*. The subjunctive is a kind of verb form (or technically, a *mood*) expressing hypothesis, conjecture, something that is imagined, wished or proposed. It's the mood of 'If . . .', the mood of 'Other things being equal . . .'

One complication about OE verbs is the use of a separate set of inflections to express the subjunctive mood. The usual or unmarked form (that is the form that is assumed in the absence of linguistic evidence to the contrary) of a verb in PDE is the *indicative mood*. All the examples we've discussed so far have been expressed in this mood. As the name perhaps implies, the indicative is a mood of direct statement, or reportage.

The most typical examples of the subjunctive in PDE are in clauses such as (31) and in formulaic expressions such as (33).

(31) If I were you [subjunctive]
(32) If I was you [Indicative]
(33) Long live the King
(34) Long lives the King [Indicative]

The first type, (31), expresses an unreal or hypothetical condition (i.e. *I can't actually be you, but* *if I were* . . .); this contrasts with the prescriptively incorrect but nonetheless common (32). (33) expresses a wish that a state of affairs should come about which does not at present necessarily exist. It differs from (34), which is a somewhat poetic statement in the indicative mood, a comment on the King's remarkable lifespan. Notice that what both (31) and (33) have in common is that the speaker is not committed to the truth of the statement. Rather, he/she either pretends it might be true, or wishes or hopes that it might be true. The subjunctive, then, is the mood of hypothesis, and perhaps also the mood of conjecture or recommendation.

A nice example of the use (and non-use) of the subjunctive in PDE comes from the wine shelves of a giant UK supermarket chain. On bottles of wine retailing there for under £5 (cheap plonk), a recommendation runs as follows: 'It is recommended that this wine *is drunk* this year'. The indicative. On (some) bottles of wine retailing above £10 (classier stuff), there stands the following: 'It is recommended that this wine *be drunk* after 2006'. The subjunctive, yes . . . but at a price.

Hypothesis and conjecture – these are the keys to the use of the subjunctive in OE. There, it's used freely to indicate that the speaker (or writer) isn't committed to the literal truth of his or her statement. Therefore the subjunctive is used both for unreal conditions (as in (31)) and wishes (as in (33)). But it's also used in situations where PDE wouldn't have the same grammatical opportunities. For example, it's quite often used in reported speech to indicate that the speaker is uncertain about the truth of the statement being reported (in PDE we use emphasis for this, as in 'He *said* he votes Conservative (but I don't believe him)'). In this context, OE would use the subjunctive.

There are several other uses of the subjunctive, which you'll find amply discussed in Mitchell and Robinson (1992) and other standard handbooks, and which don't need to be repeated here. The only other point to mention is that the subjunctive inflection is quite straightforward. In the singular it's *-e* and in the plural it's *-en* regardless of number, or whether the verb is weak or strong, or in the present or past tense.

In the above passage, the subjunctive is introduced with *swylc swā* at the beginning of line 3. *Swylc swā* plus the subjunctive have the PDE equivalent 'It's as if . . .' or perhaps even 'imagine that . . .' What follows, as the speaker invites the king to imagine that he is sitting with his high priests and thanes at a banquet in winter time, is cast in the subjunctive.

Notice that in line 6 a non-referential or dummy subject, *it*, is used. We have this construction still today in PDE, in which *it* or *there* are used almost as place markers for a subject because English has apparently always demanded that there be *something* in subject position. The *it* is not referential in the sense of (35), in which *Paul's new car* and *it* are co-referential:

(35) I saw Paul's new car, but I didn't like it much.

Summary

We began this unit by recounting the well-known story of Augustine's mission to Britain, sent by Pope Gregory in 597. We then turned our attention to a somewhat lesser-known story, the contribution of the Celtic Church to the conversion of what is now England. Our first reading selection was from the OE translation of Bede's account of the conversion of King Edwin. We read the words of one of Edwin's witan, Cefi, who counselled acceptance of the new religion chiefly because he personally had not received any material benefits from his years of devotion to the old gods and hoped he might fare better with a new religion. In our discussion of the first reading we considered word order in OE, pronouns, present participles, relative clauses and how *thou* and *you* were deployed in OE. Then, in some detail, we began to analyse the behaviour of OE verbs. Finally, we concluded with a second reading from the OE translation of Bede, and in that context discussed the subjunctive mood.

Study questions

1. Why is the Christianisation of Britain important from a linguistic point of view?
2. One kind of word-order in OE sentences was SVO, but there were several other possible and common word-orders. What were they? Looking back at the originals of the passages you've translated, can you identify principles that trigger particular kinds of word-order? (Hint: one place to look is sentences that begin with adverbs of time like 'then' or 'when'.)
3. We claim that part of the story of English is the story of language moving from a synthetic to an analytic language. Giving examples, show what such a claim might involve.
4. What was the difference between the OE equivalent of *you* (*gē*) and *thou* (*þē*) in OE? What's the relationship between OE *gē* and *ēow*? Where does PDE *you* come from?

5. Which inflections (both nouns and verbs) do we still have in PDE, and which parts of speech inflect? Which PDE inflections do you think are relics of earlier bits of English morphology?
6. Does PDE have a future tense? Why – or why not? Did OE? In what ways can we indicate 'future action' in PDE VPs? How might OE have indicated 'futurity'?
7. How many classes of strong verbs were there in OE? Why are we able to analyse strong verbs into such classes? Are there any exceptions you've found in your experience of OE verbs to date?
8. *drīfan* is a class I strong verb. What were its inflections in present tense? Past tense? *scīnan*, to shine, is also a class I strong verb. What are the principle parts (that is, what is the gradation 'tune') of this verb? What are the inflections for present tense? For past?
9. What is the subjunctive? How does it differ from the indicative? Taking any OE weak verb, compare its set of indicative inflections to the set of subjunctive inflections.

Websites that you may find useful

- www.members.aol.com/burrrtrousch/augustine
  This website talks about the background of Augustine's mission, his journey from Rome to Kent, and a history of the period from 597 to 604. It also contains a number of links to other sites
- www.members.tripod.com/babaev/archieve/grammar41.html
  Students have recommended this site for information on phonetics, adjectives, pronouns, numerals, adverbs, verbs and more. The site includes the history of Old English and its development, and students say 'it really is a great help in understanding all those complicated endings . . .'
- http://www.britannia.com/church/bond3.html
- http://www.augustana.edu/users/enmcdowell/bede.htm
  According to one student, 'the Medieval Sourcebook is an excellent internet source. All of the pages are copy-permitted. There is a lot about Bede, and the story of the conversion of England comes alive on the pages. The history starts with the arrival of the missionaries in Kent. It continues with the conversion of Northumbria and even goes into the controversy over the date of Easter, which was very interesting. A must read.' [Note: we didn't pay this student anything to write that. What? On these royalties?]
- http://christusrex.org/www1CDHN/saints.html
  Look at 'Our Christian heritage'
- http://www.willa.demon.co.uk/info/nor.htm
  Look at 'Edwin: King of Northumbria'

- http://www.cushnieent.force9.co/uk/extent.html
  This site talks about the Celtic Church

References and suggestions for further reading

In general, if you continue to work with some of the references we detailed in Units 2 and 3, you'll be doing well, and will have quite enough of the earliest English to think about.

Translation: Exercise 4.3.0

þā hæfde hē gesprec and geþeaht mid his witum and syndriglīce	1
Then had he speech and thought with his witan and individually	
Then he deliberated with his counsellors, and kept asking	
wæs fram him eallum frignende hwylc him þūthe and gesawen	2
was from them all asking what to-them seemed and seen	
them all individually how this new learning seemed to them, and was seen by them,	
wæs þēos nīwe lār and þǣre godcundnesse bīgong þe þǣr lǣred wæs	3
was this new lore, and the divinity that there taught was.	
. . . along with the form of divinity that it taught.	
Him þā andswarode his ealdorbisceop, Cēfi wæs hāten:	4
Him then answered his high priest, Cefi was called:	
Then his (pagan) high priest, who was called Cefi, answered him:	
'Geseoh þū, cyning, hwelc þēos lār sīe þe ūs nū bodad is. Ic þē	5
Consider, king, just what this newly offered teaching might be.	
sōðlīce andette þæt ic cūðlīce geleornad hæbbe, þæt eallinga	6
I truly confess to you that I have learned very clearly that	
nāwiht mægenes ne nyttnesse hafað sīo ǣfæstnes þe wē oð ðis	7
the religious practice we kept until now had nothing of power or benefit,	
hæfdon and beēodon, for ðon nǣnig þīnra þegna nēodlicor ne	8
and indeed none of your counsellors more diligently or	

gelustfullīcor hine sylfne underþēodde tō ūre goda bīgange þonne	**9**
earnestly devoted himself to our former gods than	
ic, and nōht þon lǣs monige syndon þā þe māran gefe and fremsumnesse	**10**
I myself; nonetheless there are many who received more gifts and benefits	
æt þē onfēngon þonne ic, and in eallum þingum māran gesynto hæfdon.	**11**
from you than I, and had more prosperity in all things.	
Hwæt, ic wāt, gif ūre godo ǣnige mihte hæfdon, þonne woldan hīe mē mā fultumian	**12**
In sum, I know that if our gods had truly had any power, then they would have blessed me more,	
for þon ic him geornlīcor þēodde ond hȳrde. For þon mē þynceð wīslic, gif þū	**13**
because I served and obeyed them so diligently. Therefore to me it seems wise, if you	
gesēo þā þing beteran and strangran þe ūs nīwan bodad syndon, þæt wē þām	**14**
consider the practices newly offered to us as stronger and better, that we	
onfon.' þæs wordum ōþer cyninges wita and ealdormann geþafunge	**15**
accept them.' Another counsellor and alderman of the king assented	
sealde, and tō þǣre sprǣce fēng and þus cwæð . . .	**16**
to Cefi's speech, and spoke in his turn, saying the following . . .	

Translation: Exercise 4.12.0

'þyslīc mē is gesewen, þū cyning, þis andwearde līf manna	1
This-like by me is seen, O king, this present life of-man	
Such seems to me, great Edwin, this present life of man	
on eorðan tō wiðmetenesse þǣre tīde þe ūs uncūð is:	2
on earth to with-measure-ness the time which to us unknown is:	
on earth in comparison to the time which is unknown to us:	
swylc swā þū æt swǣsendum sitte	3
if-so thou at banquets were to sit	
It's as if you were to sit at great feasts	
mid þīnum ealdormannum and þegnum on wintertīde,	4
with thine aldermen and nobles in wintertime	
in the winter with your high priests and nobles,	
and sīe fȳr onǣlæd and þīn heall gewyrmed,	5
and might-be fire kindled and thine hall warmed	
and a fire would be kindled and your hall warmed	
and hit rīne and snīwe and styrme ūte;	6
and it would rain and snow and storm outside	
while outside it would rain, and snow, and storm;	
cume ān spearwa and hrædlīce þæt hūs þurhflēo,	7
(it's as if) a single sparrow should come, and fly quickly through the place,	
cume þurh ōþre duru in, þurh ōþre ūt gewīte.	8
(it's as if) it were to come in through one door, and depart through the other.	
Hwæt, hē on þā tīd þe hē inne bið	9
Thus, during the time he's inside	
ne bið hrinen mid ðȳ storme þæs wintres;	10
he's not touched by the winter's storm;	

ac þæt bið ān ēagan bryhtm and þæt lǣsste fæc,	11
but that's the blink of an eye, the least interval,	
ac hē sōna of wintra on þone winter eft cymeð.	12
and he'll immediately come again from winter into winter.	
Swā þonne þis monna līf tō medmiclum fæce ætȳweð.	13
So then this life of mankind appears as a brief sojourn.	
Hwæt þǣr forgange, oððe hwæt þǣr æfterfylige,	14
What comes before it, or what follows it,	
wē ne cunnun. For ðon gif þēos nīwe lār	15
we do not know. Therefore if this new teaching	
ōwiht cūðlicre ond gerisenlicre brenge,	16
should bring anything more certain and more honourable,	
þæs weorþe is þæt wē þǣre fylgen.'	17
it is worthy that we should follow it.'	

And finally . . .

Appendix 2: At-a-glance guide to OE inflections – verbs

Table 4.2 presents a guide to characteristic OE verb inflections as they might be expressed in classical WS.

Table 4.2 Weak and strong verbs

(1a) Weak verbs (-d in past tense) – indicative

Infinitive	**(i) -ian**	**(ii) -an**	**-ian**	**-an**
	Present tense		**Past tense**	
Sg.1	-ie	-e	-ode	-ede
2	-ast	-est	-odest	-edest
3	-að	-eð	-ode	-ede
Pl.	-iað	-að	-odon	-eden

(1b) Weak verbs – subjunctive

	Present tense		**Past tense**	
Sg.	-ie	-e	-ode	-ede
Pl.	-ien	-en	-oden	-eden

(2) Strong verbs (change their root vowel shape in the past tense)

Infinitive	**-an**		
	Present tense	**Past tense**	
Sg.1	-e	–	(1)
2	-est	-e	(2)
3	-(e)ð	–	(1)
Pl.	-að	-on	(2)

- Past participles occur in the frame *ge* +_____+ *en* (2, or 3)
- Numerals to the right are intended to show gradation patterns, e.g. the vowel shapes in Sg.1 and 3 are identical, as are those in Sg.2 and Pl., whereas the past participle either shares its root vowel with (2) or sometimes shows a different root vowel altogether. An example is the past tense of OE *singan*, to sing:

	singan, past tense	
Sg.1	sang	(1: <a>)
Sg.2	sunge	(2: <u>)
Sg.3	sang	(1: <a>)
Pl.	sungon	(2: <u>)
Ppl.	ge + sung + en	

Interlude

Working with dictionaries

Interlude 1: The *Oxford English Dictionary* (OED)

You've already, in Exercise 4.30, line 3, seen the OE word *lār*, teaching or doctrine. Over the course of time, the vowel shape found in the root of this word undergoes phonological change: for our present-day word 'lore' we no longer say /lɑːr/, but (BrE) /lɔː/ or (AmE) /lɔːr/. And again over the course of time, the word undergoes *semantic* change: although we can still recognise the range of meanings of the words as including 'teaching, doctrine', the present-day word 'lore' has acquired other, and possibly more central, meanings. For example, the *New Oxford English Dictionary* defines 'lore' as a mass noun meaning 'a body of traditions and knowledge on a subject or held by a particular group, typically passed from person to person by word of mouth . . .'

Clearly, words can and often do change their meaning over time. When we write 'words', we mean 'both content words and function words'. Content words – nouns, verbs, adjectives and adverbs – may change their meanings, or acquire additional functions (adjectives, for instance, may acquire the property of behaving like nouns, e.g. PDE *it was enough to wake **the dead***). Function words may both change their meaning and/or refine their range of grammatical functions.

The study of meaning – semantics – isn't just confined to word roots. Notice that in lines 9 and 10 of the translation found in Exercise 4.3.0 we have comparatives: *nēodlicor*, more diligently, and *gelustfullīcor*, more willingly. The suffix that you find here – *-or* – is the ancestor of one of the inflections that still remain in English (*happy/happi**er***). In PDE we continue to inflect adjectives for the comparative with *-er*, or with a construction such as *more* + adjective or adverb – *more beautiful; more eagerly . . .*

One source of information about semantic change and morphology is the OED, an important tool for students and professional scholars of English.

At this point in our Interlude we could immediately have directed you to one of the great specialist dictionaries of OE but, in our experience students – even advanced students – are surprisingly loath to undertake study with such a dictionary. They may feel more comfortable with the OED (and are therefore more prepared to work with it). Another reason that we direct you to the OED now is that most school and university libraries, even if they don't have, or don't have access to, a good OE dictionary, do have access to the OED, either in its hard text or on-line versions.

NB: we shall below direct you to one great *Dictionary of Old English* in Interlude 3, after we've seen some of the principles of lexicography at work in both the OED and the *Middle English Dictionary* (on which last, see below, Interlude 2).

The second edition of the *Oxford English Dictionary* – OED2, as we'll abbreviate it from this point – is arguably the single most important research resource in our discipline. (An updated 3rd edition is expected to appear in 2004/5.) It contains information not only about the etymology of words but also when they were first attested as occurring in written English, and about the texts and contexts in which those words were used. It's essential to become familiar with the layout and structure of OED2 at this point in your study of the earliest English.

For the moment, we'll focus simply on OED2, firstly because it's the dictionary which is most readily available; secondly because it's a useful research tool for tracking the histories of words from OE into ME and later Englishes, and thus highly relevant to our work in this book; thirdly because it contains a great wealth of detail regarding other Germanic word-forms (not just English); and lastly because it includes most of the information you'll ever need to work in a precise way with the history of English words, and the ways in which those words were formed and/or reformed.

The bibliographic reference you need to trace the lineage of the OED (second edition) is as follows: (i) eds. James A.H. Murray, Henry Bradley, W.A. Craigie and C.T. Onions (1933) *The Oxford English Dictionary*, 12 vols, Oxford: Clarendon Press. This last was the first edition of the OED. (ii) Then there appeared a (now-obsolete) *Supplement* (ed. R.W. Burchfield – this included addenda, corrections and revisions, and appeared in several volumes, the last being published in 1987). (iii) The two works were combined, in work prepared by J.A. Simpson and E.S.C. Weiner, in the OED, second edition (OED2), which appeared in 1989 (Oxford: The Clarendon Press).

OED2 is available in at least three different forms: a multi-volume text, a 'Compact' edition (which reproduces the entire contents of the multi-volume text, but in a small-print, single-volume work) and a CD-ROM/ on-line text. Below, we reproduce parts of the entry for the head-word *tribe* as this is found in the multi-volume edition of OED2. Immediately below you'll find just the beginning part of the OED2's entry for the word:

tribe (traɪb), n. Forms: 3 (pl.) tribuz, 4_6 tribu, (pl. -us), 5 trybu-s. _. 4_6 trybe, (7 Sc. tryb), 4_ tribe.

[In earliest form, ME. *tribu*, a. OF. *tribu*, Sp., Pg. *tribu*, It. *tribù*, *tribo*, a. L. *tribus* (u-stem); but as the OF. has not been found in the sing. before 14th c. the ME. *tribuz* of 1250 may directly represent L. *tribus* pl. The later *tribe* may have been f. L. *tribus* on the usual pattern of derivatives from L. ns. in *-us*.
L. *tribus* is usually explained from *tri-* three and the verbal root *bhu*, *bu*, *fu* to be. It is thought by some to be cognate with Welsh *tref* town or inhabited place. The earliest known application of *tribus* was to the three divisions of the early people of Rome (attributed by some to the separate Latin, Sabine, and Etruscan elements); thence it was transferred to render the Greek [cognate] . . . and so to the Greek application of the latter to the tribes of Israel. This, from its biblical use, was the earliest use in English, the original Roman use not appearing till the 16th c.]

1. a. A group of persons forming a community and claiming descent from a common ancestor; spec. each of the twelve divisions of the people of Israel, claiming descent from the twelve sons of Jacob . . .

First, the word appears in boldface. This is the *lemma*, or *head-word*, the word that is subsequently going to be defined and illustrated.

Second, there's an indication, in the form of a transcription, of the present-day *pronunciation* of the word. Interestingly, for *tribe*, the first edition of the OED, which appeared through the end of the 19th century and the beginning of the 20th, gives the transcription /trəɪb/ for this word, while OED2 gives the transcription /traɪb/. Despite the fact that you may not be able just yet to reconstruct the sounds indicated by this transcription, since those involve diphthongal vowel shapes, the difference between the pronunciations found in OED1 and OED2 suggests that some kind of phonological change has taken place in the last hundred years.

Third, OED2 gives the *part of speech* of the indicated word. Here, the word is defined as 'n.' or 'noun'. (The first edition of the OED gives 'sb.', or *substantive*, a now old-fashioned term from traditional grammar that is equivalent simply to 'noun'.)

Then there is a list of *variant chronological forms*. These entries detail some of the *written* forms in which the word has been recorded in English (or in Englishes), together with the century in which the relevant variant form was first recorded. The numerals are themselves abbreviations for centuries, thus the numeral '3' is an abbreviation for the 13th century, the numeral cluster '4–6' is an abbreviation of 'between the 14th and 16th centuries', and so on. Therefore from this bit of information you could work out that *tribe* made its first recorded appearance in English during the 13th century in the guise <tribuz> – a plural, representing 'tribes'.

Then comes a highly significant part of the definition, set in square brackets. This is the *etymology* of the word, its history as a word. From this, we find that in its earliest form in English, *tribe* is found as ME (Middle English) *tribu*, a word adopted from Old French (OF) *tribu*. So here, the etymologists who compiled OED2 are identifying for us what is a very common pattern in immediately post-Conquest English, that is in English after the Norman Conquest in 1066: *tribe* is a word originally adopted from French – borrowed, initially even with the same OF spelling, into early ME. But behind the OF form there's also some history, and the word can ultimately be traced to L(atin) *tribus*. That is, OF got the word from somewhere, and that somewhere was Latin.

In OED2 there's more information we'd want to consider: L. *tribus* itself can be derived from the root *tri-*, meaning three (think of PDE *triple*, or *tricycle* or *triad*). The root *tri-* has a link with what, OED2 tells us, was 'the earliest known application of *tribus* . . . to the three divisions of the early people of Rome . . .'

Behind the seemingly innocent behaviour of the word *tribe* in the English language lie at least 1000 years of history, and the etymology of the word tells some of this fascinatingly complex tale.

Then there's a numbered set of *definitions*, beginning with the *chronologically prior* definition as this is found in English, numbered '1a.', here 'A group of persons forming a community and claiming descent from a common ancestor; spec. each of the twelve divisions of the people of Israel, claiming descent from the twelve sons of Jacob.'

Each definition is followed by illustrative quotations, together with relevant dates. The *principle of illustrative quotation* is a key principle used in the OED2 and other great dictionaries. Not only are the meanings of words defined, but their variant forms are identified, and each form, and each meaning, illustrated by an appropriate quotation. Perhaps we should point out here that this principle, of illustrative quotation, was first developed by Samuel Johnson in his great *Dictionary* of 1755.

So what we're now looking for is an illustrative quotation for the chronologically prior meaning of the word *tribe* – the meaning that relates to the 'twelve divisions of the people of Israel'. We find it in the following:

> c1250 Gen.&Ex. 3813 Đo he wenen ðat god sal taken Of ðo xii tribuz summe mo 1449 Pecock Repr. ii. vi. (Rolls) 173 In her tribu or kinred as in the hous of Miche. The Tribu of Dan . . .

In this context, the head definition is followed by 'a. c1250 *Gen & Ex*. 3813', which is itself followed by a line of eME, in which the word *tribe* appears (here in an eME form as *tribuz*, cf. the dating of attestations of forms of the word found in the early part of the OED2 entry). We realise that the first attestation of the word *tribe*, in this sense, in the English language can be dated to around 1250, and it occurs in an eME text called *Genesis and Exodus*, and, specifically, in line 3813 of that text (see below on how to *find* the text and edition cited). The next attestation of the word, as it occurs *in this particular sense*, can be dated from 1449.

This seems almost fantastically detailed but, once again, there's a scholarly point to the detail. We need to be able to talk about words and their histories with precision; OED2 (as well as specialist dictionaries) offers that precision. We also need to be able to talk about meaning, and changes in meaning: in giving such richly detailed and organised information, OED2 offers us the chance to see meaning change take place in a wealth of examples and to trace these examples for ourselves, in order to verify the accuracy of our work. Or our hunches. And we also need to be able to see how productive words have been in the recorded history of English – how they've combined with other words, or shifted in word class (from noun to verb, for example), or lent themselves to new combinations of word-units. OED2 offers that detail. This is why we can claim that OED2 is one of the most significant research resources in our discipline. Nor have we even begun to unpack all the detail an entry such as that for *tribe* contains.

Looking down the same entry for *tribe*, for example, we look perhaps not for its sense of 'one of the twelve divisions of the tribes of Israel' but for its more familiar sense of 'family' or 'kindred'. We find that under sense 1b. of the OED2 entry:

> . . . b. A particular race of recognized ancestry; a family
> 1400 Mandeville (1839) viii. 67 With his wyf Eue he gatt Seth; of which tribe, þat is to seye, kynrede, Ihesu Crist was born . . .

(Note again that 'sense 1b' doesn't mean that this particular sense is somehow *subordinate to* 'sense 1a' – it just means that sense 1b. *post-dates* sense 1a.)

Interlude Exercise 1.0

As you no doubt have found just by studying the above fragments, in working with OED2 and with other dictionaries you need to know what some of the abbreviations in the text stand for in order to make sense of the wealth of detail in each entry.

What follows are some of the most commonly used abbreviations in OED2. Try to unpack their meanings. You'll be able to guess some of them . . . although we'd much prefer that you looked them up and worked accurately rather than by guesswork. We have supplied answers to the first two items in the list here, and supply a full set of solutions to this exercise at the end of this Interlude.

Abbreviations commonly used in OED2 (and other dictionaries)

a.	adoption of, adopted from	ad.	adaptation of
app.		arch.	
colloq.		contr.	
dial.		f.	
J.		pl.	
*			

Interlude 2: The *Middle English Dictionary* (MED)

We turn to the *Middle English Dictionary*. Is this set out in the same way as OED2? What information might the MED contain about our specimen word *tribe*?

The *Middle English Dictionary* (MED) began life as a project developed by the American academic Hans Kurath. In 1954 Hans Kurath and Sherman M. Kuhn published a book-length study titled *Middle English dictionary (plan and bibliography)* (Ann Arbor: University of Michigan Press). This not only set out the principles under which the MED was to be developed, but also included, for example, dialect maps of England 1400–1450 (pp.8–10). The dictionary then appeared in multiple volumes, being completed under the editor-in-chief, Robert E. Lewis (1956–1999, Ann Arbor: University of Michigan Press).

If we look up *tribe* in the MED, we find the lemma and the following information:

> **trībe** n. Also **tribu**; pl. **tribes, tribus** [OF **tribu** & L **tribus**, pl. -**ūs**]
> (a) A family, race, lineage; (b) one of the twelve tribes of Israel; . . . (c) a group formed by common association . . .

So there are three senses (a–c) which are explored in the MED. Notice the more limited range here, compared with OED2. Then again, that limitation of range is as it should be: this is, after all, a *Middle English* dictionary. The exploration again proceeds via the principle of *historical illustration*:

From the *Middle English Dictionary* (MED):
(a) **?a1425 (c1400)** *Mandev. (1)* 44/20: There the Aungell commaunded Adam þat he scholde duelle with his wyf Eue, Of the whiche he gatt Seth, of which tribe . . . þat is to seye kynrede, Ihesu crist was born . . .
(b) **a1325 (c1250)** *Gen. & Ex.* 3813: He wenen þat god sal taken Of þo xij tribuz summe mo . . .
(c) **c1350** *Ayenb. App.* 267/14: Ich y-zeȝ þe apostles ine tronen zittynde, þe tribus . . .

Good. But what, and where, exactly, are the works cited in these historical illustrations? One turns back to the *Middle English Dictionary (Plan and bibliography)*. There, if you look up 'Mandev. (1)' under 'Title stencils', you'll find precisely

> **?a1425** Mandev. (Tit.):: Mandeville's Travels, ed. P. Hamelius, EETS 153 (1919). 1–211.

So the work referred to in the MED's historical illustration is a medieval travel work (one might almost call it a fantasy text), detailing the travels of John Mandeville. This was edited for 'EETS' (an abbreviation of the *Early English Text Society*) and appeared in 1919 in volume 153 of the original EETS series . . . Similarly, 'Gen. and Ex.' is unpacked in the same place as 'The story of Genesis and Exodus, ed. R. Morris, EETS 7 (1865, rev. 1873, reprint 1895)'. And again, the mysterious 'Ayenb. App.' refers to 'Matter appended to the Ayenbite: Morris op.cit., pp.262 etc.' But what was the 'Ayenbite'? Further hunting reveals that it, too, is a medieval prose text (whose title is the *Ayenbite of Inwyt* – the 'Again-bite of Conscience', or just 'Prick of Conscience'): 'Dan Michel's Ayenbite of inwyt, ed. R. Morris, EETS 23 (1866, reprint 1895) . . .'

Interlude 3: The *Dictionary of Old English* (DOE)

The *Dictionary of Old English* is usually abbreviated to DOE, since 'Old English Dictionary' would abbreviate as 'OED', and we already have an OED. The dictionary project started in the mid-1980s in Toronto, Canada, and the DOE began to appear in microfiche from 1986 (Quebec: Toronto Pontifical Institute of Mediaeval Studies). From 1986 to 1996, under the general editorship of Ashley Crandell Amos, the plan, introduction, preface, list of text and index of authors, together with complete entries spanning letters A, Æ, B, C, D and E, had appeared. Volume <E>, for example, was edited by Antonette diPaolo Healey, Joan Holland and others, 'using materials originally assembled by Angus Cameron'. The DOE is another invaluable resource.

It's not possible, of course, to look up **tribe** in the DOE, since the word is first attested as appearing in English in the 13th century. And so for this part of the Interlude we've chosen a rarely occurring OE word to explore, largely because the DOE contains such a wealth of information – for nearly *all* words, content and function – that it was difficult for us to find an entry short enough to cite in a framework such as this. However, exploring this rare word, which turns out to be part of what seems to have been a specialised OE poetic vocabulary, is an interesting exercise in its own right. The word is **ellor**.

The DOE gives the lemma (in bold text). On the next line we are given the part of speech ('Adv.') and 'Att. sp.' – attested spellings. As it happens, there's only one attested spelling, <ellor>. On the next lines we are given the following information:

From the *Dictionary of Old English* (DOE)
9 occ. (in poetry; 5x in GenA and GenB) elsewhere; *ellor landes* 'in another country' GenB 770: þæt wif gnornode . . . þa heo þæt leoht geseah **ellor** scriðan

This is extremely helpful. It tells us that there are 9 occurrences of the word in the OE corpus, all of them in poetry, with 5 occurrences in the text 'Genesis B' (see below). The word is glossed as meaning 'elsewhere', and a specimen phrase is given to illustrate the semantic range of the adverb, i.e. it appears in the phrase 'ellor landes'. Then there is a historical illustration of usage, with the target word picked out in bold type.

Later in the DOE's exploration of the word *ellor* it appears that the word has a sub sense, seen in phrases such as *ellor hwearfan/sceacen*, to depart elsewhere – a euphemism, as the DOE explains, for 'to die'.

And further, it seems the word entered into compound forms such as *ellor-fūs* (ready or eager to depart), *ellor-gāst* (of Grendel and his mother: alien spirit; second element with *-æ-* has also been interpreted as a form of *giest*, visitor, guest, or word play on both senses . . .), and *ellor-sīþ* (a compound meaning 'journey elsewhere, euphemism for "death"', having just 1 occurrence, and that in poetry: *Beo*[wulf], line 2450 . . .

And how do we trace the texts from which DOE cites its information? Again we need to turn to the index of texts referred to. There we find 'Gen A,B' (two versions of the same poem, *Genesis*) as an abbreviated introduction to the following:

> 'Genesis: Krapp 1931, 1–87. Cited by line no. following ed.'

And Krapp? No, not Beckett, but the following – traceable again via the apparatus in the DOE:

Krapp, G.P. 1931 *The Junius manuscript*, ASPR 1 (New York).

And ASPR?

Why, the *Anglo-Saxon Poetic Records*, of course.

Reading you may find useful

It's a very good idea to consult the prefaces and introductions to both the DOE and the MED, for the reasons we've begun to sketch above. These will help to orientate you not only to *how* the dictionaries were constructed, but *why* a need was felt for them in the first place. Such reading will also give you a sense of the chronological and geographical boundaries other scholars have worked with as they analyse period or dialect-specific specimens of the English language. On work with the OED2, Donna Lee Berg's, *A user's guide to the Oxford English Dictionary* (1991) is a useful reference tool, though you might first like to read – indeed, everyone involved in English studies should read – the *General Preface* to the Dictionary itself. The essays collected in Lynda Mugglestone, ed. (2000) form an interesting group, and include pieces on the making of the first version of what was to become the OED together with pieces about the nature of the principles used in the OED's definitions, principles and sources. The long making of the original OED is detailed by James Murray's granddaughter, K.M. Elisabeth Murray, in *Caught in the web of words* (1977). Besides being a biography of the greatest lexicographer of the OED, it's also a stirring tale of academic rivalry, philology and tricycles (p.327).

And finally . . .

Interlude Exercise 1.0

Commonly used abbreviations in OED2 (see OED2, p.xvi)			
a.	adoption of, adopted from	ad.	adaptation of
app.	apparently	arch.	archaic
colloq.	colloquial, -ly	contr.	contrast with
dial.	dialect, -al	f.	from
J.	(quoted from) Johnson's *Dictionary*		
*	'indicates a word or form not actually found, but of which the existence is inferred' (OED2, p.xvi)		

Unit Five

OE metrics

5.0 Overview of OE metre

In Units 3 and 4 we did some work on the behaviour of nouns and verbs in the earliest phases of English. It's time now to turn to a different topic, that of metrics. We do so for two reasons. First, this topic is interesting in its own right, and significant – sometimes in unexpected ways – for the evolution of English poetic culture. Second, when we begin to work with OE metrics we must also engage with features of the OE sound system such as the nature of 'long' vs. 'short' vowel shapes, and with the form of syllables. We've not yet considered such matters in any detail, since in Unit 2 we concentrated on consonant systems, particularly as those manifested themselves in OE. Thus far in our text we have had only a cursory look at vowel shapes. First, though, some quite general remarks on the nature of OE verse.

We noted in our work on Cædmon in Unit 1 that there was apparently one, and only one, form of poetry in England during the period that spanned the 6th to 11th centuries. Such a form seems to have functioned as a cultural sign ('this form of discourse = poetry'). Towards the end of our period, true, different kinds of metrical writing, among them rhymed and *isosyllabic* (= syllable-counting) verse, began to make an impression on the culture of England, and even in late Old English we can find some scraps of rhymed verse, sometimes interspersed among prose *Chronicle* entries. Although these scraps are linguistically, and culturally, highly interesting, they by no means seem to have had the prestige of the classical alliterative form. We'll inspect some of the linguistic reasons there might be for the coming of a new, isosyllabic verse in Unit 8. For the present, we'll confine our analysis just to OE alliterative verse.

You'll recall that the structure of OE verse could be described in terms of a long line that could be, and was, structurally divided into two *half-lines*. The half-lines of the verse were bound together by relatively predictable patterns of *alliteration*. Further, it was apparent that, generally speaking, there were *two* syllables in each half-line that bore stress of some kind. These stress-bearing syllables tended to be the ones picked out for alliteration. Syllable-initial consonants bore alliteration, where present; and vowels, whatever their phonetic quality, were also able to alliterate with each other. We repeat a WS text of Cædmon's *Hymn* for convenience, where we also indicate the (editorially given) half-line divisions together with a note on the alliteration of each long line:

(1)

Nū sculon **h**erigean	**h**eofonrīces Weard,	(alliteration on /h/)
Meotodes **m**eahte	ond his **m**ōdgeþanc,	(alliteration on /m/)
weorc **W**uldorfæder,	swā hē **w**undra gehwæs,	(alliteration on /w/)
ēce Drihten,	**ō**r onstealde.	(alliteration on vowels)
Hē **æ**rest scēop	**eo**rðan bearnum	(alliteration on vowels)
heofon tō **hr**ōfe,	**h**ālig Scyppend.	(alliteration on /h/)
Þā **m**iddangeard	**m**onncynnes Weard,	(alliteration on /m/)
ēce Drihten,	**æ**fter tēode	(alliteration on vowels)
fīrum **f**oldan,	**F**rea ælmihtig	(alliteration on /f/)

In order to make the constructive principles clearer, we also offer a specimen of verse written using OE conventions, but cast in a version of PDE. (Note: we make no claim for this as fine, persuasive, or elegant poetry. It's just an explanatory construct.) In what follows, major stresses are given above each line, where they're indicated by a slash (/); alliterative segments are boldened; and alliterating syllables are marked 'a' below the relevant line; 'x' marks a stressed but non-alliterating syllable:

(2)

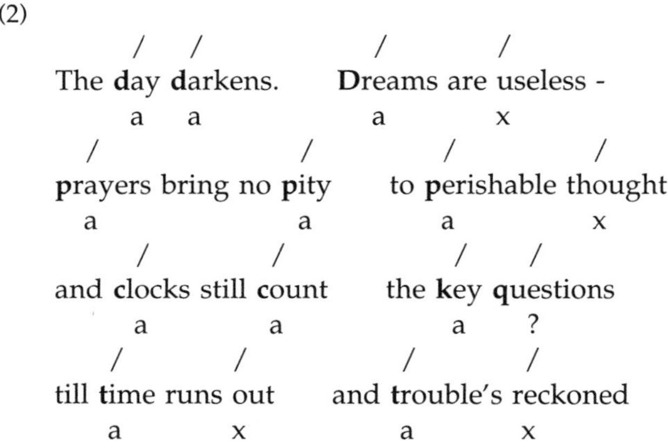

One problem we'll have to address is the patterning of alliteration, which is regularly (but not invariably) found on *two stressed syllables within the first half-line*, but is usually found only on *the first stressed syllable of the second*. (Hence our querying of the possible alliteration found in *questions* in the above construct – notice that <questions>, in spoken English, begins with the consonant cluster /kw-/, and thus would be a candidate for alliteration with <key>, /ki:/.) Are there any linguistic reasons for such characteristic structures? You'll find further work on alliteration in Sections 5.3 and 5.9 below. For the moment, it's sufficient to realise that when standard textbooks refer to the 'aa:ax' patterns of alliteration found in classical OE verse, they're referring to the kind of structures we've identified within the long lines of the *Hymn*, and within the long lines of our constructed fragment above.

5.1 Stress in OE

The bare description we've offered to this point is in fact as far as many standard teachings tend to go in their descriptions of OE metre – if they deign to describe it at all. It seems that many students have learned merely that OE half-lines thump along on two-stresses-per-half-line, where each thump of stress is surrounded by a 'gabble of weaker syllables'. This parodic view of OE metre conceals a very different kind of truth. The OE, indeed the wider Germanic, metrical form (we include here OS and OHG verse, as well as ON Eddic verse) was highly sophisticated, and beautifully adapted to the language(s) out of which it was constructed. It was also a very durable form in which there was a high degree of regularity and constraint, in both the number, type and disposition not only of stressed syllables, but also of *unstressed* syllables.

In order to see how OE verse-makers – the *scops* – were able to construct such a remarkable artefact out of their raw linguistic materials, we need to understand something of the *stress patterning* that pertained in OE. It's difficult to avoid circularity of reasoning and argument here, because much of what we know about the OE stress system depends on evidence that comes from verse. But there's independent evidence, too – we can learn a great deal about which syllables were unstressed from studying patterns of inflectional loss – and we can infer a great deal even from the stress patterning of PDE.

Exercise 5.1.1

Study the word-lists for PDE given in table 5.1. Where does the main (the heaviest, the most prominent) stress fall in each word? Are there any words where you're uncertain? Are there some words where there's no perceptible stress? Can you make generalisations about these data?

Table 5.1 PDE word-lists

Column 1	2	3	4	5	6
book-shop	garage	you	the	in	and
ironmonger	printer	they	a	by	but
picture-frame	pewter	she	some	from	
video-store	orange	your	there	through	

Comment on Exercise 5.1.1

No doubt you noticed that the words in column 1 were all *compound* words, that is, they're themselves whole 'words' – a plural inflection, for example, would be tacked on to the end of the whole string, not as in e.g. **books-store* or **hats-rack*. Such full words nevertheless contain two independent lexical words. The morphological structure of these compounds might be described as follows, where N stands simply for Noun:

(3)

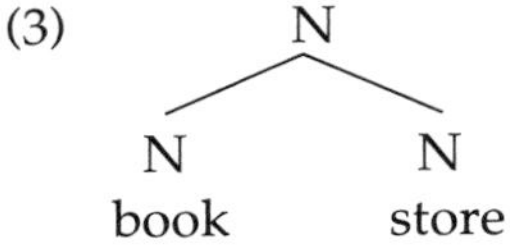

Notice also that in such compounds, *one* syllable in the first word is very strongly stressed, while *one* syllable in the second word is stressed – but not as strongly stressed as the prominent syllable in the first word. Let's refer to such stresses as *primary* and *secondary* stresses respectively. Primary and secondary stress can be schematised with / for primary stress, and \ for secondary, so that *book-store* might look as follows:

(4)

```
 /     \
book-store
```

In the compound *ironmonger* the first syllable of the word carries primary stress, the syllable *-mon-* seems to bear secondary stress (it's not as prominent as the very first syllable), while the syllables *-ron* and *-ger* seem to bear no stress at all. In fact, these last, unstressed syllables are pronounced with a 'murmur vowel' – a mid, non-tense vowel shape, very frequently occurring and technically known as *schwa*. The presence of schwa is reliably diagnostic of stressless syllables. If we designate an unstressed syllable as 'x', a graphic display of *ironmonger* might look as follows:

(5)

```
/ x    \   x
i ron mon ger
```

The falling stress contour of compounds is highly characteristic, and different from the *rising* stress contour we often apprehend in *phrases*. Thus there's a distinction in PDE between a *yellow-hammer* (which is a kind of bird, a summer migrant to Britain) and a *yellow hammer* (a tool, in this case coloured yellow, which you use to knocks nails into walls with); between a *red-cap* (another kind of bird) and a *red cap* (something you wear); and between a *greenhouse* (where you pot plants and grow tomatoes) and a *green house* (a house painted green). These differences are sometimes indicated in English graphology by the use of hyphenation (or closure between word spacing) in compounds – thus *green-house* or *greenhouse* (compounds) as distinct from *green house* (an NP). But punctuation conventions are, sometimes, inconsistent, and – where they do offer consistency – often prove to be merely stylisations of prior linguistic processes. Understanding such graphic conventions is a trivial matter compared with understanding the deeper linguistic processes themselves.

The morphological (that is, the word-building) process of compounding is still highly productive in all the Germanic languages. It is an important means by which new items are added to English vocabulary (*computer table, water sprinkler, kitchen knife, funeral arrangements*). Further, such items are often noun + noun compounds and, in this sense, the English language doesn't seem to have changed much in its morphological habits over the past 1500 years. The morphology, and the stress phonology, of compounds and compounding appear to be an interesting piece of linguistic stability, of continuity.

Look now at the words in column 2 of table 5.1. For almost all speakers of BrE these words are stressed on their initial syllables: *pewter* and *printer* have that diagnostic schwa again in their final syllables, while for many speakers, *garage* and *orange* have the vowel shape /ɪ/ in their final syllables – a vowel that proves to be in free variation with schwa in such stressless environments. AmE speakers, though, will remark that words such as *garage* are stressed on their final syllables (compare also words such as *souffle, chateau* in their AmE versions), with their initial syllables often reducing to a pronunciation in schwa. Presumably, such stressings come about because speakers have the idea that such pronunciations are 'prestige', and reflect the fact that the lexical items in question are often enough French loan-words. (Note that the word *prestige* is itself a French loan, and carries end-stress.) Perhaps this gives us a clue to a more fundamental principle that appears to be operative in English stress patterning: *historically, and before foreign influence could ever have been felt, nouns and adjectives are stressed on the initial syllables of their lexical roots.* Thus a noun such as *printer* has the morphological composition [[print] + er], and stress falls on the initial syllable, on the root of the word. Similarly *print + ing, print + able.*

Where a word has no internal morphological structure – where the word is *monomorphemic*, as in [pewter] or [orange] (cf. *[[pewt]er], whose bracketing is impossible because there is no such word, or indeed thing, process or entity, as **pewt*) – then stress seems to fall most readily on the initial syllable of the root, as we predict.

What, you might ask, about words such as *unkind*? Or *mistake*? At first hearing, such words seem to bear main stress on their final syllables, not on their initial ones. A glance at the morphology of such words shows us that *un-* and *mis-* are in these cases *prefixes* ([un[kind]], [mis[take]]): main lexical stress here falls again on the *first (in these cases, the only) syllable of the root.*

You'll also notice immediately that there are many nouns in your variety of English that are monomorphemic, yet have non-initial stress. Examples are words like *guitar, affair, bizarre, antique.* Closer inspection, however, reveals often that such words are loaned into English from French, from Latin, or from Italian, and as they're borrowed, they seem to retain their native stress-patterning. Sometimes they do not, and are thoroughly Englished: a word such as *carpenter*, for example, was used, albeit in verse, by Chaucer as end-stressed, and yet today, we pronounce the word with root-initial stress, and with schwa (or /r/, in rhotic varieties) on the final syllable. The word has been nativised. It appears, then, as if there's an historically stable process again going on here: OE nouns, like many nativised PDE nouns, have 'left-hand' stress – or more accurately, they're stressed on the initial syllables of their roots.

Look now at the words in column 3 of table 5.1. They're all pronouns. Pronouns are interesting because they may have a 'full' pronunciation – a pronunciation with a long vowel or diphthong, such as (long vowel) /juː/ for *you* or (diphthong) /eɪ/ for *they* – or they may have a 'reduced' pronunciation, a pronunciation with schwa, such as that found in *y'know*, /jə nəʊ/. This behaviour comes about because pronouns, unlike nouns, adjectives and (many) verbs, are not themselves *lexical words*, i.e. they don't carry 'dictionary meanings'. (On the distinction between lexical and non-lexical words, see Unit 1.)

The same goes for the words in columns 4 and 5 of table 5.1. They're all non-lexical words, and all of them have a possible pronunciation in schwa. Then again, they also have a pronunciation, which you can hear under emphasis, with a full vowel – compare the standard pronunciation of a phrase like *fish 'n'chips*, where the vowel of the conjunction is reduced, with an emphatic pronunciation of the same conjunction in *mayonnaise AND ketchup*. We might develop these observations by claiming that *non-lexical words are underlyingly unstressed in English*. True, they have stressed variants – and interestingly, the vowels of some of the pronouns (notably those of the 1st person singular and plural, and the 3rd person singular *he* form) eventually, in their 'full' guises, undergo the same changes as stressed vowels in other word-classes – but their typical behaviour is to function as unstressed. The same, as we'll see, appears true for the behaviour of non-lexical words in OE: under normal circumstances they're typically unstressed. This relative stresslessness goes for prepositions, articles and conjunctions, since all are non-lexical words.

Let's try to put these remarks together, and make some generalisations that might help us to understand the OE stress system.

- First, stress in OE appears to be keyed to morphology, in that it's sensitive to morphological environments such as 'root-initial syllable'.
- Second, it's the initial syllable of lexical roots that carries stress. *It follows that inflections, which are themselves never initial, will not carry stress.*
- Third, non-lexical words appear to be underlyingly unstressed, i.e. they typically have 'weak' pronunciations, but may possibly acquire stress

under certain conditions – for example, by syntactic displacement, or under emphasis.

Note again that these three principles also 'work' for some of the stress system of PDE. We still have initially-stressed compounds; many (though not all) monomorphemic nouns still carry initial stress; and non-lexical words are still reliably, in unmarked environments, pronounced 'weak'.

Returning to OE, complete the following two exercises before reading further.

Exercise 5.1.2

Using the conventions we've introduced above, mark the stress patterning for the following two lines of Cædmon's *Hymn*:

Hē **æ**rest scēop **eo**rðan bearnum
heofon tō **h**rōfe, **h**ālig Scyppend.

Comment on Exercise 5.1.2

You should have got something like the following:

x / x / / x / x
Hē **æ**rest scēop **eo**rðan bearnum

/ x x /x /x / x
heofon tō **h**rōfe, **h**ālig Scyppend.

Hē is a pronoun, and underlyingly unstressed – notice too that it doesn't alliterate; *ærest* is an adverb, a lexical word, and as such carries stress on its initial syllable (note that the word eventually becomes the now-antique *erst*); *scēop* is a verb, a content word, and so is stressed on its initial – in this case, its only – syllable; *eorðan* and *bearnum* are both content words, and both are stressed, as expected, on the initial syllables of their roots – and notice how the inflectional endings *-an* and *-um* are here unstressed.

Exercise 5.1.3

Now do the same – mark up the stresses – for the following fragment:

monncynnes Weard

Comment on Exercise 5.1.3

We hope you might have marked this fragment as follows:

/ \ x /
monncynnes Weard

You'll have noticed that *monncynnes*, mankind, is a compound ([[monn][cynn] + es]), and *Weard*, guardian is a monomorphemic lexical word. The compound word takes a pattern of primary + secondary stress on its lexical roots ([[monn][cynn] + es]) – with heaviest stress, as expected, on the initial syllable, while the genitive singular inflection *-es* is stressless. *Weard*, a noun, is a fully stressed word, of course.

We'll say more in a moment about OE metre. For the present, we simply observe, once again, that the principles that appear to obtain in OE verse-making are stylisations of morphological and phonological tendencies and structures that are already present 'in' the OE language. Though we don't know, and may never know, exactly how they were *performed*, the lines and half-lines of OE poetry don't seem to 'go to a tune', that is, be lovely, particularly euphonious, or musically assonantal. As Tolkien once claimed in a telling aside, much Germanic verse is 'more like masonry than music' (Tolkien 1936:31). From what we know of the relationship between OE verse and OE morpho-phonology, we'd fully support such a claim. Architecture, after all, can also be aesthetically pleasing, and when we think about OE metrics we could do worse than to think of ourselves as hearing, and analysing, the principles of 'aural architecture'.

5.2 Syllables in OE and PDE

Like so much else in language, syllables have a rich, and eminently describable, internal structure. Describing that structure helps us explain alliteration, among other things. So it's worthwhile saying something now about how we might begin to describe OE syllables.

If you start to think about syllables as a linguist would think about them, the more mysterious these entities seem to become. We all believe we know what syllables are: we can tap out their number in any phrase; they're undeniably parts of words; and each syllable has some kind of vowel at its perceptible centre . . . Or can we? Or are they? Or does it?

How many syllables does a word such as *fire* have? One? Or two? How many syllables does a word such as *harmonious* have? Three? Or four?

As for syllables being 'parts of words' – what part of the word might syllables be part of? In OE *bearnum*, for example, the syllable *-um* is an inflection. Is it 'part of' the word *bearn*? Or is such a syllable merely affixed somehow to the root of the word? And where does the /n/ of *bearnum* belong – to the end of the first syllable, to *bearn*, and thus to the root of the word? Or does it belong to the beginning of the second syllable, as in *bear.num*, where the little dot, '.', symbolises the division of the syllables? And if *bear.num* is the *syllabification* of the word *bearnum*, how is that related to the *morphological* division of the word, which is root + suffix – *bearn* + *um*?

And as for syllables having vowel shapes at their presumed centres – what about PDE words such as *button* or *fathom* or *chasm*? Is there in fact a vowel in the final syllables of these words? For AmE speakers – or any other English speakers whose varieties have rhoticity, that is, have post-vocalic /r/ – think also about words such as *fetter* or *butter*. Do these words have a vowel shape in their final syllables?

Syllables aren't quite the simple entities that we might believe. However, they do have an interesting, and eminently describable, structure, and the description we're about to undertake goes for OE as well as for PDE.

First, English syllables often – though by no means always – appear to begin with a consonant, or a consonant cluster. Usually, if there's a consonant *cluster* that begins the syllable, there are *two* consonants in the cluster; more rarely, there are three, and if there are three, then the first is invariably /s/ (see table 5.2). (Notice here that <sh> and <th> in the first column are the normal written versions of single phonological segments. In the second column <sch> is the written cluster for phonological /sk/, and both BrE and many AmE speakers will be aware that <pew> begins with the phonological cluster /pj/. In the third column, *sclerosis* is queried because it's the only example we can find of an English word – in fact it's a loan-word – that begins /skl/, and 'stl' is asterisked as deviant because we can't find *any* English words that begin with the phonological cluster /stl/.)

Table 5.2 Consonant word openings

1-consonant openings	2-consonant openings	3-consonant openings
need	tread	stride /str-/
bale	breed	spread /spr-/
pile	pray	scream /skr-/
sight	blight	splint /spl-/
harm	brown	sclerosis (?)
shame	school	*stl . . .
thigh	pew	
then	snow	

It seems from this list as if almost any single consonant may begin an English syllable. Immediately, though, we notice that there are some exceptions to this claim for PDE – consonants such as /ŋ/ can't begin syllables, though they can readily end them, e.g. *sing*, while consonants such as /h/ may begin syllables, but not end them; one other segment, /ʒ/, appears syllable-finally, as in *rouge* and *beige*, or between vowels, as in *leisure*, but it can't itself stand alone as a consonant opening a syllable, i.e. this segment has a *restricted distribution* in terms of English syllable phonotactics.

Of the 2-consonant openings, the second consonant seems readily to be /l,r,m,n/ (*blue*, with /bl-/ is fine, but */lb-/ would be unacceptable; /pr-/ is fine, as in *pray*, but */rp-/ is unacceptable), and almost equally readily to be /j/ or /w/ (/pju:/, /swu:n/ 'swoon'). The second consonant of a 2-consonant opening might also be /p,t,k/ – *but only after /s/*, as in 'spot, stoat, school /sku:l/'. That *only after /s/* rider is significant, because when we look at the kind of 3-consonant openings we can get in English syllables, we find that the only times you can ever get 3-consonant clusters in this position is when the first segment is itself /s/. The role of /s/ in terms of English syllable structure is, then, somewhat anomalous. It turns out to be significantly anomalous in OE, too – something that poets seemed well aware of.

Following a clear and useful linguistic tradition, let's call the consonant or consonant cluster that begins the syllable the *Onset*. Thus, in the above table, there are single-consonant Onsets /b,p,r,l . . . / etc., and bi-consonantal Onsets, while tri-consonantal Onsets are a restricted class involving that problematic /s/.

There are also, of course, syllables that begin just with vowels. These syllables apparently have no Onset – or perhaps better, we might claim that they have a *zero Onset*:

Ø + ease	ease	cf. **t**ease
Ø + isle	isle	cf. **f**ile
Ø + egg	egg	cf. **b**eg

Zero Onsets will turn out to be important later on, when we get back to describing alliteration in OE verse. It's important to notice that in syllables with zero Onsets, the Onset constituent of the syllable is still present; it simply, in these cases, happens to be filled with the null term Ø instead of with a consonant proper.

Turning now to the heart of the syllable, and again following good linguistic tradition, we can call this heart the *Nucleus* of the syllable, and note that syllabic Nuclei are typically, though by no means always, filled with *vowel shapes* (for counter-examples, think of the examples *fathom*, *fetter*, *chasm* and so forth – we noted their existence above).

And last, turning to the consonant or consonants, if any, that end the syllable, we can call this the syllabic *Coda*.

Exercise 5.2.1

Onset-Nucleus-Coda. Syllables turn out to be rather like novels, in that they apparently, in their most straightforward cases, have a beginning, a middle and an end. To make this clear, look at the following list of English monosyllables (while thinking particularly carefully how they're *pronounced*

– don't go just by the spelling), and for each instance, specify which segments belong where – to Onset, Nucleus or Coda:

beg	pack	plight
pray	trunk	snack
twice	space	spear

Comment on Exercise 5.2.1

We can schematise our answer in table 5.3, where for each word we have given the relevant phonemic transcription (as this might be found in a relatively conservative variety of BrE Received Pronunciation), and in the right-hand columns, show which segments belong to which constituent of the syllable:

Table 5.3 Internal structure of some PDE syllables

	Onset	Nucleus	Coda
beg /beg/	/b/	/e/	/g/
pray /preɪ/	/pr/	/eɪ/	None
twice /twɑɪs/	/tw/	/ɑɪ/	/s/
pack /pæk/	/p/	/æ/	/k/
trunk /trʌŋk/	/tr/	/ʌ/	/ŋk/
space /speɪs/	/sp/	/eɪ/	/s/
plight /plaɪt/	/pl/	/aɪ/	/t/
snack /snæk/	/sn/	/æ/	/k/
spear /spɪə/ (BrE)	/sp/	/ɪə/	None

One further thing we can observe is that Nucleus and Coda sub-constituents are themselves gathered into a constituent of the syllable that we can call, following traditional labelling, the *Rhyme*. Thus a syllable such as *beg* has a structure rather like the following:

(6) Syllable structure of *beg*

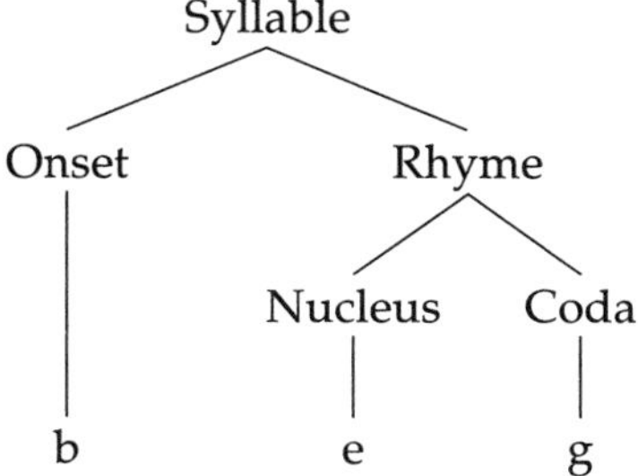

Syllables appear – like so much else in language – to have a *hierarchical structure*, where constituent bits of structure are nested within larger bits of constituency.

Why is it worth going to all of this trouble to describe something as apparently simple as the English syllable? One possible answer lies in the next observation. In both OE and PDE there's at least *a partial correlation between Rhyme structure*, in the sense that we've just described 'Rhyme', and *stressedness*. In OE, for example, just as in PDE, there are no stressed monosyllables that contain just a single, short vowel; nor are there stressed monosyllables that contain an Onset followed just by a short stressed vowel (no *ki or *fæ, though *kynn* and *fæt* are fine). On the other hand, there are very many stressed syllables that contain a single vowel in the Nucleus, when that is followed by one or more consonants (in the Coda); and there are also syllables that contain just a long vowel or diphthong in the Nucleus. Table 5.4, containing a few examples from PDE, should make this clear:

Table 5.4 Well-structured and poorly structured English lexical monosyllables

Not OK	OK
*/ba/	/bæn/
*/a/	/aɪ/ eye
*/eɪ/	/eɪl/ ail
*/frɛ/	/frɛʃ/ fresh
*/hɪ/	/hi:d/ heed

In PDE, just as in OE, stressedness seems most readily to be a property of syllables that have at least two segments in the Rhyme. It doesn't matter whether these segments are spread across Nucleus + Coda (as in *ban*), or whether both segments are found simply in the Nucleus (as in *eye*, /ɑɪ/ – the Nucleus is part of the Rhyme). We'll call syllables containing two or more segments in their Rhymes *heavy syllables*, while syllables containing just one segment in their Rhymes we can call *light syllables*. In OE, then, as well as being sensitive to the environment 'Root-initial', stress also seems to be attracted to heavy syllables. (There's an important exception to this, in which stress falls on light syllables precisely when they're root-initial. We'll cover this in Section 5.5. below.)

There's a further good reason for studying the hierarchical structure of syllables. It gives insight into what constitutes a *long vowel* as distinct from a *short vowel*. Our intuitions are usually pretty reliable: the vowel of PDE *heed* is fairly readily distinguishable (even beyond its graphological shape) from that of PDE *hid*, so what's the problem? The problem is that *phonetically*, in terms of measurable acoustic production, the vowel of PDE *hid* turns out to be longer than that of PDE *hit*. Another problem is that word-final vowels like the sort you hear in *happy* or *canny* are hard to distinguish as either short or long (our students typically don't know whether to transcribe such vowel shapes as /iː/ or /ɪ/, or as something 'in-between'). So vowel length isn't quite the simple issue it might at first appear to be. However, we can use our syllable template to help solve at least some of these difficulties, and at least enable us to distinguish long from short. Let's suppose, for instance, that we were to align each segment within the syllable one-to-one with a little 'x', and then gathered such x's, rather than the segments themselves, into the constituents of a syllable tree. Under such a procedure, the syllable *beg* would have the following structure:

(7) Syllable structure of *beg*, revisited

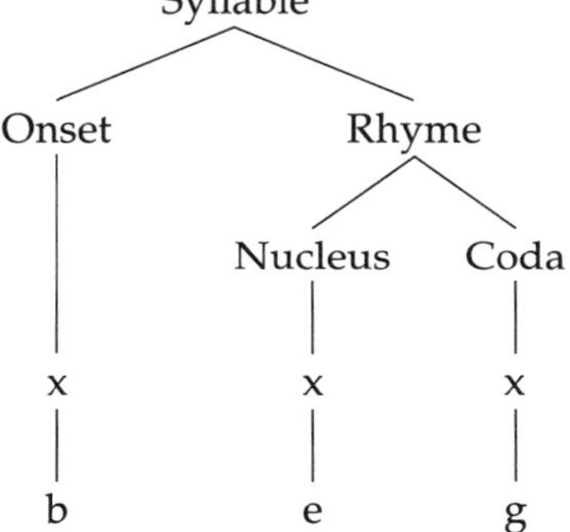

Notice that in the Nucleus, the short vowel lines up with one 'x'. But what about Nuclei containing long vowels? Consider the following, a syllable tree for PDE *heed*:

(8) Syllable structure of PDE *heed*

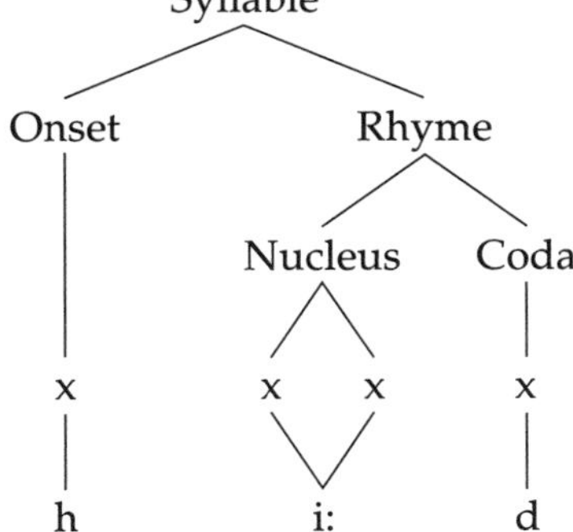

Exercise 5.2.3

To make the relevance of this kind of analysis to OE even clearer, construct syllable trees for the following OE words (taken from the *Hymn*): (i) *mōd*, spirit, (ii) *ōr*, beginning, (iii) *hrōf*, roof. Notice that each word contains a long vowel, and that *ōr* has no Onset.

Comment on Exercise 5.2.3

We trust you constructed trees as follows:

(1) Syllable structure of *mōd*

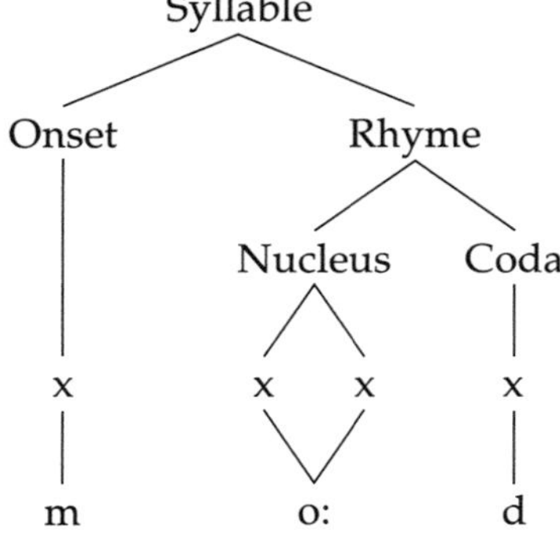

(2) Syllable structure of *ōr*

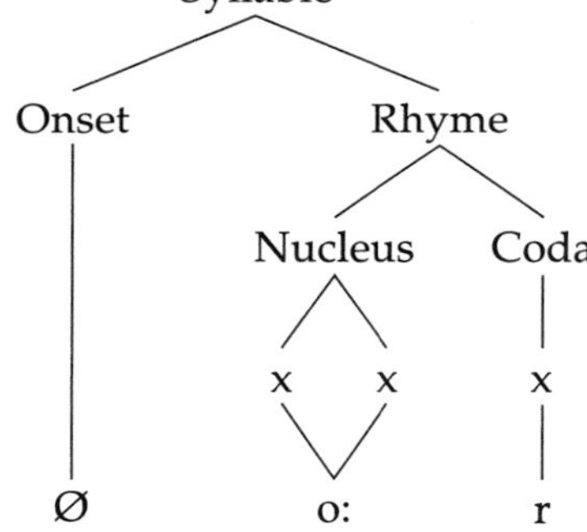

(3) Syllable structure of *hrōf*

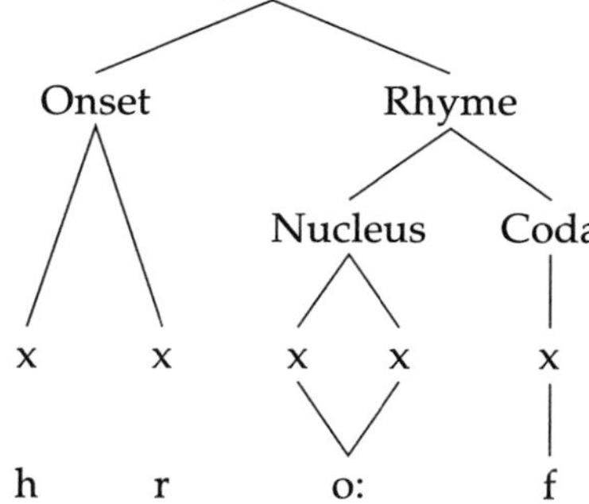

Table 5.5 Possible/impossible Onsets and Coda strings

Possible/impossible Onsets		Possible/impossible Codas	
/bl/	*/lb/	/lb/	*/bl/
/br/	*/rb/	/rb/	*/br/
/fr/	*/rf/	/rf/	*/fr/
/sw/	*/ws/	/ls/	*/sl/
/hr/	*/rh/	/χt/	*/tχ/

There's one final thing we need to notice. Study table 5.5, and see if you can make any valid generalisations about why it is that certain Onset and Coda strings are fine, while others never occur (in either PDE or OE). The last row of examples might have given you some trouble. /hr/ doesn't occur as an Onset in PDE, although it's perfectly fine in OE (think of *hrōf* again, or OE *hring*, ring); and /χt/ isn't at all a possible Coda in PDE, though it occurred readily in OE in words such as *leoht*, light, or *meaht*, power.

The point we're trying to establish is this. Onsets and Codas have a preferred structure, in that Onsets, where they contain two consonants, show that the second of those consonants is more *sonorous* than the first, while in Codas, conversely, the first consonant in a 2-consonant group is more sonorous than the second. Meanwhile, vowel shapes sit in their Nucleic peaks, the most highly sonorous segments within the syllable. Onsets, then, show an *increase* in sonority, Codas show a *decrease*. Sonority is at its least at the syllable margins, and at its greatest within the syllable Nucleus.

Defining sonority is tricky. Generally, the more 'vowel-like' a particular speech-sound is, the more sonorous it is. Therefore vowels themselves are highly sonorous segments, while stops – which are phonetically about the *least* vowel-like segments – carry little sonority. Perhaps that's one reason why stops tend to be distributed in the margins of syllables, whereas vowels function invariably in the Nucleus. But however we define sonority, we do know that there's a pattern of behaviour within English syllables that correlates with sonority, or 'open-ness', or 'resonance': *most-sonorous sounds lie towards the centre of the syllable, while least-sonorous sounds lie at the syllable's margins.*

In the preceding parts of Section 5.2 we've begun to say quite a bit about vowel shapes, and the distinction there might be between long and short vowels. In order to support our work, we need more detail on English vowel systems and, in particular, we need to examine some of the phonemic symbols we've used to transcribe vowels.

We begin by reproducing as figure 5.1 the vowel trapezium you first glimpsed in Unit 2:

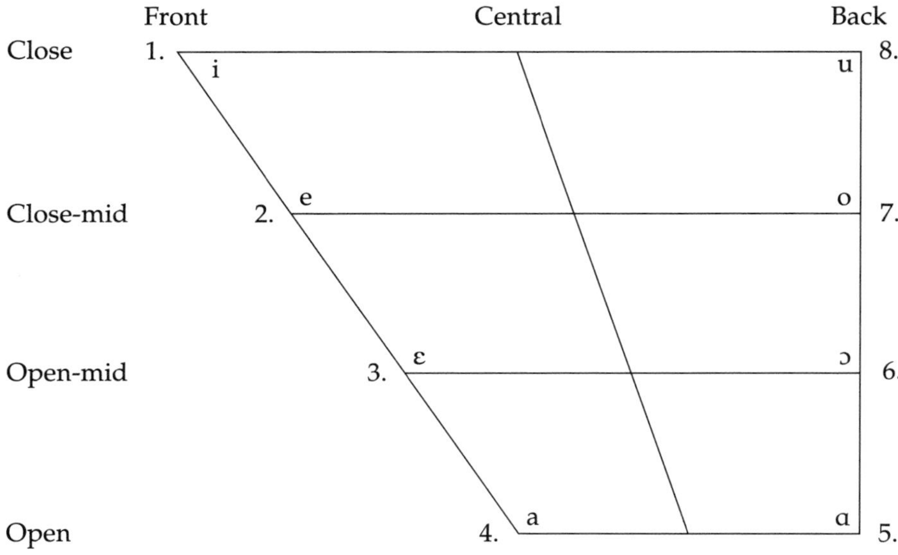

Figure 5.1 A first vowel trapezium

Although this trapezium gives some detail about how we might begin to classify vowel shapes – as 'close, front' or 'mid-close, back' – it says nothing about vowel length. The symbols in the trapezium seem to stand merely for generic shapes – 'some kind of /i/ shape', 'some kind of /a/ shape'.

Let's retain the trapezium, but modify the symbols in order to indicate vowel length. We use the diacritic mark ':' to indicate vowel length, thus a symbol such as /iː/ can be interpreted as 'the generic close front vowel shape /i/, long version'. Symbols appearing without such a following diacritic are short vowel shapes, thus the symbol /ɪ/ can be thought of as 'the generic close front vowel shape /i/, short version'. Similarly – although still theoretically – with the front vowel shapes /eː/ and /e/, with /ɛː/ and /ɛ/, and with /aː/ and /a/. This is illustrated in figure 5.2. That seems fine. But in Unit 1 we noted the existence of vowels pronounced with a rounding of the lips (do you recall the test-word *cyssan*, to kiss?). And as our text has proceeded, we have also noted the existence of the central vowel shape, schwa. Where would such a shape, and its characteristic symbol /ə/, be inserted into the trapezium?

Figure 5.3 gives a further, revised vowel trapezium, showing not only rounded vowels (the right-hand members of vowel pairs diagrammed here), but also the position of schwa. So OE *cyssan* would be produced (one might argue) with the close, front, rounded vowel shape found in the top left corner of the above trapezium, symbolised /y/.

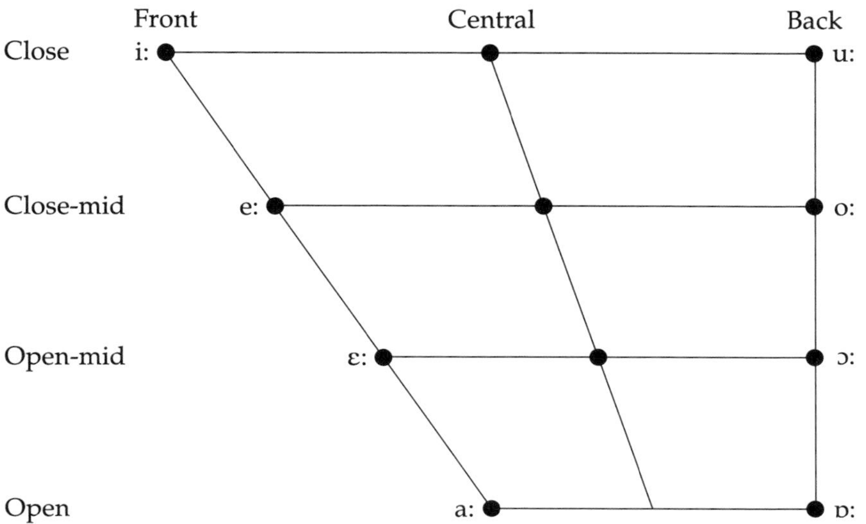

Figure 5.2 Vowel trapezium modified to indicate vowel length

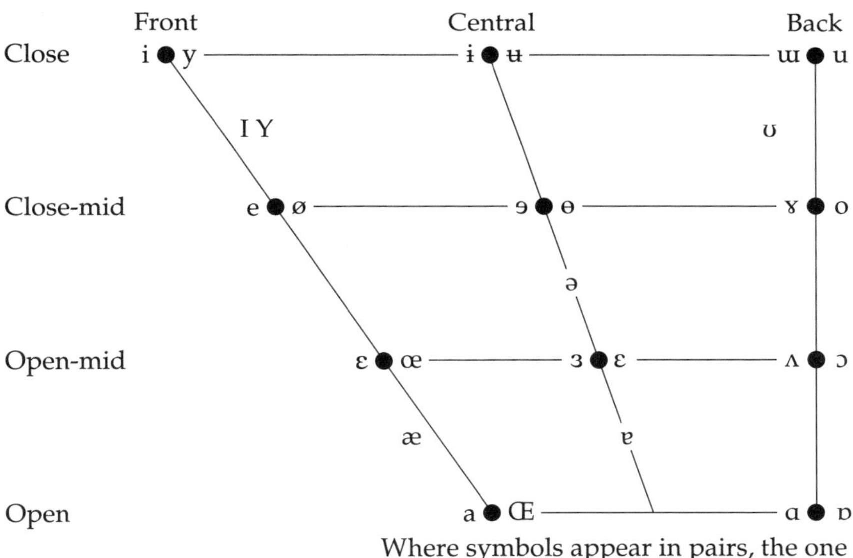

Figure 5.3 Vowel trapezium modified to show rounded vowels and the position of schwa

Source: Adapted from The IPA Chart from Ladefoged, P. (2001) *Course in Phonetics, 4th Edition*.

Table 5.6 Phonemic transcriptions of some OE words

scrūd	clothing (cf. PDE shroud)	/ʃru:d/
bāt	boat	/bɑ:t/
sellan	(to) sell	/sellən/
cræft	occupation, craft	/kræft/
hē	he	/he:/
goda (also Nbr. *godo*)	gods	/gɔdə/
wita	counsellors	/wɪtə/
tō	to, towards	/to:/
þus	thus, so	/ðʊs/

The great thing about much OE is that in terms of sound/spelling correspondence (at least as that is manifest in stressed syllables), what you see is pretty much what you get.

To illustrate this last point, think of the OE word *fisc*, fish. From two commonsense hints we can begin to infer that the word was pronounced with a short vowel: (i) the OE spelling appears without a (scribal, or editorial) macron over the vowel, and (ii) the word is pronounced with a short vowel in PDE. Moreover, the OE pronunciation appears to have contained an *unrounded* vowel. Had the vowel shape been rounded, scribes would have tended to write *<fysc> – precisely because many scribes spelled as they spoke ('what you see, in OE spelling, is what you get'). Put these observations together, and what one arrives at is /fɪʃ/.

Table 5.6 above, we give words that you have already studied in the left-hand column. These are the OE *spellings*. In the middle column, we give the translation of the word again, and in the right-hand column, we give a phonemic transcription – a more-or-less plausible reconstruction – of the word as it might have been pronounced in classical WS. Notice in particular how, for example, OE <ū> maps into /u:/, OE /ī/ into /i:/, and so on. Now you've looked at this chart, you may care to revisit the syllable trees we constructed for e.g. OE *hrōf*, /hro:f/, roof, and *mōd*, /mo:d/, courage, for example, just in order to satisfy yourselves that our work there was accurate.

We're aware that there are many vowel shapes in OE that we've not even begun to describe, especially diphthong shapes, but we'll look at these only where absolutely necessary. Studying some simple monophthongs, after all, takes us quite a long way to the heart of understanding sound/spelling correspondence in OE.

5.3 Syllables and alliteration

In OE verse, *alliteration is regularly a property of stressed syllables*. Thus, the /k/ of the first syllable of a word such as *cyning*, king, alliterates with the /k/ of a word such as *cēne*, keen. That seems straightforward, but there's a caveat. If alliteration is *regularly* a property just of *stressed* syllables in OE, then there will be occasions when stressed syllables might *appear* to alliterate with unstressed syllables, but don't. To make this clear, study the following table (examples are in PDE) and work out which pairs are instances of *true* alliteration (i.e. alliteration takes place across pairs of stressed syllables) and which pairs show instances of merely *graphic* alliteration:

(9) True alliteration and graphic alliteration

pair	prince
brown	bet
pair	dependent
prince	predictable
raid	repel
raid	derail
dream	denial
nub	neo-Classical

The first pair should have given you no trouble: both pairs consist of stressed monosyllables. In *pair – dependent*, it's the second syllable of *dependent* that is stressed, so alliteration takes place regularly in this pair. For *prince – predictable*, though, it's the antepenultimate syllable of *predictable* that bears main word-stress, so the relevant matching would be between the /p/ of *prince*, and the /d/ of *-dic(table)*. The /p/ of *pre(dictable)* is part of the prefix, and the prefix isn't stressed. Therefore, though both *prince* and *predictable* have <p> (the graphic letter shape), one is initial in a stressed syllable (*prince*) while one's initial in an unstressed syllable. There's no true alliteration here. The same goes for the pairs *raid – repel* and *dream – denial*. In the next pairing, /r/ is initial in the stressed syllable *raid*, but also initial in the *unstressed* syllable (the prefix) *re(pel)*. In this last word, /p/ begins the stressed part of the word. And in *dream – denial*, /d/ is initial in the stressed monosyllable, but also initial merely in the prefix of *denial* – and prefixes of this kind aren't typically stressed.

The final pair, *nub – neo-Classical*, is interesting. /n/ is clearly initial in the stressed syllable *nub*, and it's initial in *neo-* too. Is the first syllable of the obvious prefix *neo-* stressed? The answer is yes – notice that the first vowel of this prefix is produced long, and not with the schwa or /ɪ/ vowel shape that we've learned is diagnostic of stresslessness. We claim that the prefix *neo-* bears *secondary* stress, while the initial syllable of *-Classical* carries *primary* stress. We could still justifiably claim that in *nub – neo-Classical* we are looking at true alliteration, because our generalisation claims only that alliteration is a property of 'stressed syllables in general'. It says nothing about whether such syllables should be primary or secondary stressed.

Exercise 5.3.1

Study the sequences of OE words shown in table 5.7 (they're from an OE poem known as *The Wanderer*, and we'll be asking you to study a fragment of it later) and state which words show true, as opposed to merely graphic, alliteration:

Table 5.7 Word sets from *The Wanderer*

Row 1		
wērigmōd the one weary in spirit	wyrde destiny	wiþstondan withstand
Row 2		
hrēo troubled	hyge spirit	helpe aid (here, used as a noun)
Row 3		
dōmgeorne those eager for judgement	drēorigne sadness	oft often
Row 4		
brēostcofan breast-box	bindaþ carry	fæste . . . securely

Comment on Exercise 5.3.1

The first two words in each row alliterate in some way, while the third word in each row – with one interesting exception – appears not to alliterate with the preceding two stressed syllables of the respective preceding words.

Take Row 2: *hrēo – hyge – helpe.* All three are lexical words, and in each the initial (i.e. the root-initial) syllable bears stress (indeed, *hrēo* is a lexical monosyllable). Therefore alliteration occurs regularly on /h/.

Row 3 is more complex: *dōmgeorne – drēorigne – oft.* It seems fairly clear that whatever its stressedness or otherwise, *oft* (the adverb 'often') doesn't alliterate with any syllable of the preceding two words. That leaves *dōmgeorne – drēorigne.* For the first word, we might translate it as 'judgement-eager' – *dōm + georn(e)* – or 'those eager for judgement' in our working translation. It's a compound word and, as such, bears the normal compound stress pattern of primary + secondary:

```
/      \   x
dōm + georn(e)
```

Now look at *drēorigne*. This word has the morphological composition root + affix + affix. Neither of the affixes *-ig-* or *-ne* bears as much stress as the root-initial syllable; this itself bears primary stress. Therefore, in this row, *oft* doesn't alliterate at all, and it's just the initial syllables of ***dōm**georne* and ***drēor**igne* which alliterate.

Row 1 provides an even more interesting case. The first pair of words alliterate uncontroversially on /w/. That leaves *wiþstondan*, withstand, or resist. It's a verb, here in the 3rd person. And equally clearly, this verb has the morphological composition prefix + root + suffix, where the prefix is *wiþ* and the root *stand(-an)*: [wiþ[stand + an]]. As expected, it's the (initial) syllable of the root that receives stress, while the prefix doesn't receive any stress *despite being initial in the word*.

Now let's look at the lines of verse from which we took the words of the above exercise. They're a fragment from a well-known OE poem that scholarship has come to know as *The Wanderer*. The poem is found – untitled – in the manuscript collection known as *The Exeter Book*. As with many OE poems, it's difficult to date. Some patterns of imagery in the poem suggest a very early, even a pre-Christian, date of first composition. But then again, the distinct, and distinctive, Christian colouring in the text – with the narrator of the poem waiting for, and contemplating, what seems undeniably to be Christian revelation and 'grace' – strongly suggests a later, and clearly post-Conversion, date of composition. Whatever the case, the poem, an example of an OE elegy, was quite possibly already old by the time it was committed to parchment.

As before, we've indicated which syllables alliterate with 'a'. Syllables that are stressed – whether primary or secondary stressed – but don't alliterate are marked with 'x':

Ne mæg **w**ērigmōd	**w**yrde wiþstondan
a x	a x
ne se **h**rēo **h**yge	**h**elpe gefremman
a a	a x
Forþon **d**ōmgeorne	**d**rēorigne oft
a x	a x
in hyra **b**rēostcofan	**b**indaþ fæste . . .
a x	a x

(from *The Wanderer*, lines 15–18)

Trans.: 'Nor can the weary spirit withstand destiny, nor the troubled mind bring about help. Therefore those eager for judgement (glory?) [*dōmgeorne*] often bind sadness in their breasts . . .'

5.4 How half-lines end: poetic closure in OE

One of the regularities of metrical verse is that the relevant metrical domains of such verse – the lines or half-lines – *end in predictable ways*. If you think of the kinds of verse most familiar to you, it's probable that these kinds of verse include syllable-counting and rhymed verse-forms – perhaps sonnets, or rhymed odes in the English tradition, or octosyllabic, rhymed verse. One function of line-end rhymes is precisely to act as line-end markers: rhyme is, among other things, a *demarcative* device. It tells the reader or listener when the metrical constituents, the lines, of the verse begin and end. Further, such rhyming syllables are very often linguistically stressed. Occasionally, linguistically unstressed syllables are matched (rhymed) with linguistically stressed syllables, as in the following construct:

The Dean was sure to make a **fuss**	(*fuss*: stressed, lexical monosyllable)
about the School's new sylla**bus**	(*-bus*: linguistically unstressed)

Nevertheless the pattern of much familiar post-Conquest verse is that of regularity of number-of-syllables-per-line, plus end-rhyme, where the rhymed lines may fall into couplets (as in the above construct), or into larger groupings that we may have come to know as *stanzas*. One key point about such kinds of verse is that rhyme is a good instance of an apparently universal principle of *poetic closure*: metrical domains are demarcated by extra regularities obtaining at the end of each metrical unit (each line or, as in the case of Germanic alliterative verse, each half-line).

Line-end rhyme, and stanzas, play no part in classical OE metrical organisation. However, OE verse, precisely because it is verse, participates in the apparently universal feature of poetic closure: its half-lines end in predictable, and determinative, ways. To be sure, they don't end in the stressed thump of rhyming syllables – this is for a later tradition of verse-making – and so the constructive principles we're after may be slightly more difficult to spot. But they do most certainly exist.

Exercise 5.4.1

To make these principles of closure clear, study the half-lines both of the *Hymn* and of the fragmentary text from *The Wanderer*. Can you spot the regularities occurring at the end of each half-line? The regularities most clearly involve the stressedness, or otherwise, of the final syllable in each half-line.

The *Hymn*

Nū sculon herigean	heofonrīces Weard,
Meotodes meahte	ond his mōdgeþanc,
weorc Wuldorfæder,	swā hē wundra gehwæs,

ēce Drihten, ōr onstealde.
Hē ærest scēop eorðan bearnum
heofon tō hrōfe, hālig Scyppend.
Þā middangeard monncynnes Weard,
ēce Drihten, æfter tēode
fīrum foldan, Frea ælmihtig

The Wanderer (fragment)

Ne mæg wērigmōd wyrde wiþstondan
ne se hrēo hyge helpe gefremman
Forþon dōmgeorne drēorigne oft
in hyra brēostcofan bindaþ fæste . . .

Comment on Exercise 5.4.1

Let's take each half-line in turn, running through both texts. For each half-line, we'll state whether the final syllable is fully stressed ('stressed'), secondary stressed ('2-stressed') or unstressed ('weak'):

Nū sculon herigean	*-an*, weak
heofonrīces Weard	*Weard*, stressed
Meotodes meahte	*-te*, weak
ond his mōdgeþanc	*-þanc*, 2-stressed (2nd element of compound)
weorc Wuldorfæder	*-der*, weak (but see also Section 5.5)
swā hē wundra gehwæs	*-hwæs*, stressed
ēce Drihten,	*-ten*, weak
ōr onstealde	*-de*, weak
Hē ærest scēop	*scēop*, stressed
eorðan bearnum	*-num*, weak
heofon tō hrōfe	*-fe*, weak
hālig Scyppend	*-pend*, weak (*-pend* is a suffix)
Þā middangeard	*-geard*, 2-stressed (2nd element of compound)
monncynnes Weard	see *Weard* above
ēce Drihten,	*-ten*, weak, see above
æfter tēode	*-de*, weak
fīrum foldan	*-dan*, weak
Frea ælmihtig	*-tig*, weak
Ne mæg wērigmōd	*-mōd*, 2-stressed (2nd element of compound)
wyrde wiþstondan	*-dan*, weak
ne se hrēo hyge	*-ge*, weak
helpe gefremman	*-man*, weak
Forþon dōmgeorne	*-ne*, weak
drēorigne oft	*oft*, stressed
in hyra brēostcofan	*-fan*, weak (but see also Section 5.5)
bindaþ fæste . . .	*-te*, weak

The regularity we're looking for is as follows: half-lines apparently end on a stressed syllable **or** on one, and only one, unstressed syllable. It doesn't matter whether the domain-final stressed syllable is primary or secondary stressed – we've found both types in the data we've just covered. Yet if the half-line ends on a weak syllable, it's fairly clear that there can be *only one* such syllable in half-line-final position.

5.5 Resolution

Resolution is a verse-specific feature of OE and, furthermore, a feature grounded in the phonological structures of OE, specifically, in the structures we've adduced for the OE syllable.

To help explain this feature, first reconsider the phonological composition of lexical monosyllables. As we saw in Section 5.3, there's a limited relationship between syllabic heaviness and the stress we naturally find in the lexical monosyllables of OE (or PDE). That is, stress is attracted to heavy syllables. Recall also, again from Section 5.3, that for the purposes of calculating syllabic lightness or heaviness, Onsets were more or less irrelevant: what counted was just the number of segments – or more accurately, the number of 'x's associated with each segment – in the syllabic Rhyme. Stressed syllables in OE proved to contain a minimum of two x's. To make this clear, we repeat the syllable diagram of *ōr* we gave above.

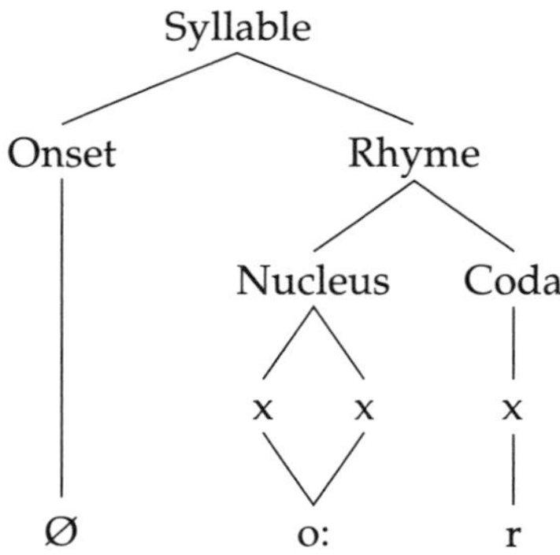

In this syllable, we get, as we expect, a minimum of two 'x's (there are in fact three, if we include, as we should, the x associated with the final consonant, since this too is in the Rhyme of the syllable).

Yet there's a class – a large class – of words for which our generalisation about stress and quantity is incorrect. Specifically, there are many polysyllables in OE where stress is root-initial – this we have come to expect – *but* where stress falls on a light syllable, not a heavy one. Examples of such words are *cyning*, king, *fæder*, father, and *biscop*, bishop.

Exercise 5.5.1

Taking the words *cyning*, king, *fæder*, father, and *biscop*, bishop, show why you think it's possible for us to claim that stress – word-initial in each case – falls on a light syllable.

Comment on Exercise 5.5.1

The answer lies in the *syllabification* of each word. In *cyning*, for instance, does the /n/ form part of the Rhyme of the first syllable, or part of the Onset of the second? In *fæder*, does the /d/ belong to the Rhyme of the first syllable, or to the Onset of the second? And in *biscop*, does the palatal fricative /ʃ/ belong to the Rhyme of the first syllable, or the Onset of the second?

In each case, such intervocalic consonants *form Onsets*. The general principle – it is in fact apparently a true linguistic universal – states that 'if you can make a well-formed Onset, do so'. In terms of building syllabic structure, languages love Onsets, and OE is no exception. We can symbolise this by using the dot, '.', to mark syllable divisions, and if we do this for our three specimen words, we come out with syllabifications as follows:

cy.ning
fæ.der
bi.scop

Notice that if you are to form an intervocalic Onset, in every case the Onset must be well-formed. So in a word such as *foldan*, the syllable division would not be **fo.ldan* (because **ld* would be an ill-formed Onset), but *fol.dan*.

If, for *cyning*, *fæder* and *biscop*, you now look at how many 'x's might be in the Rhyme of each initial syllable, there's only one, associated respectively with the vowels symbolised <y>, <æ> and <i>. All are short vowels, and associated, within their respective Rhymes, with just one 'x' apiece. Such syllables, then, are *light*. And yet they're also root-initial, and stressed.

As far as OE metre is concerned, the important observation is that under certain conditions, such light, stressed syllables *may function, and be distributed, in the metre, exactly as heavy, stressed syllables function and are distributed.*

How and why might this be so? Remember that heavy, stressed (mono)syllables minimally contain two 'x's in their Rhymes. Light, stressed syllables, though, only contain one 'x' in their Rhymes. So why the equivalence in phonological behaviour?

The solution seems to be that where the relevant syllabically light, stressed syllables occur in the half-line, they're invariably followed, in the same word, by an unstressed syllable. If you look again at our three examples, *cyning*, *fæder* and *biscop*, you'll see that this is so. In each case, the short, stressed syllable is followed by a syllable containing a short vowel (in the *-ning* of *cyning*, the *-der* of *fæder*, and the *-scop* of *biscop*). So there's one 'x' in the Rhyme of the initial syllable of such words, and (at least) one 'x' in the second syllable (the 'x' in the Nucleus of the unstressed syllable). And so for these words, we may reliably calculate *two* 'x's – one in the Rhyme of the stressed syllable, and one in the Rhyme (the Nucleus) of the unstressed syllable. If there are minimally *two* 'x's in words like *cyning, fæder* and *biscop,* and minimally *two* 'x's in words such as *ōr,* then you can see why we – and OE scops – might start to analyse such words as *equivalent* in structure. The equivalence is not a matter of stress. (Stress in words such as *cyning, fæder* and *biscop* is obviously not 'spread' across two syllables.) It's a matter of syllable weight.

This phenomenon, whereby the 'x's of unstressed syllables may contribute to the perceived metrical properties of a preceding short, stressed syllable, is technically known as *resolution.* By resolution, words (that is, word roots) such as *cyning, fæder* and *biscop* can function in OE verse 'as if' they're lexical monosyllables: they're said to be 'resolved sequences'.

To illustrate, take the word *herigean,* the last word of the first half-line of Cædmon's *Hymn.* Recall also that we claimed in our preceding section that OE half-lines ended in determinate ways, and that if a line ended on an unstressed syllable, there could only be *one* such syllable present half-line-finally. *Herigean* appears to provide a counter-example, because as well as the stressed, root-initial syllable, there's also the medial syllable, *-ri,* and the final syllable, *-gean.* Both are unstressed. (The <e> following the <g>, incidentally, is to be taken as a merely scribal gesture towards the palatal quality of the <g>; it doesn't form a vowel in its own right, and therefore could never provide the vocalic centre of a syllable; the relevant syllable is formed by *-g(e)an,* and is weakly stressed.) So on the face of it, such a half-line would appear to end on the sequence 'stressed heavy' + unstress + unstress – on '/ x x', a sequence debarred from half-line-final position.

Closer inspection, though, reveals that *heri-* is a resolved sequence (its syllabification is *he.ri-*), and thus functions in the verse equivalently to one stressed syllable containing two 'x's. 'By resolution', therefore, and as the scholarly saying is, *herigean* maps into two verse positions, one position occupied by the resolved sequence *heri-,* the other by the weak syllable *-gean.* By resolution, therefore – by the principle of syllabic equivalence we've introduced in this section – this half-line doesn't end '/ x x' but '/ x'. Linguistically, that is, *herigean* may contain *three syllables;* but metrically, and by resolution, it's enabled to occupy just *two positions* of a half-line.

5.6 The concept of metrical position in OE verse

We've begun to speak of the 'positions' of the OE half-line. What are these positions?

A *position* is, in our definition, a metrical entity, something specific just to verse. It's occupied by a stretch of linguistic material. In the simplest, indeed the prototypical case, each metrical position is occupied by exactly *one* syllable. Recall that we've seen something of the matching of syllables to positions already, in our work on how half-lines end: if, for instance, the half-line ends on an unstressed syllable, there's the special restriction there that there may be *only one* unstressed syllable in that position. A case in point is the half-line *ēce Drihten*, eternal Lord. Here, the syllable *-ten* is the one unstressed syllable at the end of the half-line.

In our view, the basic metrical structure of the half-line is most adequately described as being a set of *four positions*. Perhaps we can make this clear by looking again at our constructed lines from Section 5.1, before moving on to actual specimens of OE.

In the prototypical half-line, each position is filled by one, and exactly one, syllable, as in the construct

		/	/		/		/	
	The	**d**ay	**d**ar-	kens.	**D**reams	are	use-	less -
Position	1	2	3	4	1	2	3	4

Here, each half-line is filled by exactly four syllables (four positions). It's usually, though by no means invariably, the case that *two of the four positions contain stressed syllables*. These positions are sometimes, if traditionally, called the *lifts* of the half-line. If so, then it follows that the other two positions will contain unstressed syllables, the *dips* of the half-line – again, as in the example above: in the first half-line of our fragmentary construct, *the* and *-kens* are unstressed, in positions 1 and 4 respectively, and in the second half-line, *are* and *less* are unstressed, in positions 2 and 4 respectively.

Now take the half-line *ēce Drihten*, and apply the same kind of analysis. Again, as expected, the half-line turns out to be matched against exactly four positions, where each position is occupied by exactly one syllable:

	ē-	ce	Drih-	ten
Position	1	2	3	4

Our claim is that each normal half-line of OE verse – all classical OE verse, everywhere, of every period – is based on this four-position constraint. And in our view, *it's much more important for the metrical half-lines of OE to fulfil this constraint than it is for them to contain particular arrays of stressed and unstressed syllables*. Furthermore, for half-lines to be metrical (and not ill-formed), *it's far more important for them to fulfil constraints on what can occupy position 4 of the line than it is for them to fulfil any matching of stress and position elsewhere in the same half-line*. That is, what occupies position 4 must be some kind of stressed syllable, or it must be exactly one unstressed syllable.

This last constraint on the OE half-line is important because it may be aligned with what we know of the determination of metrical domains ('lines') in other languages. In every form of poetry studied so far, for example, it appears that special relationships hold at the ends of metrical constituents –

lines or half-lines. As we noted above, such special relationships demarcate each line, each constituent of the poetry, and among other things indicate to the listener where lines or half-lines begin and end. Yet if the end of the metrical constituent is highly constrained, the beginnings of metrical constituents can be relatively free. *Beginnings free, endings strict* is an apparently universal principle of metrical verse-making.

So we're developing three constraints on the construction of OE half-lines:

- a constraint on position: each half-line contains four metrical positions, each filled with linguistic material
- a constraint on endings: position 4 is invariably filled by some kind of stressed syllable, or with exactly one unstressed syllable
- 'beginnings free, endings strict'

Perhaps it's necessary yet again to emphasise that in our view it's more important for OE half-lines to fulfil these constraints than it is for them to contain particular arrays of stress. After all, we're constructing such constraints because they appear to have explanatory adequacy and allow us to think of OE verse-making not as some merely local phenomenon, but as a part of the universal grammar of poetry. And this, to us, is a more interesting approach to the problems.

Let's return to the 4-position half-line. It's immediately apparent that many OE half-lines contain far more than the prototypical four syllables. How do we match half-lines of more than four syllables against a metrical constraint that says 'half-lines must contain exactly four positions'?

To answer this we need to look at the behaviour of the lesser-stressed syllables, the dips, in each half-line. Dips can consist of one unstressed syllable, as in the examples we've just looked at, but they may also consist of up to three (less usually, four) unstressed syllables, while still counting as a single position. Here are some examples of metrical dips aligned with metrical positions (dips boldened and each position numbered below the line):

Forþon dōmgeorne
1 2 3 4

in hyra brēostcofan
1 2 3 4

or the following (a line you haven't studied, but again taken from *The Wanderer*)

hwær ic feor **oþþe** nēah findan meahte
1 2 3 4 1 2 3 4
where I might be able to find, far or near . . .

Each position may, then, be filled with *one or more* lesser-stressed syllables. Typically such syllables are articles, pronouns, prepositions, verbal prefixes, adverbials and other non-major-class words (i.e. they are in the class of function words). Even then, however, we haven't given a full explanation of the behaviour of dips in the OE half-line.

To help explain this, we'll do two things. One is to ask you to complete the following exercise. The other is to revise our terminology. For the *dips* of each half-line – each run of one or more unstressed syllables – we'll continue to use the symbol 'x'. For each primary *or* 2-stressed syllable that functions as accented in the half-line, we'll use the term 'Lift', and abbreviate this as 'L'. Notice that both primary and 2-stressed syllables can function as L (and there may well turn out to be other kinds of syllable that can function thus, though we haven't discussed them here).

With that slight revision in mind, we ask you to complete the following.

Exercise 5.6.1

If each OE half-line consists of four positions of which two may contain stressed syllables (L), while the remaining two contain lesser-stressed (or unstressed) syllables, what permutations of pattern are theoretically possible?

Comment on Exercise 5.6.1

One pattern might look like the following:

L x L x
1 2 3 4 (Dreams are useless; *ēce Drihten*)

This pattern is often dubbed **Type A** following the hugely influential work of the German philologist Eduard Sievers, who was the first scholar to codify the different Types of Germanic half-line in this particular way (Sievers, 1885). Statistically, this largely alternating pattern (on the definition of *alternation*, see below) was the most frequently occurring pattern of half-line. Note that it ends on *one unstressed position*.

Another kind of possible pattern is a reversal of the Type A pattern, and is known as **Type B**:

x L x L
1 2 3 4 (of mice and men; *Hē ærest scēop*)

Note that this pattern ends on *one stressed position*.

A further possibility is formed by a Type whose stresses are immediately adjacent (that is, the stresses clash). This we may call **Type C**:

x L L x (the day darkens; *ne se hrēo hyge*)
1 2 3 4

Again, note that this Type ends on one unstressed position. Note also that in the specimen of OE, *ne se hrēo hyge*, position 1 is filled by two unstressed syllables, not just one.

You'll apprehend by now that the reason behind our careful noting of how each half-line ends is that (i) half-lines are themselves metrical units, and (ii) as metrical units, we expect them *to end in predictable and determinate ways.*

5.7 Half-line patterns that never occur

There are other potential patterns of OE half-line. The first – possible, but utterly non-occurring in the OE poetic corpus – might look like the following:

```
*x  x  L  L
 1  2  3  4
```

Why doesn't this occur? Recall the remarks on unstressed syllables and their alignment with positions. Runs of adjacent weak syllables may be aligned with one position, rather than two. If we follow this principle through, the pattern 'x x L L' would be scanned as follows:

```
*x  x  L  L
 1     2  3
```

In other words, we'd have a half-line which was one short of the defining four positions, and would thus be unmetrical.

Exercise 5.7.1

Another potential half-line would be the following: / / x x. Such a pattern never occurs in classical OE verse. There are two reasons why this should be so. What are they?

Comment on Exercise 5.7.1

First, there's the same problem we noted above. Such a half-line could be scanned as containing only three positions:

```
*L  L  x  x
 1  2    3
```

Second, and more damagingly, we noted that half-lines end in determinate ways. They may end on a stressed position, or on *one and only one* unstressed syllable. Our potential line ends on two unstressed syllables and thus violates the principles of metrical *closure.*

One of the issues we've been looking at is the behaviour of unstressed syllables within the OE half-line. The position and number of such unstressed syllables is important for defining the metricality of the half-line. They are not mere fillers.

We can actually go further in analysing the behaviour of dips in OE, as Cable (1991) was the first to observe. Consider the Type B pattern, x L x L. Following the principle that dip positions may consist of more than one weak syllable, it is predicted that Type B lines such as the following would occur freely:

```
x  x  x  L  x  L
1        2  3  4    (Position 1 expanded)

x  L  x  x  x  L
1  2  3        4    (Position 3 expanded)
```

Such patterns do indeed occur. The problem is that lines such as the following, which our developing theory predicts *should* occur, rarely if ever do occur in OE:

```
*x  x  L  x  x  x  x  L
 1     2  3           4    (Expansion of Positions 1 and 3)

*x  x  x  x  L  x  x  L
    1        2  3     4    (Expansion of Positions 1 and 3)
```

Expansion of dip positions 1 *and* 3 is apparently disallowed in classical OE verse: *either* dip position 1 may be expanded, *or* dip position 3, but not both. Again the relevant pattern of *metrical constraint* involves unstressed syllables. We could state this particular constraint as 'only one expansion allowed per half-line', and add it to the list of constraints we're establishing:

- a constraint on position: each half-line contains four metrical positions, each filled with linguistic material
- a constraint on endings: position 4 is invariably filled by some kind of stressed syllable, or with exactly one unstressed syllable
- 'beginnings free, endings strict'
- only one expansion per half-line

Here are some examples of expanded dips from OE:

```
 x  x    /  x  /       /     \    /  x
siþþan geāra iū     goldwine mīnne
   1     2  3  4    1     2     3  4
```

(since long ago my gold-friend; expanded dip in position 1 of first half-line)

```
Đonne sorg ond slǣp     somod ætgædere
  1     2   3    4        1   2  3    4
```

(whenever sorrow and sleep, both together; expanded dip in position 1 of first half-line)

A more complex example is formed by *The Battle of Maldon* (late 10th century), line 268:

Hē ne wan**dode** nā   **æt þæm** wīgplegan
1   2   3   4   1   2   3 4
(He didn't hesitate at all in the battle-play)

In the first half-line, it looks as if both dips in positions 1 and 3 have been expanded. But the dip in position 1 is formed by the subject pronoun and the negative particle *ne*. If, like scholars such as Russom (1987), we view negative particles as extrametrical (i.e. invisible to metrical parsing), then *ne* is here unavailable to the scansion and the dip is formed simply by the syllable *Hē* – in which case we have an unexpanded dip in position 1 and an expanded one in position 3. (On derivative morphemes such as the past tense affix *-od(e)*, see further under Section 5.9.)

So far, we've analysed three prototypical half-line patterns, Types A, B, and C. For the sake of completion, here are the commonest forms of two further patterns, Types D and E, exemplified from the great OE epic poem, *Beowulf*:

- **Type D**
  (a) L L L x (safe sky-scraper; *ymbsittendra*, dwellers-about, *Beowulf* 9b)
  (b) L L x L (men's locker-room; *fæder ellor hwearf*, (his) father had departed elsewhere, *Beowulf* 55b)
  1 2 3 4
- **Type E**
  L L x L (sky-scrapers soar; *monncynnes Weard*)
  1 2 3 4

These Types are different from Types A–C in that they contain three, rather than two, lifts (L). However, it seems to be the case that in Types D and E we have to recognise patterns of 2-stresses working co-operatively with the stronger, primary stressed syllable(s) of the half-line. Even so, it's analytically rather difficult for us to distinguish Type E (L L x L) from the (b) variant of Type D (also L L x L), and the main reason that in the present context we do so distinguish these (sub)Types is largely, but merely, a respectful gesture towards Sievers, and to tradition. That said, there *is* a different disposition of primary and 2-stress configurations working in Type D (b) and Type E. (Can you work out what the difference is?)

5.8 The Five Types

At this point we've introduced what in traditional terms are the Five Types of metrical OE half-line that have been familiar to students since Sievers. We've also introduced some of the constraints that restrict the construction of each unit. Here's a reminder of those constraints, to which we've added a note – which is at this point a mere stipulation – about extrametrical (unscanned) material. This is followed by a list of the Types we've introduced, using our notation L for any syllable that is both linguistically stressed and functions as an accent within the half-line:

- a constraint on position: each half-line contains four metrical positions, each filled with linguistic material
- a constraint on endings: position 4 is invariably filled by some kind of stressed syllable, or with exactly one unstressed syllable
- 'beginnings free, endings strict'
- only one expansion per half-line . . . usually
- verbal prefixes, the prefix *ge-* and the negative particle *ne* may be extrametrical

- **Type A**

  L x L x
  1 2 3 4

  NB: constraints predict that only one position (position 2) of this half-line can be expanded. Position 4 can never be expanded.

- **Type B**

  x L x L
  1 2 3 4

  NB: constraints predict that position 4 can *never* be followed by any lesser-stressed syllable; they also predict that positions 1 *or* 3 may be expanded, but not both within the same half-line.

- **Type C**

  x L L x
  1 2 3 4

  NB: constraints predict that position 1 (only) may be expanded; position 4 may *never* be expanded.

- **Type D**

  (a) L L L x
  (b) L L x L
  1 2 3 4

- **Type E**

  L L x L
  1 2 3 4

  NB: Type D(b) and E could theoretically be collapsed into a single Type.

Exercise 5.8.1

Study the following passage (from *The Battle of Maldon*, written in, or very soon after, 991), and identify as many Types of half-line as you can.

Partly because of the relatively late date of composition you'll notice some problems and/or anomalies. Make a note of them for discussion.

Wōdon þā wælwulfas	(for wætere ne murnon)
1 2 3 4	1 2 3 4
wīcinga werod	west ofer Pantan
12 3 4	1 2 3 4
ofer scīr wæter	scyldas wǣgon
1 2 3 4	1 2 3 4
lidmen tō lande	linde brohton
1 2 3 4	1 2 3 4
'The slaughter-wolves advanced – the troop of vikings over the bright water the sea-men to land	they didn't care about the water – westward across the Blackwater, bore their shields, brought their linden shields'

Comment on Exercise 5.8.1

Because we wish to discuss some more urgent difficulties, we're going to do no more here than list a summary of the problems you may have encountered in completing the above exercise. The problems in Exercise 5.8.1 come about, we assume, not through poetic incompetence but because of the late date at which *Maldon* was composed (AD 991). By this time, perhaps some of the true classical principles of OE verse-making had been lost; or perhaps the vernacular was changing (indeed, it *was* changing) so that the relationship between language and verse was becoming compromised. Whatever the case, here's a summary of some of the snags you may have encountered:

Wōdon Þā wælwulfas	too much linguistic material to fill 4 positions? Is alliteration on /w/ of *Wōdon* accidental, or structural?
(for wætere ne murnon)	looks like an A-Type, with resolution on *wætere*, but there's an extra unstressed syllable half-line-initially
wīcinga werod	*werod* would be a candidate for resolution, but either resolution must be suspended here (to give an A-Type half-line) or you must allow resolution and (therefore) take the *-ing-* of *wīcinga* to be 2-stressed. This last tactic would be synchronically unlikely.
west ofer Pantan	standard A-Type half-line, with expanded position 2
ofer scīr wæter	a C-Type, but with suspension of possible resolution in *wæter*

scyldas wǣgon	standard A-Type half-line
lidmen tō lande	a standard A-Type? but only if *-men* of *lidmen* doesn't bear secondary stress (cf. PDE proper name *Goodman*)
linde brohton	standard A-Type half-line

5.9 Secondary stress, metrical position and 'L'

Some of the problems you encountered just now concern secondary stress – 2-stress, in our terminology. Syllables that bear 2-stress in OE are most clearly the second elements of compound nouns, though even here, some compounds might be analysed as 'obscured compounds', with weak second elements. 'Obscured compounds' seem to have lost the semantic transparency that normally obtains between the two elements of the compound word – for example, *filing cabinet* is a *cabinet* for *filing*, a *lawn mower* is something that *mows* the *lawn*. But the word *woman* is in fact an obscured compound (notice the pronunciation, with schwa in the second syllable) that derives from *wīf* + *mann*, and our word *lord* derives from the original compound *hlāf* + *weard*, bread-protector. This compound gradually obscures, and even in OE is regularly found as *hlaford*. However, in the process of obscuration it loses whatever secondary stress it might once have had on its second syllable.

This notwithstanding, it's clear that the (stressed syllable of the) second elements of OE compounds are candidates for secondary stress, and thus may be capable of functioning as lifts, L, in the half-line.

The problem is that there are other kinds of syllable, not nearly so obvious candidates for 2-stress, that also apparently *function* as 2-stress, and therefore are candidates for L. Take the following half-line, from *Beowulf*:

Swā rīxode   in this way he ruled, *Beowulf* 144a
  1 2 3 4

We can't simply say that the two syllables *-ode* are both unstressed, because this would violate one of our central constraints on the construction of the half-line, namely that if the half-line ends on 'x', there can be only one 'x' in position 4. If we analysed *-ode* as spanning two unstressed syllables, then (i) the half-line would be one short of the obligatory minimum 4 positions (because positions 3 and 4 would coalesce into a single position) and (ii) we'd violate a very high-ranked constraint, which is at least undesirable.

Therefore let's look again at the *-od-* of *-ode*. Historically, this syllable was in fact heavy, in that it contained a long vowel, and thus was at least capable of attracting stress. Various linguistic studies have suggested that heavy syllables like this, particularly when they belong to a particular morphological class, may indeed carry (underlying) stress. *-od-* does in fact belong to a morphological class of the right kind – it's a suffix, and part of a Class II weak verb – and, apparently, such suffixes attracted linguistic stress sufficient for them to function as L in the metrical scheme. Therefore we might choose to analyse *Swā rīxode* like this:

```
  x  L L  x
Swā rīxode
  1  2 3  4
```

Of the two L's, the second is weaker than the first, and the half-line pans out as a relatively uncontroversial C-Type.

There are other derivative syllables (in the simplest case, suffixes) that apparently behave like the *-od-* of *-ode-*. One is the suffix *-ing*. Take first another half-line from *Beowulf, Oft Scyld Scēfing* (*Beo.* 4a). You'd analyse this as a standard C-Type, right, with the *-ing* syllable unstressed and in position 4 of the half-line?

```
x     L     Lx
Oft Scyld Scēfing     Often Scyld Scefing [proper name]
1     2     34
```

Exercise 5.9.1

That's fine. But now take another half-line from *Beowulf*, this time *hū þā æþelingas*, how those princes (*Beo.* 3a). If we take *hū þā* to be relatively unstressed syllables occupying position 1, and if we allow resolution to apply on the initial two syllables of *æþelingas*, then that just leaves *-lingas*. Could we analyse these two syllables as merely unstressed?

Comment on Exercise 5.9.1

No – and for exactly the same reasons that we found in analysis of *Swā rīxode*. To allow any half-line to end on two x's is a constraint violation, and to do so would also give us an unmetrical half-line lacking an obligatory metrical position. Therefore, it seems better to take the problematic syllable *-(l)ing-* as stressed – 2-stressed – in this environment. Then we could analyse the relevant half-line as follows:

```
 x  x  L  L  x
hū þā æþelingas
    1   2  3  4
```

Notice that some of these derivative syllables are Janus-faced: sometimes they function as unstressed and sometimes they function as 2-stressed.

This variable functioning apparently depends on their position in the word: when they're followed by an inflection, they carry 2-stress; when they're in absolute word-finality, they're unstressed. This in fact gives us an important clue not only to the linguistic *stress* system of OE (and other Germanic languages of our period) but also to the *metrical* system of OE. Two principles seem to be on offer.

1. *Secondary stress*: 2-stress may be found in the following environments:
   - the (stressed syllable of the) second elements of compounds
   - derivative (and historically heavy) syllables such as the Class-markers for Class II weak verbs (*-od-*, plus, for good measure, the Class-marker *-i-*: *luf-i-an*, to love, past tense *lufode*, *rix-i-an*, to rule, past tense *rīxode*)
2. *2-stress and metrical L*: 2-stressed syllables may function as L in the verse, provided that such syllables:
   - occupy a metrical position, and
   - *are adjacent to a weaker syllable and position in the same half-line*

   It's that last, italicised clause that seems crucial. In fact, we'd go further and claim that for *any* syllable, or syllable configuration, to function as L, that L must be directly adjacent to some weaker syllable *in the same half-line*. In this way, the properties of L fairly clearly mimic what's going on 'in' the language. For a syllable, or syllable configuration, to be perceived as linguistically prominent, it's most clearly so perceived when it's adjacent to some weaker syllable. And, apparently, it's worthwhile thinking of this linguistic principle as being captured in the metrical, the verse-specific, system of OE.

   Yet this view has a further logical, and equally important, consequence:
3. *Stress- and L-adjacency in OE*
   - For any pair of directly adjacent stresses in OE, where those stresses lie within the same morphological domain, the second is weaker than the first
   - For any pair of adjacent L's in OE verse, where those L's lie within the same half-line, the second is weaker than the first

To make this clearer, try completing the following exercise.

Exercise 5.9.2

Half-lines with the morphological composition [compound] + [compound] occur frequently in OE. An example – again from *Beowulf* – is *guðrinc goldwlanc* (gold-proud warrior, or, warrior proudly adorned with gold, *Beo.* 1881a). Which syllables here bear linguistic secondary stress? And how do those syllables function in the verse, bearing in mind the principle of Stress and L-adjacency?

Comment on Exercise 5.9.2

In each case, the second member of the respective compounds is entirely capable of bearing linguistic secondary stress. But what happens to such syllables in the poetry? For any syllable to function as L, it must be adjacent to some lesser-stressed syllable, and in both cases, *-rinc* and *-wlanc* are adjacent to *more strongly stressed syllables*. Therefore, if our statement on stress and L-adjacency is correct, such syllables cannot function as L in the verse. Instead, and despite carrying *linguistic* 2-stress, they behave in the verse just like ordinary weak-stressed positions, that is, they function like this

```
L x L x
1 2 3 4
```

and not like this

```
*L L L L
 1 2 3 4
```

But there's another consequence, possibly of even more structural weight. We've claimed that for any pair of adjacent stresses within the same domain, the first is stronger than the second. This helps us to explain a problem we temporarily abandoned at an earlier point in this unit. Recall the configuration of Types D and E. There were two variants of Type D – LLLx and LLxL – while Type E had the configuration LLxL. On this analysis, Type E and the second variant of Type D are both LLxL. Is there anything that would distinguish them?

The difference is partly a matter of morphology, partly a matter of stress- and L-adjacency. The Type E pattern has the typical (morphological) configuration [[LLx]L], while the second variant of Type D has the typical configuration [L[LxL]]. Examples might make this difference clear:

- **Type D**, second variant [L[LxL]]
  [weorc [Wuldor-fæder]]
  1 2 3 4 Position 4 = \ by resolution

- **Type E** [[LLx]L]
  [[heofonrīces] Weard]
  1 23 4 Position 1 = / by resolution

We might also observe something about Type C that follows from our principles and constraints. We have notated this Type as 'x L L x', with two directly adjacent L's. In terms of the stress and linguistics of half-lines of this Type, it doesn't matter whether the second L is some kind of primary stressed syllable, or a 2-stress, since both are followed by the weaker (unstressed) syllable in position 4 and are therefore capable of functioning as L:

- **Type C** configurations

```
x      L     Lx
Oft Scyld Scēfing        (Scēfing linguistically [/ x])
1     2      3 4

  x  L L  x
Swā rīxode               (-ode linguistically [\ x])
  1  2 3  4
```

5.10 Stress, L and alliteration

One of the puzzling features about the alliteration we find in classical OE verse is that the final L of the long line – the final L of the second half-line – never alliterates. That is, and again using the short-hand notation 'aa:ax' to indicate alliterating L's, the characteristic alliterative pattern of OE verse is as follows:

- *Characteristic alliterative patterning in the long line*

```
[....L.....L.]    [....L   L.]
     a     a           a   x
```

However, there's a significant, and common, variant on this basic pattern. Often, it's just the *first* L of the first half-line, and the *first* L of the second, that alliterate – an 'ax:ax' pattern rather than the standard 'aa:ax':

- *Variant alliterative patterning in the long line*

```
[....L.....L.]    [....L   L.]
     a     x           a   x
```

Can we explain this?

Following some brilliant research by Russom (1987, 1998) we can use some of the constraints and principles we've already examined to explain both kinds of alliterative patterning. Russom develops a theory of OE (indeed, in his later work, of Germanic) metrics rather different to the sketch we've provided here, and there are clear differences between our approaches. However, Russom has also provided some of the most linguistically cogent work on alliterative form we've seen, and his research is full of interest. One of the features of his 1987 monograph, for example (and a claim developed for Germanic in the 1998 work), is his claim that the half-lines of OE verse 'mimic' the behaviour of linguistic compounds. In fact, many of the lines we've examined *are* compounds, with that characteristic 'falling' stress pattern. Such patterns are predicted in our own constraints and principles, notably in the 'adjacency' principle. But Russom goes further, and claims that the long line itself behaves rather like a massive compound, with strongest prominence at its *left* edge, i.e. within the (first element of the) first half-line.

To capture this, we need to view the half-lines, and the long line, as *hierarchical* constructs, not just linear arrays of stresses, unstresses, Lifts and weak positions. In the following diagram, for example, we claim that the first L of a half-line is stronger than the second L. Therefore S stands for 'stronger than' and W for 'weaker than':

- *Relative strength of elements within the half-line*

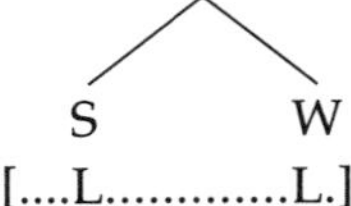

We can adopt the same notation for the long line:

- *Relative strength of elements within the long line*

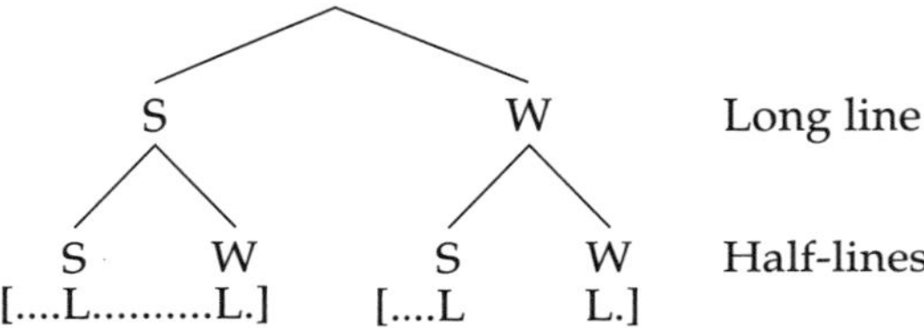

And from this, it's but a small analytical footstep to the following two claims:

- *Alliteration and relative strength in OE*
  - A weak position within a weak position can never alliterate
  - Alliteration migrates to the strongest positions within each half-line

If you look carefully at the last diagram, can you find the 'weak position within a weak position'? Right – it's the very final L of the entire line. Following Russom's work, of which we provide the crudest of summaries here, we predict that it's exactly and precisely this L that will *never* alliterate. And for many thousands of lines of the OE poetic corpus, this is just what we do find.

Then there's the claim that alliteration migrates to the strongest positions it can find within the half-line, bearing in mind that half-lines are behaving rather like linguistic compounds, with strongest prominence towards their leftmost edges.

Look again at both diagrams above. The fact that alliteration falls quite regularly on the *strongest* (S) positions of each half-line is easily detectable. But what about the second L of the first half-line? This is W – weaker than the first L of the half-line, which is labelled S. But critically, this W-labelled position is itself part of a S(trong) constituent of the entire line, and thus may readily alliterate: it's not a 'weak position within a weak position'.

Summary

Structure, constituency – and hierarchy. In our view, these are three key principles of OE metre, existing within a close relationship between the fabric of the language (both its morphological and phonological fabric) and the form of its intricately constructed verse. It's observing this relationship, between language and verse form, that helps us to explain not only why this verse is so wonderfully adapted to the language out of which it's written, but also helps us to explain its durability (a set of clear principles had been found by which language could become high art) . . . And, not least, it helps us to explain 'the miracle of Cædmon'. After all, you might think that the material in this unit has been 'technical' or 'complex' and, in truth, some parts of the analysis we've offered are tricky, while some are controversial – though all are testable. However tricky or controversial, it's a salutary thought to remember that an unlettered animal husbandman from Whitby, living towards the end of the 7th century, mastered the principles and the constraints of OE verse in a single night.

Study questions

1. There are some relatively unusual metrical half-lines that we've not examined in this Unit. One is the Type of half-line that Sievers analysed as 'D*'. This has the shape [[L x] [L L x]] or [[L x] [L x L]. It differs from the normal D Type half-lines by having an extra unstressed position after the first L, and is apparently the only half-line to allow 5 positions. See if you can find any examples in the readings we've set for this unit, and then try to explain why a 5-position half-line might be permissible. There will be no clear answers, but one clue might lie in one of our constraints: *beginnings free, endings strict*.
2. There are some unstressed syllables that never bear linguistic stress, nor function as L. Among these are the prefix *ge-* and the negative particle *ne*. Russom (1987, 1998) claims that these syllables are extrametrical in the verse, and this is a claim we'd support. Using examples from our exercises and readings in this unit, or better, from new material you've collected yourself, try to find examples of half-lines that contain these syllables, and verify that they may behave as extrametrical.
3. One of the apparent peculiarities of the OE stress system is that prefixes on verbs are unstressed, whereas noun prefixes bear linguistic stress. Examples are *aweallan*, to well up (verb) vs. *æwielm*, fountain (noun), or *onsacan*, deny (verb) vs. *andsaca*, apostate. What reasons might there be for this linguistic behaviour?
4. There are many half-lines where resolution is apparently 'suspended'. You will find several examples in the exercises and reading for this unit. What reasons might there be for 'suspending' resolution? And are

there any environments in which resolution is obligatorily suspended? (Hint: look at the heaviness or otherwise of the syllable that precedes the string in which resolution is suspended.)

5. Many scholars have suggested that OE poetry is full of *formulas*. Formulas are ready-made pieces of language, of the right linguistic and metrical shape, that may be inserted into any correctly made OE poem. Examples from Cædmon's *Hymn* might be half-lines such as *ēce Drihten*, everlasting Lord. This half-line – metrically, an A Type – could apply to any lord, secular or temporal, and thus could be inserted at will into almost any praise-poem. It's arguable that OE *scops* – and particularly, the Germanic scops of the pre-literate tradition – had a mental stock of these formulas. In your reading, have you found any other pieces of language that have been replicated from poem to poem? Or, if your reading in OE isn't yet extensive, can you identify half-lines that, metrically and thematically, might be useful to a poet as formulas?
6. OE poetry derives from a pre-literate tradition. Verse, and verse-making, were exclusively oral, and therefore the knowledge of both poetry, and how to make poetry, would be passed orally from generation to generation. What kinds of principles – we might call them 'constraints' – would an aspiring poet have to learn in order to be able, apparently spontaneously, to compose hundreds of well-formed lines in his native language?
7. OE poetry was written out in manuscript margin to margin (parchment was expensive). The familiar division into lines and half-lines is a matter of editorial intervention, though in some OE manuscripts there is a (usually inconsistent) form of punctuation, or pointing, that separates one half-line from another. Imagine you are an editor of OE poetry confronting an original manuscript that has never been studied before. On what grounds would you decide 'this is verse, not prose'? And how would you begin to find the half-lines of the poem you were editing?
8. Looking ahead to Unit 7, we will read and study a later form of literary composition that scholarship has come to know as 'rhythmical prose'. This form was apparently pioneered by Ælfric at the beginning of the 11th century, though it was also employed by others, notably Archbishop Wulfstan of York. What linguistic features exist in OE as a pre-condition for the writing of such rhythmical prose? If you were to begin writing rhythmical prose in OE – or in PDE – how would you set about it? And how would you convince your listeners that such prose was even more rhythmical than 'normal' English?
9. Why, throughout this unit, have we made a distinction between the terms 'stress' and 'lift' (L)?
10. Many commentators argue that alliteration in OE verse is a *structural* property of that verse. We believe that alliteration is merely an interesting

ornament, a kind of superficial decoration – in the same way that rhyme sometimes functions as a superficial decoration of the later pentameter line. Is alliteration a structural property of OE verse? Or just an interesting ornament? Which view is better justified?

Websites that you may find useful

To date we've been unable to find websites on this topic that are both comprehensive and reliable, and certainly there are none that develop the kind of analysis we've offered in this unit.

References and suggestions for further reading

The prime source for any work on OE metre is still Sievers. Sievers' two great essays on OE alliterative poetry first appeared in 1885, while his monograph on alliterative verse in the Germanic language family appeared in 1893. Unfortunately, these works have never been fully or usefully translated into English. There are, however, summaries of Sievers' analysis in Mitchell and Robinson (1992, Appendix C, pp.161–167). An important and interesting recent theory of OE, OHG, OS and ON alliterative verse is that of Russom (1987, and particularly, 1998), while one of the most important recent monographs on the form and development of OE verse is Fulk (1992). Neither Russom's nor Fulk's work is for the beginning student, but both richly repay study – and among other things, Fulk gives the most convincing demonstration of how the great epic *Beowulf* might be dated that we have ever seen.

On *Beowulf*, no scholar can do better than to use Klaeber's great edition of the poem (1950). His introductory material also includes quite full remarks on the metre of the poem. An invaluable resource.

Of other recent scholarship, Cable (1991) looks at OE verse and its relationship with alliterative writing in Middle English. Cable was the first to spot constraints on dips within the OE half-line, and his work is full of acuity and interest. The essays collected in McCully and Anderson, eds. (1996) are also devoted to OE and ME verse and verse-making, and include contributions from Russom, Cable, and other distinguished scholars.

Unit Six

Standards and crosses

Poetry is a wind which bloweth where it listeth: a barbaric people may have great poetry, they cannot have great prose. Prose is an institution, part of the equipment of a civilisation, part of its heritable wealth, like its laws, or its system of schooling, or its tradition of skilled craftsmanship.

J.S. Phillimore, *Dublin Review* CLIII (1913:8). Quoted by R.W. Chambers (1932) *The continuity of English prose from Alfred to More and his School.* [Early English Text Society vol. 191A]

6.0 Poetry and prose

In this unit we're going to introduce you to some more OE prose, and also look (in Section 6.6) at a short excerpt from a justly renowned poem that has come to be known as 'The Dream of the Rood' (*rood* < OE *rōd*, cross). Both topics are, perhaps surprisingly, linked.

Although English prose had of course been composed before the 9th century, it had typically been written at need, more or less sporadically, and for either Christian or utilitarian or administrative, purposes. In the former category are items like sermons (many of which have not survived); in the last are things like wills and charters. In the 9th century, though, and in particular under the inspiration and aegis of Alfred, King of Wessex (reigned 871–899), vernacular prose is written more purposefully – one might even say, more systematically. From this period come the first of the great translations of parts of the Bible; there come saints' *Lives*, homilies; other translations; historical narratives in the form of chronicles (including the beginnings of the *Anglo-Saxon Chronicle*); there is even travel literature. As Alfred himself put it, in a passage we'll study in this unit, it seemed vital to him that freeborn Anglo-Saxons had access to books that 'nīedbeðearfosta sīen eallum monnum tō wiotonne' – books that it would be most needful (*nīedbeðearfosta*) for all men to know. Under Alfred's leadership, vernacular prose, written in what became a standard literary language, that of *West Saxon* (WS), becomes the medium through which a whole cultural programme is enacted.

How does this link with 'The Dream of the Rood'? The language of the written text of the *Dream* is again West Saxon, though it's a WS that, like much of the poetry of the period, shows marked Anglian (crudely, at this stage, Northern and/or Midland) characteristics. But we need to think about this: (i) how do we know that the language of a particular text is 'West Saxon' (as opposed to Mercian, Northumbrian or Kentish)? And (ii) how can we identify 'Anglian' colouring in what is otherwise a piece of West Saxon?

Behind these philological puzzles is a further, and somewhat deeper, question: how does a 'standard language' emerge in any culture? What kind of 'standard' do we mean? With WS, we're dealing with a *written* standard language, not a spoken one – but what are the pre-conditions for the emergence of a written standard? Are they linguistic pre-conditions? Or cultural ones? Or is language so inseparable from 'culture' that such a question ultimately makes no sense?

For Alfred, and on his own testimony, language and 'culture' did seem inseparable. By insisting on that linkage (through developing learning and literacy in the vernacular), he not only played one of the leading roles in the programme of cultural reform he himself instituted, but also furnished the beginnings of what was to be 'English' society with what the epigraph to this unit claims is the 'equipment of a civilisation'. Although a politically unified England is still some way off, it's not insignificant that Alfred is the first writer, writing in English, to use the term *Angelcynn*, English people.

6.1 The emergence of Wessex

In Unit 4 we looked at some aspects of the cultural and political dominance of Northumbria in early Anglo-Saxon times, that is, during the later 7th through to the mid-8th centuries. This is the 'Golden Age' of Bede and of Cædmon, of Aidan and Oswald. Nor is it an insular – one might almost say, a parochial – period. One feature of Northumbrian Christianity, for instance, is precisely its outward-lookingness, its cosmopolitanism. Not only was it a church and society hospitable to preachers trained on the Continent, its leaders also visited Continental Europe – in particular, Rome – themselves. The founder of Bede's own monastery at Jarrow, Benedict Biscop, had himself visited Rome on five separate occasions, and developed as a result of these contacts one of the finest libraries in Europe.

Through the 8th century, Northumbrian civilisation, despite incessant royal feuding, continued to flourish, and produced at least one churchman and scholar of an international repute almost rivalling that of Bede. This was Alcuin, a Northumbrian by birth, who was subsequently trained in the cathedral school at York, then became a leading clerical figure at the court of Charlemagne. And yet . . . and yet the achievements of Northumbrian culture and scholarship were, at the end of the 8th century, to be destroyed in less than a generation. In 793, Lindisfarne was attacked and raided by

Vikings; in 794, Jarrow; in 795, Iona. It's easy to imagine the plate – the elaborate, animal-carved crucifixes, the preaching staffs, the ornamented bookmarks – carried off, while the wrought, gold-trimmed manuscript pages of the Gospel were torn out, one by one. And afterwards, the roof-beams rotting; and after the rot, broken stone, fallen masonry, the chancel standing open to the sky.

Throughout the 8th century, though, one other kingdom was gaining power. This was the kingdom of Mercia, whose extent lay northwards up to (but not including) Northumbria, and then southwards, to include East Anglia, Sussex and Kent, as well as territory into the south Midlands, as far as Wessex. Wessex remained autonomous, though even this rich, independent kingdom was obliged to concede to Mercian 'protection' during the last years of the 8th century.

Mercia, then, in the 8th century was the political and military centre of the factions and kingdoms that made up what was to become England. Its most significant leader – and the most significant Anglo-Saxon king before Alfred – was Offa (reigned 757–796).

Of Offa, we know that he aspired to be not only an 'English' but also a European figure. He corresponded with the Frankish emperor Charlemagne (who addressed him, perhaps diplomatically, as an equal), and under Offa's leadership, too, there developed many, and important, trading links with the Franks – a north European network. For some areas of 'England', this meant the development of ports – Southampton, Ipswich, London. It's a period of overseas trade. For trade, money is needed: Offa's coinage is the best-minted since Roman times. With trade, with money, comes the population expansion consequent on relatively easier living, and that means a need for easily supplied food. What is clear from the Mercian supremacy is that it had a large network of sub-kingdoms – from Kent to parts of what is now south Yorkshire – on which to draw for its internal resourcing. And what's equally clear is that Offa adopted a containing strategy that would prevent the westerly parts of his kingdom being raided by the Welsh: the huge defensive structure that is still called 'Offa's Dyke' runs almost the whole length of the English–Welsh border. As Blair (2000:32) puts it, the fact that Offa's Dyke exists at all 'is proof of the huge resources which Offa commanded'.[1]

Shortly after Offa's death, however, Mercian power began to decline:

> [T]he balance of power [between Mercia and Wessex:McC/H] was then overturned at the battle of *Ellendun* (now Wroughton, in north-east Wiltshire): Egbert, king of Wessex (802–39), defeated Beornwulf, king of Mercia (823–5),

[1] John Blair. 2000. *The Anglo-Saxon age: a very short introduction*. We are indebted to Blair's masterly, and admirably concise, introduction. We base part of Section 6.1 on some details of his text, and gratefully acknowledge the fact.

> and as a direct consequence the people of Kent, Surrey, Sussex, Essex and East Anglia submitted to King Egbert. Four years later, in 829, Egbert conquered the kingdom of Mercia and everything else south of the Humber, and in this connection the West Saxon chronicler exclaimed enthusiastically that "he was the eighth king who was Bretwalda" ['king of "Britain"': McC]. In the same year Egbert led an army to Dore, in north Derbyshire, and secured the submission of the Northumbrians; in 830 he is said to have extended his authority over the Welsh.
>
> Egbert's achievements in 825–30 established him momentarily in a position that no king before him had enjoyed, though he seems not to have tried or to have been able to consolidate whatever power he exercised in Mercia, East Anglia, Northumbria and Wales.
>
> (Keynes and Lapidge 1983:11–12)

In fact, Egbert seems to have been tactically over-stretched. Moreover, in parts of his putative kingdom, Viking raids, and subsequent settlement, were gathering in intensity. As we've mentioned, parts of Northumbria had been ravaged in the late 8th and early 9th centuries. By the 830s, Vikings were attacking parts of southern England (as they were also making incursions into the kingdom of the Franks). By the 850s, Viking raiding parties changed tactics and, instead of conducting what seem to have been largely hit-and-run sorties, began to overwinter in England. As raiding parties became fleets, as fleets bore armies, it was clear that the Viking settlement of large parts of England was irrevocably underway.

To gain some idea of how near-contemporaries viewed the Norse incursions, one turns to the account of the *Anglo-Saxon Chronicle*. It's true that the *Chronicle* was compiled very much later, but it gives a retrospectively stark, and often true, account, of events.

Exercise 6.1.0

What you're about to study is a *Chronicle* entry for the year 991 – 150 years and more later than the events we've described so far in this unit. Nevertheless, the entry sums up what had become a common pattern: where peace cannot be maintained by defensive force, it has to be bought. Perhaps, too, by this time Viking raids had become so common that they merit no more than the chronicler's somewhat laconic opening clause.

The text is that of the Laud MS of the *Anglo-Saxon Chronicle*. We have based our presentation closely on that found in Quirk *et al.* (1975:12–13). Again, you should use the selective glossary here in order to complete a translation, noticing that there are some forms in the present text (*worhtan* is a nice example) that are not quite as might be found in 'classical' WS (where one might expect *worhton*). Remember that this text dates from shortly after the year 991, and is thus a relatively late piece of OE. By this date, linguistic change, in the form of inflectional reduction and loss, was well underway.

991. Hēr wæs Gypeswīc gehergod; ond æfter þām	1
swīþe rāðe wæs Brihtnōð ealdorman ofslægen æt Mældūne.	2
Ond on þām gēare man gerǣdde	3
þæt man geald ǣrest gafol Deniscan mannum	4
for þām mycclan brōgan þe hī worhtan be þām sǣriman;	5
þæt wæs ǣrest tȳn þūsend punda.	6
Þæne rǣd gerǣdde Siric arcebiscop.	7

Selective glossary

ǣrest adj.; first.

Brihtnōð ealdorman Byrhtnoth, ealdorman of Essex [His doomed skirmish with one Viking raid is vividly described in *The battle of Maldon*, composed soon after 991. We looked at a fragment of that poem in the last unit]

brōgan noun; weak; terror (dat. sg.)

Deniscan (to the men) of the Danes [The Vikings are here referred to generically as Danes, even though by the end

	of the 10th century England was also under attack from Norwegians]
gafol	noun; tribute (acc. sg.) [Money was recorded as having being paid to marauding Danes over one hundred years before. Perhaps the year 991 was the first time that the leaders of Kent, Sussex and Essex had decided together to buy peace]
geald	verb; 3sg. indicative from paid (the meaning here is more like 'should pay')
Gypeswīc	Ipswich, a coastal town in Suffolk
Hēr	adverb; lit. 'here'; [The adverb was often used at the opening of *Chronicle* entries to mean 'in this year']
gehergod	verb; ppl., plundered (see Section 6.1.1 below)
man	impersonal pronoun; one (*man gerǣdde*, lit. 'one decided' – 'it was decided (that)'
mycclan	adj.; great (weak, dative sg.)
ofslægen	verb; ppl. slain (see Section 6.1.1 below)
gerǣdde	3sg., past, decided
rāðe	adverb; soon
sǣriman	compound noun, weak; sea-coast dat. sg.
swīþe	intensifier; very
Þæne	a variant form of *þone*, acc. sg. (*Þæne rǣd*, this decision – Archbishop Siric took this decision)
þe	relative pronoun; which
worhtan	verb, strong; 3pl. past indicative, brought about

Exercise 6.1.1

As a short supplementary exercise to your translation work, think of the verb forms that we've described in the Glossary as 'participles'. Identify each of the participles in the passage, and then find the tensed auxiliary verb to which each participle belongs.

Comment on Exercise 6.1.1

There are two examples in the passage:

wæs . . . gehergod	was . . . harried (In this year Ipswich was harried)
wæs . . . ofslægen	was . . . slain (Byrhtnoth was slain)

Notice how in each group of verbs the *tensed* verb form comes first, and is followed by its participle. In these examples, *wæs* is the tensed form of the verb *to be*. Very often, one can recognise verb participles by the fact that many of them begin with the unstressed prefix *ge-* (*gehergod*). Moreover, the *-od* ending indicates that the verb in question is a so-called weak verb, one that forms its past tense by adding *-ode* in the third person singular, or *-odon* in the 3rd person plural. On these grounds, one might confidently classify *gehergod* as the past participle of a weak verb. Still further, one might reconstruct the infinitive form of the verb (the 'to X' form) as *hergian*, to harry, to plunder.

ofslægen behaves rather differently. There's no *-d-* element of the past participle, so one might infer – correctly – that this isn't a weak verb. It's a strong verb. Instead of forming their past tenses by adding a suffix containing a *-d-* element, strong verbs form their past tenses by changing the vowel found in the root. Think of how the verb *slay* behaves in PDE:

Infinitive	*Present Tense*	*Past Tense*	*Past Participle*
(to) slay	slay	slew	slain

Notice the change of vowel in the past tense, and also the fact that the participial form ends in *-n*. In our example *ofslægen*, we're dealing with a participle whose infinitive form looks rather different (i.e. it has a different vowel in the infinitival root): it is *ofslēan*. And the vowel changes, as we expect, in the past tense:

Infinitive	*Present Tense*	*Past Tense*	*Past Participle*
ofslēan	ofslēa	ofslōg	ofslægen

As you're beginning to think about the historical linguistic configurations of English verbs, you might also consider the fact that for many present-day speakers of languages developed out of the WGmc family, forming past participles very much in the way we've just described for OE is the norm. Present-day Dutch, for instance, looks strikingly reminiscent of OE, even down to the preservation of the *ge-* participial prefix:

Het was gedogen	It was permitted
Ik heb gelezen	I have read
De tram is gestopt	The tram has stopped

The point we're making is that in beginning to describe the language structures of the past we are also helping to ascertain the extent to which these structures speak unavoidably into our linguistic present. Many 'old' structures have a remarkable historical persistence, so that today, they form parts of our linguistic competence, our (usually) tacit knowledge of the principles and structures of our native language. The past informs the present, and one can scarcely understand the present without engaging on a study of the past – sometimes, what seems the rather remote past.

6.2 Alfred's programme of cultural reform

It's a similar situation to the one described in the *Chronicle* passage above into which Alfred, later king of Wessex, is born (849), and into which he succeeds his elder brother, Æthelred, as king in 871. In fact, as Keynes and Lapidge make clear (1983:17), the military and political situation Alfred faced on his accession was appalling: East Anglia had been overrun in 869–870, and then

> [t]owards the end of 870 [the Vikings] moved westwards and established themselves at Reading, and from there struck deeper into the heartland of Wessex. During the opening weeks of 871 King Æthelred and his brother Alfred fought a series of battles against them, but despite an apparently notable victory at Ashdown they failed to achieve any decisive advantage. The situation was made still more desperate for the West Saxons by the arrival at Reading of a second Viking army, and by the death, after Easter, of Æthelred their king.

One of the achievements that earns King Alfred his colloquial epithet 'the Great' is not so much that he was a durable, even formidable, military and political tactician, under whose leadership there emerged among 'the English' some sense of common identity and purpose. This would be a half-truth: throughout Alfred's reign, the territories of the English kingdoms were subject to relentless Viking attack, and in 886 London was captured, forcing Alfred into a treaty with Guthrum, leader of the Vikings in East Anglia. One can't really look back at Alfred's military campaigns and say that these, whatever their ingenuity and endeavour, met with unbridled success.

Yet one can say, with justice, that after the general submission of the English kingdoms, around the year 890, it seemed that Alfred was regarded as the remaining leader who commanded widespread English assent – someone who had 'English' interests at heart, and whose constituency comprised what remained of 'England'. This is not, let us repeat, a unified England: it is, rather, an England whose unity is still to come, yet one whose identity is being forged out of the remains of a shattered culture, and out of a willed, resistant, cultural rebirth.

It's Alfred's role in this renascence that merits his epithet, 'Great'. In one of the most significant documents in early English history, Alfred himself tells his advisers of his ambition to revitalise the cultural life of what he surely viewed as a kind of proto-nation state. (It's significant that in this document Alfred surveys England as it extends both *behionan Humbre*, this side of the Humber, i.e. from the perspective of Wessex, and *begiondan Humbre*, beyond the Humber, i.e. into the kingdom that had been Northumbria.)

Alfred sets out his programme in a Preface, a prefatory letter, addressed to Wærferth, bishop of Worcester, whom Alfred himself recruited into his campaign for reform. Alfred's chronicler and biographer, the Welsh-trained cleric Asser, records that Wærferth was 'a man thoroughly learned in holy writings who at the king's command translated the *Dialogues* between Pope Gregory and his disciple Peter from Latin into the English language, sometimes rendering sense for sense, translating intelligently and in a very polished style' (Keynes and Lapidge 1983:92). To Wærferth, and to a handful of other bishops (each, again, the king's recruits), and at some point after 887, Alfred sends his own translation of Pope Gregory's *Liber Regulae Pastoralis* (or the *Pastoral Care*, the 'care of the Christian flock').

Exercise 6.2.0

We're going to study a fairly long section of this text – but we don't ask you to translate the whole piece. Instead, we ourselves will begin the translation, and ask you to pick up the translation at two points (only) during our work.

We have based our text on the version given in Mitchell and Robinson (1992:204–207). The original text from which they derive their version is MS Hatton 20, in the Bodleian Library, Oxford. It is a manuscript of Alfred's time.

Alfred begins his letter with a formulaic flourish. (This is something Alfred had perhaps learned for himself during his studies of Latin texts.)

Text

Ælfred cyning hāteð grētan Wǣrferð biscep his wordum luflīce ond frēondlīce;
King Alfred commands Bishop W. to be greeted with his loving and friendly words

ond ðē cȳðan hāte ðæt mē cōm swīðe oft on gemynd
and commands you to be informed that it has very often come into my thoughts

hwelce wiotan iū wǣron giond Angelcynn
which kinds of learned men there once were among the English
[notice how Alfred here speaks for the 'Angelcynn']

ǣgðer ge godcundra hāda ge woruldcundra;
both of religious and of secular orders
[notice the nice lexical parallelism between 'god-kind' and 'world-kind']

ond hū gesǣliglica tīda ðā wǣron giond Angelcynn;
and how there were blessed times then among the English
[Alfred here invokes the Golden Age of Bede]

ond hū ðā cyningas ðe ðone onwald hæfdon ðæs folces
and how the kings who then had authority over their people

Gode ond his ǣrendwrecum hīersumedon;
gave obedience to God and to his ministers

ond hīe ǣgðer ge hiora sibbe ge hiora siodu ge hiora onweald innanbordes gehīoldon,
and they maintained both their peace and their morality and their power at home
[we translate 'innanbordes' as 'at home'; an alternative might be 'within England']

ond ēac ūt hiora ēdel rȳmdon;
and also extended their territory outwards

ond hū him ðā spēow ǣgðer ge mid wīge ge mid wīsdōme;
and how they were successful then both in war and in learning
[notice the implicit linkage, suggested by the alliteration, between 'war' and 'wisdom'; for Alfred, it seemed inconceivable that military success should not be accompanied by subsequent cultural reform: the sword might have been mightier than the pen – as the Viking settlement was proving – but in Alfred's programme, the sword was but an inevitable precursor to the pen]

ond ēac ðā godcundan hādas, hū giorne hīe wǣron
and (I) also (brought to mind) the religious orders, how assiduous they were

ǣgðer ge ymb lāre ge ymb liornunga,
both about wisdom and (about) learning

ge ymb ealle ðā ðīowotdōmas ðe hīe Gode dōn scoldon;
and about all the customary offices that they had to perform for God

ond hū man ūtanbordes wīsdōm ond lāre hieder on londe sōhte;
and of how one might seek from abroad for learning and wisdom here in this country

ond hū wē hīe nū sceoldon ūte begīetan, gif wē hīe habban sceoldon.
and of how we would now have to look abroad for them, if we were to have them.
[as Alfred himself had done, recruiting churchmen to what was left of England from different parts of northern Europe]

We now ask you to translate the following. (Why should we have all the fun?) In the opening line, Alfred is still remembering 'learning' (*liornung* is a feminine noun and is the antecedent of the feminine pronoun *hio*, which you will of course translate as 'it'). In this part of his preface, he is deliberately contrasting the Age of Bede, with its peace, learning and prosperity, with the period of relative religious and cultural decline he sees around him in the late 9th century.

Swǣ clǣne hīo wæs oðfeallenu on Angelcynne	1
ðæt swīðe fēawa wǣron behionan Humbre	2
ðe hiora ðēninga cūðen understondan on Englisc	3
oððe furðum ān ǣrendgewrit of Lǣdene on Englisc āreccean;	4
ond ic wēne ðætte nōht monige begiondan Humbre nǣren.	5
Swǣ fēawa hiora wǣron ðæt ic furðum ānne ānlēpne ne mæg geðencean	6
be sūðan Temese ðā ðā ic tō rīce fēng.	7

Selective glossary

ān one (*ānne* is masc. acc. sg.)
ānlēpne adj.; single (here acc. sg.)
āreccean verb; infinitive; to translate
ǣrendgewrit noun; letter (neut. acc. sg.)
clǣne adverb; completely (cf. idiomatic PDE, I clean forgot)
fēng verb; receive, catch (*fēng tō rīce* is an idiom that means 'succeeded to the kingdom')
furðum adverb; even
nǣren contracted form of *ne wǣren*, were not

oðfeallenu	verb participle; fallen away, declined (infinitive *oðfeallan*)
ðā ðā	adverb; then when (or, better, just 'when')
geðencean	verb, infinitive; think
ðēninga	noun; church services (fem. acc. pl.)
wēne	weak verb; think (1sg., infinitive *wēnan*)

Idiomatic translation

'It (learning) had declined so completely among the English that there were very few on this side of the Humber who were able to understand their church services in English, or even translate one letter from Latin into English, and I don't believe that there were many (who could do so) on the far side of the Humber. There were in truth so few of them that I can't think of a single one living south of the Thames when I succeeded to the kingdom.'

Alfred continues by contrasting such a dearth with his current situation in Wessex. Recall that he had recruited churchmen and intellectuals – men like Asser and Wærferth, also Grimbald (who had been recruited from Flanders), John (probably from Germany), and Plegmund (recruited more locally, this time from Mercia).

Text

Gode ælmihtigum sīe ðonc ðæt wē ǣnigne onstal habbað lārēowa.
Thanks be to God Almighty that we now have any supply of teachers.

Ond for ðon ic ðē bebīode ðæt ðū dō swǣ ic geliefe ðæt ðū wille,
And therefore I command you to act as I believe you (already) intend,

ðæt ðū ðē ðissa woruldðinga tō ðǣm geǣmetige, swǣ ðū oftost mǣge,
so that you should disengage yourself from worldly affairs, as often as you are able,

ðæt ðū ðone wīsdōm ðe ðē God sealde ðǣr ðǣr ðū hiene befæstan mæge, befæste.
in order that you may apply the wisdom that God ordained to you just as often as you can apply it.
[Not the most gloriously elegant sentence Alfred ever constructed.]

Geðenc hwelc wītu ūs ðā becōmon for ðisse worulde,
Think what punishments happened to us in this world,
[the 'punishments' seem to be Alfred's reference to the Viking invasions: 'we neglected our own culture,' he seems to be saying, 'and we were rewarded for that neglect in the worst possible way']

ðā ðā wē hit nōhwæðer ne selfe ne lufodon, ne ēac oðrum monnum ne lǣfdon;
when we neither loved it (learning) ourselves, nor even passed it on to others;

ðone naman ǣnne wē lufodon ðætte we Crīstne wǣren, and swīðe fēawa ðā ðēawas.
we loved only the name of being Christians, and very few respected (Christian) virtues.

Ðā ic ðā ðis eall gemunde, ðā gemunde ic hū ic geseah,
When I brought all this to mind, I also remembered how I saw,

ǣr ðe hit eall forhergod wǣre and forbærned,
before it was all ravaged and burnt,
[*wǣre* is technically in the subjunctive mood, following the conjunction *ǣr ðe* – 'before it had become . . .' Perhaps, given his immersion in learning Latin, Alfred is trying to render something like a Latin passive, and reaching for an OE subjunctive to fulfil that function]

hū ðā ciricean giond eall Angelcynn stōdon māðma ond bōca gefylda,
how the churches throughout all England stood filled with books and treasures,
[*giond eall Angelcynn,* lit. everywhere among the English people]

ond ēac micel mengeo Godes ðīowa;
and also with a great multitude of God's servants;

ond ðā swīðe lȳtle fiorme ðāra bōca wiston
but they derived little benefit from those books
[we translate *ond* as *but;* literally, 'and they knew very little use of those books']

for ðǣm ðe hīe hiora nānwuht ongietan ne meahton,
since they weren't able to understand any part of them,

for ðǣm ðe hīe nǣron on hiora āgen geðīode āwritene.
because they weren't written in their own language.
[After the Golden Age, literacy had declined; few were able to translate from Latin into English, and the 'books' that had been inherited were written in Latin]

Swelce hīe cwǣden:
It was as if they had said:
['They' are the clerics who had inherited the riches of the Golden Age. *cwǣden* is in the subjunctive mood: 'it was as if they were to have said . . .']

'Ūre ieldran, ðā ðe ðās stōwa ǣr hīoldon, hīe lufodon wīsdōm,
'Our ancestors, those who formerly inhabited these places, they loved learning

ond ðurh ðone hīe begēaton welan ond ūs lǣfdon.
and through it they acquired wealth and bequeathed it to us.

Hēr mon mæg gīet gesīon hiora swǣð,
Here one may still see their path,

ac wē him ne cunnon æfter spyrigean.
but we don't know how to follow after them.

Ond for ðǣm wē habbað nū ǣgðer forlǣtan ge ðone welan ge ðone wīsdōm,
And therefore we've abandoned both the wealth and the learning,

for ðǣm ðe wē noldon tō ðǣm spore mid ūre mōde onlūtan.
because our minds were unable to incline to that track.
[lit. 'because we were unable to bend our minds to that trace']

At this point in his Preface, Alfred asks himself why it was that the churchmen and scholars of the Golden Age hadn't translated any religious literature from Latin into English. Having posed this question to himself, he answers it directly ('Ac ic sōna eft mē selfum andwyrde'): the scholars of the Golden Age would never have believed that men would become so careless, and learning, so declined. Perhaps after all they *intended* that with continuing scholarship, there would be *more* learning in England the more languages, including Latin, were studied.

Alfred then reminds himself of historical precedent, invoking both Greek and Roman examples: 'The Law' (*sīo ǣ*: either the entire Old Testament, or, more likely, the first six books – the Hexateuch – of the Christian Bible) had been translated into both Greek and Latin. And, continues Alfred, 'ealla ōðra Crīstna ðīoda sumne dǣl hiora on hiora āgen geðiode wendon' – all other Christian peoples have translated some part of them [the books of the Bible] into their own language.

With these august precedents in mind, Alfred then recommends to Wærferth that books 'most necessary for all men to know' should be translated into English. There's a wistful and interesting parenthesis here: 'we should translate such books,' Alfred writes, '*gif wē ðā stilnesse habbað*' – if we have the peace to do so. Remember that Alfred was writing amid a continuing war with Vikings, whose settlements and armies encroached on Wessex from both the east and the north. This makes Alfred's vision all the more remarkable. In it were included all the free-born laity of England: free-born young men, he writes, should be educated – if they can be spared from military service – until the point that they're easily able to read English. Then, from that base of literacy, one may wish to educate some young men further, in Latin, and train them for the priesthood.

More remarkable still is Alfred's assumption of a key role in his own reform programme. In a touching (and famous) passage, which we ask you to translate, Alfred details how many pains it took for him to play such a role.

Exercise 6.2.1

Đā ic ðā gemunde hū sīo lār Lǣdengeðīodes ǣr ðissum āfeallan wæs	**1**
giond Angelcynn, ond ðēah monige cūðon Englisc gewrit ārǣdan,	**2**
ðā ongan ic ongemang ōðrum mislicum ond manigfealdum bisgum	**3**
ðisses kynerīces ðā bōc wendan on Englisc ðe is genemned on Lǣden	**4**
Pastoralis, ond on Englisc 'Hierdebōc', hwīlum word be worde,	**5**
hwīlum angiet of angiete, swǣ swǣ ic hīe geliornode	**6**
æt Plegmunde mīnum ærcebiscepe, ond æt Assere mīnum biscepe . . .	**7**

Selective glossary

andgiet noun; neut. (dat. sg., *andgiete*)
bisgum noun; concerns (fem. dat. pl., root *bisgu*, cf. PDE business)

hīe	pronoun; it (fem. 3sg.) (Alfred had learned to translate 'it' – the *Pastoralis*)
hwīlum	noun; sometimes (fem. dat. pl., root *hwīl*, cf. PDE (a) while)
lār	noun; learning (fem. acc. sg., cf. PDE lore)
geliornode	verb, weak (-d in past tense); learned (indicative) (infinitive *geliornian* or *geleornian*)
manigfealdum	adj.; manifold (here dat. pl.)
mislicum	adj.; various (here dat. pl.)
monige	adj.; many (used here as a noun) – but, given Alfred's remarks on the general decline of literacy and translation skills, perhaps better translated as 'several', i.e. 'there were still several in the kingdom who knew how to read English, but nevertheless I myself began . . .'
gemunde	verb; remember (1sg. past, infinitive, *gemunan*)
ond ðēah	adverbial; and though, or better, even though
ongemang	prep., among
wendan	verb, infinitive; to turn, to translate (cf. PDE to wend)

Idiomatic translation

When I recalled how Latin learning had earlier declined among the English, even though many still knew how to read English writing, then – among many other pressing and abundant cares of this kingdom – then I began to translate into English the book that is called in Latin *Pastoralis,* and in English 'Book-of-the-flock', sometimes word-by-word, sometimes sense from sense, just as I had learned it from Plegmund, my archbishop, and from Asser, my bishop . . .

The image of this harassed, middle-aged king spending parts of his days (and, let's assume, his nights) in translation exercises, painfully puzzling out his translation 'word for word, and sense from sense', should strike a chord with scholars of language everywhere – including you, the present, and patient, reader.

That Alfred took considerable personal trouble with his translations is apparent a few lines further on in the letter, when he confesses that 'after I had learned it' (presumably, the literal sense), 'and as I understood it' (presumably, the colloquial sense), 'and as I might most intelligibly [*angitfullīcost*, lit. most sense-fully] translate it', then – one infers, only then – 'ic hīe on Englisc āwende', then I turned it into English.

The letter concludes with a royal exhortation. In his conclusion, Alfred made clear his intention of sending a copy of his translation to each bishopric in his kingdom. Each book would be accompanied by a costly bookmark. These precious objects – some bore a valuable jewel, it seems – were to remain in church, unless they were to be loaned, and/or further translations copied from them.

Alfred's Preface is unique in many ways. Perhaps most tellingly, it affords one of those very rare moments in early English history when one can study vivid, and first-hand, testimony – a form of witness that concerns not just 'events' as they seem to have happened, but how it was to respond to those events. Further, Alfred explicitly spoke for a vision of 'England', a vision that included literacy, and the English language, as central to political stability, to prosperity, even (eventually, and a pious hope) to peace. In short, the Preface embodies a key moment not only in the development of a proto-nation state, but also the maintenance of the language and literature that would underpin that sense of cultural identity.

Beyond the Preface, Alfred was hard at work: he himself translated three other key texts – the *Consolation of Philosophy* by Boethius (fl. late 5th century); the *Soliloquies* of St Augustine of Hippo; and the first 50 psalms of the Psalter (Keynes and Lapidge 1983:30–31). As Keynes and Lapidge, among others, note, Alfred was throughout his literate career linguistically thoroughgoing, even to the point of self-consciousness: 'Alfred's translation of Boethius reveals the mind of a translator who has pondered deeply on the significance of his text and who has recast its sophisticated philosophical problems in terms at once familiar and immediately comprehensible' (30–31; for a good modern translation of Boethius, see the References section at the end of this unit).

6.3 What makes West Saxon West Saxon?

We've claimed that Alfred was writing in 'West Saxon' (WS), a form of language that became a written Standard. One thing we might want to ask ourselves is what made this written form of OE distinctive? Why does it become a prestige form?

It's unlikely that Alfred thought of himself writing in any form of 'standard' – however much, given his programmatic ambitions, he might have wished that the English of his translations might give rise to such a thing. We assume he was simply writing, with as much formal consistency as possible, in the form of 'English' that came closest to hand. It's not at all clear that Alfred *intended* the future to see the written form of English he employed as in some sense a 'prestige' or 'standard' form – however much he might have wished it. Nor is it clear that a written standard language could (or can) be somehow willed into existence.

We also assume, perhaps over-simply, that at least some of Alfred's scribes were attempting to write in a consistent form of English. If a local 'house style' developed, again it's not clear that scribes *intended* this to become a 'standard'. (As his recruitment of scholars and churchmen bears witness, those he recruited to Wessex – and this will have included scribes – need not necessarily have been born there. Some will have been trained in other parts of the country, or even abroad.)

Nevertheless, it's customary for linguistic historians to think of, and speak about, 'West Saxon'. It's obviously true that this is to some extent a merely geographical label – Alfred was writing and working in the kingdom of Wessex. It's also, and equally obviously, true that 'West Saxon' is a label applied with the dubious wisdom of hindsight. Is 'West Saxon', then, *really* a written dialect, a prestige form of English that becomes a Standard? Or is it just a convenient label, perhaps of interest to a handful of scholars? What makes West Saxon West Saxon?

The preconditions for the rise of a written Standard clearly include the spread, and maintenance, of literacy in the vernacular. And Alfred had insisted on literacy, *at least* in the vernacular, for free-born English youth. That very insistence, however, is telling: Alfred would not have needed to protest that requirement had literacy not been imperilled. It's perhaps more important to ask how literacy, once it became established, could be maintained. The answer lies in a system of education. Yet 'education' wasn't, in 9th century Wessex, the property of schools and colleges. It was found in the monasteries. And again, what Alfred seems to have envisaged, by recruiting churchmen to spearhead his cultural programme, is a revitalisation of monastic life.

There's another factor that bears on the development of a written Standard. The language in which the Standard is written must have had prior, and continued, exposure to other forms of written language, whether such a language is native (a written dialect of OE), or non-native (Latin). By these measures, and perhaps too, with the precedent of Latin in mind, an incipient Standard has the means both to define and to maintain itself – given the prior condition of (monastic) literacy. Haunting this issue is also the relationship between written and spoken forms of English. There doesn't seem to be any question that Alfred and his teachers encouraged the use of written English in what amounted to an act of intellectual assertion – assertion against the intellectually and culturally destructive force that presently occupied much of what became England. This assertion seems to have been a deliberately political act.

Even having exposed some of the pre-conditions for the development of West Saxon, we still haven't answered the question 'What makes West Saxon West Saxon?' To give a more precise answer, we must turn to the forms of English we find in that written dialect. And we say immediately that the distinctions between West Saxon and other forms of written English of the period (of which we have very few surviving records) are a matter of *degree*, and a matter of *comparison*. There are, however, some hallmarks of WS that enable us to distinguish it both from other forms of English of the period, and from later forms of English. They are as follows:

- WS is a written variety of English that, while impoverished in terms of its inflectional morphology compared with other, and earlier, dialects of (Continental) West Germanic, still retains a relatively systematic inflectional morphology on its nouns, adjectives and verbs. (That is, it's a written variety that's apparently not yet been subject to the still further erosion of inflectional morphology that would take place during the 10th and 11th centuries in other varieties of English . . . and may well have been taking place, in those varieties, during the 9th.)
- WS is a written variety of English that still employs a relatively 'free' word order within sentences. (That is, this grammar did not yet evidence the relatively fixed positional syntax that would develop in some later varieties of Old English . . . and may well have been there developing during the 9th century.) To confirm this, you might like to look back at the syntax of the two passages from Alfred's Preface that you've already translated. One idea is to look for the position of each finite (= tensed) verb in each clause; as in the following examples.

  Swǣ clǣne hīo **wæs** oðfeallenu on Angelcynne

  (verb in second position, after the subject)

  ðæt swīðe fēawa **wǣron** behionan Humbre

  (a *that*- clause; verb again in second position, after the subject of the clause; this is unexpected – and perhaps, a token of ongoing change; one expects the tensed verb to be final in a *that*- clause)

  ðe hiora ðēninga **cūðen** understondan on Englisc

  (a *who*- clause; again, one expects the tensed verb to be absolutely final in the clause, but instead it comes in a position after the object. Notice that in PDE we'd expect *who were able to understand their holy services*)

  oððe furðum ān ǣrendgewrit of Lǣdene on Englisc āreccean

  (a conjoined clause [the conjunction is *oððe*, 'or']; here, the non-finite part of the Verb Group that is introduced by *cūðen*, were able/knew how to, appears last in the sentence. Notice that in PDE we'd expect this to occur directly after the conjunction – *or translate even one letter from Latin into English*)

But there's one other factor that allows us to distinguish WS from other written varieties of OE, and it is this:

- the spoken variety of WS had apparently undergone certain sound-changes that either did not take place, or did not take place regularly, in other spoken varieties of English of the period. The set of WS changes seems to be, often imperfectly, but still recognisably, captured in the written form of WS that eventually evolved.

To make this last point clearer, we offer a somewhat artificial, but nevertheless instructive, comparison. It is between two versions of a poem we've already studied (in Unit 1), Cædmon's *Hymn*. In what you're about to read, the text found towards the left margin is a WS version of the *Hymn*; the text found towards the right margin is a Northumbrian version of the same text. (Smith 1968: 38–39 makes a similar comparison, and we acknowledge again his great work on the linguistic and palaeographic history of different versions of the *Hymn*.)

Cædmon's *Hymn*: a dialectal comparison

West Saxon version (manuscript spellings 'normalised')		**Northumbrian version** (manuscript spellings retained)	
Nū sculon herigean	heofonrīces Weard,	Nu scylan herȝan	hefaenricaes uard
Meotodes meahte	ond his mōdgeþanc,	metudaes maecti	end his modȝidanc
weorc Wuldorfæder,	swā hē wundra gehwæs,	uerc uuldurfadur	sue he uundra ȝihuaes,
ēce Drihten,	ōr onstealde	eci dryctin	or astelidae;
Hē ærest scēop	eorðan bearnum	he aerist scop	aelda barnum
heofon tō hrōfe,	hālig Scyppend.	heben til hrofe,	haleȝ scepen,
Þā middangeard	monncynnes Weard,	tha middunȝeard	moncynnæs uard;
ēce Drihten,	æfter tēode	eci dryctin	æfter tidæ
fīrum foldan,	Frea ælmihtig	firum foldu,	frea allmectiȝ.

We emphasise that the WS text is merely 'a version', a kind of compromise, or composite. Students of the earliest English, if they study this text at all, usually access it in just such an editorialised version, with its regularised capitalisation and punctuation, its length-marks supplied (for ease of reading, and just possibly for comparative purposes), and its character set (the <w>, the <g>) adapted to more modern conventions.

The Northumbrian version we have here taken from Smith (1968:38–39), who in turn took his text from a manuscript copy in Cambridge University Library [Kk, 5.16]. This manuscript copy is called the *Moore* manuscript and is one of the earliest, if not the earliest, datable texts of the *Hymn*. It can be dated to the year 737 (Smith 1968:20–23), and the manuscript entry that includes the *Hymn* seems to have been the work of one hand, one scribe.

For our purposes in this unit, what's important is not so much the distinctive spelling conventions of the Northumbrian version as they relate to certain consonants (the <uu> for conventionalised <w>, for instance, or the use of <ȝ> for what we now expect as <g>), but rather, to the nature of the *vowel sounds* indicated by the spellings found in the manuscript.

We select three examples to think about:

West Saxon (WS)	**Northumbrian (Nbr)**
Weard	*uard*
meahte	*maecti*
bearnum	*barnum*

You'll immediately notice that the WS spellings for these words uniformly have the spelling (the digraph) <ea> representing the vowel shape in the root of each word, whereas the earlier Nbr spellings of the same words have either <a> or <ae> as the spellings of the root vowel. Now, when confronted with a scrap of linguistic evidence like this, we could do one of two things: we could either say, 'this is merely a matter of how the scribes "heard" the words in question', i.e. we could dismiss these spelling differences as little more than an accident of scribal interference; or we could begin to ask ourselves whether these apparent spelling differences manifested something more linguistically interesting, namely, a distinction between the spoken forms of two dialects. And because it's both more interesting, and ultimately, a more convincing explanation of such spelling differences, it's this last position we're going to explore. That is, 'something happens' – and happens fairly systematically – in, and by the time of the development of, WS that may not entirely happen, or happen so systematically, in other dialects. It's on this kind of thinking, observation and analysis that we base parts of philological reconstruction.

So what is it that 'happens' in (or 'by the time of the development of') WS, in terms of these <ea> spellings?

BrE speakers, in particular, should first think not directly of the vowel in the syllabic Nucleus of the words in question, but of the sound spelt <r>. Whatever its phonetic quality, this sound was indeed pronounced post-vocalically (i.e. after vowels) in both WS and Nbr – as it still would be for some speakers of BrE, and very many speakers of AmE (consider how you'd pronounce a word like 'barn', or a BrE dialect word like 'bairn'). Therefore, when we construct the pronunciation of the words we're interested in, we pronounce *all* the consonants surrounding each vocalic Nucleus.

Now to the vowels. The easiest assumption to make – and it will turn out to be the right one – would be to think the Nbr forms, being earlier than WS, are a manifestation of *prior* forms. Although this would be an over-simplification, we could claim that it's precisely these prior forms to which 'something happens': their pronunciation is modified, and modified fairly systematically in certain dialects (but not others), so that we get the 'later', modified, WS forms. (We put the word 'later' into scare quotes because there are some, still early, MSS of the *Hymn* whose date is contemporaneous with WS, and where the spelling evidence for reconstructing sounds and sound-changes is somewhat messy.)

What is the 'something' that happens? What we're looking at is a very well-known OE *sound change*, quaintly, and somewhat inaccurately, known as 'Breaking'. Our philological claim would then be that Breaking occurred fairly systematically in WS, but didn't take place so systematically (or hadn't had time to take place fully) in early forms of Nbr.

Breaking has spawned a vast technical literature. The most detailed description of the change can be found in Hogg (1992a:84ff.). Here's a simplified version of Hogg's opening description of Breaking:

> Very early in the prehistoric OE period the front vowels [long and short *æ*, long and short *e*, and long and short *i*: McC/H] were diphthongized when immediately followed by a velar or velarized consonant or consonant group. The consonant and consonant groups before which diphthongization occurred are: (1) the voiceless velar fricative /x/, usually spelled <h> . . . ; (2) the velarized liquid [ɫ] when covered by a following consonant, including itself; (3) the liquid /r/ when it was similarly covered, which was either velarized or had an articulation similar in effect to velarization . . . ; (4) the labiovelar approximant /w/. *Between the front vowels and the consonants there developed a transitional glide which in the first instance would be a non-low, nonsyllabic back vowel, that is, /u/ or /o/. At a later stage, certainly by the time of the earliest written texts, this glide developed into a nonsyllabic back vowel of the same height as the preceding front vowel . . .*
> (Hogg 1992:84–5; our emphasis, McC/H)

This looks and sounds quite technical, and it might help to go through it slowly. The first stage envisioned is that of a group of front vowel shapes, both long and short. In the prehistoric OE phase, these were (or can be regarded as) pure vowel shapes, that is, in the case of the long vowels /iː/, /eː/ and /æː/, the one long vowel shape was related to, and indeed an exponent of, the two x's occupying the relevant syllabic Nucleus.

The next phase envisioned is that of a pressure for these pure vowel shapes to diphthongise. Diphthongs can be thought of (and heard) as vowel shapes that are not 'pure', but are gliding movements. Table 6.1 contains examples from PDE to help you hear the difference between pure vowel shapes and diphthongs.

Table 6.1 Pure vowel shapes vs. diphthongs

Pure vowel shapes	Diphthongal glides
heed /hiːd/	hide /haɪd/
feed /fiːd/	fade /feɪd/
heart (BrE) /hɑːt/	height /haɪt/
bead /biːd/	beer (BrE) /bɪə/
bored (BrE) /bɔːd/	bared (BrE) /beəd/
whose /huːz/	house /haʊs/

As you'll see, diphthongs are vowel shapes comprising two non-identical vowel segments within a syllabic Nucleus. What Hogg seems to be suggesting about Breaking in the above quote is that there was pressure for erstwhile pure vowels to become diphthongs – to acquire gliding elements. What caused that pressure?

This is the third phase. The pressure for change is supplied by the phonetic environment – specifically, by the phonetic nature of the consonants that followed the vowel shape that was to be affected. Where a consonant was produced with the body of the tongue raised towards the soft palate, or velum, for example, one can speak of a 'back' consonant and, in producing the preceding vowel shape, one anticipates the backness of the following consonants, thereby transferring the 'backness' to the vowel shape – that is to say, the vowel shape acquires a back glide.

We see from the quote that the speech-sound /r/ (here called a 'liquid', which can be glossed as a highly sonorous consonant) did in an early stage of OE have a 'velar' or 'velarized' pronunciation. This exerts pressure on the preceding vowel shape to acquire 'backness' as part of its phonetic quality – in other words, to diphthongise. The part of Hogg's text that we've italicised tells you just how this 'backness' was acquired.

Whatever the phonetics of Breaking, it had apparently occurred 'by the time of the earliest written texts', and thus before even the earliest, Nbr written version of the *Hymn*. If so, then how do we explain the <a> or <ae> spellings in Nbr? Breaking had taken place earlier than they were written. Do these Nbr spellings reflect vowel sounds that had undergone Breaking, but then were in some inexplicable sense 'reverting' to an earlier (indeed, a prehistoric) pronunciation? Or do we take the simpler position that in the early Nbr version in question (with a spelling system largely like that manifested in the Moore MS), Breaking just hadn't happened?

Some more reconstruction. It seems fairly likely that the vowels of the words we're thinking about (WS *Weard, meaht, bearn*) were in WGmc pronounced /æ/ and written <a>. (Notice that this is a *short* vowel sound – to produce something like it, have a go at pronouncing *cat, mat* and *sat* as they might have been pronounced by a Gaumont-News announcer from the 1930s (an RP speaker): the result is an 'e-coloured *a*', symbolised /æ/.) Incidentally, we can with some justice claim that this /æ/ was 'West Germanic' because of records from other Germanic dialects. OHG, for example, regularly has spelling of <a> for this vowel shape: <arm> arm, <hard> hard, etc. (Jones 1989:39), cf. OE (WS) *earm, heard*.

It's this sound (together with some other front vowels, both long and short) that undergoes modification *in certain environments*. That is, more economically

WGmc /æ/ > later /æɑ/ *when followed by certain consonants*

It's /æɑ/ that is regularly spelled <ea> in many varieties of OE. And our claim would be that this change occurs rather systematically in WS.

And to account for the Nbr spellings? We think we have to claim that these spellings sometimes reflect the 'unbroken' WGmc forms – the original 'a-forms'. Smith (1968:29) wrote as follows of the phonology of the early MS versions of the *Hymn*: 'Breaking: (a) WGerm *a* before *r* + consonant remains mostly unbroken: [*Hymn*, Moore and Leningrad MSS] *uard* (twice), *barnum*, [Leningrad MS] *ȝard* . . .' In a footnote, Smith also pointed out that 'In other Angl[ian] texts there is also fluctuation between broken and unbroken forms' (1968:29).

This helps us. Because there is precisely 'fluctuation' between broken and unbroken forms of the interesting vowels (look back, too, at the form *-ȝeard* – a broken form – that occurs elsewhere in the Moore MS), it looks like the Moore MS version of the *Hymn could not be West Saxon*. It's from a northern dialect area, from Mercia or Northumbria. A cover term for this non-West Saxon dialect area is 'Anglian'.

Since it's a 'major diphthong producing phonological process' (Jones 1989:49), Breaking is worth spending more time on. Recall we said that /æ/ was affected ('in certain environments'). Other front vowels affected – in the same environments – are /e/ and /i/. Both the long versions of these phonemes (/e:/, /i:/) and the short are apparently affected by the change. Thus in WS we get forms such as *heort(e)*, heart (where the original vowel was /e/, cf. OS *herta*) and *liornian*, to learn (where the original vowel was /i/, cf. Gothic *lirnojan* – see again Jones 1989: 43, 45). Schematically –

ǣ̆ }
ē̆ } diphthongised in certain environments
ī̆ }

The key question, and one on which much earnest philological ink has been spent, is 'what are these "certain environments" that apparently make vowel shapes begin to wander through articulatory space?'

Exercise 6.3.0

Look at the following WS spellings. The 'broken' vowel shape is shown in each case. Try pronouncing the words in question. *Now try again*, less self-consciously and more slowly. (It might help you to remember that the post-vocalic sound spelled <h> is pronounced /x/ – a bit like the *ch* in Scots *loch*.) When you've done that, try to work out what, if anything, the *consonant, or consonant groups, following the broken vowels might have in common, in terms of their articulation*.

WS **earm** arm
WS **weall** wall
WS **Piohtas** Picts

Comment on Exercise 6.3.0

The 'broken' vowel shape is followed either by <**r**> (plus consonant), <**l**> (plus consonant, in this case, another <l>), and <**h**> (plus consonant, although the <t> of *Piohtas* properly belongs to the second syllable of the word, not the first). So it looks as if originally monophthongal vowel shapes start to diphthongise when they're followed by (crudely) /r/, /l/, and /x/ or /χ/. The question we're really asking – and which you should now be asking yourself – is 'what do these speech sounds have in common'?

One possible answer is that they're all some kind of 'back' sound. As we mentioned a little time ago, one possible pronunciation of <r> was as a velarised or even uvular fricative (phonemically /r/, phonetically [ʁ]). Such a realisation does in fact still exist: one of your authors heard this realisation (in words like *brown, crude*) throughout his boyhood in different parts of the north of England. And we also know that <h> – here, the speech sound /x/ – is a voiceless velar fricative (pronounced with the back of the tongue vibrating briefly at the very back of the palate). And we *also* know that /l/, when it occurs after a vowel, has a 'back' resonance, i.e. it is velarised. (Students of phonetics and phonology know this speech sound, an allophone of /l/, as 'dark *l*', symbolised [ɫ].) This realisation of /l/ still occurs: speakers of Cockney English, for example – and this feature has also leaked into Estuary Englishes – often produce a word such as 'milk' as something like 'miwk', where the realisation of /l/ is very highly velarised. (Note: the speech sound /w/ is technically a labio-*velar* approximant.)

Where does that leave us? It leaves us with 'backness' – better, and more accurately, with *velarity* – as a possible conditioning factor of the sound change known as Breaking. And it's useful to have evidence from contemporary Englishes that such changes aren't merely one-offs.

Exercise 6.3.1

Take the following three examples and, for each one, try to reconstruct what the historically prior vowel would be (i.e. the vowel that would occur in earlier varieties of WGmc):

WS	**eorl** earl	WGmc?
WS	**weall** wall	WGmc?
WS	**Piohtas** Picts	WGmc?

Comment on Exercise 6.3.1

WS	**eorl** earl	WGmc <e>, /e/. OS <erl>
WS	**weall** wall	WGmc <a>, <æ>, /æ/. OS <wal>
WS	**Piohtas** Picts	WGmc <i>, /i/. OS *<Pihtas>

[The asterisk covering <Pihtas> in the last example indicates that this is a hypothetical, reconstructed form, one not apparently attested in any written form of WGmc. But just because it's not written down doesn't mean it didn't or can't exist.]

6.4 Quibbling with 'Breaking'

There are a couple of further points to make about 'Breaking'. We make them because (i) they're interesting, and controversial, and (ii) because they introduce you to some notions that are everywhere present in linguists' thinking as they conduct comparative or historical research.

First, and as will have been evident from our use of scare-quotes around the term 'Breaking', we need to ask about the accuracy of the descriptive terminology we employ. We don't ourselves like the term 'Breaking': the term suggests that an originally pure vowel (long or short) was somehow 'divided into halves'. But how would you 'divide' a short vowel into two shorter halves? That doesn't seem intuitively plausible. We don't like the term 'Fracture' either, and for the same reasons. After all, it may well be more accurate, as well as more intuitively plausible, to claim that in what is known as 'Breaking', *a glide is <u>added</u> to a vowel shape*, which itself, and during the process of addition, becomes modified. That is, we're not dealing with 'division', but with *addition*.

Second, we also need to ask whether this process of addition was in fact a 'sound change' at all. Perhaps scribes were just simply 'writing what they heard' and, therefore, what they wrote as a digraph merely indicated that a 'pure' vowel had acquired some sort of resonance only because it was followed by a consonant with a causative (back) resonance. Or perhaps, the second element of the vocalic shapes written <ea>, <eo>, etc., was just a graphic indication of the quality of the following consonant and, thus, was itself not a 'proper vowel', but a diacritic? In other words, what linguistic historians know as 'Breaking' might have been merely a matter of *graphic convention*.

Let's revisit that first point, the notion that 'Breaking' is a matter of *addition*. In one of the simplest and most intellectually satisfying accounts of the process that we know, Jones (1989:33ff. – a work we have already cited several times in our work on this phenomenon) makes the point that vowels can be thought of as 'conceptual spaces', rather than (or perhaps better, as well as) discrete segments. Further, he makes the point that these 'conceptual spaces' occur at the heart of *the syllable*, and therefore, syllable structure can't be entirely discounted as we try to relate the story of vowel shifts. And last, Jones makes the point that the addition of off-glides to pre-existing 'pure' vowels is a very common process, one that has occurred at every phase of the phonological development of English. OE sound changes, he writes, including 'Breaking', '. . . are of a type which occurs over and over again in the history of the English language, one indeed which is still observable . . . in the phonology of many dialects today' (1989:33–34). This gives his – and our – narrative more explanatory power when considered in the light of the Uniformitarian Hypothesis, to which we introduced you in Unit 1.

Let's try to yoke the idea of vowel shapes as 'conceptual spaces' together with the second point we raised above, that of syllable structure.

Exercise 6.4.0

Take the example *arm* (WGmc, arm), and construct a tree diagram of its syllable shape. (Hint: before doing this exercise, you may wish to revisit Unit 5, Section 5.2.) One thing to think about is where the /r/ belongs – to the Nucleus? or to the Coda?

Comment on Exercise 6.4.0

You may well have constructed a syllable diagram like the following:

(1) Syllable structure of WGmc *arm*, arm

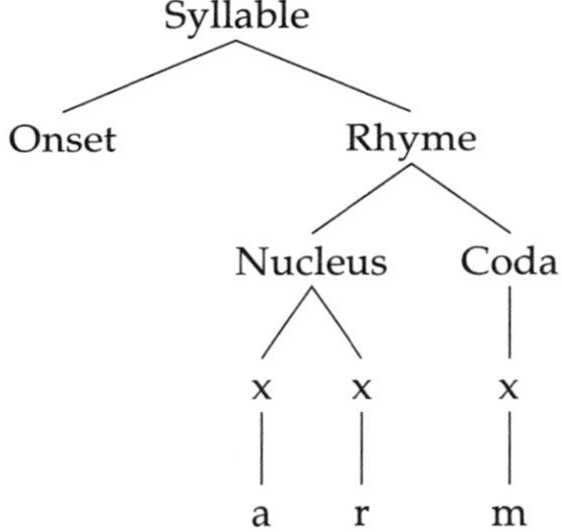

The Onset is null (a zero Onset, see again Section 5.2). The /r/, as a sonorant segment, can follow a short vowel shape in the *Nucleus* of the syllable, leaving the /m/ to be syllabified as a (single-member) Coda. Note that the /a/ is indeed a *short* vowel shape: it's aligned with just one x on the 'x-tier' (the tier of structure that expresses syllable weight).

Exercise 6.4.1

Repeat the exercise, but this time using the example WS *earm*, arm.

Comment on Exercise 6.4.1

Your diagram might look like the following. Note especially what happens to the first position of the Nucleus:

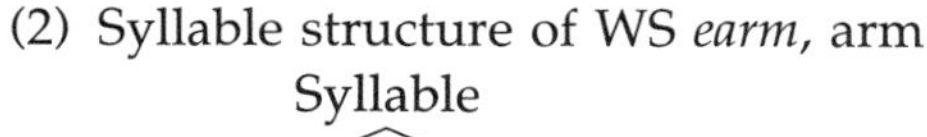

(2) Syllable structure of WS *earm*, arm

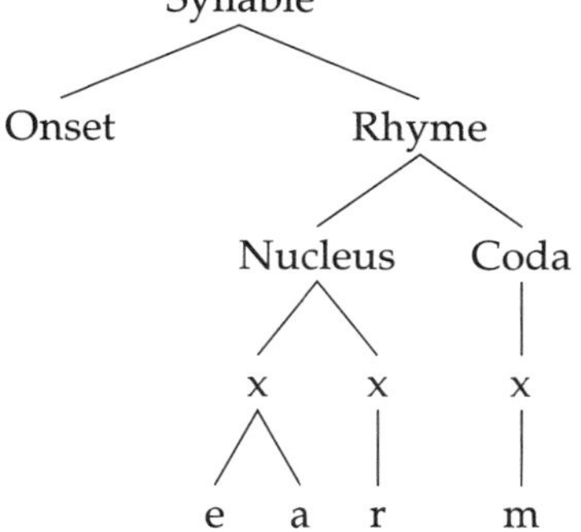

The crucial point is that the original Nucleic configuration isn't 'broken'. Rather, *something is added to it* – in this case, the off-glide that is symbolised by the <a> graph (written symbol). The spelling <ea>, we'd claim (following a long line of writers), is what is pronounced /æɑ/ in WS.

That syllable structure plays a further role in 'Breaking' is further suggested by studying where 'Breaking' *doesn't* happen where expected. For instance, Jones makes the point that in the OE word *Alfred*, the initial vowel is followed by /lfr/ – by /l/ plus a consonant cluster, which on the face of it, looks like the environment for 'Breaking' (Jones 1989:41). Yet nowhere is there the expected post-Breaking spelling *<Ealfred>. Breaking appears not to happen here. Why not? Precisely because the 'back' consonant (or consonant cluster) that apparently triggers the change *must be tautosyllabic with* (belong to the same syllable as) *the affected vowel*. In <Alfred>, the syllable division would be <Al.fred>, where <fr> would form the Onset of the second syllable. This would leave a single post-vocalic /l/ as a possible trigger for 'Breaking' – and whereas 'l + consonant' seems readily to trigger 'Breaking', 'l + nothing' doesn't seem to be 'strong enough' to cause the change with total consistency.

We can map that mystery into syllable structure, too. It seems as though for 'Breaking' to occur, *ideally, a Coda must be present*. (Check this with figures 1 and 2 above, where there is indeed the required consonant in the Coda.) We'd go further and claim that *a Coda must be present in the root*: thus, in *liornian*, to learn, the syllable structure of the full infinitival form would be *lior.nian* (where the first <n> forms an Onset), but in the root, the structure would be *liorn* +, where the <n> forms a Coda constituent.

There's an apparent exception to this: <h> (the speech sound /x/) appears to trigger 'breaking' even when it isn't followed by another consonant in the Coda. Still, this is only an apparent exception: /x/, as one of the most consonantal of consonants (i.e. one of the least sonorous), *can never stand in the Nucleus*, unlike the resonants /r/ and /l/. Therefore, whereas in *arm* or *ald* (arm, old) the /r/ and /l/ stand in the second slot of the Nucleus, in a word such as OHG *sehs*, WS *seox*, six, the /x/ will invariably be in the Coda and be 'available' as it were to trigger the change – if the change is in fact conditioned by syllable structure in the way we're beginning to suggest.

All this leaves one infuriating question dangling: was 'Breaking' a real sound change? Or was the second element of the 'broken' shapes <ea>, <eo> and so forth in WS merely a diacritic that indicated the back (velar) nature of the following consonant? That's a possible view, and one that's haunted the nightmares of many enthusiastic phonologists over the years, particularly following the work of Daunt (1939), who proposed that the 'Breaking' spellings were a 'purely orthographic convention [which] Old English scribes inherited from an Old Irish spelling system in which it [i.e. the use of vowel graphs as diacritics: McC/H] was commonplace and with which they were very familiar' (Jones 1989:49).

We remain undaunted by the possible counter-arguments. To sustain our own view that 'breaking' is a sound change, and not a piece of Irish-derived orthography, we suggest the following:

- vowel shifts of exactly the type manifested in Breaking are common throughout the history of English
- syllable-conditioned changes, of the type manifested, we believe, in Breaking, are evidenced throughout the history of English
- as many studies of both past and present forms of English have shown, speakers are aware of the 'conceptual spaces' that are vowels, of distinctions between 'long' and 'short', tense and lax, etc. . . . and therefore
- the view that Breaking is a sound-change would be supported by (i) phonetic character, (ii) syllable-conditioned plausibility, (iii) intuitive awareness, (iv) the historical persistence of (i–iii) . . . and therefore, by the Uniformitarian Hypothesis

If you wish, as we're sure you will wish, to pursue this controversy to its uttermost limits – and in doing so encounter the work of some of the greatest linguists and philologists of past and present generations – we refer you to the Further Reading section at the end of this unit.

6.5 What is 'an account of linguistic change'?

Despite having spent some time on the sound-change known as Breaking, we've really only scratched the surface of the problems involved in constructing an account of it. And because we've only given a very partial account of the problem here, it's a good opportunity to stand back from it and think about the procedures involved in 'giving an account' of this particular change – and many others. What is it that philologists and historical linguists actually do when they 'give an account'? What makes studying Breaking – and other problems – so interesting, even compelling?

First, an intellectually satisfying account has the ability to *relate apparently unrelated 'facts'*.

With Breaking, for example, and once the basic (supposed) mechanisms of the change are understood, we're in a surprising position to explain something about OE verb morphology. There is in OE, for example, a class of strong verbs – these are verbs, like PDE *ride/rode,* that form their past tense by changing the vowel found in the root – where some knowledge of Breaking helps us to understand some otherwise unexpected forms.

The class of verbs in question is labelled Class III, largely because the vowel alternations in the root are more or less predictable, and distinctive of these kinds of verb, i.e. these verbs behave unlike the verbs in Class I, II, or any other Class of strong verb. They could almost be thought of as going to a kind of 'tune' – a particular kind of vowel alternation, found in the root (see Unit 4). In the infinitive, the *to-* form, for example, the expected vowel is <e>. Thus we have Class III infinitives like *stregdan,* to strew, *berstan,* to burst, and *þerscan,* to thresh (Mitchell and Robinson 1992:38 – an economical account of Breaking). In the 3rd person singular past tense, the root vowel changes to <æ>, thus *strægd,* he strewed. In the past tense plural, the vowel changes again, to <u>, thus *strugdon,* they strewed. This gives the expected vowel gradation series for such Class III verbs as

Infinitive	*Past Tense 3sg.*	*Past Tense pl.*
<e>	<æ>	<u>

The interesting thing is that there are verbs belonging to Class III which *do not show* the expected gradation pattern. An example is WS *weorpan,* to throw. If it's a Class III verb, we expect the vowel <e> in the infinitive; instead, we get <eo>. Again, we expect <æ> in the past tense 3rd person singular; instead, we get <ea>. And we expect <u> in the past tense plural; and this time, we do get what we expect (*wurpon,* they threw').

So what's happening? Breaking can help us explain. Recall that <e> (the speech sound /e/) normatively underwent Breaking – certainly in WS – when it preceded a consonant group such as /r/ + consonant (when these consonants were tautosyllabic in the root). The Breaking process would be something like [e] becoming [eʊ] or [eo] (in the written alphabet, words spelt with original <e> turning up with <eo>). And this is what we find in the infinitive of *weorpan*: the expected <e> spelling doesn't occur and we get the <eo> spelling that reflects the aftermath of the Breaking process. Similarly in the past tense singular: we expect the vowel spelled <æ>, but instead get a vowel shape spelled <ea>. This spelling reflects the Breaking process again – <æ> becoming <ea>, capturing the movement of the speech sound /æ/ moving to /æa/. And in the past tense plural of this verb, as we've mentioned, we get entirely expected <u> – *wurpon,* they threw. But why so? Well, Breaking primarily affected *front* vowels such as /e/ and /æ/. It did not seem to affect back vowels such as /u/ or /o/ (or /o:/ or

/u:/, the long back vowels). This suggests that the phonetic mechanism of Breaking was the addition of an off-glide, of a 'back' character, to short and long front vowel spaces. Back vowels didn't apparently undergo the change precisely because they were *already* 'back'.

So 'Breaking' isn't just a matter of 'messing with prehistoric spelling', as one of our students put it. It interacts with, and helps explain, other, and apparently unrelated, facts – including this last fact, concerning the phonology and morphology of OE strong verbs.

There's another apparently unrelated fact that Breaking helps us to think about, if not 'explain', and that is syllable structure, and the process of syllabification (= how syllables are put together, and/or linked, and/or divided). We hinted above, for instance, that Breaking took place most readily when the trigger consonants were *tautosyllabic* in the word's root form – belonged to the same syllable as the vowel that would undergo the process. But this means that the *syllable*, and not the whole word, is a conditioning factor of the change – otherwise we would get Breaking in the *word* **Ealfred*. Yet for syllable structure to function as a conditioning factor on the process, *syllabification must have applied before the process could take place*. And even more interestingly, it's the syllabification of the *root* that seems to 'count' as the relevant conditioning factor. Thus, in *weorpan*, which we've just studied, the syllable structure of the WGmc infinitive would be *wer.pan*. In such a form, /r/ is alone in the Coda of the first syllable, while /p/ forms the Onset of the second syllable. Now, /r/ *on its own* often isn't 'strong enough' to trigger Breaking, whereas /r/ + consonant is. So where do we find this trigger? Precisely: in the root, WGmc *werp-*, OE *weorp-*. (This still leaves a puzzle, though: what about postulated WGmc *berst-*? Why didn't Breaking take place in that root?)

So – if we're right about syllabification being a conditioning factor here – an account of Breaking means that we have to start thinking about syllabification and how that takes place. And as we think about that, we also have to begin to think about the interaction between OE syllabification and morphology, between sound structure (putting together the syllable) and word-building (morphology = constructing words from roots plus accompanying morphemes, if any are present).

Let's make a second point about historical reconstruction of this kind: an intellectually satisfying account *is based on the widest possible range of evidence*.

When we study the earliest English, the evidence often comes, frustratingly, from languages, or varieties of a particular language, where there are few written records (WGmc). But even scraps of evidence can, to some extent, confirm the interest and consistency of our linguistic narratives. And of course we can also begin to study OE manuscripts themselves for evidence of expected or unexpected spelling forms. This would be the place where historical linguistics interacts with *palaeography*, the study of the history and transmission of manuscripts themselves, together with the spelling conventions that may (or may not) apply to each manuscript. So in an account of something *apparently* rather idiosyncratic, like Breaking, we begin to engage with another, sometimes rather distantly related, discipline, *palaeography*, and in doing so, gain another perspective on the history that is embedded in 'historical linguistics'.

A third and final point: *studying the linguistic changes of the past (often, what seems to be the remote past) helps to give a surprising authenticity to the changes we can study in the present.*

We've suggested everywhere in our work that the structures we can find in the present can help to give authenticity to our narratives and explanations of the linguistic past (remember the Uniformitarian Hypothesis?). But nevertheless, the fact that current and ongoing change can be anticipated by changes that apparently took place (in English and other languages) at much earlier periods of development gives us reassurance that languages – like human beings themselves – do not really pass through 'phases'. Whatever they have been, and however they have developed, in some sense they are still, and in some sense, they must develop still. If we can find cross-linguistic evidence for these pieces of change and continuity, so much the better: they help to give our linguistic story even more consistency, and begin to allow us to think about change (and continuity) as something ongoing, and universal, and (therefore) unavoidable.

In summary:

- an account of any one change requires theoretical consistency, and that desideratum is challenging, therefore (usually) intellectually interesting
- an account of any one change usually requires the relation of apparently unrelated facts – in order to be internally consistent, and explanatorily adequate
- an account of any one change requires authentication from the widest possible range of linguistic evidence, and is often therefore inter-lingual, even inter-disciplinary – something that enhances its intellectual interest
- while all are explanatory fictions, some accounts of linguistic change are *better* than others, precisely because they fulfil the requirements of *consistency* and *adequacy*. They have, that is, an empirically derived *authenticity*. They become that fascinating thing, a true story – and contain all the complexities and even contradictions that the phrase 'true story' implies.

6.6 Crosses

Let's turn our attention to one of the most justly famous OE poems, one that has come to be known as 'The Dream of the Rood' (or the 'Vision of the Cross'). We do so for two main reasons. First, the poem is a remarkably beautiful and memorable artefact in itself, and one with a particularly interesting history. Second, it's claimed that the language of one version of the text – a 10th century WS version – contains some non-WS, specifically Anglian, forms (see e.g. Swanton 1970:7ff.). We need to puzzle about such 'Anglian colouring'. What are the forms, in what is otherwise a late WS manuscript, which can be identified as 'Anglian'? How do we know? What, precisely, does 'Anglian' mean?

The written text of the *Dream* (as we'll continue to refer to it) is found in a codex that contains OE homilies, at least one saint's *Life* and other poems. The manuscript as a whole is known as the *Vercelli Book*, since the text somehow found its way from 10th century England to the cathedral library at Vercelli, in north-west Italy. (You will find Vercelli on present-day maps, situated between Milan and Turin.) We don't know precisely how, or why, the manuscript travelled: it may well have accompanied an English monk on a journey from England to Rome, since 'Vercelli was an important staging post for the not inconsiderable traffic between England and Rome at this time, and the existence of a "hospitalis Scottorum" there probably dates from before the beginning of the twelfth century' (Swanton 1970:3). ('Hospitalis Scottorum'? Roughly, a 'hostel for Northerners'.)

So the *Dream* survives, by accident one might say. And although we can reconstruct its language, and know that the written version of the text came from part of the WS area, we don't know who its author was.

There's one additional piece of information about the *Dream* that must inform any work on the piece. We've referred in our introductory paragraphs to the 'written text' of the poem. This careful phrasing implies that there's another, non-written text of the *Dream* . . . And indeed, there is. A fragment from the poem is found *carved* on a stone cross that is today found in the church at the village of Ruthwell, near Dumfries in SW Scotland. Although the carving is partly made using letter shapes from the runic alphabet, the verbal parallels between it and the WS version of the *Dream* mean that the identity of the two pieces can't be questioned: we're dealing with 'the same' poem. Yet the Ruthwell Cross dates from the late 7th or early 8th centuries, from the Golden Age of Northumbria, whereas the written text of the *Dream*, as it's found in the Vercelli Book, dates from the 10th century (and from a different OE dialect area). Clearly, the poem was known in different areas, perhaps treasured for three centuries, perhaps being written and copied more than once, in Northumbria, possibly Mercia and in Wessex. We don't know. All we have is the substantial, early fragment of the poem as it exists on the Ruthwell Cross and the later, WS version in the Vercelli Book.

To look at photographs of the Ruthwell Cross, you might like at this point to explore some of the websites listed at the end of the chapter. This remarkable, richly carved stone cross, like the Bewcastle Cross – an artefact that dates from the same period and milieu, and is found less than 30 miles away – is clearly a monument that was used for Christian preaching, for spreading the Gospel. It doesn't seem to be entirely coincidental that the *Dream* contains a vision of a Christian way of life, centred on the crucifixion of Christ, but set in an eschatological framework. ('*Eschatology*: the part of theology concerned with death, judgement, and the final destiny of the soul and of humankind', *New Oxford Dictionary of English*.)

What makes the *Dream* so remarkable, so innovative, even possibly unprecedented, is that it is no mere piece of sermonising dressed up as verse. It is an intensely dramatic narrative, in which the human narrator has a vision of the cross in which the cross itself is endowed with human attributes, including speech and the capacity to suffer. As its drama unfolds, the cross itself narrates the events on Calvary, before the human narrator, the dreamer of the *Dream*, is left to draw out the meanings of the cross's narrative in the final section of the poem. The result is an expression of the drama and meaning of the Christian revelation.

The poem opens with the human narrator stating that he wants to explore 'the most important of visions'. The vision seems to have been manifested to him alone, since he was granted it 'while other speech-bearers were at rest', i.e. while they were asleep. Implied here is the view that human beings are often careless about the Christian message; they are 'asleep', spiritually negligent.

The dreamer's vision is of a 'most beautiful tree, one raised aloft, one wound round with light'. It's significant that the word first used to introduce the cross is the everyday word *trēow*, tree – on the face of it, just like any growing piece of wood you'd find in any forest (but about to become a much more multi-faceted, poetically useful symbol later in the text). Behind the vision is a set of images whose significance wouldn't have been lost on a Christian audience in 8th century Northumbria, or 10th century Wessex. The symbol of a tree 'raised aloft, wound round with light' evoked what Swanton (1970:45) calls the 'living tradition' of the veneration of the cross in early Northumbria. This had gained in impetus from Latin sources, including accounts of cross relics and the discovery of the 'true cross' by the mother of the (Christian) Roman Emperor Constantine in 326. Notably, Constantine himself had been granted a heavenly vision of the cross in 312 . . . just before his victory in battle. That some of these accounts and legends were known in 8th century Northumbria is attested by the fact that Aldfrith (reigned 685–704) ordered copies of some 'cross stories' to be made available throughout his kingdom. There is, too, the fact that '. . . in 633, at Heavenfield, Oswald of Northumbria had re-enacted the original Constantinian story, erecting a great wooden cross and praying for the assistance of God before engaging battle, the wood of this cross being subsequently believed to work miracles. And what is believed to be the sole surviving coin-type of Aldfrith's predecessor, Ecgfrith, bears a cross surrounded by rays of light and the inscription +LUX' (Swanton 1970:45).

As the first part of the poem continues, the dreamer's vision of the cross becomes more colourful, and more complex. The 'tree' is 'sprinkled with gold'; he sees it studded with precious stones ('there were five [symbolising the five wounds of Christ] up on the cross-beam'); all creation gazes at this lovely adornment, lost in adoration, rapt with attention. And yet, in contrast to the pristine radiance of his dream, the narrator is aware of himself 'stained with sin'. Furthermore, as he looks on, the cross changes in appearance, sometimes appearing radiant, yet at other times, streaming with blood, dripping with sweat. It is at least a dual image, of triumph and of suffering. This duality is made explicit – for the first time – on line 25, where the text, and the dreamer, make reference to *Hǣlendes trēow*, the cross of the Saviour. Even more surprisingly, at this point in the poem the cross is endowed with a speaking voice, and takes up the narrative.

Exercise 6.6.0

A short piece of translation, from lines 28–34 of the *Dream*. What you are translating are the opening words of the cross as it takes up the narrative of the *Dream*. The first text you'll find below is an editorialised version of this fragment of the poem, typographically set into half-lines and lines. The second, boxed text is a reproduction of that found in Swanton's great edition of the poem (1970), which is based on the Vercelli text. As before, translate into idiomatic PDE, using the Selective Glossary below the translation box, and then answer the supplementary questions you find in the immediately following exercise.

þæt was geāra iū, (ic þæt gȳta geman), (line 28)
þæt ic wæs āhēawen holtes on ende
āstyred of stefne mīnum. Genāman mē ðǣr strange fēondas
geworhton him þǣr tō wǣfersȳne, hēton mē heora wergas hebban.
Bǣron mē ðǣr beornas on eaxlum, oððæt hīe mē on beorg āsetton
gefæstnodon mē þǣr fēondas genōge. Geseah ic þā Frean mancynnes
efstan elne mycle þæt hē mē wolde on gestīgan.
(line 34)

þæt was geāra iū, (ic þæt gȳta geman),
þæt ic wæs āhēawen holtes on ende
āstyred of stefne mīnum. Genāman mē ðǣr strange fēondas

geworhton him þǣr tō wǣfersȳne, hēton mē heora wergas hebban.	**31**
Bǣron mē ðǣr beornas on eaxlum, oððæt hīe mē on beorg āsetton,	**32**
gefæstnodon mē þǣr fēondas genōge. Geseah ic þā Frean mancynnes	**33**
efstan elne mycle þæt hē mē wolde on gestīgan.	**34**

Selective glossary

āhēawen ppl.; cut down (here masc. nom. sg., agreeing with 'I', cf. PDE 'hew')
āstyred ppl.; moved, removed (here masc. nom. sg., cf. PDE stirred)
bǣron verb; carried (3pl. past, infinitive *beran*, cf. PDE bear)
beorg noun; mound, hill (masc. acc. sg.)
beornas noun; men, warriors (nom. pl.)
eaxlum noun; shoulders (fem. dat. pl., cf. PDE axle)
efstan verb, infinitive; hurry, hasten
elne noun; zeal (masc. dat. sg., root *ellen*)
ende edge (masc. dat. sg.)
gefæstnodon verb; fasten, make fast (3pl. past, infinitive *gefæstnian*)
fēondas noun; enemies (nom. pl., cf. PDE fiend)
Frean noun; Lord (masc. acc. sg., root *Frea*)
geāra lit. of years; *geāra iū*, once, long ago
genōge adj.; enough (masc. nom. pl., cf. Mod German *genug*)
gȳta adverb; yet, still
hebban verb, infinitive; to raise up, bear aloft (cf. PDE heave)
hēton verb; commanded (3pl. past, infinitive *hātan*)
holtes noun; forest (masc. or neut. Gen. sg., cf. PDE holt)
iū adverb; once
geman verb; remember (1sg. pres., root *gemunan*)
mycle adj.; great (masc. dat. sg., cf. PDE dialectal 'mickle')

genāman	verb; seize (3pl. past, infinitive *geniman*)
stefne	noun; root (masc. dat. sg.)
gestīgan	verb, infinitive; mount, ascend
strange	adj.; strong (masc. nom. pl.)
wǣfersȳne	noun; spectacle (fem., dat. sg.)
wergas	noun; criminals, outlaws (masc. acc. pl.)
geworhton	verb; made (3pl. past, infinitive *gewyrcan*, cf. PDE wrought)

Idiomatic translation

It was long ago – I still remember it – that I was cut down at the edge of the forest, stripped from my root. Powerful adversaries seized me there, made me into a spectacle for themselves (*him*), enemies enough made me fast there. But then I saw the Lord of mankind hasten (towards me) with great zeal, because he wanted to ascend onto me.

Here is no stripped, scourged Christ – a figure that may be familiar to us from the post-medieval tradition of graphic representation. Instead, the cross seems to participate in a Germanic drama, in which it is seized by 'enemies', and in which Christ is presented as an Anglo-Saxon warrior, eager to embrace the challenge of battle.

Exercise 6.6.1

There are a couple of supplementary questions we'd like to ask, one relating to the language of the text and its 'Anglian colouring', and another relating to the metre of some (but by no means all) lines of the *Dream*.

First, study the form *wergas*, criminals, paying particular attention to the stressed vowel you find in the root (*werg*). In what ways is the written form of this vowel distinct from what you might regularly expect in classical WS?

Second, can you find any ways in which the metre of some of the lines you looked at in the last exercise offers any challenges to the metrical description we sketched in Unit 5?

Comment on Exercise 6.6.1

First, the written form *wergas*. You might have noticed (we hope you did) that the stressed vowel of the root is followed by <r>, plus a following consonant (the <g> that itself begins the final syllable in the form *wergas*). Now, supposing the original stressed vowel of the root was something like /æ/, what we're looking at is precisely the environment that triggers Breaking, at least in classical WS varieties of OE. Therefore, in WS, we might quite reasonably expect the surface form <wearg>. So in this little fiction, we would have the following development in the root of the word:

wærg > *wearg*. Instead, we get *werg(as)*. What's happened? Has Breaking somehow failed to take place? Is it just a copyist's slip, some kind of mistake?

In fact, what we're looking at seems to be a peculiarly Anglian feature of OE phonology, called 'Smoothing'. Hogg's description of this process is again quite complex, but it's the best there is:

> In the Anglian dialects of OE, at or shortly before the time of the earliest texts . . . the short and long diphthongs . . . of whatever source were monophthongized when followed, either immediately or with an intervening liquid [/l/ or /r/: McC/H], by the velar consonants /k,x,ɣ/.
>
> (Hogg 1992:142)

Notice the dating of this postulated process: 'at or shortly before the time of the earliest texts'. This suggests strongly that Smoothing takes place *after* Breaking – in Anglian dialects. In other words, in Anglian areas, Breaking does take place, only for the results of Breaking to be 'undone' by a subsequent change, Smoothing, in particular environments. We're encouraged in this chronology by the phrase 'the short and long diphthongs . . . of whatever source', i.e. whether they were originally diphthongal shapes or whether they were the diphthongal shapes produced by Breaking. And we're still further encouraged by looking at the small print of Hogg's description: 'the short and long diphthongs /ĭu, iu, ĕo, eo, æ̆ɑ, æɑ/ . . . were monophthongized . . .' Now, if you check the shapes /æ̆ɑ, æɑ/ with Section 6.3, you'll find that these are precisely the shapes produced (from original short and long /æ/) by Breaking. So Breaking appears to be 'undone' in certain dialect areas.

The environment for Smoothing is stated as monophthongisation *when followed by a velar consonant*, when this consonant either (i) stands on its own after the affected vowel, or (ii) follows the affected vowel plus 'a liquid'. We know well by now that very often, the letter shape <g> (as in <werg>) is pronounced as a velar fricative; that leaves the sound spelled as <r> as our 'liquid'. What, precisely, is a 'liquid'? One obvious candidate is /l/ – one might say, carelessly but intuitively, it just '*sounds* liquid'. But it quickly becomes clear, if you study the environments affected by Smoothing, that the class of 'liquid' consonants includes /l/ *and* /r/. What do these sounds have in common? Notably, they're both quite vowel-like sounds (in OE, as in PDE, they can function as vocalic peaks), that is, they're quite sonorant (though nevertheless consonantal) and they are both alveolar or post-alveolar in character. That is, they're (i) fairly consonantal, but (ii) they're not stops, and (iii) they're 'continuants', i.e. the air escapes in a (relatively non-fricated) stream.

It's this environment, working in conjunction with that provided by a following/final velar, which seems to provide the trigger for Smoothing – in Anglian dialect areas.

If we can find at least some spelling evidence for 'Anglian colouring' in the written text of the *Dream*, can we find any other evidence? Swanton –

with some circumspection, because the evidence isn't totally conclusive – gives the following examples of *lexical items* (not just spellings) in the *Dream* 'that have been considered specifically or predominantly Anglian . . . *bearn, (ge)frīnan, hlēoðrian, sigor(fæst), sceððan,* or *on* in the sense 'upon'. In the formation of place-names the second element of *feorgbold – bold,* thus – certainly is characteristic of Anglian regions, *boðl* being chiefly Northumbrian and the form *bold,* chiefly Mercian' (1970:8–9; we omit Swanton's meticulous line-referencing). Nevertheless, Swanton's conclusion is tepid: 'In general, however, it may be concluded that the linguistic character of the Vercelli Book version of the *Dream* simply conforms with the standard literary language in which the majority of Old English poetical manuscripts were written, that is, predominantly late West Saxon with a strong Anglian element' (1970:9).

Anglian? Clearly, at this stage this (still) means little more than 'with Mercian and/or Northumbrian features'. However, the presence of such features in the *Dream* shouldn't surprise us, given what we know of the history of the text, and, in particular, its partial, sculptural existence on a cross-shaft in the former OE kingdom of Northumbria. And further, should we wish to identify 'Anglian' colouring in an OE text, we know what kinds of features to look out for – for evidence of Smoothing (where WS would still have spelling evidence of Breaking), and possibly, too, for some *lexical* evidence, for words that seem to 'belong' most readily to one dialect area rather than to another.

The second question we left you with was a question concerning metre. In Unit 5, we claimed that the usual metrical shape of each half-line of OE spanned *exactly four positions*. Yet in the *Dream* excerpt you looked at, there are several half-lines that seem exceptionally long: they can't easily be made to fill 'exactly four positions', neither do they have the minimum one or maximum two main lexical stresses:

> Bǣron mē ðǣr beornas on eaxlum
>
> (**Problem**: if we allow *Bǣron* to be stressed, as the alliteration suggests we should, then *Bǣron, boernas* and *eaxlum* are all stressed, and one ends up with a three-lift half-line. The alternative would be to regard *Bǣron mē ðǣr* as altogether 'unstressed', but that doesn't seem very satisfactory either.)
>
> gefæstnodon mē þǣr fēondas genōge
>
> (**Problem**: if we allow *gefæstnodon* to be stressed – as, once again, the alliteration suggests we should – then the verb, *and* the words *fēondas* and *genōge,* all contain stress, and one ends up with a three-lift half-line.)

There's a somewhat unexpected solution to this difficulty. It's to regard such lines not as 'deviant' or badly constructed, but as *systematically different*. Scholars give such 'long' half-lines a special name: they're *hypermetric verses*.

No-one quite knows what the precise structure (or, for that matter, purpose) of such long half-lines is: 'Occasionally Old English poets shift in the course of a poem to an expanded form of verse which we call hypermetric. Hypermetric verses have three rather than two accented syllables in each half-line; they seem to be composed of a regular verse-type with another half-verse added on . . . Hypermetric lines usually occur in groups of three or more and must have had some kind of special effect for an Anglo-Saxon audience, but we do not know what the effect was' (Mitchell and Robinson 1992:166–67).

In the verses we picked out –

> Bǣron mē ðǣr beornas on eaxlum
> gefæstnodon mē þǣr fēondas genōge –

the 'regular' half-lines would be, in respective cases, 'beornas on eaxlum' (an A type verse), and 'fēondas genōge' (another A Type). Both 'kernel' half-lines have had something extra added to their beginnings. Now, whatever hypermetric verses might be, structurally speaking, it isn't odd that extra material is added to the *beginnings* of constituents, since it's exactly in that place where there's most metrical freedom. Remember one of the key metrical constraints of OE (or for that matter, any other form of metrical verse, in any language)? Right: 'beginnings free, endings strict'. It is a principle of *closure*.

Perhaps the stylistic point of hypermetric verses is merely to add variety. Perhaps at least part of their function is to slow down what would otherwise be a rapidly paced narrative. Perhaps they induce a particular type of concentration in an audience. We don't know. We only know that the existence of such structures seems to be otherwise unparalleled in the English tradition of verse-making.

Summary

For all the uncertainties of historical reconstruction, some of which we've introduced you to in this unit, there's one point we wish to emphasise by way of conclusion. Swanton mentions a 'standard literary language'. In our work in this unit, we've seen something of how such a literary standard evolved, and how it was (rather self-consciously) promoted by King Alfred. Along the way, we've also said something about how different dialects of OE can be identified – about how written evidence can be interpreted, and about how we can begin to think through some of the problems posed by that evidence, particularly with respect to those sound-changes that seem to have affected certain OE dialects. In the next unit, we're going to look at how that written, literary standard (WS) flourished in the early 11th century, aware that this was in many ways a final flourish. Throughout the

11th century, 'Old English' itself was beginning to change with what was apparently great rapidity, especially in northern dialect areas; there was progressive settlement by Vikings (both by Danes and later, Norwegians, who invaded and colonised from the west); and ultimately, in 1066, southern England was invaded by Norsemen who had settled in northern France. This politically and culturally cataclysmic event forms just part of the framework we need for studying 'late Old English', and it's to that topic, and that synchrony, we now turn.

Study questions

1. Consider the word <work>. For many BrE speakers, this word is pronounced with some kind of long (tense) vowel in its Nucleus, and for many of these speakers, there is no post-vocalic /r/. For AmE speakers, while some may have a long (tense) vowel in the Nucleus, others may have a short vowel – and very many AmE speakers will follow the vowel with /r/.

   What interests us is the phonological history of the word. How would you go about reconstructing this, while recalling that the WS form of the word was <weorc> and the Anglian (Northumbrian) form <werc>? Where does the <or> spelling of contemporary Englishes come from?
2. What evidence can you find that sound changes relating to vocalic shapes are taking place in your own variety of English? (Hint: try pronouncing the word 'milk' once at a normal tempo, once at a deliberately slow tempo, and once as it might be pronounced by a Cockney [re-read Section 6.3 if necessary]. Now try the same exercise with the word 'feel'. What happens to the vowel in the different pronunciations as you attempt these exercises?)
3. Are sound changes merely a matter of users of English 'speaking sloppily'?
4. In the preceding units, you've come across (or been deliberately introduced to) words whose inflectional syllables show spelling variation. An example from this unit is *worhton*, they made (spelled *worhtan* in the *Chronicle* entry we studied). Another example, from the *Chronicle* narrative of Cynewulf and Cyneheard, is the spelling *wærun* for expected/regular *wæron*. Why would an expected inflectional ending like <-on> be spelled <-un> or <-an> – or sometimes as both, in the same text?
5. We spent some little time in Unit 6 thinking about the structure of finite verbs and past participles, and their relationship within the Verb Group. Study the following Verb Groups, and in each case identify the tensed (finite) verb, and the past participle:

   They had enjoyed it.
   He had ridden over from the south of the city.

She'd swum for miles.
She'd been thinking a great deal.

6. Find the tensed verb in the following OE examples.

   ic sceolde āwendan 'I had to translate'
   hē nolde ābūgan 'he didn't want to give way'
   hē wolde āhīeran 'he wished to listen to'

   What other verbs are there in OE that can function like the tensed (finite) verbs you have just spotted? What do these verbs become in PDE?
7. Try to find any ONE piece of contemporary English that is written in a 'non-standard' variety? What makes the piece 'non-standard'? Does 'non-standard' mean 'sub-standard' – and if so, to whom?
8. Last, a reprise on sound change. Consider the PDE word <old>. Its WS spelling was regularly <eald>. What would its Anglian spelling have been? Which variety do we take our present pronunciation from?

Websites that you may find useful

- http://www.oxlink.co.uk/wantage/index.html
  This website has a picture of a statue of Alfred the Great, and yields some interesting facts about the great ruler as well as interesting links to other sites and information about films and books
- http://coral.lili.uni-bielefeld.de/Classes/Winter96/Dialects/dialects/node33.html
  This is a very helpful website – e.g. look at 'History of English maps and illustrations' – and shows the dialect areas we talked about in this unit as well as other interesting maps, including diocesan boundaries
- http://www.wmich.edu/medieval/rawl/keynes1/map1.htm
  Map 1 on this site shows the location of the monasteries mentioned in our work as well as diocesan boundaries and the political changes from 700 to 1000
- http://www.newadvent.org/cathen/02441b.htm
  This site lists a number of Roman (and Anglo-) Catholic Saints who also happen to be key figures in the history of English. One can go through the list and click on many individuals mentioned in this chapter (and in others) and from there go to any number of other interesting and helpful sites
- http://www.newadvent.org/cathen/02441b.htm
  This is a small but informative site devoted to Benedict Biscop, founder of the religious houses of Jarrow and Monkwearmouth
- http://www.castlewales.com/offa.html
  For a picture of Offa's coinage and an aerial view of Offa's Dyke

- http://web.ukonline.co.uk/zamberlan/hist-geog/odyke.htm for further pictures of Offa's Dyke
- http://ccat.sas.upenn.edu/jod/boethius.html is an excellent site on Boethius and *The Consolation of Philosophy*
- http://www.flsouthern.edu/eng/abruce/rood/CROSS.HTM is a site devoted to the Ruthwell Cross, with excellent pictures and information
- For a text of 'The Dream of the Rood' and the fragmentary text on the Ruthwell Cross, see http://www.georgetown.edu/labyrinth/library/oe/vercelli.html+%22Vercelli+Book%22&hl=en&ie=UTF-8
- For pictures of the Ruthwell Cross as well as the manuscript that contains 'The Dream of the Rood' see http://www.wmich.edu/medieval/grad/engl676/rood.html+%22Vercelli+Book%22&hl=en&ie=UTF-8
- See also http://www.dumfriesmuseum.demon.co.uk/ruthwellcross.html for information on the Ruthwell Cross . . . and a lovely picture
- For a picture of Bewcastle Cross and some information about it, see http://www.flsouthern.edu/eng/abruce/rood/Bew.htm

References and suggestions for further reading

An intuitively attractive treatment of some of the major phonological developments in OE can be found in Charles Jones (1989) *A history of English phonology*. The most detailed and comprehensive coverage of OE phonology may be found in Richard M. Hogg (1992) *A grammar of Old English: Vol 1. Phonology*. This last work is for specialists, but it's full of detail, it formulates some of the changes in ways that would make sense to a present-day linguist, and it doesn't eschew controversy. As such, it's as much a replacement for as it is a supplement to Campbell's great *Old English grammar* (1959).

Basic, but useful and readable, linguistic introductions to this phase of the development of English include those found in Charles Barber (1993) *The English language: a historical introduction*, and Barbara A. Fennell (2001) *A history of English: a sociolinguistic approach*. Chapter 3 of Fennell's work is recommended.

Material on Alfred may be found in translation (we bet you never thought we'd get round to recommending that) in Simon Keynes and Michael Lapidge (ed. and trans. 1983) *Alfred the Great* (published as part of the Penguin Classics series). Fennell's book (see above) includes a WS excerpt from 'The voyages of Ohthere and Wulfstan', together with an interlinear gloss. The same passage, indeed the whole account of the 'Voyages', may be found in *Sweet's Anglo-Saxon reader in prose and verse* (15th edition, ed. Dorothy Whitelock, 1967).

Some of the history we sketch in this unit is much more adequately covered in Peter Hunter Blair (1970) *An introduction to Anglo-Saxon England*, while John Blair's *The Anglo-Saxon Age: a very short introduction* (1984/2000) is actually more detailed and sophisticated that its title suggests, and a small masterpiece of compression. It may be read in an evening.

A.H. Smith's edition of Cædmon's *Hymn*, Bede's *Death Song* and the *Leiden Riddle* may be found in A.H. Smith (ed. 1968) *Three Northumbrian Poems*. One recent work which looks again at the dating of the Moore MS of the *Hymn* is R.D. Fulk, *A history of Old English meter* (1992). The dating of the Moore MS is discussed in Appendix D of this wonderful work (p.426ff.).

Swanton's edition of the *Dream* is noted in-text. The full reference is Michael Swanton (ed. 1970) *The Dream of the Rood*. This edition includes a very full and useful introductory essay that looks at the linguistic and cultural backgrounds of both the written text of the *Dream* and the fragment that appears on the Ruthwell Cross.

A good modern translation of Boethins is V.E. Watts (ed. and trans. 1998) *Boethins: The Consolation of Philosophy*.

Unit Seven

Twilight

> 1066 marks the division between an age that, if not Golden, is Silver, and one that if not Dark, is Twilight. These changes are vividly reflected in the kinds of English used, and the kinds of evidence we have about them.
>
> Barbara Strang, *A history of English* (1970:284)

7.0 A 'Silver Age'?

In this unit we're going to examine English as we find it, in different varieties, in the 11th century, during the period that precedes the Norman Conquest. In what sense might we claim that this was a 'Silver Age'? And in what sense might we claim that the century following 1066 was a period of cultural, perhaps even of linguistic, 'twilight'? Can there be such a thing as a 'linguistic twilight'? In terms of *evidence*, perhaps; in terms of the *competence of speakers*, probably not.

The distinction that Strang makes (above) runs counter to several intuitions about the English language (and 'the English' as a culture) that we might have previously acquired. Given our relative unfamiliarity with the varieties of OE, and the difficulties we sometimes encounter when reading it, it's tempting to suppose that the Norman Conquest somehow brings a dark and backward language and culture – 'English' – blinking, somewhat nervously, into the early European sunlight of what historians would later dub 'the Middle Ages'. That is, it seems somewhat easier to read and understand this:

> þa þe king Stephne to Englaland com, þa macod he his gadering æt Oxeneford. 7 þar he nam þe biscop Roger of Serebyri 7 Alexander biscop of Lincol 7 te canceler Roger, hise neues, 7 dide ælle in prisun til hi iafen up here castles . . .

than it does this:

> Sē ferde on his iugoðe fram his freondum and māgum tō Scotlande on sǣ, and þǣr sōna wearð gefullod, and his gefēran samod þe mid him sīþedon . . .

The first passage was written during the middle of the 12th century (Clark 1958; we'll encounter this text again in Unit 8 here); the second was written at the very end of the 10th. Our apparent familiarity with the one – the 12th century text – and the apparent ease of reading and understanding it, can translate misleadingly into the supposition that the earliest English was somehow 'primitive', whereas the later, post-Conquest varieties of English were more 'sophisticated', acquiring their patina of Continental modernity from the dubious cultural and linguistic accoutrements of early French, and/or later ('vulgar') Latin.

As we've been at pains to emphasise throughout this work, such a supposition would be very much mistaken. The English language, as we find it in its different varieties through the pre-Conquest 11th century, is quite as sophisticated as any other medium of linguistic communication, and it is perceived as such by some contemporary writers and educators. But while it would be a great mistake to imagine that, after the events at Hastings, the English language somehow ceased to be used (being dispreferred to Norman French), it would be true to claim that English *as a literary and cultural medium* went into a period of relative decline.

We must also note that it's quite possible to over-estimate the immediate linguistic significance of the Norman Conquest. The Conquest didn't mean that English ceased to be used overnight. It didn't mean that the political and clerical institutions of England and the English were, wholesale and everywhere, subject to drastic and *immediate* change (though change there indeed was); nor did it mean *immediate* change in the morphology, or the phonology, or even the syntax of 'English'. In truth, the English language had been subject to pressures for change long before the Norman Conquest, and at least one variety of English – a variety we'll study in this unit – had evolved what seems an astonishingly modern morpho-syntax long before the thought of England was ever a mote in William of Normandy's eye.

7.1 The reinvention of West Saxon prestige

After the death of Alfred (899), and throughout the 10th century, England was more or less a divided entity. Sometimes it was more legislatively unified; at other times it was less politically integrated. During certain decades of this epoch, large areas of the northern Midlands and the North were more a Scandinavian country than an English one, and owed allegiance to Scandinavian overlords. During the same periods, areas of the south and west Midlands, together with the kingdom of Wessex, could claim with justice to be 'English', tracing their language, their political institutions and their royal genealogies back through the Anglo-Saxon generations.

In the period 899–954, Alfred's successors attempted to reconquer the Danelaw – and eventually did so. By 920, English rule was secure south of the Humber, and in the tumultuous decade that was the 920s, Alfred's grandson, Athelstan, pushed the boundaries of England back still further, to the Tees, annexing the kingdom of York and defeating a combined force of Norse and Scots at Brunanburh (the exact site of the battle is unknown) in 937. At this point, Athelstan could almost justifiably claim to be 'king of all the English' (Blair 2000:46; Hunter Blair 1970:85–87).

Such a claim would have been short-lived. Shortly after Athelstan's death, Olaf Guthfrithson, the Viking (Norwegian) leader who had been defeated at Brunanburh, returned to England, re-took the kingdom of York and invaded the eastern part of the Midlands. Yet his exercise of power was in turn brief: Athelstan's brother, Edmund, recovered land south of the Humber and moved northwards, on the kingdom of York, even receiving the loyalty of Malcolm, king of the Scots, after English forces had invaded Strathclyde.

In 946, Edmund was succeeded by his younger brother Eadred. Under Eadred's rule, Eric Bloodaxe, the Scandinavian ruler of the kingdom of York, was overthrown and expelled from England. Thereafter, until the later part of the century, England was almost unified and enjoyed a short period of peace and prosperity: as a political and military force, 'the English' had withstood the first set of Viking invasions. Subject to the pressures of linguistic contact, however – and you'll recall that Danish and, later, Norwegian incursion had been underway for over 100 years – English as a language must clearly have been exposed to circumstances that would catalyse change. One such circumstance is the settlement of Norwegians in parts of Northumbria – particularly in areas of what is now called Cumbria – and in SW Scotland. Even after the expulsion of Eric Bloodaxe, it's safe for us to assume that Norse influence – linguistic and cultural – persisted in these areas of the north and west, reinforced as it would have been by emigration from the Norse kingdom of Dublin.

Let's look for a moment at the closing decades of the 10th century. An area where the English language continued to be used to great effect was in monastic (and, therefore, in cultural) life. One chief exponent of English as a cultural medium was the cleric and scholar Ælfric (c.955–c.1010), whom we have met before in our text.

Ælfric's literary output was vast – it included sermons, saints' *Lives*, a grammar, even a layman's introduction to the Bible (plus a planned, but never completed, translation of the Old Testament). He wrote in both Latin and English. What interests us is the fact that, in his English writings, Ælfric used a form of late West Saxon, a literary variety – a Standard – that had had its beginnings under the sponsorship of Alfred over 100 years earlier (see Unit 6). Even more significant is the fact that Ælfric, like some of his august clerical predecessors, was concerned with revitalising English monastic life, which had declined through the earlier parts of the 10th century: 'True Benedictine monasticism seems to have been almost dead in early tenth-century England. Several great and innumerable small minsters had been destroyed by the Danes, while those which survived had tended towards a more secular lifestyle. Groups of minister priests lived in separate houses with their wives and children. . . .' (Blair 2000:50)

In the second half of the 10th century, and led by (arch)bishops such as Dunstan, Æthelwold and Oswold, Benedictine monastic life was to be revitalised. What's especially interesting for our purposes is that Ælfric, as an important contributor to the continuity and enhancement of that life, chose to write many of his works in the vernacular, in late West Saxon. No doubt his choice of West Saxon was helped by the fact that he had been trained in the heart of Wessex, in Winchester – the most important English monastic school of its period – and had subsequently taken up positions at Cerne Abbas (in present-day Dorset) and (as abbot) at Eynsham, near Oxford. Even more important than the geographical accident of his birth and education is the fact that he chose to write *at all* in a particular variety of English. The new monasticism could, on the face of it, have been developed, and possibly, sustained, in Latin. However, since part of Ælfric's vocation was to train English priests, his decision was that such priests would be more effectively trained in English (which, after all, they knew) than in Latin (which, after all, they might not have known at all). One is reminded of Alfred's prior decisions concerning the literacy of the English. In its own way, Ælfric's scholarship provided just as significant a stimulus to the maintenance of the English language as a medium of culture as did Alfred's desiderata for educational reform. And it is a scholarship based in West Saxon, endowed, however precariously, with the prestige accruing from English courtly patronage and imbued with the ethics – they were no less – of English educational procedures. After all, of how many European languages could it be said, at this point in history, that their educational systems comprised the development and transmission of literacy in the vernacular? How many European cultures believed that the point of such transmission was the endowment of a sense of cultural identity, rooted precisely in the vernacular?

7.2 Alliterative prose (1): Ælfric

As we examine the following specimen of Ælfrician prose, one thing we might ask ourselves is what makes this variety of written English '*late* West Saxon'? Another question we might ask concerns the *form* of this kind of prose: what syntactic and rhythmical shape do these sentences have?

The text is taken from Sweet's *Anglo-Saxon Reader* (ed. Whitelock 1967: 77). That text in turn is taken largely from a contemporary manuscript (Julius E. vii (W), currently in Cambridge University Library), though it exists in two other MSS, one from the mid-11th century, and another from the 12th. As noted in the helpful introduction to the text in Sweet's *Reader*, the fragment we're going to examine is from 'No. XXVI in Ælfric's *Lives of*

Saints, a set of homilies issued between 992 and 1002, probably not later than 998, for the feast-days of saints which the monks observed. Like most of this work, it is in [Ælfric's] fully developed rhythmical style. It is a good example of straightforward narrative; the material comes from Bede, but has been selected and rearranged with great skill' (ed. Whitelock 1970:77).

We provide a translation immediately below the text, but would ask you to complete the exercises following the translation before reading further in this unit.

Æfter ðan ðe Augustinus tō Engla lande becōm, wæs sum æðele cyning, Ōswold gehāten, on Norðymbra lande, gelȳfed swȳþe on God. Sē fērde on his iugoðe fram his frēondum and māgum tō Scotlande on sǣ, and þǣr sōna wearð gefullod, and his gefēran samod þe mid him sīþedon. Betwux þām wearð ofslagen Ēadwine his ēam, Norðymbra cyning, on Crīst gelȳfed, fram Brytta cyninge, Ceadwalla gecīged, and twēgen his æftergengan binnan twām gēarum; and se Ceadwalla slōh and tō sceame tūcode þā Norðhymbran lēode æfter heora hlāfordes fylle, oð þæt Ōswold se ēadiga his yfelnysse ādwǣscte.

Literal translation

After that (time) which Augustine to the land of-the-Angles had come, was a certain noble king, Oswold called, very believing in God. He travelled in his youth from his friends and kinsmen to Scotland by sea, and there immediately became baptised, and his companions together who with him travelled. Between-that became slain Edwin his uncle, of-Northumbrians the king, believed in Christ, by of-Britons the king, Cadwallon named, and twain his successors within two years; and this Cadwallon slew and to-shame ill-treated the Northumbrian people after of-their-lord (the) death, until Oswold the blessed his evilness extinguished.

Idiomatic translation

Some time after Augustine had come to England, there was a certain noble king in Northumberland, called Oswald, greatly confirmed in the faith of God. In his youth, Oswald had travelled by sea – far from his friends and kinsmen – to Scotland [to Iona, then part of an Irish kingdom], and was soon afterwards baptised there, together with the companions who had made the journey with him. Meanwhile, King Edwin, his uncle, another Christian believer, had been slain by Cadwallon, king of the Britons, and within two years, two of Edwin's successors had also been slain. And Cadwallon butchered, and shamefully ill-treated, the Northumbrian people after their lord's death, until the blessed Oswald ended Cadwallon's evil.

Exercise 7.2.0

One clue to the fact that the original is written in a later form of WS may be found by looking carefully at the following words and phrases: *Engla lande*;

fram; and; yfelnysse. To ascertain why such forms are distinctive of this phase of WS, think back to how such forms might have appeared in a WS manuscript of Alfred's time – and think also of how such forms come to be spelled in post-Conquest varieties of English (including PDE varieties).

Comment on Exercise 7.2.0

Trivia first. *Engla lande*, here with the head noun *land* in the dative singular. (thus *land* + *e*), will of course come to be spelled as <England>, as one word. *Engla* is genitive plural, 'of-the-Angles'. At this date, then, *Engla* + *land* still seem to be characteristically spelled as two separate words; by the 12th century they will be spelled as one – as *Englaland* (cf. excerpt in Section 7.0 above). Eventually, the fossilised genitive plural inflection on *Engla* will be lost. Such a childishly simple observation could help us to date this text, albeit in a very crude fashion: it's unlikely to date from a post-Conquest period.

The forms *fram* and *and* are interesting insofar as their vowels were characteristically spelled <o> in earlier WS (<from>, <ond>: these spellings occur in Alfred's *Preface to the Pastoral Care*, which you looked at in the last unit). In post-Conquest Englishes, *and* often retains its <a> spelling, whereas *from* (re-)acquires its <o> graphic shape. You might also care to think for a moment about how such words are often pronounced in PDE: in low-stress (non-emphatic) environments, such as *fish and chips, hidden from view*, the vowel is characteristically, even predictably, schwa – /ən(d)/, /frəm/. Notice, too, that in both cases the vowel is followed by a nasal consonant.

Reconstructing the history of a seemingly innocuous non-lexical word such as <and> isn't altogether a straightforward task, but we'll offer a sketch here, if only to persuade you that the historical linguistics of 'mere function words' is often highly interesting. Take the case of <and>.

In late WGmc and proto-OE, what we know as the familiar conjunction <and> had a form we may reconstruct as something like **andi* (Hogg 1992: 126). The vowel shape of the initial syllable, spelled <a>, undergoes mutation – caused by the presence of a high vowel (in the reconstructed form, spelled <i>) in the immediately following syllable. That is, speakers modify their production of particular vocalic shapes *in anticipation of* the quality of following speech-sounds. We noted something similar in our discussion of Breaking, in the last unit. In this instance, it seems as if the 'a-coloured' vowel raised and fronted in quality, to something like /æ/. How do we know this? In the earliest OE records, our familiar conjunction appears as <ænd> (Hogg 1992:126). In the Moore MS of Cædmon's *Hymn* the word is spelled <end> (*end his modȝidanc*, see Section 6.3). Both the <æ> and the <e> spellings strongly suggest that fronting and raising had taken place.

However, when this 'a-coloured' vowel appeared immediately before a nasal consonant such as /n, m/, its production appears to have been modified again: the vowel acquired a nasal resonance and, for some speakers, may even have been produced as a more retracted vowel shape.

In Alfredian Wessex, the short 'a-coloured' vowel was very typically spelled as <o> when it occurred before nasals, giving the <ond> and <from> that we find in, for example, Alfred's *Preface*. By Ælfric's time, however, all was confusion: since the vowel shapes in *from* and *and* occur so often in unstressed syllables, which by this period were highly likely to have been pronounced with schwa anyway, how should the puzzled scribes actually spell the vowels in question? <a>? <o>? or something else? <u> perhaps?

Connected with <a/o> spellings before nasals in *unstressed* syllables is the spelling of *stressed* vowels in the same environment. Strang comments as follows: '. . . *o* is also used in alternation with *a* in environments where an original short /a/ occurred before a nasal consonant, as in *mann*, *lang* (man, long). It seems likely that the sound in question must have been nasalised /ã/, and that those who devised the writing system were uncertain whether to interpret it as /a/ or /o/. By the late OE period we are here concerned with the most likely situation . . . that in the E[ast] the sound, even if phonetically distinct, was treated as a member of the *a*-phoneme . . . while in the W[est] it had fallen together with /o/' (1970:286).

So by Ælfric's time, the late WS synchrony appeared to lack the relatively systematic solution to the 'a/o before nasals' problem that had appealed to WS scribes 100 years earlier. They had spelled the relevant vowels (in unstressed syllables, and before nasals) typically with <o>. Ælfric and (one infers) his scribes weren't able to adopt such a quick fix, largely because the vowel shapes in question were, in pronunciation, so difficult to distinguish. At least one scribe of the late 10th century, perhaps trained outside Wessex, thought it most convenient to spell <ond> as <and>.

It's this seeming lack of regularity, in something as apparently insignificant as the spelling of unstressed syllables, that gives us a clue as to the fact that we're dealing with *later* WS prose – with Ælfrician, rather than Alfredian, WS.

Exercise 7.2.1

Whitelock comments that the passage from Ælfric we're looking at was written 'in his fully developed rhythmical style'. For this exercise, revisit Ælfric's text, and attempt to specify what this 'rhythmical style' might be. Further, if you can spot the structures that would be the hallmark of a rhythmical prose style, consider the extent to which such a prose style might be distinct from the structures of metrical (OE) verse that we introduced in Unit 5.

Comment on Exercise 7.2.1

One thing you may have noticed is that the passage seems to have been composed in syntactic groups that themselves comprise two-stress rhythmical phrases. This observation might be clearer if we re-lineate the passage, showing the structural groupings we mean:

Prose relineated into rhythmical groups

Æfter ðan ðe Augustinus
wæs sum æðele cyning,
on Norðymbra lande,
Sē fērde on his iugoðe
tō Scotlande on sǣ,
and his gefēran samod
Betwux þām wearð ofslagen
Norðymbra cyning,
fram Brytta cyninge,
and twēgen his æftergengan
and se Ceadwalla slōh
þā Norðhymbran lēode
oð þæt Ōswold se ēadiga
tō Engla lande becōm,
Ōswold gehāten,
gelȳfed swȳþe on God.
fram his frēondum and māgum
and þǣr sōna wearð gefullod,
þe mid him sīþedon.
Ēadwine his ēam,
on Crīst gelȳfed,
Ceadwalla gecīged,
binnan twām gēarum;
and tō sceame tūcode
æfter heora hlāfordes fylle,
his yfelnysse ādwǣscte.

Mitchell and Robinson (1992:196) conduct much the same kind of exercise with another specimen of Ælfric's prose (from the *Life of St Edmund*) commenting that this form of writing is 'an ornamental style which [Ælfric] devised early in his career and used in many of his works. Alliterative prose consists of 4-stressed units bound by alliteration. Ælfric adapted these features from Old English poetry . . . The difference between Ælfric's prose and Old English verse is that he avoids the distinctive poetic vocabulary characteristic of verse . . . and ignores the strictly ordered stress-patterns of verse' (1992:196).

All of which is quite true. We would add, though, that Ælfric's adoption of this style was not 'merely' ornamental. It allowed him to write measured, dignified prose whose form was appropriate to its solemn religious subject matter. It's worth noting, too, that this is prose designed to be read aloud. The rhythmic character of the prose helped the rhetoric of performance. The rhythmic phrasing could be an effective instrument for a grandly paced form of thematic emphasis. We say more about this below. For now, let's try to be more explicit about the characteristics of Ælfric's prose style as it's found in our chosen excerpt.

First, it appears that the units of Ælfric's rhythmical prose style are indeed paired groups of (largely) two-stress units. However, if you recall the most highly ranked constraints of OE verse, as we introduced these in Unit 5, they are that the OE half-line had *exactly four positions*, and that it had *a strict principle of closure*, i.e. it had a very highly ranked constraint on what kind of material could align with position 4, the final position of the half-line.

If you try to coerce Ælfric's rhythmical prose into verse, you'll immediately find it doesn't 'fit'. There are many Ælfrician units that contain more material than would easily slot into the 4 positions of the classical half-line.

Equally, there are many units (particularly in the first 2-stress unit of the Ælfrician line) where there's no strict principle of closure:

1. *More material than would fit into 4 positions*

   oð þæt Ōswold se ēadiga
   1 2 3 4...5.... ?

2. *No fixed principle of closure*

   oð þæt Ōswold se **ēadiga**
   [long, stressed syllable followed by **two** weak syllables]

For these reasons, it's impossible to talk about 'resolution' in Ælfrician rhythmical prose: there's no motivation for it, since there are no *metrical positions*. Equally, it's impossible to talk about the systematic patterning of alliteration, as one would expect to find in classical OE verse. It's quite true that Ælfric uses alliteration prodigiously, but it's not aligned with *metrical positions*. Often, for example, the first 2-stress unit contains one alliterating syllable in its final stressed word: this would be an unexpected, even an impossible, pattern in many kinds of classical OE half-line (specifically, in those half-lines that contain two potential Lifts).

We might question ourselves further as to why Ælfric chose to compose in this style. As far as we know, it was his invention. Nothing quite like it seems to have existed before – although, as we'll shortly see, something very like it, issuing from a different cleric, existed contemporaneously.

One possible reason is that 2-stress units are *comfortable breath-groups* for English speakers (of whatever period). Remember that Ælfric was primarily concerned with promoting the vernacular *for teaching and preaching*: 2-stress units are somewhat more wieldy in performance than, say, 5- or 7-stress units. A related reason is that 2-stress units are often *memorable*, particularly when their structure is enhanced by alliteration. A third possible reason is that the repetition of equivalent structures – in this case, 2-stress units and 4-stress 'lines' – lends itself very readily to *parallelism*, a notable stylistic feature of very many forms of English rhetorical writing (again, writing of any period). Parallelism in turn lends itself readily to patterns of *cumulation* and thematic *climax*. As an educator, a preacher, and as someone vitally concerned with promoting education in English, Ælfric would have been well aware of the stylistic potential of the medium he developed. His genius was to exploit it.

7.3 Alliterative prose (2): Wulfstan

Ælfric was not the only English writer of his period to have developed such a prose style. Another exponent of a highly rhetorical prose, structured in much the same way, was Wulfstan, bishop of Worcester and (simultaneously) archbishop of the war-torn kingdom of York. His renowned sermon, 'Sermo Lupi ad Anglos' – *the Sermon of the Wolf to the English* – was delivered in 1014 and provides a spectacular example of the Wolf (as he punningly styled himself for this purpose) in full cry. Significantly, and rather like Alfred before him, Wulfstan sees the Norse incursions as a punishment for English degeneracy. It's also interesting to note that Wulfstan was a diplomat and statesman as well as a cleric, and someone who was to exert a distinguished, and native, influence on the Danish-born 'king of all the English', Cnut.

Sermo Lupi ad Anglos

Excerpt

Hēr syndan þurh synlēawa, swā hit þincan mæg, sāre gelēwede tō manege on earde. Hēr syndan mannslagan and mǣgslagan and mæsserbanan and mynsterhatan, and hēr syndan mānsworan and morþorwyrhtan, and hēr syndan myltestran and bearnmyrðan and fūle forlegene hōringas manege, and hēr syndan wiccan and wælcyrian, and hēr syndan rȳperas and rēaferas and worolstrūderas, and, hrædest is tō cweþenne, māna and misdǣda ungerīm ealra. And þæs ūs ne scamað nā, ac ūs scamað swȳþe þæt wē bōte āginnan swā swā bēc tǣcan, and þæt is gesȳne on þysse earman forsyngodan þēode. Ēala, micel magan manege gȳt hērtōēacen ēaþe beþencan þæs þe ān man ne mehte on hrædinge āsmēagan, hū earmlīce hit gefaren is nū ealle hwīle wīde gynd þās þēode . . . Ac lā, on Godes naman, utan dōn swā ūs nēod is, beorgan ūs sylfum swā wē geornost magan, þē lǣs wē ætgædere ealle forweorðan.

Idiomatic translation

In this time many on earth are severely blemished, it appears, by the injuries of sin. In this time are homicides and slayers of family and priest-killers and church persecutors, and there are perjurers and murderers, and here there are harlots and infanticides, and many fornicators committing lewd acts, and in this time there are witches and harpies, and here there are plunderers and predators and spoliators and, to be brief, a countless number of all manner of crimes and misdemeanours. And this causes us no shame! Rather, it should concern us that we begin atonement, as the books teach, and that this should be witnessed among this wretched and sin-corrupted people. Alas! a great deal may still be all too easily called to mind that would escape the hasty consideration of just one man, a great deal that would show just how continually wretched things are at this time everywhere among this people . . . But lo! in the name of God, let us act as is necessary for us, and protect ourselves as we best may, else we were all to perish together!

Table 7.1 Some features of later OE phonology and morphology, compared with classical WS

Wulfstan	'Classical' WS
syndan	sindon
-wyrhtan	-weorhtan
āginnan	onginnan
mehte	meahte
gynd	geond

A 'wretched and sin-corrupted people'. Wulfstan here sounds rather like one of today's more dubious television evangelists. Nevertheless, his work should not be dismissed as 'mere' rhetoric from the Early Bible Belt. The fact that he chose to invoke such a thunderous list of crimes is itself important evidence as to the state of proto-England as he (and his congregations) might have seen it: harried, perilously uncultured, lacking in clear (that was to say, Christian) principles. A people at war, a culture at war – not least, at war with itself.

For our purposes in this unit, one particularly interesting aspect of this excerpt from Wulfstan's writings is provided by some of the differences shown in phonology and morphology from the language of classical WS. Some few differences are shown in table 7.1. Some spellings provide inconclusive evidence for the provenance of Wulfstan's variety of English (or that of his scribe): *mehte*, for instance, against the 'classical' WS form *meahte*, reflects a process whereby a monophthong, spelled <e>, <mehte>, apparently coexists with the regular form containing the diphthong developed by Breaking (<meahte>). But these 'smoothed' (monophthongal) forms existed in WS as well as in Anglian varieties. Hogg (1992: 170) calls this smoothing process 'a somewhat sporadic tendency' – so the <mehte> spelling doesn't help us much. A form like <gynd>, on the other hand, does help us *date* Wulfstan's text: it's a spelling that captures the fact that by this period, the short diphthongs /eo/ and /io/ (with <eo> and <io> spellings) had begun to merge.

The spelling *syndan* (expected WS <sindon>) is more significant. The second, unstressed syllable is spelled <-(d)an>. Classically, and regularly, we expect the <-on> inflection in the 3rd person plural here. So why does an <-an> spelling show up? Is it just a scribal slip? Or at this period are <-an> and <-on> *indistinguishable in terms of pronunciation*? If so, scribes would have been puzzled as to how to spell such inflections – as <-an>, <-on>? . . . or even as <-en> or <-un>?

What's at issue here is nothing more or less than *inflectional reduction and inflectional loss*. Since this is such an important topic in the development of the earliest English, it deserves some sections to itself.

7.4 Inflectional loss: introductory questions

It's a commonplace of historical linguistic guides to English that the language went from being a richly inflected, 'synthetic' language to being a less-inflected, 'analytic' language. As Fennell recently put it, '[t]he major changes from Old to Middle English are the loss of inflections, and with it the development of more fixed word order' (2000:97). You will find some comment to that effect in almost any standard history of the language.

We need to ask ourselves the following questions:

- what was actually lost?
- why was it lost?
- when was it lost?

And as linguistic historians, we also need to ask ourselves some supplementary questions:

- what evidence is there for inflectional loss?
- is inflectional loss paralleled in other languages?
- where does the 'lost' material go? (We simply pose this question, because we think it's interesting. We won't attempt to answer it in these pages.)

We'll try to provide at least partial answers to most of these questions. Some answers will be quite well developed; others will be no more than sketches but, for the sketches, we'll provide a list of further reading for you to look at, should you care to develop your thinking about this topic.

From our questions, we'll focus to begin with on just one, since it's procedurally sound to begin with *evidence*: what kinds of evidence do we have for inflectional loss?

7.5 Inflectional loss (1): evidence from the late 10th century

It's tempting to suppose that inflectional loss was a consequence of the Conquest. Our students often claim this, but it is, and was, by no means true. Inflectional loss had begun very much earlier. In fact, we could claim quite accurately that inflectional loss had already begun in WGmc, and continued through proto-Old English into classical OE and later Old Englishes. After all, the inflectional paradigms one finds on nouns (for example) in the classical phase of OE (in WS Standard) are a much reduced set from the paradigms one might have found four centuries earlier in the WGmc dialects of Continental Europe.

But the process of reduction (a term which we'll redefine shortly) and loss seems to have been accelerated in certain varieties of *English* well before the Conquest. Perhaps the rate of change was stimulated by contact with other Germanic languages and dialects; perhaps OE, in some of its varieties, had simply become rather inefficient at developing and maintaining the necessary grammatical distinctions it needed.

One key piece of evidence is provided by the interlinear gloss to the *Lindisfarne Gospels*. These splendidly illuminated and illustrated gospels were written in Latin by Eadfrith, bishop of Lindisfarne 698–721, but they were glossed (translated) line by line into OE by a priest named Aldred 250 years later.

Exercise 7.5.0

Study the following excerpt from the glossed *Lindisfarne Gospels*. The gloss appears in bold font on the top line of text, the original Latin on the middle line, while KJV refers to the version of the text given in the King James version of the Bible. The abbreviation <vel> in the MS seems to act here as an intensifier 'even' or 'so that' (somewhat equivalent to OE *oþþe*), whereas the symbol <7> is equivalent to *and*.

Note each instance of inflectional oddity (principally in nouns and verbs). You should be able to find at least three clear examples of words where the ending differs (and markedly) from what you'd expect to find in WS. Specify which ending should have occurred given what you know already of the classical OE noun and verb paradigms, list what actually occurs and consider how this provides evidence for inflectional change.

(NB: (i) you can achieve a great deal in this exercise just by considering the language of the gloss in relation to your own variety of English. How 'modern' does the language of the gloss seem to you?

(ii) if you need further information on the paradigms of OE inflections, skip forward to the next section before returning to complete the present exercise.)

Gospel of Matthew, chapter VI, vv.1–2

1. **behaldas þæt soðfæstnisse iuerre gie doas before monnum**

Attendite ne justitiam vestram faciatis coram hominibus
KJV: Take heed that ye do not your alms before men

þæt gie se geseno from him eaðe mæg mearde nabbas ge

ut videamini an eis; alioquin mercedem non habebitis
to be seen of them: otherwise ye have no reward

mið fader iurre se þe in heafnas is

apud patrem verstrum qui in caelis est
KJV: of your Father which is in heaven

2. **mið ðy ðonne ðu doas ælmessa nelle þu bema vel stocc singa**

cum ergo facies elemosyna, noli tuba canere
KJV: Therefore when thou doest thine alms, do not sound a trumpet

before þec suæ legeras gewyrcas in somnungum <7> in londum

ante te, sicut hipocritae faciunt in synagogis et in vicis
KJV: before thee, as the hypocrites do in the synagogues and in the streets

vel in gemærum þæt hia se gearðad from monnum

ut honorificentur ab hominibus.
KJV: that they may have glory of men.

soðlice vel soð is ic cueðo iuh to hie gefengon mearde hiora

amen dico vobis, receperunt mercedem suam.
KJV: Verily I say unto you, They have their reward.

There are many varietal spellings here, such as *gie* for what we'd expect as WS *gē*, you (plural), and the OE text may look unfamiliar on that account. Still, in this two-verse extract we can see several features of 10th century Nbr which suggest that, even at this early date, such a northern dialect was losing – or at least, modifying – some of its inflections.

Consider the opening word, *behaldas* (compare WS *behealdan*, watch over). Imperative plural forms in WS had the inflection *-aþ*, thus *fremmaþ*, Do! or *hīeraþ*, Hear! Clearly, Nbr is in the process of modifying this inflection – which will eventually be lost altogether. (And although we didn't ask you to spot this, you may also have noticed that the spelling *-hald-* is distinctly non-WS.)

A similar example is formed by Nbr *doas*. If one reads this as an indicative form – and this is the likeliest reading – the inflection would have been *-(a)þ* in WS; here in the gloss to *Lindisfarne Gospels* we have a form rather like 'you does' compared with 'you doeth'. If, on the other hand, we read this as a form that might have been cast in the subjunctive ('Therefore, should you perform your alms . . .'), then the WS inflection would have been *-en* (*gē dōen*). Interestingly, in a Mercian (Midland) form of the same text, the gloss to the *Rushworth Gospels* (another 10th century MS), the phrase appears as *ne doan fore monnum*. Either, then, the Nbr word shows that the dialect was in the process of modifying its indicative plural verb morphology or that it was in the process of modifying the subjunctive . . . or both.

A striking example of inflectional modification in nouns is provided by the word *heafnas*. In WS, this word would regularly have appeared in the dative plural as *heof(e)num*, and in fact appears as *heofunum* in the Rushworth text. Yet in 10th century Nbr we seem to have a form much closer to PDE *heavens*, with a plural *-s* ending rather than WS dative plural *-um*.

With further study of even this fragmentary text you'd be able to identify several other instances of inflectional erosion or loss (the verb morphology is especially interesting), but the point's been made: when linguistic historians of English speak of inflectional loss, they're not altogether indulging in a tidy retrospective fairy-tale. The evidence for erosion and loss is there. Judged from the perspective of what morphology remains in 'classical' OE, the process begins very early . . . and it begins in the North: 'if we turn to writings not in the Standard language, we find in Northumbria a phase of grammatical development almost as far advanced towards modernity as the Standard language of the 15th [century]' (Strang 1970:294).

7.6 Inflectional loss (2): what was lost?

To answer this question, it's convenient to study inflectional loss from the perspective of the set of inflections a user of classical WS might have maintained. There are other perspectives we could take: as we've pointed out, should we choose to study inflectional loss from the perspective of WGmc, 600 years previous to the 11th century, we'd find that even classical WS showed a markedly reduced set of inflectional endings. But for our purposes the simplest thing is to study inflectional loss against the context provided by WS Standard – largely because we have established that this was a 'Standard', but also because it provides a convenient, though arbitrary, point of reference.

First we need to look again at some *strong noun* paradigms. Nouns behaving in this way are called 'strong' largely because they are distinct from *weak nouns*, which characteristically have many of their plural forms in *-an* (recall Unit 3). Strong nouns show some case-dependent variety in the ways in which they form their plurals. Additionally, the strong nouns of OE, as they appear in WS, have themselves descended from different classes of nouns in WGmc. You'll very often find references in standard handbooks of OE to 'a-stem nouns' or 'o-stem nouns'. These references can at first glance seem puzzling, but matters become clearer if you remember that references to 'such-and-such-a-stem noun' refer to the forms historically underlying their residues in OE. Of recent commentators, Fennell makes this particularly clear:

Nouns in Old English are divided into vocalic or consonantal stems, depending on the element in which the noun-stem originally ended. There are four vocalic stems *-a, -o, -u,* and *-i,* though the vowel itself was often lost in Old English, the declension being actually inherited from an earlier form of Germanic. The *-i* stems, e.g. *wine* 'friend', for the most part joined the masculine *-a* nouns . . . The largest group of consonantal stems was marked by the presence of *n* in Indo-European. Among vocalic stems, masculines consist of *a*-stems (and old *i*-stems), neuters of *a*-stems and feminines of *o*-stems, while *u*-stems were either masculine or feminine. Consonant stems could be any of the three genders'.

(Fennell 2000:65)

With these comments in mind, let's look again at a list of OE noun inflections as we might expect to find these in classical WS. Tables 7.2 and 7.3 show inflectional endings for both strong (vocalic) and weak (consonantal) nouns.

In terms of loss, it's clear that English (eventually) sheds every inflectional ending in the strong paradigms *except for genitive singular -es and nominative/accusative plural -as.* Further, the system of grammatical

Table 7.2 Strong inflection of OE nouns

		Masculine	Neuter	Feminine
Sg.	N	cyning, king	word, word	lār, lore
	A	cyning	word	lār-**e**
	G	cyning-**es**	word-**es**	lār-**e**
	D	cyning-**e**	word-**e**	lār-**e**
Pl.	N	cyning-**as**	word	lār-**a** (~-**e**)
	A	cyning-**as**	word	lār-**a** (~-**e**)
	G	cyning-**a**	word-**a** (~-**ena**)	lār-**a** (~-**ena**)
	D	cyning-**um**	word-**um**	lār-**um**

Table 7.3 Weak inflection of OE nouns

		Masculine	Neuter	Feminine
Sg.	N	nam-**a**, name	ēag-**e**, eye	abudiss-**e**, abbess
	A	nam-**an**	ēag-**an**	abudiss-**an**
	G	nam-**an**	ēag-**an**	abudiss-**an**
	D	nam-**an**	ēag-**an**	abudiss-**an**
Pl.	N	nam-**an**	ēag-**an**	abudiss-**an**
	A	nam-**an**	ēag-**an**	abudiss-**an**
	G	nam-**ena**	ēag-**ena**	abudiss-**ena**
	D	nam-**um**	ēag-**um**	abudiss-**um**

gender is (and again, eventually) modified. In the weak paradigms, virtually everything is lost, albeit slowly (we no longer inflect plural nouns regularly in *-en*, though in Midland varieties of Middle English this was still a regular way of inflecting many nouns for plurality). And as everything begins to become 'lost', the former weak nouns begin to pattern with the surviving strong nouns, starting to take their plurals in *-s*, rather than in *-an*.

Once so many nominal inflections have vanished, what remaining point is there in a language maintaining a full set of case distinctions? Can case distinctions be maintained if they have no inflectional exponents? In the longer term, one wouldn't think so, no. And therefore, English slowly begins to lose its system of grammatical case, at least case as marked on nouns. We no longer speak of 'nominative' and 'accusative', but of Subject and Object, grammatical entities whose existence we infer from their relationship with verbs, and from syntactic constituency and position, rather than from inflectional endings. (Note: *pronouns* in PDE still show (relics of) case. To think that observation through, look at the Study Questions at the end of this unit.)

Eventually, the system of grammatical case is modified and grammatical gender is lost. Yet, as we know, WS had also had a *definite article* that inflected for case, gender and number. Further, if an *adjective* was preceded by a definite article, the adjective inflected 'weakly' (typically, in *-an*), whereas if the adjective stood alone ('strong ships'), then it took a 'strong' range of inflections. Both adjectives and articles had of course to show agreement (in case, gender, number) with the noun they modified. This material will be familiar from Unit 3, but for ease of exposition, we give summaries below (tables 7.4 and 7.5).

What happens to this range of adjective inflections? It's almost wholly lost. There are some sporadic (largely rhythmically driven) survivals – we would tend to say *a drunk**en** sailor*, not *a drunk sailor*, *a wood**en** box* not *a wood*

Table 7.4 Strong inflection, adjectives

		Masculine	Neuter	Feminine
Sg.	**N**	glæd	glæd	glad-**u** (~ -**o**)
	A	glæd-**ne**	glæd	glad-**e**
	G	glad-**es**	glad-**es**	glæd-**re**
	D	glad-**um**	glad-**um**	glæd-**re**
	I	glad-**e**	glad-**e**	glæd-**re**
Pl.	**N**	glad-**e**	glad-**u** (~ -**o** ~ -**e**)	glad-**a** (~ -**e**)
	A	glad-**e**	glad-**u** (~ -**o** ~ -**e**)	glad-**a** (~ -**e**)
	G	glæd-**ra**	glæd-**ra**	glæd-**ra**
	D/I	glad-**um**	glad-**um**	glad-**um**

Table 7.5 Weak inflection, adjectives (preceding article also shown)

		Masculine		Neuter		Feminine	
Sg.	N	se	gōd-**a(n)**	þæt	gōd-**e**	sēo	gōd-**e**
	A	þone	god-**an**	þæt	gōd-**e**	þā	gōd-**an**
	G	þæs	gōd-**an**	þæs	gōd-**an**	þǣre	gōd-**an**
	D/I	þǣm/þȳ	gōd-**an**	þǣm/þȳ	gōd-**an**	þǣre	gōd-**an**
Pl.	N	þā	gōd-**an**	þā	gōd-**an**	þā	gōd-**an**
	A	þā	gōd-**an**	þā	gōd-**an**	þā	gōd-**an**
	G	þāra	gōd-**ra**	þāra	gōd-**ra**	þāra	gōd-**ra**
		~	gōd-**ena**	~	gōd-**ena**	~	gōd-**ena**
	D/I	þǣm	gōd-**um**	þǣm	gōd-**um**	þǣm	gōd-**um**

Table 7.6 Inflection in present-day Germanic languages

	Gender maintained?	Infl. def.art.?	Adj. infl.?	Nouns infl. for case?
English	No	No ('the')	No	No
Dutch	Partly	For gender	Partly (-e/-zero)	No
German	Yes	Yes	Yes	Yes

box – but they are vanishingly few. And the inflected definite article largely disappears . . . in English, although it survives, as students of German will know to their cost, in other Germanic languages.

It's instructive to think of the differences in the *present-day* inflectional structures (or lack of them) in three Germanic languages (table 7.6) in order to emphasise the distinctions English was to lose. (One question you might like to begin thinking about now is why English lost so many of its inflections whereas German *maintained* so many, particularly where these are exponents of case in articles, and in the system of adjectives.)

Returning to WS, we can also observe the verb morphology was about to undergo extensive modification (we spotted the first traces of change in the fragment from the *Lindisfarne Gospels*). As we've seen from some of our translations, verbs, at least in WS, regularly inflected for *number* (whether singular or plural), *person* (1st, 2nd, 3rd), *tense* (present or past) and *mood* (indicative, subjunctive, or – something we've only mentioned in this text – the mood of command, the imperative). This pattern of inflection obtained whether the verb was historically 'strong' (i.e. whether it changed the vowel in its root in the past tense: *ride/rode*) or 'weak' (i.e. whether it formed its past tense forms by suffixation (*-ed-/-od-*): *arrive/arrived*). Again, these

Table 7.7 Inflection of OE strong verbs

Infinitive	wrītan	cēosan	sēon
PRESENT			
Ind. 1. Sg.	wrīte, write	cēose, choose	sēo, see
2. Sg.	wrīt(e)st	cyst	syhst
3. Sg.	wrītt	cyst	syhð
1.–3. Pl.	wrītað	cēosað	sēoð
Subj. Sg.	wrīte	cēose	sēo
Pl.	wrīten	cēosen	sēon
PRETERITE			
Ind. 1. Sg.	wrāt	cēas	seah
2. Sg.	wrīte	cure	sāwe
3. Sg.	wrāt	cēas	seah
1.–3. Pl.	writon	curon	sāwon~sǣgon
Subj. Sg.	write	cure	sāwe
Pl.	writen	curen	sāwen
Imperative 2. Sg.	wrīt	cēos	sēoh
2. Pl.	wrītað	cēosað	sēoð
Present Participle	wrītende	cēosende	sēonde
Past Participle	gewriten	gecoren	gesewen

distinctions should be clear to you from the work we did in Unit 4 here, but we give summaries above and below (tables 7.7 and 7.8).

In terms of linguistic change, again we can observe that there have been several simplifications in the verb system. We pick out only some of the more striking changes and simplifications in what follows.

1. OE verb infinitives are signalled by the morphology [[root] + (i)an]. In PDE, infinitival structure consists of [(to +)[root]]
2. OE strong verbs are distinguished by the fact that they change the vowel of the root in their past tense. Such verbs, and their morphological behaviour, often survive into PDE ('ride–rode–ridden'), but significantly, some originally strong verbs sometimes begin to pattern with the weak paradigm, that forms its past tense using a suffix containing a <-d->. Many speakers of PDE, for example, vacillate when asked to form the past tense of a verb such as *dive*: is it *dove*? (it would be for many AmE speakers)? Or is it *dived*?
3. OE weak verbs, and their morphological behaviour, become numerically the preponderant class of verbs: verbs loaned into English in the ME

Table 7.8 Inflection of OE weak verbs

Infinitive	Ia: settan	Ia: herian	Ib: dēman	II: lufian
PRESENT				
Ind. 1. Sg.	sette, set	herie, praise	dēme, judge	lufie, love
2. Sg.	set(te)st	herest	dēmst	lufast
3. Sg.	sett	hereð	dēmð	lufað
1.–3. Pl.	settað	herıað	dēmað	lufiað
Subj. Sg.	sette	herie	dēme	lufie
Pl.	setten	herien	dēmen	lufien
PRETERITE				
Ind. 1. Sg.	sette	herede	dēmde	lufode
2. Sg.	settest	heredest	dēmdest	lufodest
3. Sg.	sette	herede	dēmde	lufode
1.–3. Pl.	setton	heredon	dēmdon	lufodon
Subj. Sg.	sette	herede	dēmde	lufode
Pl.	setten	hereden	dēmden	lufoden
Imperative Sg.	set(t)e	here	dēm	lufa
Pl.	settað	heriað	dēmað	lufiað
Present Participle	settende	heriende	dēmende	lufiende
Past Participle	gesetted	gehered	gedēmed	gelufod

period, for example, form their past tenses by adding <-d->. This behaviour still occurs today. If we coin a nonce-verb, for example – say, the verb *to snorp* – how would you form its past tense? You'd have no hesitation in saying 'The past tense form is *snorped*'. Even if we were to form another nonce-verb, with a high, tense front vowel in its root – say, the verb *to flike* – again you'd very probably form its past tense as *fliked* (rather than *floke*).

4. In the present tense plurals, OE forms the relevant morphology by adding <-(i)að>. Today, we don't add any inflectional morphology to present tense plural verbs: *I ride, we ride*; *I talk, they talk*. This isn't the case with other Germanic languages: present-day Dutch, for example, adds *-en* (*ik loop*, I walk, *wij lopen*, we walk). Interestingly, many varieties of ME behaved the same way as present-day Dutch, adding *-en* to indicate 'present tense plural'.

What these remarks intend is an observation of some of the morphological changes that were underway in English before the Conquest and that continued after it. The verb morphology changes; the system of inflections on nouns simplifies. There is further change in the inflectional structure found on adjectives and, eventually, wholesale remodelling of the system of the definite article.

Since the Norman Conquest, and socio-political events subsequent to it, form the cultural backdrop to the 11th and 12th century linguistic drama that is English, before continuing with the analysis of what was lost, how it was lost and when it was lost, we ought to look at some further external history. We introduce that at the beginning of the following, and final, unit.

Summary

In this unit we've studied a prestige model of late WS prose and contrasted it with another specimen of prose that displayed some non-WS characteristics. Both specimens of prose we studied were written in an alliterative style and we tried to work out what the features of that style might have been, noting that such ornamental prose could never be analysed as verse. We then turned to the topic of inflectional loss, asking some leading questions along the way, and began to analyse how the system of case began to modify, how case-marking via inflection was in many cases lost, and how the system of grammatical gender changed. Using the inflections of classical WS as a comparative baseline, we tried to identify what was lost of the OE inflectional system, particularly in the patterns of noun, adjective and verb inflections.

Study questions

1. Frequently we think of the English language as being radically 'changed' by the events of the Conquest. Is this an accurate perception? Why – or why not?
2. The text mentioned Cnut, who reigned 1016–1035. Who was he? Why is he important in the story of English? Under his reign, what happened to the English language?
3. Why is the work of Ælfric important in chronicling the story of English?
4. In your own words, give the linguistic history of the word *and*. What does the linguistic term 'mutation' mean?
5. On what grounds might you claim that Ælfric's rhythmical prose was written in 'an ornamental style'? What forms of 'ornamentation' were involved?
6. Why is loss of inflection important in the overall story of English?
7. When and where does evidence of inflectional loss begin to appear in English?
8. What evidence do we have of inflectional modification and/or loss in PDE (or in other present-day Germanic languages), and what explanatory value does this evidence have for analysing inflectional loss as it took place in OE and eME?

9. To what extent does the pronoun system of your variety of English still show evidence of grammatical case? (Hint: particularly interesting evidence might be found by considering relative pronouns.)

Websites that you may find useful

- http://www.georgetown.edu/cball/oe/oe-map.html
  This site contains a map of Europe showing Danish settlements, the Danelaw and the Anglo-Saxon kingdoms c.830
- http://www.mirror.org/ken.roberts/king.alfred.html.
  Links on Alfred the Great
- http://www.ogdoad.force9.co.uk/alfred/alfredintro.htm
  Some 9th-century English towns
- http://sunsite.berkeley.edu/OMACL/KingAlfred/part1.html
  More links on Alfred the Great
- http://www.britannia.com/history/histmaps.html
  Useful maps
- http://orb.rhodes.edu/encyclop/early/pre1000/ASindex.html
  Very detailed map section – you'll have to go down about three-quarters of the way through to find it
- http://www.rook.org/heritage/german/anglosaxon.html
  General principles
- http://www.maldavies.ic24.net/vikings.html
  Dramatic website, with a good map section (Danelaw)

References and suggestions for further reading

Charles Barber's *The English language: a historical introduction* (1993), Chapters 6 and 7. Strang, *A history of English* (1970) gives much more detail. Her Chapter V (detailing English linguistic history in the pre- and post-Conquest period) is essential reading.

Unit Eight

Rebuilding English

> A point of great interest in the development of English is why a Germanic language very similar to the ancestor of Modern German became an SVO language depending on prepositions and lost the inflexions, the three Germanic element orders, and such things as the strong and weak declensions of the adjectives – features which are all retained in modern German. My own view, shared by others, is that a major factor was the Scandinavian invasions and the consequent establishment of bilingual communities of speakers of English and Scandinavian dialects – all Germanic in origin. As a result, the inflexional endings (which differed from dialect to dialect) were confused and reduced so that they were no longer distinctive.
>
> (Mitchell 1988:342)

8.0 Hastings and after

In June 1066 an English person, if he or she thought about it at all, would recognise that one of the problems facing 'the English' was the fact that the monarch, a pious but ailing Edward ('the Confessor'), had produced no direct heir. The indirect heir to Edward's crown was his nephew's son, Edgar, but Edgar was too young to rule a turbulent nation in turbulent times. Besides, there were more powerful claimants to the English throne.

Harold, the son of Godwine, earl of Wessex, was certainly one of the most powerful magnates within England, and in the seventh decade of the 11th century had already enjoyed considerable political success. His political ambitions commanded widespread assent among those volunteering for, or pressed into, his service.

Across the North Sea, however, the king of Norway, Harold Hardrada, saw himself as the historically legitimate heir to what had been Cnut's kingdom.

Across the English Channel, there was William of Normandy, who rightly or wrongly considered himself to have been promised the English throne by both Edward and (perhaps, to us, more surprisingly) by Harold of Wessex. It is known, for example, that Harold of Wessex had visited William of Normandy's court in 1064 or 1065, and there had apparently sworn an oath of allegiance to William. Thus much is implied by the Bayeux Tapestry, but it's impossible to be sure whether such a story was a piece of Norman embroidery or encodes the historical truth.

What is certain is that William of Normandy's political ambitions were an approaching problem. In the autumn of 1066, the problem materialised in person, accompanied by a formidably equipped army, transported over the Channel by the fleet that William had taken care to assemble through the early months of the year. Meanwhile Harold of Wessex, who had duly, if not happily, succeeded Edward the previous January, was in Yorkshire, countering the attack of Harold, King of Norway, who had chosen this moment to mount his claim to the English throne.

While Harold of England was in Yorkshire, William and his army landed in Pevensey (Sussex) on 27 September. They were unopposed. Since it provided a more secure strategic position than Pevensey, William and his forces occupied Hastings at the beginning of October. As Stenton tellingly puts it, William can at that stage have known nothing of the events occurring in the English North: '. . . several days must have passed before [William] could be certain that his opponent would be Harold of England and not Harold of Norway' (1947:583).

In the event, it was Harold of England who, having won an astonishing victory over the Norwegian invasion forces in the North, brought his troops southwards to face William. Battle was engaged at Hastings on 14 October. By the evening of the same day, it was clear not only that Harold had been killed (probably by a random arrow), but that the English forces had been vanquished.

8.1 English, Norman and Anglo-Norman

Our students sometimes tell us that it was the Norman Conquest that immediately gave rise to that staple of undergraduate essays, the 'French loan-words' that at first trickled, then flooded into the English language. But loans from French had begun to infiltrate at least some varieties of English years – if not decades – before the autumn of 1066. That would not be surprising, given the cultural contacts that had already taken place between English and French courts (see above). As Strang writes:

> It should not be supposed that borrowing from French is merely due to the Norman Conquest. The cultivated and outward-looking society of late Anglo-Saxon times already had relations with France, and in accordance with the late tendency to borrow rather than form calques [loan-translations of phrases: McC/H] a number of French words had been taken in even before the Conquest. Examples are *prūd*, 'proud', *sōt*, 'foolish' (which seems to have been borrowed in slightly different forms from both Latin and French before the Conquest), *tūr*, 'tower' (which also had been borrowed very early in the form *torr*, from L *turris*), *capun*, 'capon', and a few others. Before 1100 we have (and now the

> subject-matter of the loans is highly significant) *arblast, serfise, prisun, castel, market, cancelere* (a Norman form). Between 1100 and 1170 some thirty others, including *abbat, capelein* (Norman), *cardinal, clerc, cuntesse, duc, legat, prior, curt, rent, tresor, iustise, miracle, standard.*
>
> (1970:316)

Generally, many of the French loans from this early period of contact were concerned with legal and political matters, with the exigencies of government. Some concerned the partial remodelling of the clerical system. There is not among this group of loans evidence of the same intimacy of contact that was simultaneously taking place (in non-southern areas) between varieties of English and Scandinavian dialects – linguistic borrowing (in some cases, replacement) in which pronouns, prepositions and even parts of the verb *to be* made their way into English.

We'll look at some Scandinavian loans in the subsequent section of this unit. For the moment, it seems worthwhile to look in a little more detail at the language of the invaders, the Normans. What kind of language did they bring with them to England? What impact did such a language have on England and the English? After all, if the Normans were ultimately Scandinavians, how come their language was by 1066 effectively an early form of French?

Parts of Normandy, and what is now Brittany, had been invaded by Scandinavian forces – mainly by Danish armies, and their subsequent settlers – in the mid-9th through the early 10th centuries (Haugen 1976:136). But as Haugen points out, early forms of French language (and culture) had in this instance assimilated the Dane, rather than Danish usurping early French. The impress of Scandinavian loans was, in Normandy and Brittany, fairly slight. Haugen also makes the point that in Normandy of the 10th and 11th centuries, 'Sc[andinavian] can hardly have lasted more than a generation or two' (1976:135). Given the cultural prestige of forms of French, and the political and cultural necessity to trade with other kingdoms within France, the originally Scandinavian kingdom of Normandy had become 'continental'.

In post-Conquest England, then, the language of the Norman invader was not that of a more or less mutually intelligible Germanic dialect, as was the case with Scandinavian contacts in parts of the north, the north-east and the north-west of the country. It was a different language entirely – different in its pronoun system, its verb morphology, its patterns of noun and adjective inflection, its syntax and its lexicon. It had different linguistic manners. It follows that whatever linguistic impact Norman French was to have on English, it would take time for such changes to develop. Given the differences between the two languages, it would be logical to assume that the apparent changes would at first be largely lexical, i.e. to do with loanwords and loaning processes.

It's worthwhile looking behind the surface of 'loaning' for the cultural and linguistic relationships that underlie the process. Haugen (1976) follows in a long line of historical linguists (e.g. see Wyld 1927:51) in describing the procedures that emanate from linguistic contact:

> It is well known that the influence exerted by one language on another is in some degree correlated with the social and political relationships of their speakers. The connection is neither simple nor fully understood, but it has been observed in many times and places that dominance by one people over another stimulates dominated people to learn the language of the dominant one. There is a greater pressure on the dominated than on the dominant to become bilingual. If the dominance endures for any length of time, the bilinguals are fairly certain to do one or both of the following: (a) *adapt* their own language to resemble the dominant one, primarily by borrowing words and phrases from the latter; (b) *adopt* the dominant language as their only language, while gradually forgetting their own. It is important to note that (b) does not necessarily follow from (a); there are numerous contrary instances. But it is conspicuous that when (a) does occur, it is nearly always a one-way street: borrowings move primarily from the dominant to the dominated.
>
> (Haugen 1976:64)

Is language contact simply a matter of 'adopt or adapt'? Clearly, what had happened to the Scandinavians in Normandy seems to have been a matter of adoption, i.e. they 'adopted' French. And what happened to some varieties of English, post-Conquest, appears to have been that they 'adapted' – primarily by borrowing words, by which is meant 'borrowing lexical (to a greater extent than non-lexical) items'. Notably, some varieties of English also, in the post-Conquest period, borrow *phrases* from French, which are then calqued into English, as in the English expression 'to do justice', which begins life as a calque (a loan-translation) on Fr 'faire iustise'.

It is clear that William of Normandy wished to rule as a legitimate English king. For three years subsequent to 1066, he appears to have

> made a serious attempt to govern England through men who had held high office in King Edward's day. For the greater part of 1067 the natural leaders of the English people were in eclipse, as hostages with the king in Normandy. But they reappear on the establishment of a regular administration in England after his return, and thenceforward until the summer of 1069 there is no question of their importance in the state. None of the lesser materials for the history of William's reign are more interesting than the charters which show Edwin, Morcar, Waltheof, and Archbishop Stigand associated in council with Odo of Bayeux, Geoffrey of Coutances, Earl William fitz Osbern, and Count Robert of Mortain.
>
> (Stenton 1947:615)

For men such as Odo of Bayeux or Geoffrey of Coutances, what motivation would there have been to learn English? How much time did they actually spend in England, among the English?

For Norman landowners like these – men now endowed with lands across the English Channel, as well as with their home estates in France – the answer to both questions would be 'not much'. Yet we can't simply interpret that lack of motivation to mean that they, or their retinues, and still less, their own successors, were *never* present in England. One of William's innovations, for example, was to call a Great Council that met three times each year (held respectively at Gloucester, Winchester and Westminster, at Christmas, Easter and Whitsuntide). On those peripatetic occasions, which were political as well as merely ceremonial, William's barons were expected to be present. And not just on those occasions. Stenton states that 'the duty of this kind which [his barons] paid [William] went far beyond these formal occasions. The witnesses to his charters suggest that some of the greatest men in the land must have spent an appreciable proportion of their time in his company . . . Other lords of the first importance repeatedly appear at court . . . From one or other of these men the king could obtain first-hand information about every part of England, except the extreme north' (Stenton 1947:623–624).

What's at issue here is the character of William's administration, and the language spoken by his administrators, including his sheriffs. These men, through self-interest, through financial inducement, or through the pressings of the need to find (English) bodies to coerce into military service, were often – one might say 'normally' – resident in England. And although neither they, nor their immediate successors, might have had any motivation to learn English, it is certain that in political and military circles there would be a motivation for the English to learn French. French is prestige. French is get-ahead. But there is still no pressure for English to be adapted to French immediately. The process – if it takes place at all – is necessarily bound to take at least two generations, as (possibly bilingual) children exposed to the 'adapted' variety of English in turn bring up a new generation of speakers for whom the 'adapted' tongue is a first language (L1). Alongside the evolution of an Anglo-Norman *society*, for example, one looks also for the emergence of an Anglo-Norman (A-N) *language*. Does such a language come to exist? And if it does come to exist, what kind of language is it? What is its cultural status? Is it supported by a literature, and through the desire of people to use it as their prestige L1?

A preliminary answer is that through the 12th century A-N does indeed come to exist. It is not, as one might expect, a widespread language and, since one of its roots is in a French that becomes increasingly insular, it is not going to be a long-lived language, except in certain specialised registers such as that of the law. Its use seems to have been confined to the administrative, mercantile and professional classes (in which last we include the class of clerics and academics, many of whom were also able to write in Latin). And again, as one might expect, it is a prestige variety. Happily, we have near-contemporary accounts of the prestige of A-N and insular French.

Although it is written in the 13th century, the chronicler of Robert of Gloucester's comment that 'If a man does not know French he is little esteemed' would seem to hold good for the 12th century, a time when the English court was almost wholly French-speaking. Later, but still relevant, and often cited in textbooks on the history of the English language, come the remarks of the 14th century chronicler Ranulf Higden, who wrote (in Latin) that 'children in school, contrary to the usage and customs of all other nations, are compelled to abandon their own language, and to construe their lessons and their tasks in French, and have since the Normans first came to England. Moreover, gentlemen's children are taught to speak French from the time that they are rocked in their cradle . . . and rustic men want to make themselves like gentlemen, and strive with great industry to speak French, in order to be more highly thought of' (cited in Barber 1993:142).

Higden's comment that schoolchildren had construed their lessons in French 'since the Normans came to England' is interesting. It's possible that Higden was exaggerating. It's certainly probable that his remarks didn't apply to all English children, but only to the children of the well-born, at a time when there was no universal literacy. It's possible, too, that his remarks are only relevant to the language contact situation as this obtained in schools in certain parts of England. And yet we can infer that some bilingualism existed, and we surely know that there was a literature written in A-N. Throughout the post-Conquest period, native 'English' literary production appears to come almost to a standstill: one looks in vain, for example, for the continuity of classically made OE alliterative verse. Instead, and in the south-east and the southerly midland regions, one finds a new genre, that of the prose romance, together with psalters (books of the Psalms) and saints' *Lives* written in the new prestige language. Perhaps the most well-known of these literary productions is the verse that celebrates the *Voyage of St Brendan* (12th century; see Legge 1963:8ff.). At the same period, one also finds Arthurian materials, notably the story of Tristan, appearing in A-N versions (Legge 1963:45ff.). What poetry there is appears to be composed in forms very different from that of the native OE alliterative half-line.

We've claimed that A-N was not a durable variety. For any variety of language to be durable, it must have a constant resupply of native speakers, that is, the variety must renew itself continually within its host communities. In 1204, however, the kingdom of Normandy passed out of English control, and a new law required landowners to hold estates either in England or in France, but not both (Strang 1970:217). By the 13th century, too, English clerks might prefer to acquire their prestige education at Oxford, rather than at Paris. In 1258, Henry III published one of his charters in both French and English 'to all his faithful, learned, and lay' (Pope 1934:421), 'and towards the end of the [13th] century we learn from the author of *Arthour and Merlin* that he had seen many a nobleman who could not speak a word of French' (Pope 1934:421).

By political accident, A-N had been cut off from its host communities. As an educational medium, it was under pressure from Latin; as a literary medium, it came under increasing pressure both from continental French and from a resurgent English; and as a vernacular, it came under two further pressures, the first from a new prestige variety of French, the second from a native, though changed, English – the language that never went away.

8.2 Was English ever a creole?

If we think about language-contact situations and processes in general it's useful to think about them not just in terms of the 'adopt or adapt' distinction we considered in the last section, but in terms of a theoretical framework that involves the linguistic processes of *pidginisation* and *creolisation*.

In an admirably concise introduction to pidgin and creole languages, Todd (1990) writes as follows:

> A *pidgin* is a marginal language which arises to fulfil certain restricted communication needs among people who have no common language. In the initial stages of contact the communication is often limited to transactions where a detailed exchange of ideas is not required and where a small vocabulary, drawn almost exclusively from one language, suffices. The syntactic structure of the pidgin is less complex and less flexible than the structures of the languages which were in contact, and though many pidgin features clearly reflect usages in the contact languages, others are unique to the pidgin . . .
>
> A *creole* arises when a pidgin becomes the mother tongue of a speech community. The simple structure that characterized the pidgin is carried over into the creole but since a creole, as a mother tongue, must be capable of expressing the whole range of human experience, the lexicon is expanded and frequently a more elaborate syntactic system evolves.
>
> A creole can develop from a pidgin in two ways. Speakers of a pidgin may be put in a position where they can no longer communicate by using their mother tongues . . . But a creole is not always the result of people being deprived of the opportunity to utilize their mother tongue. A pidgin can become so useful as a community lingua franca that it may be expanded and used even by people who share a mother tongue. Parents, for example, may use a pidgin so extensively throughout the day, in the market, at church, in offices and on public transport, that it becomes normal for them to use it also in the home. In this way children can acquire it as one of their first languages. This second type of creolization can probably occur only in multilingual areas where an auxiliary language is essential to progress.
>
> (1990:2–3)

Like some scholars working on the history of English we might ask whether there were circumstances and pressures for some varieties of the earliest English to creolise. The creolisation that some scholars have envisaged is not a process that involves English and French, but English and Old Norse (ON).

The idea was first developed by Poussa (1982), and in essence claims that Middle English (ME) developed partly as a result of the emergence of a Scandinavian/English creole in the E Midlands.

The circumstances for possible creolisation seem to have obtained in parts of England during the period following Scandinavian settlement – that is, either the *dialects* that were OE and ON were mutually intelligible, or, if one conceives OE and ON as two separate languages, there was very widespread *borrowing*, not only of lexical items but also of non-lexical ones. Recall how a creole language develops:

> A *creole* arises when a pidgin becomes the mother tongue of a speech community. The simple structure that characterized the pidgin is carried over into the creole but since a creole, as a mother tongue, must be capable of expressing the whole range of human experience, the lexicon is expanded and frequently a more elaborate syntactic system evolves . . .
>
> (Todd, cited above)

So if we were to argue that in parts of England, at least, an OE/ON creole language develops, and is the basis of early ME, we would first have to argue that in these same areas a pidgin language developed first, and eventually became the mother tongue of the English speech-community in those areas.

There has been over two decades of work by linguistic historians on this question (e.g. see Poussa (1982), Danchev (1997), Görlach (1986)), but we are going to sum it up here by saying 'Middle English a creole? No . . .'

Of recent commentators, Allen (1997) gives the most useful – and in our view, compelling – summary of the arguments *against* ME ever having creolised. Allen's arguments are in essence these:

1. Although OE had 'a healthy case-marking system, syncretism of forms was already considerably advanced' before pressure for pidginisation and creolisation might have been felt (Allen 1997:65). On syncretism – which in this case can be conceived of as the falling together of forms in just two grammatically marked categories, the 'subject' and 'non-subject' – see below.
2. Regularisation of OE noun paradigms was already apparent in the very earliest OE, for example at a very early period masculine u-stems had started to pattern with a-stem nouns. This happened long before Scandinavian pressure on the forms and case system of OE might have been felt.
3. In terms of the OE pronoun system, already in later OE the dative form (crudely, the *him* form) had 'usurped the functions of the accusative in the first and second person, becoming a general object marker' (Allen 1997:67). Again, this seems to be a language-internal change, rather than a change driven by language contact.
4. In terms of evidence, a 9th century Nbr version of the *Leiden Riddle* shows loss of final *-n* and evidence of vowel reduction in unstressed syllables.

> One might interpret such evidence as an instance of the kind of simplification that occurs in a language-contact situation, but Allen (1997:68) points out that loss of final *-n* must have been underway long before 900 and that, again therefore, this is a change internal to, and specific to, OE: 'It is likely that the Scandinavian settlers in the north reinforced this variant in northern English and contributed to its spread, but they did not introduce it into English'.

Further, on Allen's view, English nowhere shows the 'confusion' that would have otherwise provided evidence for pidginisation and creolisation. (The term 'confusion' is also, and unfortunately, used in some standard textbooks to describe the linguistic state of affairs in eME.) On the contrary, Allen distinguishes three stages of the internal development of OE. It's worthwhile looking at these postulated stages of development, since they contain one important piece of evidence as to why it's *most unlikely* that eME developed as an OE/ON creole.

- *The early OE stage*: Early on, there is widespread syncretism, with identical *forms* in, for example, the nominative and accusative inflectional exponents of case. There is, too, a reduction in the number of inflectional classes as these had been inherited from WGmc (u-stems> a-stem pattern).
- *The later OE stage*: In the pronoun system, the dative *form* had usurped the functions of the accusative: the *him* form, for example – an originally dative form – came readily to be used in 'direct object' positions. And in the inflectional system, final *-n* was lost, or in the process of being lost, especially in the North. In the phonology of vowels, there was widespread neutralisation of front vowel shapes in a sound spelled as <e>. And in terms of case? While case-marking categories seem to have been maintained, there was a further syncretism of *form*, especially in the North.
- *The terminal OE stage*
  - (a) the genitive *-es* form spread to genitives of all classes/genders (that is, 'genitive' was retained as a grammatical case, but the *form* that marked it changed (in former feminine nouns, for example) when grammatical gender marking was compromised)
  - (b) the nominative *-(a)s* form spread to other classes/genders (that is, 'nominative' was retained as a grammatical case, a 'general subject-case')
  - (c) unstressed vowels were neutralised in schwa (although the beginnings of this change can be traced to the 'later OE' stage . . . and were indisputably taking place long before Scandinavian influence could have been felt in the system)
  - (d) loss of final *-n* feeds further syncretism, for example the obliteration of the distinction between nominative and accusative in masculine weak nouns
  - (e) and finally . . . there appears to have been analogical levelling in the system of masculine and feminine *determiners*, so that the old *s*-forms

> (masculine *se*, feminine *sēo*) were replaced by dental fricative forms (spelled with <þ> or, later, with <th>). Interestingly, intimations of this change can be found earlier, in the *Lindisfarne Gospels*. By this change, the 'new' article <þe> could be used for nominative and accusative, with older <þone> reserved only for the accusative. In this situation, the use of non-specialised <þe> is bound to spread . . . irrespective of any Scandinavian influence. ON, in any case, had *s*-forms, so the development and spread of the definite article <the> in English cannot have been a contact-induced change.

These seem compelling counter-arguments to the 'creolisation hypothesis'. If they're correct, the earliest English was undergoing a *long, continuous process of internal remodelling*. It seems to be indisputable that certain aspects of that remodelling were given a healthy push – in the direction of disambiguation, in the direction of simplification – by the pressure for change caused by the language-contact situation in parts of England through the 10th–12th centuries. And while this pressure is not unique to England and the English, the existence of the pressure helps to explain why OE seems to undergo such a rapid (even a spectacular) remodelling, while cognate languages on the European mainland did not.

8.3 Remodelling the pronoun system

One of the most spectacular features of the earliest English is the remodelling of its pronoun system. Studying that set of changes helps us think some more about the nature of the Scandinavian contact. It's also revealing on phonological grounds, and it's with those phonological grounds that we'll begin our analysis of the remodelling process.

It appears that in spoken language, pronouns – those familiar entities including *I*, *me*, *he*, *she*, *her*, *they*, *them* – actually have two *forms*. (Note again that there's a distinction between *form* and *function*. It's entirely possible to have two forms – in PDE, say, *them* and *'em* – that are exponents of the same function.) They have a stressed form and an unstressed form. The stressed form tends to appear under conditions of syntactic focus and/or thematic emphasis, while the unstressed form appears in virtually all other positions and conditions: it is the 'normative' form.

The distinction between stressed and unstressed forms appears readily in other present-day Germanic languages. Take the case of present-day Dutch. Every teaching handbook of Dutch includes some paradigm such as that shown in table 8.1. The text from which we've adapted this diagram makes the point that 'some pronouns have an unstressed form . . . [This] is the one commonly used in speech unless special emphasis is required. The unstressed forms given in brackets are never written. The other unstressed

Table 8.1 Subject pronouns in present-day Dutch

Singular		Stressed	Unstressed	
1st pers		ik	('k)	I
2nd pers	**(informal)**	jij	je	you
2nd pers	**(formal)**	u		you
3rd pers		hij	(ie)	he
		zij	ze	she
		het	't	it
Plural				
1st pers		wij	we	we
2nd pers	**(informal)**	jullie	je	you
2nd pers	**(formal)**	u		you
3rd pers		zij	ze	they

Source: Adapted from Fenoulhet, J. (1997) *Hugo: Dutch in Three Months*, pub. Great Britain: Dorling Kindersley, p. 18. Copyright © Dorling Kindersley. Reproduced by permission of Dorling Kindersley Ltd.

pronouns – the ones without brackets – are used in less formal writing' (Fenoulhet 1997:18).

Under the general terms of the Uniformitarian Hypothesis we have no reason to expect that the pronoun system of OE, or eME, behaved differently. Given the abundant present-day evidence that speakers find it useful to have a system of pronouns that may be distinct from the set that is actually written, then it's likely that a speaker of English in, say, 875 or 1205, found it useful to employ the same kind of distinction. That leaves the historical linguist with a problem, since all of the evidence we have for linguistic change at these early periods is *written evidence*. Nevertheless, the evidence we have for the structure of pronoun systems, written and spoken, in present-day languages, urges us to treat the written evidence from earlier periods as an inherently conservative medium, one that doesn't tell the whole story of innovation and change.

We also study pronoun systems in terms of their morpho-syntax – how these linguistic elements can form different kinds of pronoun (e.g. object *them*, reflexive *[[them]selves]*) and how they function in terms of the syntax of clauses and phrases. Today, for example, in English as in Dutch there seem to be a set of general 'subject' pronouns and a set of general 'object' ones. What, you may ask, about the case-marking system of OE (and other Germanic languages)? 'We've learnt, at tedious length' (you complain) 'about stuff like nominative and dative. Do we have to forget about that stuff now, and simply think of pronouns in terms of "subject" and "object"?' Indeed not. One of the changes we're going to observe is precisely a remodelling which involves the widespread replacement of a case-marked pronoun set with a set that is marked for 'subject-hood' and 'object-hood', where 'object-hood' captures the functions both of the former accusative (direct object) case *and* the former dative. That is, in later Englishes, one tends to find 'subject' forms in constituents fulfilling the role of grammatical subject and 'object' forms elsewhere. The move is from a system where pronoun forms are exponents of grammatical *case* (and in some instances, of *gender*), to one where they are largely – but not quite entirely – exponents of grammatical *function*.

Third, as the Dutch data begin to suggest, there are sometimes fudges in any linguistic system. These fudges are interesting, since languages generally don't tolerate too many of them. Fudges usually get fixed . . . sooner or later. In the present-day Dutch system, for instance, the form <je> /jə/ can be employed in four functions in the spoken language – as 2nd person singular and 2nd person plural subject, and as 2nd person singular and 2nd person plural object. And <ze> /zə/ can function as 3rd person singular subject (she) and as 3rd person plural object (them). That is, there are some forms that appear to have dual, or even multiple, functions. Multiplicity of function leads to fudging, and since fudging gets fixed, sooner or later, that multiplicity usually means 'change'.

Consider also how impoverished many varieties of present-day English seem, in terms of their pronoun systems, when compared with the richly differentiated pronoun system of OE: PDE <you>, for example, can function as both 2nd person singular and plural, in both subject and object positions. Further, in many spoken forms of English, <'m> /əm/ can function as both 3rd person singular object (him) and 3rd person plural object (them). And in some spoken varieties, <her> (often /ə/) can function both as an object form, and as a possessive ('her car' /ə kɑː/ . . . which last form runs the risk of being confused with the indefinite article (compare informal 'her car' with 'a car')).

With these remarks in mind, let's turn to the OE pronoun system as we'd find it in 'classical' (written) OE (in WS or late WS), remembering that these paradigms very possibly reflect a rather conservative variety. Table 8.2 repeats the standard paradigms, as they're found in virtually all handbooks and grammars, omitting the 'dual' forms of the pronouns (*wit*, we two, *unc*, us two). Look at these paradigms carefully, and then, before reading further, attempt to answer the questions that follow.

Exercise 8.3.0

Look over the paradigms, and identify instances where there's possible ambiguity in the OE system. (Hint: as well as considering the different functions particular pronouns might have had, consider also how pronouns might have been *spoken*.)

Table 8.2 The OE pronoun system

First person forms, singular			**First person forms, plural**	
Nom.	ic	I	wē	we
Acc.	mē	me	ūs	us
Gen.	mīn	my	ūre	our
Dat.	mē	(to) me, etc.	ūs	(to) us, etc.
Second person forms, singular			**Second person forms, plural**	
Nom.	þū	thou	gē	ye
Acc.	þē	thee	ēow	you
Gen.	þīn	'thine'	ēower	your
Dat.	þē	(to) thee, etc.	ēow	(to) you, etc.
Third person forms, singular, masculine				
Nom.	hē	he		
Acc.	hine	him		
Gen.	his	his		
Dat.	him	him		
Third person forms, singular, neuter				
Nom.	hit	it		
Acc.	hit	it		
Gen.	his	its		
Dat.	him	(to) it, etc.		
Third person forms, singular, feminine				
Nom.	hēo, hīo	she		
Acc.	hī(e)	her		
Gen.	hire	her		
Dat.	hire	(to) her, etc.		
Third person forms, plural, all genders				
Nom.	hīe, hī	they		
Acc.	hīe, hī	them		
Gen.	heora, hiora	their		
Dat.	him, heom	(to) them, etc.		

Comment on Exercise 8.3.0

There are numerous instances worthy of comment, especially those where pronoun forms correspond to more than one function:

Form	Functions
ūs	acc.pl., dat. pl.
mē	acc.sg., dat.sg.
þē	acc.sg., dat.sg
hit	nom.sg., acc.sg.
him	dat. sg (masc.), dat. pl. (all genders)
hī(e)	acc.sg. (fem. her), nom.pl. (they), acc. pl. (them)

Another form you may have spotted, although in its written form it looks distinct from any other pronoun, is *hēo/hīo*, she. It looks suspiciously similar to *hīe*, they.

Exercise 8.3.1

In this exercise, try to work out *what distinctions are lost*. To do this, a good starting point is your own pronoun system. Do you yourself maintain, for example – as on this evidence many OE speakers did – a distinction between object forms of 'feminine' pronouns and possessive forms of the same set? Do you make a distinction between 2nd person singular subject and object forms, or between 2nd person possessive singular and plural?

Comment on Exercise 8.3.1

You very probably do *not* make all the distinctions evidenced by the OE pronoun set (that is, you'll use a simplified set of *forms* to cover the different possible functions). For 'feminine' pronouns, you won't make a distinction between the form written <her> (object) and <her> (possessive). Nor is it likely you'll make a distinction between possessive singular (written) <your> (cf. OE *þīn*, thine) and possessive plural <your> (cf. OE *eower*, your). It's unlikely, too, that you'll make a distinction between second person singular (written) <you> (cf. OE *þū*, thou) and second person plural <you> (cf. OE *ēow*, you) – though you may possibly, particularly if you're a Scouse, Dublin or AmE speaker, have a distinction between <you> (/ju:/) singular and <y'all> (AmE) or <youse> (Scouse, Dublin) plural(s). (Remember our comment above about multiplicity of function? Many varieties of English have the single pronoun *you* in singular and plural, subject and object. It's very useful to speakers to be able to make singular and plural distinctions, and so *y'all* and *youse* are, we think, spreading – an instance of ongoing, present-day change. A fudge is slowly being fixed.)

What we're emphasising is that many distinctions that were made in OE are remodelled, and some former distinctions become wholly or partly obliterated in PDE. Some OE forms, indeed, are *replaced* by borrowed pronouns.

Exercise 8.3.2

What 'classical' OE forms appear to have been lost – or better, lost-and-replaced-by-something-else? If you think a pronoun form has been 'replaced', where did the replacing form come from?

Comment on Exercise 8.3.2

The most spectacular examples of loss/replacement are in the plural. OE had *hī(e)* to do duty for both nominative and accusative plural ('they' and 'them' forms). But clearly, in these positions and functions, PDE has precisely that <they, them> contrast. In other words, the original <h-> form was largely replaced by new <th-> forms. Where did the replacing <th-> forms come from? And why?

Another example of 'loss/replacement' (we insert that term in scare-quotes since it may turn out to involve a different process from that of plural <h-> pronouns being replaced by <th->) is provided by OE *hēo/hīo*, she. Since the PDE form is unambiguously <she>, where did the <sh-> form originate? And why?

The <th-> pronoun set (*they, them, their*) were *borrowed* from the dialects brought with them by the Scandinavian settlers. These <th-> pronouns weren't all borrowed wholesale, or at the same time. A supplementary question, then: given what you know of possible ambiguity in the OE pronoun system, which OE 3rd person plural pronoun do you think might have been replaced first?

The answer is OE *hī(e)*. The OE form *<he(o)m>*, after all – the exponent of the dative – is a form whose phonological shape is closed by a consonant (written as <m>), and which is therefore quite distinct from anything else in the OE pronoun set. The form *hī(e)*, though, if pronounced 'weak', threatens to be non-distinct from OE *hē* or indeed *hēo* (she).

This observation helps us to explain some features of later (eME and ME) English. Chaucer, for example, readily uses the <they> form, but retains the <h> form in <hem>. Describing the pilgrims who travel to Canterbury, Chaucer writes as follows:

> And specially from every shires ende
> Of Engelond to Caunterbury **they** wende,
> The hooly blisful martir for to seke,
> That **hem** hath holpen whan that they were seke . . .
>
> And specially from every shire's end
> of England they journeyed to Canterbury
> in order to seek out the holy, blissful martyr [Thomas Becket]
> who has helped them whenever they were sick . . .
>
> (*Canterbury Tales,* General Prologue, lines 15–18. ed. Robinson 1957:17; our trans.)

Table 8.3 Some third person plural pronouns

(1) Classical OE			
Nom.	hīe, hī	they	(Ambiguity of Nom./Acc. forms)
Acc.	hīe, hī	them	
Dat.	him, heom	(to, for, by) them	
(2) Early ME			
Subject	they	(borrowed < ON; EMidl. <*þeȝȝ*>, c.1200)	
Non-subject	hem, (h)em	(OE *hem, heom*; <*þeȝȝm*> not unknown, but rare)	
(3) Later ME			
Subject	they		
Non-subject	them, (h)em	(*(h)em* < OE, now in unstressed positions; *them* < ON)	

We might present these changes as in table 8.3 above.

And how are we to explain the pronoun form *she*? Recall that the classical OE form was *hēo* (later WS *hīo*). Was the form in /ʃ/ also a borrowing? Or does such a form develop somehow from the OE /h-/ form?

The answer to this last question is 'we don't know'. It's conceivable that the English *she*-forms were adapted from the ON demonstrative pronoun *sjá* (Gordon 1957:295). If so, we would have a situation where a demonstrative pronoun, with a primarily deictic (a pointing and indexing) function (cf. PDE ***this*** *book*, as distinct from ***a*** *book*), is borrowed with a new kind of function into a different, though cognate, language.

It's not unprecedented for demonstrative pronouns to be used in a personal function. This happens widely in present-day Dutch:

Q:	*Waar is Georgette?*	Where's G.?
A:	***Die*** *is ziek.*	She's sick.
		(That one, i.e. the one you just mentioned, is sick)
cf.		
	Zij *is ziek.*	She's sick.

This seems to happen only where the referent of the pronoun (here, the referent of **Die**) has been mentioned already in the discourse.

Then again, it's unlikely that English *she* is an adaptation of a non-demonstrative ON 3rd person pronoun. The ON form we find is nom. *han*, acc. *hana*, gen. *hennar*, dat. *henni*, and it's hard to see how any of these forms might give rise to newly minted English forms in /ʃ-/.

An alternative explanation might be that the OE original *hēo/hīo* was subject to a pattern of language-internal change. This is one of the explanations countenanced by Clark (1958) in her work on *The Peterborough Chronicle* (see especially pp. lxii–lxiii). The original OE form comprised a *falling* diphthong, i.e. a diphthong with most prominence on its first vocalic component. If (one might argue), the prominence-relations within the original diphthong were switched so that the diphthong became *rising*, then phonetically, one would produce (and perceive) a form something like (<*seō*>, <*siō*>) /sjo:/. Look carefully at the consonant cluster that begins this putative 'new' pronoun: the /s/ is alveolar, and fricative, while the /j/ is a palatal glide. How easy it is for these sounds to assimilate – specifically, for the frication of the /s/ to anticipate the palatality of the /j/ – with the result of the assimilation being the palatal fricative /ʃ/ . . . If that is the case, we would expect eME spellings of later *she* in <sho> or <scho>. Such spellings do occur:

> *heo* was used in the SW and Wmid . . . and *he* or *hi* in the SE, the EMid had *sche*, and the NMid had *sche* or *ho* in E, *ho* or *scho* in the W. The far N, so far as it is documented, had *scho* . . . The new element in the feminine pronouns is probably to be explained by a . . . disambiguating process, giving rise to /ʃ/ forms; they may have arisen as phonetic variants rather than as new words, borrowed or otherwise. What is clear is that a similar structural weakness in the S forms of the language led to the spread of the EMid forms southwards by internal borrowing . . .
>
> (Strang 1970:236–237)

The weakness of the former postulation ('*she* was a borrowing from ON') is that it would instance an unusual form of cross-linguistic contact – and one that is, unhelpfully for our purposes, undocumented. The weakness of the second postulation ('*she* evolved from internal change and spread by internal borrowing') is that it's hard to see *why* the triggering phonetics – the change of an originally falling diphthong to a rising one – could have taken place. Prominence changes within diphthongs do occur, but they're relatively rare, and in other instances of such change, the remnant of the vowel stranded by the evolving phonetics (in the case of OE *hēo* this remnant would be the vowel-shape spelled as <o>) is *copied* from x-position to x-position within the new syllabic Nucleus. In our context, this would leave /ʃo:/ (note the long /o:/ shape) as the 'new' *she*-pronoun, which would have been variously spelled as <sho> or <scho> . . . whereas what is actually documented, first of all in the East Midlands of the early 12th century, is the spelling <scæ>.

It's a puzzle. For our money, the 'Norse' explanation seems slightly stronger. Or perhaps we could suggest – playing both unreliable ends against an equally unreliable middle – that native remodelling was given a healthy push, a linguistically disambiguating push, by the simultaneous existence, in parts of England, of the Norse demonstrative <sja> form.

What we do want to suggest is that the factors we are beginning to consider that bear on 'how OE changed' are important when we come to assess the plausibility of our narrative concerning the language of the earliest English. The factors we've been considering are these:

- external borrowing
- language-internal remodelling
- a linguistic intolerance of too much structural fudging
- a linguistic intolerance of too much ambiguity in the spoken system
- language-internal borrowing of forms (i.e. 'change spreads')
- speakers' awareness of a distinction between *form* and *function*

In terms of the evolution of OE into eME, we could also point to the following specifics (among others):

- *inflectional erosion and loss*, beginning in the N
- a reformed, positionally based *syntax*
- a simplifying of *case-relations*, the simplification being in the direction of binary subject/non-subject, and therefore
- case syncretism (the 'falling together' of the exponents of former cases, e.g. the old accusative/dative cases)
- loss of much grammatical *gender* marking
- remodelling of the *pronoun* system

8.4 The *Peterborough Chronicle*: reading and study passage

It seems arid to make these points without closer exemplification. In what follows, you will be able to see some of the changes we've been discussing in action, as it were. The text we're going to use is an excerpt from *The Peterborough Chronicle* (PC). The PC is a continuation of the *Anglo-Saxon Chronicle*, begun so long ago under the direction of Alfred. Notably, there were different 'continuations' of the *Chronicle*, but the continuation(s) found in Peterborough are the most durable and contain entries relating to the later 11th and the early to mid-12th centuries. The 'Second Continuation' of the PC runs up to the year 1155, at which time the PC was discontinued. The Second Continuation details events spanning 1080–1155, and must have been written retrospectively (possibly at the dictation of an old monk, see Bennett and Smithers 1968:202). The entry you're about to read relates to the year 1137 and describes the period of anarchy under King Stephen. For ease of reference in the subsequent exercise, we've split the text into alphabetic paragraphs. Read both the original and the translation provided very carefully:

A. [an. 1137] þa þe king Stephne to Englaland com, þa macod he his gadering æt Oxeneford. And þar he nam þe biscop Roger of Serebyri, and Alexander biscop of Lincol and te canceler Roger, hise neues, and dide ælle in prisun til hi iafen up here castles.

When King Stephen came to England, he called his Council together at Oxford, and there he seized Roger, bishop of Salisbury, Alexander, bishop of Lincoln, and the Chancellor, Roger, his nephews, and put them all in prison until they had surrendered their castles.

B. þa þe suikes undergæton ðat he milde man was, and softe and god, and na iustise ne dide, þa diden hi alle wunder. Hi hadden him manred maked and athes suoren, ac hi nan treuthe ne heolden. Alle he wæron forsworen and here treothes forloren, for æueric rice man his castles makede and agænes him heolden, and fylden þe land ful of castles.

When the traitors realised that he was a kind, gentle and good man, who inflicted no punishment, then they all performed atrocities. They had done homage to him and sworn oaths, but they kept no pledge. They were all forsworn and their pledges broken, because every powerful man built his castles and held them against him, and filled the land full of castles.

C. Hi suencten suyðe þe wreccemen of þe land mid castelweorces. þa þe castles uuaren maked, þa fylden hi mid deoules and yuele men. þa namen hi þa men þe hi wenden ðat ani god hefden, bathe be nihtes and be daies, carlmen and wimmen, and diden heom in prisun and pined heom efter gold and syluer untellendlice pining, for ne uuæren næure nan martyrs swa pined alse hi wæron.

They severely oppressed the poor men of the country with the building of castles. When the castles were built, they filled them with devils and evil men. Then they seized those people who they believed had any property, both by night and by day, both men and women, and put them in prison and tortured them with unspeakable torture in pursuit of gold and silver – no martyrs were ever so tortured as they were.

D. Me henged up bi the fet and smoked heom mid ful smoke; me henged bi the þumbes, other bi the hefed and hengen bryniges on her fet; me dide cnotted strenges abuton here hæufed and uurythen it ðat it gæde to þe hærnes. Hi diden heom in quarterne þar nadres and snakes and pades wæron inne, and drapen heom swa. Sume hi diden in crucethur – ðat is, in an ceste þat was scort and nareu and undep – and dide scærpe stanes þerinne, and þrengde þe man þerinne ðat him bræcon alle þe limes . . .

Some they hung up by the feet and suffocated them with foul smoke. Some they hung by the thumbs, others by the head with coats of mail hanging from their feet. They tied knotted rope around their heads, and twisted it so that it cut through to the brains. They put them in a dungeon where there were adders, snakes and toads, and thus killed them. Some they put in a torture box – that is in a chest that was short, narrow and shallow – and put sharp stones in it and crushed the man inside until they broke all his bones . . .

E. I ne can ne I ne mai tellen alle þe wunder ne alle þe pines ðat hi diden wreccemen on þis land. And ðat lastede þa xix wintre wile Stephne was king, and æuere it was uuerse and uuerse. Hi læiden gæildes on the tunes æuere umwile, and clepeden it 'tenserie'.

I am unable to nor can I tell of all the atrocities nor all the tortures which they inflicted on the poor men of this country; and that lasted the 19 years that Stephen was king, and always it grew worse and worse. They imposed taxes on the villages every so often, and called it 'protection money'.

F. þa þe wreccemen ne hadden nammore to gyuen, þa ræueden hi and brendon alle the tunes, ðat wel þu myhtes faren al a dæis fare, sculdest thu neurer finden man in tune sittende ne land tiled. þa was corn dære, and flesc and cæse and butere, for nan ne wæs o þe land. Wreccemen sturuen of hungær. Sume ieden on ælmes, þe waren sum wile ricemen; sume flugen ut of lande . . .

When the wretched people had no more to give, then they ravaged and burned all the villages, so that you could easily travel a whole day's journey and never find a man sitting in a village or land cultivated. Then corn was expensive, and meat and cheese and butter, for there was none in the country. Poor men died of hunger. Some who were once powerful travelled for alms; some fled the country . . .

G. War sæ me tilede, þe erthe ne bar nan corn, for þe land was al fordon mid suilce dædes. And he sæden openlice ðat Crist slep and his halechen. Suilc, and mare þanne we cunnen sæin, we þoledon xix wintre for ure sinnes . . .

Wherever one ploughed, the earth bore no corn, for the ground was completely destroyed by such acts, and they said openly that Christ and his saints slept. Such, and more than we are able to say, we endured for 19 years because of our sins . . .

H. [an. 1140] þa ferde Eustace, þe kinges sune, to France and nam þe kinges suster of France to wife – wende to bigæton Normandi þærþurh. Oc he spedde litel, and be gode rihte, for he was an yuel man; for warese he com he dide mare yuel þanne god: he reuede þe landes and læide micele geldes on. He brohte his wif to Engleland and dide hire in þe castel on Cantebyri. God wimman scæ wæs, oc hedde litel blisse mid him. And Crist ne wolde ðat he sculde lange rixan; and wærd ded, and his moder beien.

Then Eustace the king's son travelled to France and married the king of France's sister. He thought he would thereby inherit Normandy. But he prospered little, and rightly so, for he was an evil man; for wherever he went he did more harm than good: he plundered the lands and imposed huge taxes. He brought his wife to England and put her in a castle in Canterbury. She was a good woman, but she had little joy with him. And Christ did not wish him to reign long, and he died, and his mother too.

Exercise 8.4.1

How often is case marked in the singular of nouns? How often is case marked in the plural of nouns? What plural inflections can you find that are *different* from the inflections you'd find marked on those same nouns, in their same functions, in classical OE?

Comment on Exercise 8.4.1

How often is case marked in the singular? It must be confessed that one shouldn't expect, at this date in the development of the earliest English, to find much case-marking in this part of the grammar (i.e. the singular), since the OE system has already begun its long movement of radical simplification. There are some interesting instances, though. One comes in para. **C** – *bathe be nihtes and be daies.* You might have been tempted to translate this as 'both by nights (plural) and by days (plural)', but if you look carefully at our gloss, you'll see there 'both by night (singular) and by day (singular)'. What we're in fact looking at here is the reinforcement of an old adverbial genitive by preposition. Mustanoja (1960:88) points out that 'In OE the genitive is occasionally used adverbially to indicate relations in time and space. This practice continues into ME . . .' He also notes (1960:89) that 'This adverbial use of the genitive seems to be paralleled by present-day American English expressions like *winters, summers* and *nights* "in winter, in summer, by night"'. So when an AmE speaker says something like 'Winters we go skating . . .', *winters* isn't clearly 'plural'. Rather, it seems to originate in the old pattern of the adverbial genitive *singular*.

Elsewhere in our passage, one can readily find instances of the survival of the genitive singular, for example in para. **F**, *al a dae**is** fare*, and in para. **H**, *þe king**es** sune.* That is quite expected (and notice that the reflex of the genitive is *always* apparently some form of '-(e)s'; it is *never* the '-e' termination that would betoken a survival of the OE genitive from the old feminine gender).

Staying with the genitive, there's one interesting example of a compound or split genitive in para. **H**, *þe king**es** suster **of** France*, the sister of the king of France. This usage in fact looks back to OE: 'In OE, in the genitive is followed by another noun in apposition, the noun governing the genitive is usually placed between the genitive and the noun in apposition' (an example is *Ælfred**es** sweostor cyning**es***, the sister of king A., where *sweostor*, sister, is the 'governing noun'). And, further, Mustanoja records that the split genitive is common in ME, is the only type to appear in the great 14th century alliterative poem *Piers Plowman*, and that the PDE type of expression *the king of France's mother* 'is first recorded in Chaucer's works, where, however, the usual type is the split genitive' (Mustanoja 1960:79). Note, though, the refinement of the function of the preposition *of*, which is here coming to be associated with the notion of grammatical possession (cf. also Dutch *van – het boekje van Monika*, Monika's book).

Can one find relics of other case-marking in the singular in our passage? Yes, but barely. Two examples might be para. **D**, *in an ceste* (OE (Anglian) *cest*), and para. **F**, *in tune* (OE *tūn*, neuter). These look like inflectional relics of the OE dative. But despite these examples, one gets the distinct impression of a variety of language where case-marking has been all but obliterated in the singular, with one notable exception – the old genitive.

The plural is another story. What one expects to find, given the date of the passage, is widespread plural marking in '-(e)s'. Generally speaking, that's just what you will find, but it's worth spending a moment looking both at some of these 's' plurals, and at some other types of plural.

Englaland, para. **A**, shows a survival of the ancient *-a* inflection in the genitive plural. Presumably it is merely fossilised. *halechen*, saints, para. **G**, is more interesting, since in OE *halga*, saint, was a weakly declining noun, i.e. one of those nouns that inflected in the nominative and accusative plural in *-an* (OE *halgan*, saints). So the *-en* termination here seems to be a survival of that old 'weak' pattern. Indeed, one of the features of many ME dialects – particularly of South and West dialects, the 'conservative' varieties – is the widespread tendency to form plurals in precisely that '-(e)n'. Such a termination had the merit, after all, of being *relatively* distinctive. But again, such a termination was already under pressure from the survival, and then the internal borrowing, of the old masculine nom. and acc. plural in '-(e)s', which had long been current in N dialect areas, and was at this period (mid-12th century) in the process of its long spread southwards and westwards.

Can we see this form of plural-marking at work in the passage? Consider para. **A**, *his neues*, his nephews. *nefa*, nephew, was an OE weak noun, that is, one would expect it to form its nominative and accusative plural with the inflection *-an* (OE *nefan*, nephews). Here, though, quite unambiguously the termination is an '-s' form. This looks, in other words, like a noun that is jumping – which already has jumped – from the old weak declension into the survival of the old strong masculine declension, with its '-(e)s' genitive singular and its generalised '-(e)s' plural.

A further interesting example comes in para. **C**, *mid deoules*, with devils. In classical OE, *deofol* was a masculine noun, and one would expect a dative plural in *-um*. But look at what's happened here: plural '-(e)s' is spreading across the old plural inflectional structure, until it occurs even in the old dative plural slots. The same tendency can be seen at work in phrases from our passage such as *mid castelweorces, bi the þumbes, to the hærnes, on þe tunes, on ælmes*.

Finally here, notice also the tendency for loan-words from Norman French to pattern very readily with the '-(e)s' plural. A good example is from para. **A**, *castles*.

Exercise 8.4.2

Staying with nouns and their structure, can you identify OE nouns, originally belonging to the feminine or neuter genders, which appear to have transferred into the simplified 's-plural' pattern?

Comment on Exercise 8.4.2

It's difficult to complete this exercise without reference to an OE dictionary, one that will give the original gender of the relevant noun. But here are some examples to think about:

- *treothes*, para. **B**. Originally a strong feminine noun in OE, with accusative plural in *-e*.
- *ælmes*, para. **F**. Originally a weak feminine noun, with dative singular in *-an*, dative plural in *-um*.
- *landes*, para. **H**. Originally a strong neuter noun, with zero plural in the accusative case. Here with an '-(e)s' plural, and a clear case of transfer.

Exercise 8.4.3

What has happened to the highly inflected definite article of OE?

Comment on Exercise 8.4.3

The inflected definite article – recall that it inflected for gender, number and case – has been almost altogether scrapped in favour of some form of *the*. One should begin to ask questions, though, concerning the origin of the form *the*. Where did it originate? How did usage spread? What chronology are we looking at? Unfortunately, there are no absolutely satisfactory answers. It seems clear that the 'new' definite article originated in the old demonstrative system (*se*, nominative masculine singular, *seo*, nominative feminine singular, *þæt*, nominative neuter singular, see Mustanoja 1960:234–237; see also Allen 1997 and her remarks on the evolution of <the> – we cited these at the end of the last section of our text). And of course it's fairly useful for any language to have a system of pointing and indexing words (words with deictic functions), so that, for example, 'the book', 'the books' and 'this book' can be distinguished from 'a book' or just 'books'. But the precise origins of *the* can't satisfactorily be traced. Once some form of <th-> (<þ->) article was incipiently in existence, though, its rate of deployment was bound to spread analogically as the distinctions of grammatical gender were blurred, then largely lost. Its later *spelling*, however – its <th-> – can be identified as Latin-derived, possibly via A-N, in the sense that <th> for OE <þ> seems to have been largely an A-N innovation (Scragg 1974:46).

While we're working with the definite article, and its range of deictic functions, notice too that form ***þa*** in ***þa*** *men*, those people, para. **C**. It's possible that this phrase is to be translated as 'the people', but we've here translated it as 'those people' (i.e. they seized, in particular, those people that they thought had property). As Strang points out, most ME dialects have *þa* for the demonstrative plural, with *þat* in the demonstrative singular. Historically, the demonstrative plural *þa*, those, originates in the North, whereas the Midlands and South had *þo*; 'from the early 13C the regularising N uses an analogical plural in *-s*; only in the 15C do we find the S adopting this . . .' (Strang 1970:268)

Exercise 8.4.4

Consider the structure of the pronoun system, as this is evidenced in our passage from the *Peterborough Chronicle*. What changes can you identify between this system and the system of classical OE?

Comment on Exercise 8.4.4

There are many quite expected survivals, among them *he, his* and *him*. The form *hi* in para. **A** (*hi iafen up*, they gave up) is a straight survival from OE, too, but in precisely this dialect area, the E Midlands, it will not be very long before we begin to see the impress of borrowed Scandinavian forms in *th-*.

thu, in para. **F** is a straightforward survival from OE (though, trivially, its spelling has changed). Here it's used in a context of address – the narrator is addressing the reader. That is, the reader is here conceived as an imaginary audience. We know independently that *thou* and *you* are going to take on respectively different functions, and perhaps we get an inkling of the impending change here (see also Strang 1970:139–141 and, on later history, Mustanoja 1960:124ff., and especially 224).

Another noteworthy form is *me*, para. **G** (*War sæ me tilede*, wherever *one* tilled). In *War sæ me tilede, me* is an indefinite pronoun form (one). Another way in which this indefinite form was rendered, at least in eME, was by the form *man* or *men* (cf. PDG *man*). Mustanoja (1960:16) points out that although the *me* (indefinite pronoun) form was very common in eME, it slowly disappears from Standard, the last recorded instance coming in the works of Caxton (late 15th century).

Turning to para. **H**, we find the phrase *God wimman scæ wæs*, she was a good woman. This isn't merely an interesting attestation of the new *she* pronoun, it is a very new form in English of the period, and in fact, our example here seems to be the first attestation of the new *sh-* form anywhere in English.

Exercise 8.4.5

What loan-words can you identify in the passage? And what do such loans tell you about linguistic patterns of borrowing as these might be related to patterns of settlement and social governance?

Table 8.4 Norman and ON loans

List (i)	List (ii)
canceler, 1066	carlmenn (ON *karl*, man)
castel, 11th century; in this sense, 1050–1070	bryniges (ON *brynja*, coats of chain mail)
iustise, first attestation	hærnes (brains)
prisun, 1123, *Chronicle*	drapen (ON *drapa*, kill)
tenserie (?L.), first attestation	oc (but)
	bathe (both)
	til (until)

Comment on Exercise 8.4.5

We pick out here merely some spectacular instances of respectively different kinds of borrowing. Notice, too, that in the following, we use the word 'attestation'. What we're emphasising is that words may be borrowed into a language, and used in that language, long before they're written down. The 'first written occurrence' is evidence of the *attestation* of word. It is not necessarily the 'first recorded use' of the word. In table 8.4 List (i) details loans which are fairly unambiguously from (Norman) French, together with the date at which such loans are first attested in English; while List (ii) is a lightly annotated list of loans from ON.

It's readily apparent that the loans from Norman French are almost invariably nouns. Moreover, the register of these nouns seems chiefly to concern government and administration. The ON loans, on the other hand, include nouns, but generally these are nouns that have to do with parts of the body, or with things you might wear (a 'brinie' is a coat of chain-mail, here the torturer's equivalent of a concrete overcoat, a means of torture and death). But again, the ON loans included verbs – a synonym for the verb 'to kill' – and even more significantly, the ON list includes conjunctions and prepositions (on *til*, which does appear in OE, but only in Nbr, see Mossé 1952:338). One notes again how the apparent pattern of borrowing tells us something about the nature of linguistic contact. From the Scandinavian *settlers* come the 'everyday words' – some function words, some pronouns and a synonym for the verb 'to kill'. From the Norman *conquerors* come, in the first instance, nouns to do with administration, political repression, castle building.

There's more to say about interesting linguistic features of this passage – about its verb morphology, in particular (notice the prevalence of Midlands plural inflections in *-en*), and about its principles of word-order. But now, rather than continue with our narrative reconstruction of some of the linguistic principles behind the PC, in ever more intricate detail, we choose to turn to a different topic, that of the evolution of English verse. This is the final topic we'll study in this unit.

8.5 New models of verse

Whether 'evolution' is a useful term in describing the development of a language we're not entirely sure: are we really dealing with 'the survival of the most apt', in a Darwinian sense? What, linguistically, would be 'most apt', anyway? Still, as we look at the . . . let's choose a relatively neutral term . . . as we look at the *change* there is in the manifestation of English verse, as we find it in the 12th century, we can with some justice think about the death of the classical OE alliterative form, a death that came about because the form wasn't (or was no longer) 'apt'. That is, alliterative verse in its classical OE form appeared no longer to be suited to the language that had originally developed and sustained it. At this period we can also begin to trace the beginnings of an entirely new kind of verse, one that counted stresses and syllables, rather than being expressed in the 'positions' of half-line structure. It's this form – a stress-timed, preferentially alternating form – that wins out as an expression of culturally refined, canonical English verse, perhaps not only for reasons of its continental origins and its prestige – again derived from the continental, outward-looking behaviour of the English royal courts of the 12th century, which derived their aesthetics more from Provençal than from Peterborough – but also because it, in turn, was felt to be 'most apt', i.e. best suited to the language from which it was derived.

By the second half of the 12th century, and certainly by 1200, new forms of accentual-syllabic poetry had made their impress in England. These forms were not merely *isosyllabic* – syllable-counting. In addition to syllable-counting regularity, the English forms also contained a regular number of metrical accents per line and were typically rhymed. Many of the relevant, continentally borrowed forms may be said to be thus *accentual-syllabic*. One critical handbook puts the supposed state of affairs this way:

> The conquered Saxons may have kept up their old songs, but for more than a century after the Conquest there was no *written* verse in England, and by the time it came to be written the language had changed considerably. That it had shed many of its inflections was perhaps no great loss; but its vocabulary too had been sadly impoverished, especially in culture words, and had to be replenished from French. Then it had to learn a new tune, to change its native prosody of stress and alliteration for the syllabic rhymed system of France . . . The French system won first in the East and South – a decisive victory, for the capital and the Universities were there. By 1250 Nicholas of Guildford was writing very fair rhymed couplets in his *disputoison* of *The Owl and the Nightingale*. By 1300 or thereabout English lyric was beginning to run smoothly enough in the fetters of rhyme . . .
>
> (Grierson and Smith 1956:9)

This is an over-simplified picture. Mid-11th century English culture was very far from being 'impoverished'. There were extensive cultural links between the French court and the court of Edward the Confessor, many loan-words from the French of that period were from courtly or ecclesiastical registers and, elsewhere, poetry and prose continued to flourish in the 'Silver Age'. On the other hand, the observation that alliterative poetry constructed along classical OE lines was obliterated, at least in writing, seems to be essentially correct – although again, one wonders how much written verse might have been lost. The geographical distribution of much of the 'new' poetry is also well attested. Let's look immediately at a specimen of it.

Exercise 8.5.1

What follows is the opening of *The Owl and the Nightingale*, a debate-poem ('disputoison') written towards the end of the 12th century, almost certainly in the SE during the 1180s. As Bennett and Smithers put it, the poem 'reveals a masterly skill in naturalising French metres' (1968:1).

Try to discern what metrical principles are at work here:

***The Owl and the Nightingale*, extract**
(late 12th century, SE; Bennett and Smithers 1968)

Ich was in one sumere dale
In one suþe diȝele hale;
Iherde Ich holde grete tale
An hule and one niȝtingale.
Þat plait was stif an starc an strong,
Sumwile softe an lud among;
An eiþer aȝen oþer sval
An let þat vuele mod ut al;
An eiþer seide of oþeres custe
Þat alreworste þat hi wuste . . .

(I was in a valley one summer, in a greatly hidden hollow. There I heard an owl and a nightingale hold severe debate. The suit was hard and fierce and strong, sometimes soft, sometimes loud. Each swelled up against the other, and gave out all their evil thoughts – each said the very worst they knew of the other's qualities)

Comment on Exercise 8.5.1

Perhaps the first thing to notice is that the poem is composed in rhyming couplets. Despite the blithe ascription of authorship to 'Nicholas of Guildford' by Grierson and Smith (above), we don't actually know who wrote the poem. A 'Nicholas of Guildford' is certainly *associated* with the poem, but whether he is the author, or the designated, and honoured, recipient of the poem is unclear. (On this question, see the scrupulous discussion in Stanley 1972:20–22.) Whoever he might have been, the poet seems to have inherited his form from French models, and he appears to have been 'familiar with the Anglo-Norman culture of the court – a culture epitomized in the *Fables* of Marie de France, which he appears to have drawn on' (Bennett and Smithers 1968:1; see also Stanley 1972, Appendix, p.159ff.).

A problem is formed by the role of word-final -e, whether this was an inflectional survival or whether it had been borrowed with its French (or Latin) etymon. At this period, word-final -e was almost certainly pronounced in the SE dialect area. Assuming that, a phrase like *holde grete tale* would scan as follows:

      / x   / x / x
. . . holde grete tale

There's one environment, though, where word-final -e may not have been pronounced. This is where such an -e occurs before a following vowel (i.e. in the opening syllable of the next word). This metrical phenomenon is known as *elision*. If we take elision into account of the metrical pattern, we might plausibly scan line 4 of the above excerpt as follows, where '. . .' represents the elided string. (We ignore the problem posed by the penultimate syllable of *nightingale*, which probably bore secondary rather than primary word-stress):

x   / **x......** / x   / x   / x
An hul**e and** one niȝtingale

And similarly

x   /x / **x......** /   x /
Sumwile soft**e and** lud among

If we take elision into account, we can arrive at a provisional statement of the poem's metre. (Indeed, the assumption about the form of the metrical pattern is one of the prime motivating factors for assuming elision to operate – a nice piece of circular reasoning whose problematic explanatory value we'll simply ignore.) The metre seems to be largely octosyllabic, rhyming aabb, etc., and it also seems to fall into an *alternating* pattern, where each pair of syllables has a weaker (W) first member, and a second, stronger member (S). (We're not justified in calling this pattern 'iambic' at this stage of the evolution of English, though WS pairings do indeed look suspiciously iambic.) Moreover, each octosyllabic line may end on a further, unstressed syllable, *providing this is unstressed, word-final -e*. These supernumerary, line-final syllables are sometimes called 'extrametrical' syllables: they're not part of the core metrical description of the line.

Another problem is posed by trisyllabic words such as *sumere, diȝele* and *oþeres*. If we regard these words as truly trisyllabic then they provide counter-examples to the generalisation that the underlying metre is strictly alternating and octosyllabic:

x / x / x / **x x** / x
In one suþe **diȝele** hale

These trisyllables, though, have two things in common: their initial stressed syllables are (typically, but here with the exception of *oþeres*) light; and their second, unstressed syllables begin with a single consonant, with a further, resonant consonant (most clearly, /r/ or /l/) after the second vowel of the word. We could in fact regard these last resonant consonants not as Codas to syllables, but as Onsets, and we could regard them too, as 'swallowing' the syllabic force of the preceding unstressed vowel (written <e> in each case here). If so, then we'd be able to scan the words in question as disyllabic, not trisyllabic, and would thus preserve the adequacy of our earlier prosodic generalisation:

/ x   / x   / x   / x
sum(e)re   diȝ(e)le   oþ(e)res   also   vu(e)le

This solution seems to have been produced out of a hat in order to preserve metrical tidiness ('Eight syllables per line, plus one extrametrical syllable!'), but in fact there's clear evidence from elsewhere in the (post-)medieval English poetic tradition that poets often allow words of this form –

#(X)V(V).CV.C̲V(Y)#

– as disyllabic. How to read this graphic? X = any Onset, including null string; V = single vocalic x-slot; C = any single consonant; C̲ = /r/ or /l/; Y = any Coda, including null string. Therefore, a word such as *sumere* matches that description as follows:

#(X)V(V).CV.CV(Y)#
s u   me r e

And *oþeres*, with its initial heavy syllable (heavy since it contains a 2-x vowel):

#(X)V(V).CV.CV(Y)#
o o þe r e s

Seven hundred years later, Tennyson allows a similar reading of the word 'cataract' in the line 'In cataract after cataract to the sea' – which scans as an unremarkable pentameter:

#(X)V(V).CV.CV(Y)#
c a   t a r a ct

Exercise 8.5.2

There are lines in the poem where elision doesn't seem to operate as expected, and lines that are metrically odd for other reasons. Study the following and detail the metrical irregularities:

The Owl and the Nightingale, **lines 171–180**

Þe niȝtingale was al ȝare;
Ho hadde ilorned wel aiware:
'Hule,' ho seide, 'seie me soþ:
Wi dostu þat unwiȝtis doþ?
Þu singist aniȝt an noȝt adai,
An al þi song is 'wailawai'.
Þu miȝt mid þine song afere
Alle þat inhereþ þine ibere;
Þu schrichest an ȝollest to þine fere,
Þat hit is grislich to ihere . . .

(The nightingale was very eager. She'd learned well everywhere. 'Owl,' she said, 'tell me truly: why do you do what evil creatures do? You sing at night and not by day, and all your song is 'wailawai' [horrible]. You're able to frighten with your song everyone who hears your awful clamour. You shriek and yell to your companions, and it's grisly to hear it . . .)

Comment on Exercise 8.5.2

One problem relates to the 2nd person singular verb inflection *-est* (*singist*, *ȝollest*, *schrichest*). Although we've claimed that what remained of inflectional endings (especially word-final -e) were probably pronounced in this dialect area, in our text it may well be that the words in question were produced as monosyllables (*sing'st*, etc.). This would be quite in line with our general comments about inflectional reduction and loss. Notice also that in the words in question, the first syllable contains a stressed, short vowel.

There also appears to be a failure of elision in line 10 –

x / x / x / x / x
Þat hit is grislich **to i**here

Elision seems to be a strongly preferred, but ultimately optional metrical feature: 'elide wherever possible, but only where the identity of the metrical pattern isn't compromised by the result'.

Another problem relates to the stress-pattern of *nightingale*. In line 1, the word seems to have functioned as quadrisyllabic:

x / x / x /
Þe niȝtingale was al ȝare

Yet there are other lines in the same text where the same word seems to have a trisyllabic pronunciation:

x / x / x /
Þe niȝtingale bigon þe speche . . .

Failure of elision; problems relating to the pronunciation of inflectional syllables and final -e; metrical difficulties concerning the scanning of (Romance) trisyllables . . . It's beginning to look as if these couplets are, after all, 'very fair' rather than 'perfect'. Yet they're among the earliest rhyming couplets to have been produced in England after the French manner (see also Legge 1963:14ff. on A-N sources for the rhymed octosyllable), and they're considerably more regular than the couplets found in, for example, the 13th century *King Alysaunder*, and in many other contemporary eME poems in the same ostensible form.

The standard textbook assumption is, as we've seen, that accentual-syllabic, rhymed forms of verse were borrowed into English from French. There's clearly much to support this view, not least the relationship between a culture of high prestige and that of a native, eME low; the composition and nature of the 12th century English court (which was largely French-speaking); and the patronage extended to the troubadours by, for example, Eleanor of Aquitaine, wife of Louis VII of France and, subsequently, of Henry II of England. Eleanor 'was an immensely influential patron of the arts, particularly in her patronage of the development of courtly poetry in Poitiers . . .' (ed. Drabble 2000:319).

Still, in literature as in language, the idea of 'French influence' can be over-stated as an explanation of change. English had been itself changing radically, as we've begun to see. Inflectional erosion and loss were accompanied by grammatical changes such as the remodelling of the definite article, the redeployment of the function and meaning of prepositions, and the development of a more rigid word-order. In addition, new words were being borrowed, at an increasing rate in the 13th century, from French (and from Latin). Many of these words were polysyllabic – we got a hint of the nature of some of these polysyllabic loan-words when we considered items like *canceler*, chancellor, during our work on the PC. Taken together, these changes mean not only that traditional alliterative poetry would cease to be composed – since its ancient principles would no longer be happily compatible with a changed, and changing, English language – but also, more intriguingly, that new forms of poetry would develop in English *quite apart from French (or Latin) influence.*

Given the paucity of written records it's difficult to be certain that new *native* forms of poetry were being written in English after the Conquest. But there is one place we can look for evidence, and that is the *Anglo-Saxon Chronicle. Chronicle* entries from the 10th and 11th centuries do include specimens of verse, and these provide interesting evidence not only for the development of the alliterative line in late OE (Turville-Petre 1977:6) but also about the development of what is effectively a native, and rhymed, couplet. In the late OE and eME phase of its evolution, therefore, English hosted both the remains of the alliterative metrical system *and* a newer, possibly 'popular', type of verse. Oakden (1930–5), for instance, argued that *Chronicle* entries for the years 959, 979, 1067, 1075, 1077 and 1078 show verse exhibiting a mixture of the alliterative long line with couplets, where rhyme becomes a structural feature of the texts:

> These entries are very important, because they are sufficient to show that popular rhythms did exist, and subsequently developed along certain lines, until rhyming couplets were evolved. *All this took place before French influence could have been felt*, and it is almost equally certain that the use of rhyme was not due to the influence of the Latin Hymns of the Church, but to popular tradition
>
> (Oakden 1930:135)

The subsequent fusion of the classical OE metrical system and the newer system of popular verse can be seen, Oakden suggested, in poems such as the *First Worcester Fragment* (c.1170, SW Midlands) and in *The Departing Soul's Address to the Body* (c.1170, again SW Midlands), in the latter of which there are 29 syllabic couplets 'due to the encroachment of rhyme and assonance from the popular poetry' (Oakden 1930:139). The emergence of a native couplet can also be discerned in *The Proverbs of Alfred* (c.1180, South-west).

The fusion, or at least the co-existence, can be argued to underlie such important subsequent texts as *The Harley Lyrics*, assembled in the Midlands around 1340, whose poets 'achieved a fusion of the alliterative long line with syllable verse in rhyming stanzas' (Turville-Petre 1977:8). This is outside our period, true, but the fact that such subsequent verse is arguably a *synthesis* is suggestive of the nature of verse composition during the later 12th and earlier 13th centuries.

In terms of borrowing of poetic form from one language to another, it may be that such borrowing is not merely a matter of prestige. It can't in our view be coincidental that the rhymed octosyllable entered the language from French (and probably A-N) sources at exactly the time when English was developing a native, and rhymed, couplet which in turn had evolved from the 'popular rhythms' evinced by certain *Chronicle* entries. It may well turn out to be the case that language change is itself a pre-condition not only for literary borrowing but also of more structural forms of poetic change (see also McCully 2003 for a fuller account).

8.6 Orm

Written in the East Midlands in the late 12th century by an Augustinian canon called Orm, the *Ormulum* is one of the most remarkable pieces of eME verse. It has long been the object of philological interest, largely because of its idiosyncratic, quasi-phonetic spelling system (Orm's invention), which – precisely because it is an invention, and is quasi-phonetic – offers rich insights into the nature of English phonology of the period. But it's also of interest for metrical reasons: it's a long text (20 000 lines – about one-eighth of the work as planned; see Bennett and Smithers 1968:174); it's a native English text; and its form is remarkably – one might say tediously, or hypnotically, or even 'disastrously' – regular:

7 tærfore hafe icc turnedd itt
Intill Ennglisshe spæche,
For þatt I wollde bliþeli
Þatt all Ennglisshe lede
Wiþþ ære shollde lisstenn itt . . .

NB. The MS symbol '7' indicates 'and': 'And therefore I have turned it [the Gospel] into the English tongue, because I gladly intend that all English people should listen to it with reverence . . .'

The form itself – whose alternating . . . one hesitates to call it a 'pulse', it's more of a nightmarish, inescapable jog-trot . . . whose alternating hypnotics one can hear even in a short fragment – has come to be known as the *septenarius* (from L *septem*, seven: 'A line of seven feet, especially the trochaic or iambic tetrameter catalectic' – where *catalectic* means 'lacking a syllable in the final foot'). This last definition is both complex and problematic, as we'll see. For the moment, the form – the *formulum?* – can perhaps best be described as evincing a binary pattern, where one octosyllabic (part-)line containing alternating [WS] syllables is followed by a second, six-syllable (part-)line ending on a seventh, final, yet obligatorily unstressed syllable:

x / x / x / x / 7 tærfore hafe icc turnedd itt	(8 syllables, alternating)
x / x / x / x Intill Ennglisshe spæche,	(6 syllables, alternating, + one final unstress)

In the final (part-)line cited above, it seems that Orm violated normal accentuation on the word *English* in order to maintain his rigid metrical pattern. And how rigid the pattern is: only in line-initial positions do 'trochaic' [SW] patterns occur, and these are infrequent (see also Minkova 1996: 101):

To frofrenn swillke senndeþþ godd:
Enngless 7 hallʒe sawless (English and blessed souls)

Long-hand statements of Orm's *formulum* aren't very useful ('a binary pattern . . . an octosyllabic line followed by . . .'). They lack explanatory adequacy. If the constituent in which Orm composed spanned 14 syllables, with an unstressed extrametrical syllable at the end of the constituent, why should any inversions occur mid-line? How can we justify the traditional claim that the metrical form is catalectic? And, most significantly, what

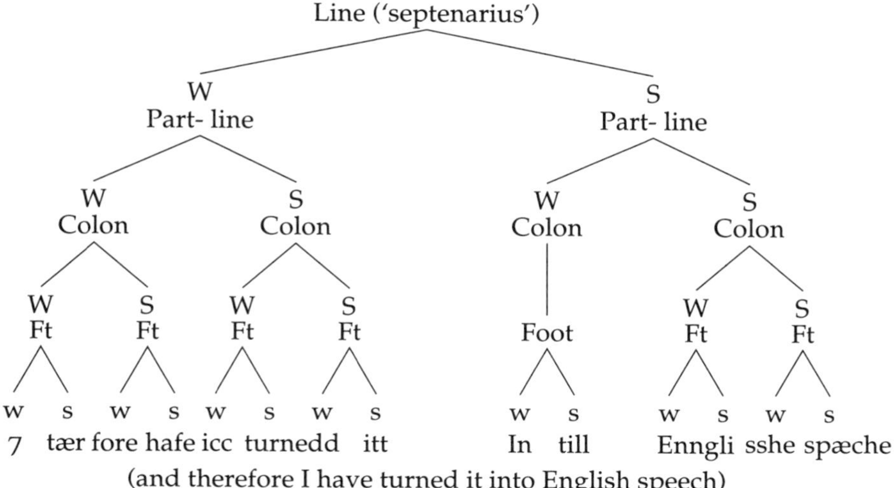

Figure 8.1 *Ormulum*. Metrical template
(adapted from Minkova 1996: *Ft* stands for 'verse-specific foot'. Here W stands for 'weaker than' and S for 'stronger than')

factors govern the realisation of the final positions of the couplet, the metrical domain?

These questions can be answered most elegantly by following Minkova (1996), who handles the metre of the poem – if it can be called a poem – using a theory of metrical domains as these are expressed through a non-linear template (figure 8.1). Such a graphic representation isn't merely a pictorial convenience. Notice that the 'Line' constituent (which spans two printed lines in modern editions of Orm) is split into two asymmetrical constituents (we call these 'part-lines' to avoid possible ambiguity with the term 'half-line'). It's precisely in constituent-initial position that we expect to find inversions (cf. trochaic substitution in the standard pentameter, for instance, which is commonest line-initially, and after a mid-line caesura). In Orm, what little inversion there is occurs exactly in the first or the fifth constituent ('Ft'). Further, the tree above (figure 8.1) claims that Orm's underlying metre consists of 14 syllables, not the apparent 15 of the printed page. That's actually a gain, because the fifteenth syllable of the 'Line' constituent is, as claimed, 'extrametrical' – it falls outside the base metrical description. Furthermore, on the MS evidence, this fifteenth syllable is *always unstressed*, and we can readily infer this stresslessness because the fifteenth syllable is *always spelled with* <e>.

As Minkova shows, we can incorporate this observation into the analysis by showing that the distribution and nature of constituent-final syllables in Orm is governed by an auxiliary template in which the final two

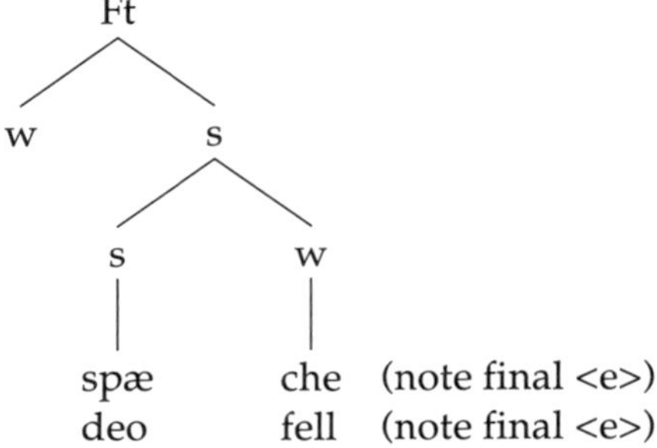

Figure 8.2 *Ormulum*. Auxiliary template, constituent-final position

syllables of the 'Line' constituent are nested within the final Ft, as shown in figure 8.2. The non-linear analysis makes special predictions about the right edge of the metrical domain: (i) it is a uniquely strong metrical position (if you look at the penultimate diagram, you'll see that the final Ft is dominated by S all the way up the hierarchy); and (ii) the fact that the fifteenth and final syllable of the domain is *always* unstressed follows nicely from the *depth of embedding* of that particular syllable. No other syllable apart from an unstressed one, spelled with <e> in its Nucleus, can be buried that deep in this particular metrical hierarchy.

If you compare the kind of description we're giving, following Minkova (1996), to the metre of the *Ormulum* with the description of classical OE alliterative metre we gave in Unit 5 you'll see how very different the two descriptions are. In the earlier, alliterative form the metre is to be described, we argued, primarily in terms of abstract *positions*. In that metre, we didn't use the term or the concept of 'foot' (Ft), nor did we privilege the idea that the ideal metrical form was *alternating*. With Orm's metre, however, we're beginning to think in terms of alternation, of 'strong' and 'weak' parts of a verse-specific foot and of syllable-counting. These lines, unlike the lines and half-lines of OE metre, are not simple structures, static and strong (Tolkien 1936:31); they are lines that, however rudimentarily, are beginning to go to a tune.

Exercise 8.6.1

It's interesting to observe what happens if we ignore the domain-final, extrametrical syllable in Orm and look again at the main template governing the line. Can you think of any other verse, or specimen of verse, from later periods of English that might match this template?

Comment on Exercise 8.6.1

The template fits a form that has come to be known, rather unsurprisingly, as the *fourteener* – known as such since most of its constituents count 14 (sometimes 13) syllables. The fourteener clearly underlies, and is therefore related to, the ballad stanza:

> While shepherds watched their flocks by night,
> All seated on the ground,
> The angel of the Lord came down,
> And glory shone around.
>
> 'Fear not,' said he; for mighty dread
> Had seized their troubled mind:
> 'Glad tidings of great joy I bring
> To you and all mankind'. . .

(While shepherds watched their flocks. English Christmas carol, first two verses. 'The tune first appeared in Este's *Psalter*, 1592. The words by Nahum Tate appeared in a supplement to a book of Psalms in 1700' (Anon. *Christmas melodies*, n.d.:35).)

Fourteener isn't, in fact, a particularly useful description of this metre, which came to be particularly popular in, and throughout, the 16th century. Metrically, the line divides into two asymmetrical parts, and there are major syntactic boundaries that appear to readily (but non-coincidentally) match the boundaries of major metrical constituents. A mere statement of syllable-count ('the line has 14 syllables') ignores this isomorphism.

We have come a long way, culturally and linguistically, from classical Old English. However we begin to describe the form and the language of, say, *The Owl and the Nightingale*, or of the *Ormulum*, we've said enough to show that we must begin to think of new varieties of English, and a new variety, or set of varieties, of verse-form. We are beginning to describe the verse-forms, in particular, using terminology and descriptions that might be familiar to any student of later English verse – with notions like 'inversion' and, in the *Ormulum* at least, with the verse-specific, alternating foot.

8.7 Envoi: The 'Alliterative Revival'

The *Ormulum* may be a philologists's goldmine, but it's only questionably a poem, and we don't wish to leave our story of the earliest English with Orm's intricate albeit interesting disaster. To conclude, we're going to step beyond our period and look forward to some literary artefacts of later ME. We'll very briefly look at two excerpts from poems that belong to a period of literary production that scholars have called the 'Alliterative Revival'.

The first excerpt comes from *The Vision of Piers Plowman*, which was written by William Langland probably in the 1360s and 1370s (Schmidt 1978:xii). We know little of Langland's life, but know that he was a native of Worcester. The language used in the original manuscripts of the poem also belongs to the South West dialect area. In the following, which is taken from Passus XVIII of the B-text (we have merely added graphic half-line divisions), you might make an appropriate comparison between Langland's handling of Christ's death and the poetic sublime achieved by, for example, the poet of the OE 'The dream of the rood':

> *'Consummatum est,'* quod Crist, and comsede for to swoune,
> Pitousliche and pale as a prison that deieth;
> the lord of lif and of light tho leide hise eighen togideres.
> The day for drede withdrough and derk bicam the sonne.
> The wal waggede and cleef, and al the world quaved . . . (ll.57–61)
>
> 'It is finished,' said Christ, and began to faint,
> Pitiable and pale as a dying prisoner;
> the lord of life and of light then laid his eyes together.
> The day declined from dread and the sun became dark.
> The wall [of the temple] tottered and split, and the whole world quaked . . .

If you look for a moment at Langland's metre you'll see it will by no means fit the verse-specific constraints we adduced for the metrical structures of classically constructed OE verse. To take but one issue: in Langland's a-verses there are often three chief stressed syllables (the **lord** of **life** and of **light**), and such patterns are not at all accommodated by one of the central constraints of OE alliterative verse, which requires that well-made half-lines have exactly four positions (where these positions usually contain two chief stresses). It's true that in some of its diction, and in the overall alliterative pattern, such a form recalls OE alliterative verse. But, we suggest, it does not derive directly from the tradition of verse-making in OE.

A second excerpt, this time the opening lines from the poem known as *Sir Gawain and the Green Knight*. The author is unknown, but it's relatively clear from the language of the text that the poem issued from a North West or North West Midlands dialect area, and was probably composed towards the end of the 14th century. We have used the edition of Tolkien and Gordon (1967), but have again added graphic half-line divisions:

> Siþen þe sege and þe assaut watz sesed at Troye,
> þe borȝ brittened and brent to brondez and askez,
> þe tulk of þe trammes of tresoun þer wroȝt
> Watz tried for his tricherie, þe trewest on erthe . . . (ll.1–4)
>
> After the siege and battle at Troy had ceased,
> the city sacked and burnt to brands and ashes,
> the man who had there wrought treason's plots
> was tried for his treachery, the most certain on earth . . .

Here, too, the half-lines don't seem to fit the constraints of earlier alliterative verse as this was written and composed in OE. Further, the *Gawain* poet doesn't just use alliterative lines in his poem. His alliterative stanzas conclude with a five-line block of rhymed syllabics, a two-syllable 'bob' followed by a rhyming syllabic 'wheel':

> I schal telle hit as-tit, as I in toun herde
>   with tonge,
> As hit is stad and stoken
> In stori stif and stronge,
> With lel lettres loken,
> In londe so hatz ben longe (ll.31–36)
>
> I shall tell it at once, as I heard it in town
>   spoken;
> as it's set down and fixed
> in brave and strong fable,
> locked in linked letters, [a reference to alliteration]
> as has long been a custom in this country

The unique stanza-composition of *Gawain* doesn't look back directly to OE verse traditions, however the poet may protest that his largely alliterative telling 'has long been a custom'. Instead, the form offers a fusion between the consciously antique prestige of the one, alliterative line and the consciously 'new', rhymed and syllable-counting lines of the bob and wheel that conclude each stanza. It is the work of a consummate literary artist.

Perhaps this almost-final flourish of alliterative poetry was not a 'revival'. There was, perhaps, a consciousness that this form of composition was burnished by august Germanic precedent, but it seems likely that the principles of composition of OE-style alliterative verse had by this date been altogether lost and that what we are hearing, with both *Piers Plowman* and *Gawain*, is the *re-invention* of alliterative verse writing. The basis of this verse seems different: syllable length plays much less of a prominent role than it did in OE verse; in ME verse the constraints on the number and disposition of unstressed syllables seems more relaxed, particularly in the a-verse; and the metrical unit of ME alliterative verse seems to be the line rather than the half-line.

If this is so, we should ask – and it will be the final question we do ask – what prior literary artefacts enabled such a re-invention to take place. As we've said, these prior works seem unlikely to be alliterative poems composed on the OE model. But one possibility, explored more fully in, for example, Cable 1991 (and see also Turville-Petre 1977), is that some texts of the 'Alliterative Revival' were enabled, and perhaps conditioned, by the prior existence of a tradition of *alliterative prose* writing that had flourished largely in the West and South West Midlands through the earlier ME period. You might like to recall Strang's comment about verse-making that we cited in Unit 1. In the classical OE phase, she wrote, '[t]here was one metre; you used it or you did not. You might compromise and conform to some but not all of its rules, writing a kind of semi-verse, and you could add patterning of your own selection to the basic form; but you could not write a verse of a different form' (1970:323). One intriguing possibility is that it is precisely the 'semi-verse' of alliterative prose writers – such as, most evidently and prestigiously, Ælfric (Unit 6) – that provides the ultimate origin of the great texts of the English 'Alliterative Revival'.

Summary

In this unit we've looked at some, though by no means all, of the linguistic pressures that were bearing on the earliest English in the period c.1066 until the 12th century. Some of these pressures came about because of ambiguities or other weaknesses intrinsic in the systems of OE; other pressures came from external factors, such as the Norman Conquest. We have tried to look at the respective importance of such factors in the development of the earliest English, and along the way have started to think about matters such as inflectional erosion and loss, case syncretism, patterns of loaning, the modification of the English pronoun system and the death of one kind of verse-form along with the invention, or the adaptation, of other, new forms of metrical writing in and into English. In the 12th century the linguistic landscape looked very different to the one inhabited by speakers of the 10th, or for that matter the 8th, century.

What we've written is by no means a complete linguistic history, and still less is it a complete cultural or political history. We have sometimes been very partial in our coverage. Nevertheless, our hope is that the present text will help you to continue to think about all aspects of the development of English – including the narrative that is your own account of your own English – and that you'll at least be equipped with the curiosity to consult the more advanced handbooks that are there for your use as you continue to work in this area of historical English language and linguistics.

Study questions

1. If you read that 'the English language underwent widespread case syncretism in the early Middle English period', how would you argue for or against that proposition?
2. The regular dative plural inflection on nouns in many varieties of OE was *-um*. Such an ending seems entirely distinctive, in that it ends with a bilabial, nasal consonant. What was the history, and what the eventual fate, of this inflectional ending?

3. Many ME dialects, particularly those of the Midlands, form regular plurals by adding the inflection -en. (You can find a relic of this process by thinking of PDE words such as *ox*, plural *oxen*.) Why was that a productive way of forming plural nouns? Why does -(e)s eventually win out over -en as the regular plural inflection?
4. Why does English lose so many of its inflectional endings, while German appears to retain a fairly fully inflected noun and verb system?
5. What do the nature, category and grammatical function of loan-words tell us about the evolution of the English language during the period 1000–1250?
6. If you wanted to write English verse at the end of the 12th century, which metrical form(s) could you have chosen to compose in? Which form would you eventually have chosen, and why?
7. Determine the nature of the pronoun system you yourself use as a speaker of PDE. Then consider the following sub-questions: (i) does your own pronoun system make use of 'strong' and 'weak' forms of pronouns? (You can think about this by considering where, and the extent to which, you might use unstressed pronouns.) (ii) Does the pronoun system you use show traces of grammatical case?
8. It's clear that the syntactic system of English changes so that word-order becomes a key grammatical principle. And we also know that OE inflections were subject to wholesale change. Which do you think came first – syntactic change or phonological change? Can we, in fact, claim that one change *caused* the other? How have other languages behaved with respect to syntactic and phonological change?
9. What pressures are there on *you*, a speaker of PDE, that might mean you feel obliged to adopt, or try to adopt, a more 'prestigious' variety of English? What aspects of your language-use do these pressures seem most to affect – phonological aspects? syntactic aspects? the lexicon?

Websites you may find useful

- http://www.chass.utoronto.ca/~cpercy/courses/6361Heys.htm
This site features an accessible article on French as a mother tongue in medieval England. It explains what Anglo-Norman was, and how it came about. It also gives excellent suggestions for additional reading
- http://faculty.uml.edu/jgarreau/FromFrenchtoEnglish.htm
This site gives the history of a number of words that came into English from Anglo-Norman. It also provides links to other interesting sites, gives additional sources and includes etymologies from Latin. Recommended
- http://members.tripod.com/nicolaa5/articles/names.html
This is an interesting site. Its title is 'Statistical survey of given names in Essex . . . England, 1182–1272'. It lists names, details the frequency of their

occurrence and gives some information about naming practices during this period

- http://mockingbird.creighton.edu/english/fajardo/teaching/ENG340/mideng.htm
  '... Middle English and Early Renaissance Periods: Historical and Cultural Outline'. This site is organised like a time line and details (in order, with dates and brief discussions) important cultural events and significant works of literature. It starts with Edward the Confessor and ends with *Dr Faustus*
- http://www.orbilat.com/Influences_of_Romance/English/RIFL-English-French-The_Domination_of_French.html
  This is an excerpt from *A history of the English language* (3rd ed.) by Albert Baugh and Thomas Cable. It has some links to other articles within the encyclopedia, and is part of the Orbis Latinus site
- http://www.georgetown.edu/faculty/ballc/oe/pater_noster.html
  On this site you can see the Lord's Prayer from various sources in eME. This is a site we talked about earlier in the text
- http://www.soton.ac.uk/~wpwt/notes/metrans.htm
  This site provides excellent, concise information about eME grammar and pronunciation. It also gives sources for downloading fonts that can be used for graphic representations of eME. It also touches on the issues of spelling and dialects
- http://ets.umdl.umich.edu/m/mec/
  This site's homepage states 'The Middle English Compendium has been designed to offer easy access to and interconnectivity between three major Middle English electronic resources: an electronic version of the Middle English Dictionary, a HyperBibliography of Middle English prose and verse, based on the MED bibliographies, and a Corpus of Middle English Prose and Verse, as well as links to an associated network of electronic resources.' It's produced by the University of Michigan, and is a particularly rich resource. There's limited access to the *Middle English Dictionary*, but one can apply for temporary access. The vast corpora, however, can be accessed and read from home at will

References and suggestions for further reading

As always, to get an overview of the main features of this phase of the development of the English language you should consult one of the standard *Histories* of the language, perhaps starting with Barber (1993, Chapters 6 and 7), following up with Baugh and Cable (1993, or later edition), and with a further consultation of Strang (1970). (Note: if you're going to take on this reading, we suggest you undertake it in that order.)

If you wish to read further around the arguments for and against the 'creolisation hypothesis', a good though quite advanced starting point would be Allen (1997; Allen's paper includes a section (pp.77–80) specifically on the PC). If that proves too advanced to begin with, try looking at Todd (1990) on pidgins and creoles first. Then go back to Allen's fine paper.

For work on the PC, Clark (1958) is indispensable, and you should make particular use of Clark's apparatus and notes. These will help to orientate you to the distinctive nature of the EMidlands variety of English in which the Continuations to the *Chronicle* were composed, and allow you to begin to assess how E Midlands English of the period differs from, say, W Midlands or Southern varieties.

If you wish to work further on the *syntax* of the PC, a starting-point is Mitchell (1964), but you should also, and without delay, consult Denison (1993), which is a single-volume history of English syntax, and a fine work in its field.

For work on the history of English verse, you should look at e.g. Cable (1991, particularly Chapter 2, 'Old English rhythmical prose and early Middle English meter') and Turville-Petre (1977) for some discussion of the death – and the re-invention – of alliterative poetry in English. McCully and Hogg (1994) suggest that the dialectal distribution of later alliterative writing – poetry from the 14th century, in particular, and the great works of the 'Alliterative Revival' – isn't a cultural accident, but is at least in part linguistically determined. We have not made more of these texts in the present work because the analysis of poetic death and re-invention, as this takes place in ME, falls outside both the theoretical and chronological scope of a textbook such as this. McCully (2003) provides some ideas about how we might begin to analyse poetic change as this is manifest in the English language of different periods.

Appendix 1 (repeated from Unit 3): At-a-glance guide to OE inflections – nouns and adjectives

Tables A1.1 and A1.2 present a somewhat simplified guide to OE article, adjective and noun inflections, as these might be expressed in classical WS.

Table A.1 Nouns and strongly declining adjectives

If you wish to find the strongly declining adjective, together with the inflections on the head noun, then just cover the left-hand part of the table (i.e. the articles). If an article is present in a given, then of course the following adjective will decline weakly, if present, and you should look up the relevant inflection in Table A1.2.

We use the abbreviations M(asculine), F(eminine) and N(euter), and in the left-hand rows, N(ominative), A(ccusative), G(enitive) and D(ative). N+A here means 'both nominative and accusative'.

Inflections appearing in parentheses are often phonologically conditioned, e.g. they appear after light syllables in roots. Thus *scip* (neuter, n+a sg., with zero inflection) and *scipu* (n+a pl.)

	Articles ('the/that')			**Adjectives**			**Nouns**		
	M	**N**	**F**	**M**	**N**	**F**	**M**	**N**	**F**
Sg.N	se	þæt	sēo	–	–	(-u)	–	–	(-u)
A	þone	þæt	þā	-ne	–	-e	–	–	-e
G	þæs		þære	-es		-re	-es		-e
D	þæm		þære	-um		-re	-e		-e
Pl.N+A		þā		-e	(-u)	-a	-as	(-u)	-a
G		þara			-ra			-a	
D		þæm			-um			-um	

Table A1.2 Weakly declining adjectives (and nouns)

Recall that weak adjectives are preceded by a definite article or possessive pronoun. Here's how adjectives behave in that circumstance. Nouns – 'weak nouns' – inflect this way as well. Notice the prevalence of the inflectional ending *-an*.

	M	N	F
Sg.N	-a	-e	-e
A	-an	-e	-an
G		-an	
D		-an	
Pl.N+A		-an	
G		-ena	
D		-um	

Appendix 2 (repeated from Unit 4): At-a-glance guide to OE inflections – verbs

Table A2.1 presents a guide to characteristic OE verb inflections, as there might be expressed in classical WS.

Table A2.1 Weak and strong verbs

(1a) Weak verbs (-d in past tense) – indicative

Infinitive	**(i) -ian**	**(ii) -an**	**-ian**	**-an**
	Present tense		**Past tense**	
Sg.1	-ie	-e	-ode	-ede
2	-ast	-est	-odest	-edest
3	-að	-eð	-ode	-ede
Pl.	-iað	-að	-odon	-eden

(1b) Weak verbs – subjunctive

	Present tense		**Past tense**	
Sg.	-ie	-e	-ode	-ede
Pl.	-ien	-en	-oden	-eden

Table A2.1 (*cont'd*)

(2) Strong verbs (change their root vowel shape in the past tense)

Infinitive	**-an**		
	Present tense	**Past tense**	
Sg.1	-e	–	(1)
2	-est	-e	(2)
3	-(e)ð	–	(1)
Pl.	-að	-on	(2)

- Past participles occur in the frame ge +_____+ en (2, or 3)
- Numerals to the right are intended to show gradation patterns, e.g. the vowel shape in Sg.1 and 3 is identical, as is that in Sg.2 and Pl., whereas the past participle either shares its root vowel with (2), or sometimes shows a different root vowel altogether. An example is the past tense of OE *singan*, to sing:

	singan, past tense	
Sg.1	sang	(1: <a>)
Sg.2	sunge	(2: <u>)
Sg.3	sang	(1: <a>)
Pl.	sungon	(2: <u>)
Ppl.	ge + sung + en	

References

As well as including all the works to which we have referred in-text we have also included other useful references that have gone into the making of this book. If you wish to find bibliographic information about the dictionaries we've used, you're referred to the Interlude, where fairly comprehensive information about OED2, MED and DOE is given.

Allen, Cynthia. 1997. 'Middle English case loss and the "creolization" hypothesis.' *English Language and Linguistics* 1: 63–89.

Anon. n.d. (no date) *Christmas melodies*. London: The Dickens Press.

Barber, Charles L. 1993. *The English language: a historical introduction*. Cambridge: Cambridge University Press.

Barney, Stephen A. 1985. *Word hoard: an introduction to Old English vocabulary*. Second edition. New Haven and London: Yale University Press.

Baugh, Albert C. and Thomas Cable. 1993. *A history of the English language*. Fourth edition. London: Routledge.

Beekes, Robert S.P. 1995. *Comparative Indo-European linguistics*. Amsterdam/ Philadelphia: John Benjamins.

Bennett, J.A.W. and G.V. Smithers. 1968. *Early Middle English verse and prose*. Second edition, with a Glossary by Norman Davis. Oxford: Clarendon Press.

Berg, Donna Lee. 1991. *A user's guide to the OED*. Oxford: Oxford University Press.

Biddulph, Joseph. 1995. *Notes on Frisian*. Pontypridd, Wales: Joseph Biddulph Publisher.

Blair, John. 2000. *The Anglo-Saxon age: a very short introduction*. Oxford: Oxford University Press.

Blair, Peter Hunter. 1970. *An introduction to Anglo-Saxon England*. Cambridge: Cambridge University Press.

Blair, Peter Hunter. 1990. *The world of Bede*. New edition, revised by Pauline Hunter Blair. Cambridge: Cambridge University Press.

Bliss, A.J. 1958. *The metre of Beowulf*. Oxford: Blackwell.

Bliss, A.J. 1962. *An introduction to Old English metre*. Oxfrod: Blackwell.

Bolton, W.F. 1982. *A living language. The history and structure of English*. New York: McGraw-Hill Publishing Company.

Booij, Geert. 2002. *The morphology of Dutch*. Oxford: Oxford University Press.

Bradley, S.A.J. 1982. *Anglo-Saxon poetry*. London: Dent.

Brook, G.L. 1955. *An introduction to Old English*. Manchester: Manchester University Press.

Brundage, James. 1987 (paperback edition, 1990). *Law, sex, and Christian society in medieval Europe*. Chicago and London: The University of Chicago Press.

Bryson, Bill. 1991. *Mother tongue*. London: Penguin.

Busse, W.G., J. Krings and U. Schemman. 1995 (corrected repr. 1997). *An Introduction to Old English: A Workbook*. University of Düsseldorf.

Cable, Thomas. 1991. *The English alliterative tradition*. Philadelphia: University of Pennsylvania Press.

Campbell, Alistair. 1959. *Old English grammar*. Oxford: Clarendon Press.

Campbell, J.J., E. John and P. Wormald. 1982. *The Anglo-Saxons*. Oxford: Phaidon.

Cassidy, Fred. J. and Richard Ringler. 1971. *Bright's Old English grammar and reader*. Third edition. New York and Chicago: Holt, Rinehart, and Winston Inc.

Chambers, R.W. 1932. *On the continuity of English prose from Alfred to More and his school*. London: Early English Text Society (EETS vol. 191A).

Clark, Cecily. 1958. *The Peterborough Chronicle 1070–1154*. Oxford: Oxford University Press.

Clemoes, Peter. gen. ed. 1976. *Anglo-Saxon England*, 5. Cambridge: Cambridge University Press.

Crossley-Holland, Kevin. 1984. *The Anglo-Saxon world*. Oxford: Oxford University Press.

Crystal, David ed. 1995. *The Cambridge encyclopedia of the English language*. Cambridge: Cambridge University Press.

Danchev, Andrei. 1997. 'The Middle English creolization hypothesis revisited'. In Fisiak, Jacek (ed.). *Studies in Middle English linguistics*. Berlin and New York: Mouton de Gruyter (*Trends in Linguistics/Studies and Monographs* 103), 79–108.

Daunt, Marjorie. 1939. 'Old English sound changes reconsidered in relation to scribal tradition and practice'. *Transactions of the Philological Society*, 108–37.

Davies, N. 1999. *The isles: a history*. Oxford: Oxford University Press.

Denison, D. 1993. *English historical syntax*. London: Longman.

Derry, T.K. and M.G. Blakeway. 1973. *The making of early and medieval Britain*. London: John Murray.

Dorian, Nancy C. ed. 1989. *Investigating obsolescence*. Cambridge: Cambridge University Press.

Drabble, Margaret. ed. 2000. *The Oxford companion to English literature*. Oxford and New York: Oxford University Press.

Fennell, Barbara A. 2001. *A history of English: a sociolinguistic approach*. Oxford: Blackwell.

Fenoulhet, Jane. 1997. *Dutch in three months*. London: Dorling Kindersley.

Finegan, Edward. 1987. 'English'. In ed. Bernard Comrie, *The World's Major Languages*. New York: Oxford University Press, 77–109.

Fowler, H.W. 1996. *The new Fowler's modern English usage*. ed. R.W. Burchfield. 3rd edition. [First edition 1926.] Oxford: Clarendon Press.

Fox, Anthony. 1990. *The structure of German*. Oxford: Clarendon Press.

Framer, D.H. 1988. *The age of Bede*. Trans. J.F. Webb. London: Penguin.

Freeborn, Dennis. 1992. *From Old English to Standard English*. London: Macmillan.

Fulk, Robert D. 1992. *A history of Old English meter*. Philadelphia: Pennsylvania University Press.

Godden, Malcolm R. and M. Lapidge. eds. 1991. *The Cambridge companion to English literature*. Cambridge: Cambridge University Press.

Godden, Malcolm R. 1992. 'Literary language'. In ed. Richard M. Hogg, *The Cambridge history of the English language* I: *the beginnings to 1066*. Cambridge: Cambridge University Press, 490–535.

Gordon, E.V. 1957. *An introduction to Old Norse*. Second edition, revised by A.R. Taylor. Oxford: Clarendon Press.

Görlach, Manfred. 1986. 'Middle English – a creole?' In Kastovsky, Dieter and Aleksander Swedek (eds., with Barbara Płocińska), *Linguistics across historical and geographical boundaries: in honour of Jacek Fisiak on the occasion of his fiftieth birthday*, vol. 1. Berlin, New York and Amsterdam: Mouton de Gruyter (*Trends in Linguistics/Studies and Monographs* 32), 329–44.

Graddol, David, D. Leith and J. Swann. 1996. *English: history, diversity, change*. London: Routledge.

Greenfield, S.B. 1965. *A critical history of Old English literature*. New York: New Ryork University Press.

Greenfield, S.B. and D.G. Calder. 1986. *A new critical history of Old English literature*. New York: New York University Press.

Grierson, H.J.C. and J.C. Smith. 1956. *A critical history of English poetry*. London: Chatto and Windus.

Hall, J.R. Clark. 1960. *A concise Anglo-Saxon dictionary*. Fourth edition, with a supplement by Herbert D. Merritt. Toronto and London UK: University of Toronto Press.

Hamer, Andrew. 1970. *A choice of Anglo-Saxon verse*. London: Faber.

Haugen, Einar. 1976. *The Scandinavian languages: an introduction to their history*. London: Faber and Faber.

Hill, David. 1981. *An atlas of Anglo-Saxon England*. Oxford: Basil Blackwell.

Hock, Hans Heinrich and Brian D. Joseph. 1996. *Language history, language change and language relationship*. Berlin and New York: Mouton de Gruyter.

Hogg, Richard M. 1992a. *A grammar of Old English. Vol. 1: phonology*. Oxford: Blackwell.

Hogg, Richard M. 1992b. 'Introduction'. In ed. Richard M. Hogg, *The Cambridge history of the English language* I: *the beginnings to 1066*. Cambridge: Cambridge University Press, 1–25.

Hogg, Richard M. 2002. *An introduction to Old English*. Edinburgh: Edinburgh University Press.

Howe, Stephen. 1996. *The personal pronouns in the Germanic languages*. Berlin and New York: Walter de Gruyter.

Jespersen, Otto. 1964. *Language: its nature, development and origin*. New York: W.W. Norton.

Jespersen, Otto. 1965. *The philosophy of grammar*. [First edition 1924.] New York: W.W. Norton.

Jones, Charles. 1989. *A history of English phonology*. London and New York: Longman.

Jones, Gwyn. 1984. *A history of the Vikings*. Oxford: Oxford University Press.

Keynes, Simon and Michael Lapidge. ed. and trans. 1983. *Alfred the Great*. London: Penguin.

Klaeber, F. 1950. *Beowulf and the Fight at Finnsburg*. Third edition. Lexington, Mass.: D.C. Heath & Co.

Lass, Roger. 1994. *Old English: a historical and linguistic companion*. Cambridge: Cambridge University Press.

Lass, Roger. 1997. *Historical linguistics and language change*: *Cambridge Studies in Linguistics* 81. Cambridge: Cambridge University Press.

Legge, M. Dominica. 1963. *Anglo-Norman literature and its background*. Oxford: Clarendon Press.

Leith, D. 1983. *A social history of English*. London: Routledge and Kegan Paul.

Loyn, H.R. 1984. *The governance of Anglo-Saxon England*. London: Edward Arnold.

Marsden, John. 1992. *Northanhymbre saga: the history of the Anglo-Saxon kings of Northumbria*. London: Kyle Cathie Ltd.

Mattingly, H. trans (rev. trans. S.A. Handford) 1970. *Tacitus: Germania*. London: Penguin.

McCully, Christopher B. 2003. 'Towards a theory of poetic change'. *Language and Literature* 12(1): 5–25.

McCully, Christopher B. and Richard Hogg. 1994. 'Dialect variation and historical metrics'. *Diachronica* XI/1: 13–34.

McCully, Christopher B. and J.J. Anderson. eds. 1996. *English historical metrics.* Cambridge: Cambridge University Press.

McMahon, April. 1994. *Understanding language change.* Cambridge: Cambridge University Press.

Minkova, Donka. 1984. 'On the hierarchy of factors causing schwa loss in Middle English'. *Neuphilologische Mitteilungen* 80: 445–454.

Minkova, Donka. 1985. 'The prosodic character of early schwa deletion in English'. In A.G. Ramat et al., eds., *Papers from the 7th International Conference on Historical Linguistics.* Amsterdam: John Benjamins, 445–459.

Minkova, Donka. 1991. *The history of final vowels in English.* Berlin: Mouton de Gruyter.

Minkova, Donka. 1996. 'Nonprimary stress in early Middle English accentual-syllabic verse'. In eds. McCully and Anderson, *English historical metrics*, 95–119.

Mitchell, Bruce. 1964. 'Syntax and word-order in *The Peterborough Chronicle* 1122–1154.' *Neuphilologische Mitteilungen* 2, LXV: 113–144.

Mitchell, Bruce. 1988. *On Old English.* Oxford: Basil Blackwell.

Mitchell, Bruce. 1995. *An invitation to Old English and Anglo-Saxon England.* Oxford UK and Cambridge USA: Blackwell.

Mitchell, Bruce and Fred C. Robinson. 1992. *A guide to Old English.* Fifth edition. Oxford: Blackwell.

Mossé, F. 1952. *A handbook of Middle English.* trans. J.A. Walker. Baltimore: Johns Hopkins Press.

Mugglestone, Lynda. ed. 2000. *Lexicography and the OED.* Oxford: Oxford University Press.

Mustanoja, Tauno F. 1960. *A Middle English syntax. Part 1: parts of speech.* Helsinki: Société Néophilologique.

Oakden, J.P. 1930–5. *Alliterative poetry in Middle English.* 2 vols. Manchester: Manchester University Press. (Reprinted in one vol., Hamden, Conn.: Archon Books, 1968).

Partridge, A.C. 1982. *A companion to Old and Middle English studies.* Totowa, New Jersey: Barnes and Noble Books.

Pope, Mildred K. 1934. *From Latin to modern French with especial consideration of Anglo-Norman.* Manchester: Manchester University Press.

Poussa, Patricia. 1982. 'The evolution of early standard English: the creolization hypothesis'. *Studia Anglica Posnaniensia* 14: 69–85.

Pyles, Thomas. 1964. *The origins and development of the English language.* New York: Harcourt, Brace and World, Inc.

Pyles, Thomas and J. Algeo. 1993. *The origins and development of the English language.* Fourth edition. Orlando, Florida: Harcourt Brace Jovanovich.

Quirk, Randolph and Charles L. Wrenn. 1957. *An Old English grammar.* Second edition. London: Methuen.

Quirk, Randolph, Valerie Adams and Derek Davy. 1975. *Old English literature: a practical introduction.* London: Edward Arnold.

Robinson, F.N. 1957. *The complete works of Geoffrey Chaucer.* Oxford: Oxford University Press.

Robinson, Orrin W. 1992. *Old English and its closest relatives.* Stanford, CA.: Stanford University Press.

Roesdahl, Else, James Graham-Campbell, Patricia Connor and Kenneth Pearson. eds. 1981. *The Vikings in England*. Exhibition catalogue. London: The Anglo-Danish Viking Project.

Russom, Geoffrey. 1987. *Old English meter and linguistic theory*. Cambridge: Cambridge University Press.

Russom, Geoffrey. 1998. *Beowulf and Old Germanic metre*. (Cambridge Studies in Anglo-Saxon England 23.) Cambridge: Cambridge University Press.

Schmidt, A.V.C. ed. 1978. *The vision of Piers Plowman. A complete edition of the B-text*. New York: E.P. Dutton, and London: J.M. Dent.

Scragg, D.G. 1974. *A history of English spelling*. Manchester: Manchester University Press.

Sherley Price, Leo. ed. and trans. 1955. *Bede: History of the English church and people*. London: Penguin.

Sievers, Eduard. 1885. 'Zur Rhythmik des Germanischen Alliterationsverses: I'. *Beiträge zur Geschichte der Deutschen Sprache und Literatur* X: 209–313.

Sievers, Eduard 1893. *Altgermanische metrik*. Halle: Max Niemeyer.

Smith, A.H. 1968. *Three Northumbrian poems*. Second edition. London: Methuen.

Stanley, Eric G. ed. 1972. *The Owl and the Nightingale*. Manchester: Manchester University Press.

Stenton, F.M. 1947. *Anglo-Saxon England*. Second edition. Oxford: Clarendon Press.

Strang, Barbara M.H. 1970. *A history of English*. London: Methuen.

Swanton, Michael. ed. 1970. *The dream of the rood*. Manchester: Manchester University Press.

Swanton, Michael. 1975. *Anglo-Saxon prose*. London: Dent.

Swanton, Michael. 1987. *English literature before Chaucer*. London and New York: Longman.

Sweet, Henry. 1897. *First steps in Anglo-Saxon*. Oxford: The Clarendon Press.

Sweet, Henry. 1967. *Sweet's Anglo-Saxon reader in prose and verse*. Fifteenth edition, revised by Dorothy Whitelock. Oxford: Clarendon Press.

Todd, Loreto. 1990. *Pidgins and creoles*. Second edition. London: Routledge.

Tolkien, J.R.R. 1936. '*Beowulf*: the monsters and the critics'. (The British Academy Sir Israel Gollancz Lecture, 1936). Reprinted from the *Proceedings of the British Academy*, Vol. XXII. Oxford: Oxford University Press.

Tolkien, J.R.R. and E.V. Gordon. eds. 1967. *Sir Gawain and the Green Knight*. Second edition ed. Norman Davis. Oxford: Clarendon Press.

Turville-Petre, Thorlac. 1977. *The alliterative revival*. Cambridge: Brewer.

Visser, F. Th. 1963–73. *An historical syntax of the English language*, parts I–III. 4 vols. Leiden: E.J. Brill.

Watts, V.E. 1998. *Boethius: The consolation of philosophy*. London: The Folio Society.

Whitelock, Dorothy. 1952. *The beginnings of English society*. Harmondsworth: Penguin.

Whitelock, Dorothy. 1967. *Sweet's Anglo-Saxon reader in prose and verse*. 15th edition. Oxford: Clarendon Press.

Williams, Joseph M. 1975. *Origins of the English language*. London and New York: The Free Press.

Woolf, Rosemary. 1976. 'The ideal of men dying with their lord in the *Germania* and in *The Battle of Maldon*'. In Peter Clemoes (ed.) *Anglo-Saxon England*, 5. Cambridge: Cambridge University Press, 63–81.

Wrenn, Charles L. 1958. *Beowulf*. Second edition. London: George Harrap & Co.

Wyld, H.C. 1927. *A short history of English*. Third edition. London: John Murray.

Index

References are to pagination. The abbr. 'ff.' stands for 'and following page(s)'